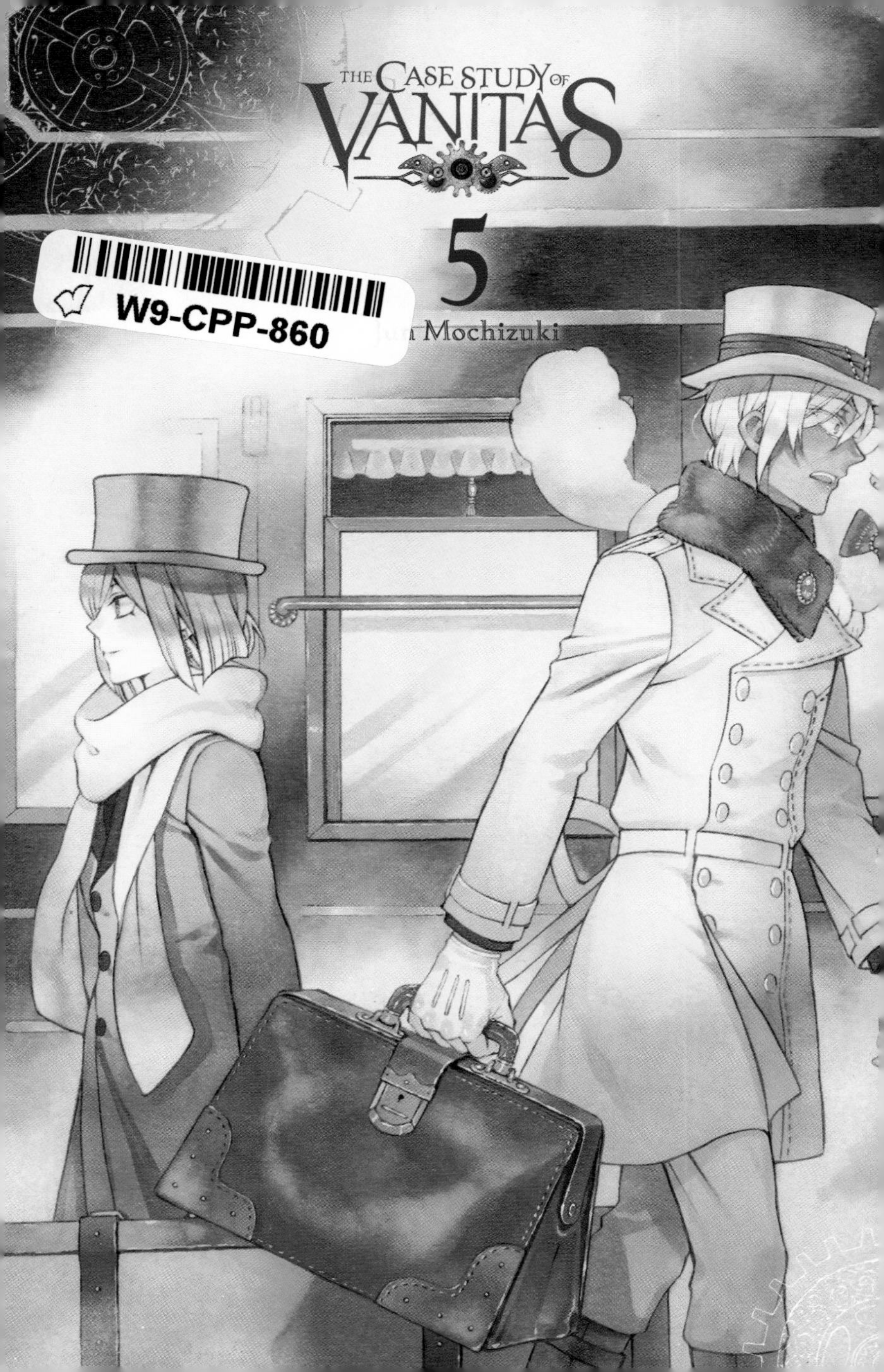
THE CASE STUDY OF
VANITAS
5
Mochizuki

THE CASE STUDY OF VANITAS 5

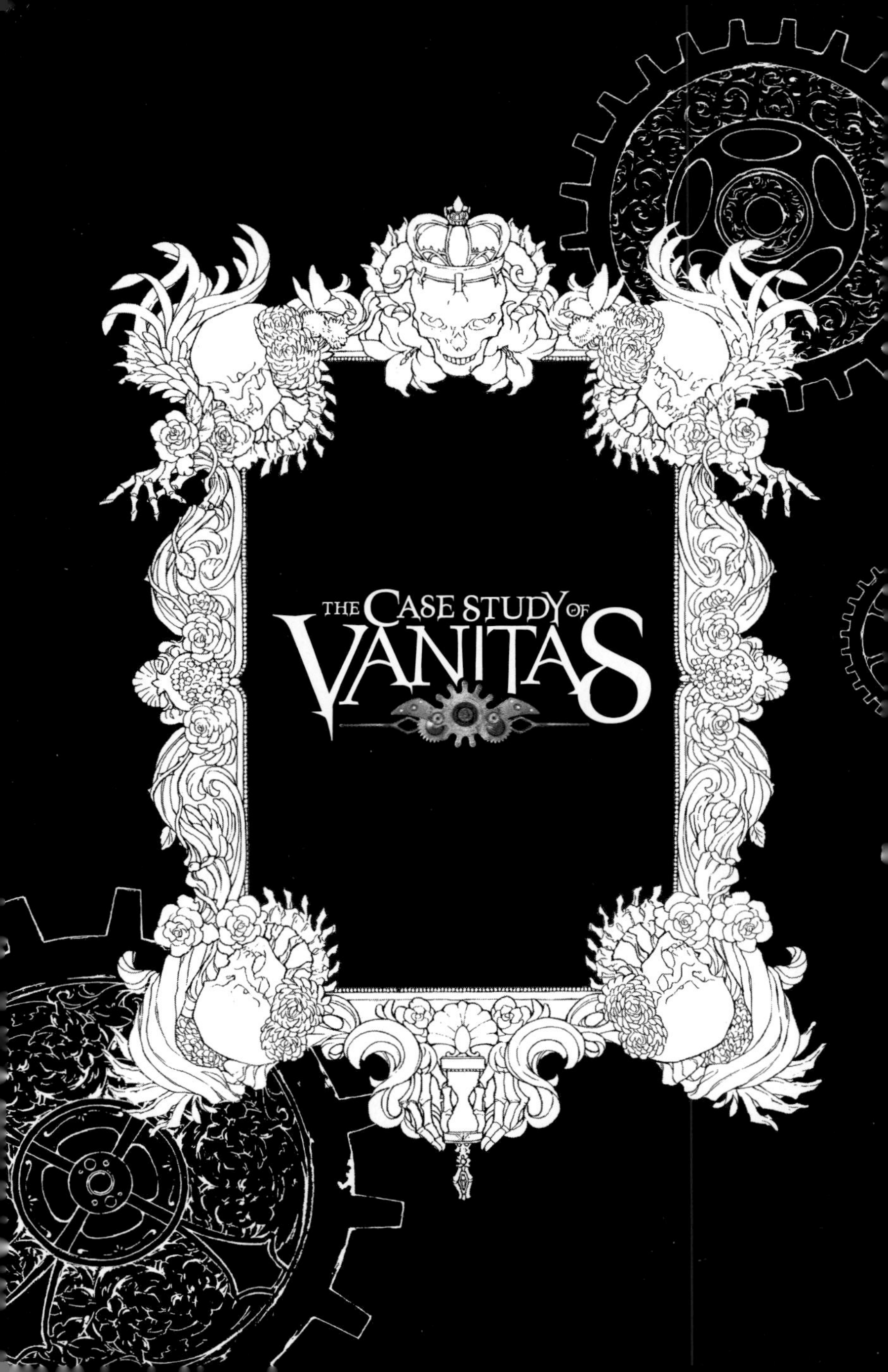
THE CASE STUDY OF
VANITAS

Mémoire 22 Hurler A CALLING VOICE

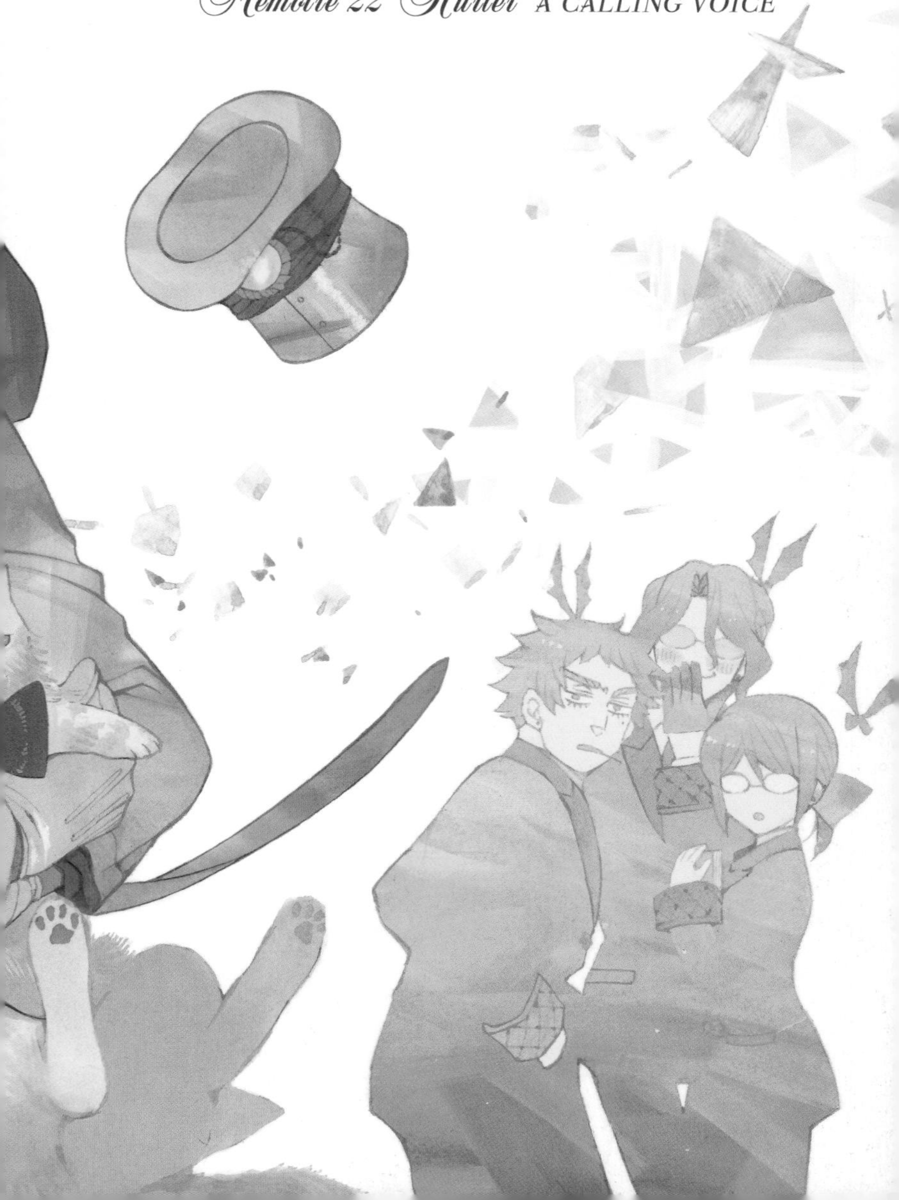

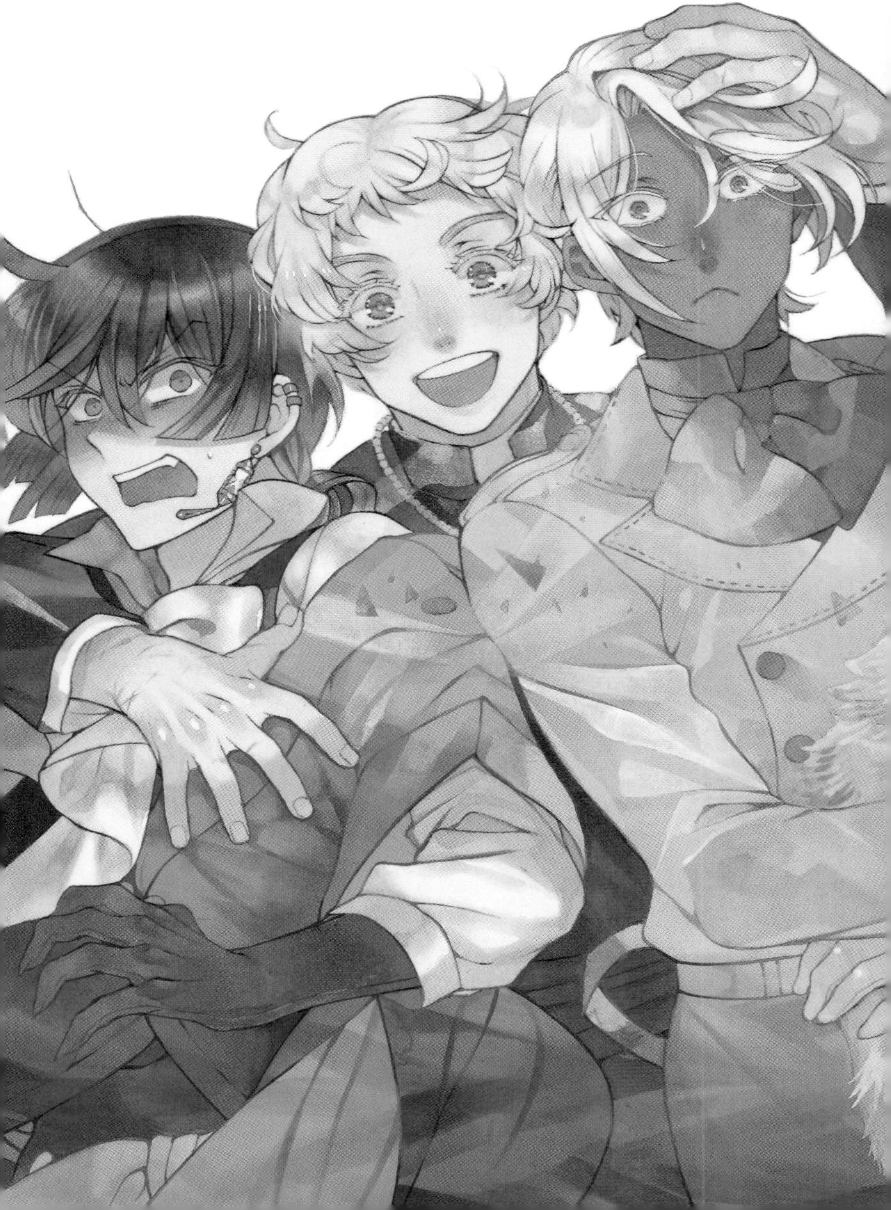

Les Mémoires de Vanitas

THE CASE STUDY OF VANITAS

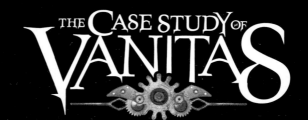

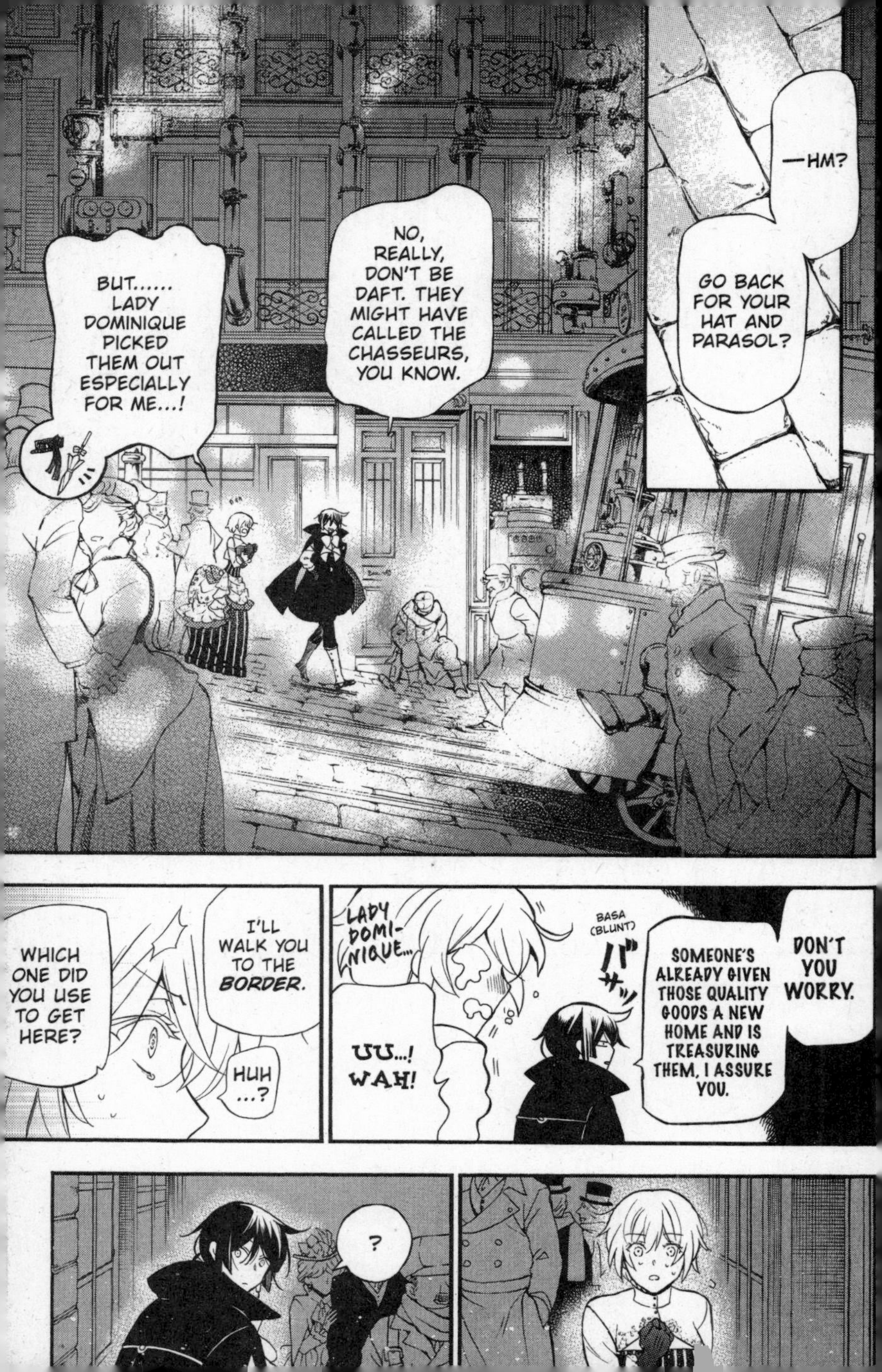
—HM?
GO BACK FOR YOUR HAT AND PARASOL?
NO, REALLY, DON'T BE DAFT. THEY MIGHT HAVE CALLED THE CHASSEURS, YOU KNOW.
BUT...... LADY DOMINIQUE PICKED THEM OUT ESPECIALLY FOR ME...!
DON'T YOU WORRY.
SOMEONE'S ALREADY GIVEN THOSE QUALITY GOODS A NEW HOME AND IS TREASURING THEM, I ASSURE YOU.
BASA (BLUNT)
バサッ
LADY DOMI-NIQUE...
UU...! WAH!
I'LL WALK YOU TO THE *BORDER*.
WHICH ONE DID YOU USE TO GET HERE?
HUH ...?
?

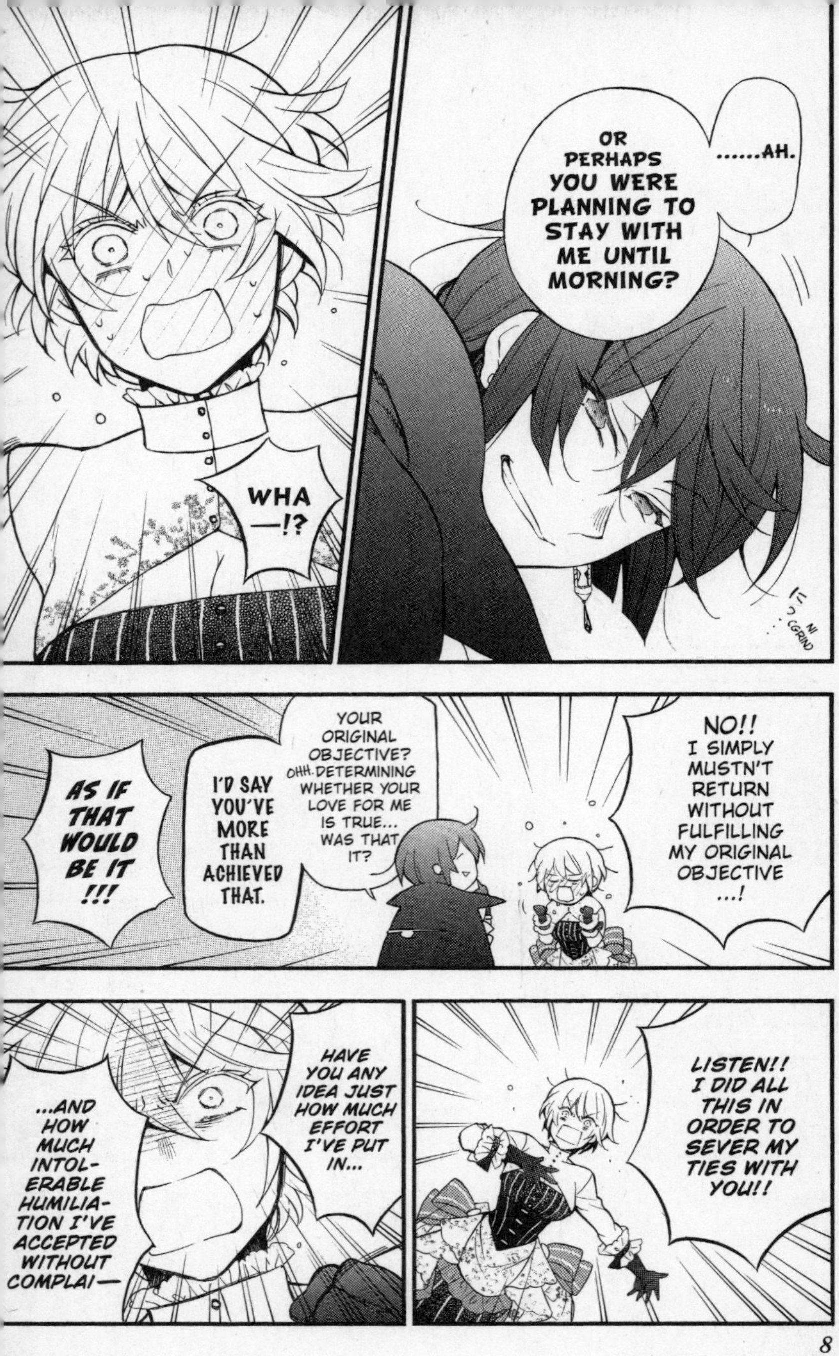
......AH.
OR PERHAPS YOU WERE PLANNING TO STAY WITH ME UNTIL MORNING?
NI (GRIND)
WHA—!?
NO!! I SIMPLY MUSTN'T RETURN WITHOUT FULFILLING MY ORIGINAL OBJECTIVE ...!
YOUR ORIGINAL OBJECTIVE? OHH. DETERMINING WHETHER YOUR LOVE FOR ME IS TRUE... WAS THAT IT?
I'D SAY YOU'VE MORE THAN ACHIEVED THAT.
AS IF THAT WOULD BE IT !!!
LISTEN!! I DID ALL THIS IN ORDER TO SEVER MY TIES WITH YOU!!
HAVE YOU ANY IDEA JUST HOW MUCH EFFORT I'VE PUT IN...
...AND HOW MUCH INTOL-ERABLE HUMILIA-TION I'VE ACCEPTED WITHOUT COMPLAI—

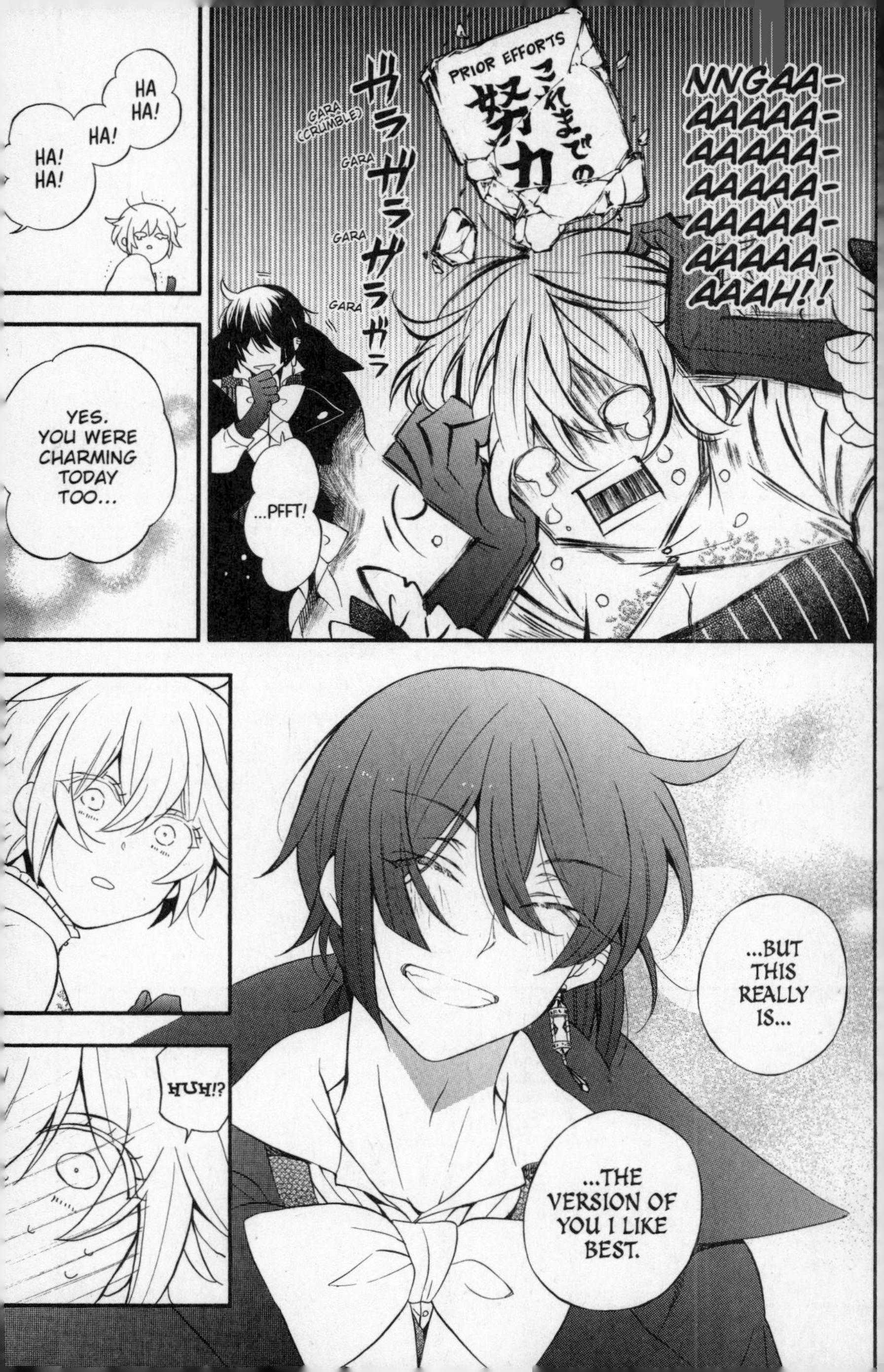
NNGAA-AAAAA-AAAAA-AAAAA-AAAAA-AAAAA-AAAH!!
PRIOR EFFORTS
これまでの努力
GARA (CRUMBLE)
GARA
GARA
GARA
...PFFT!
HA HA!
HA!
HA! HA!
YES. YOU WERE CHARMING TODAY TOO...
...BUT THIS REALLY IS...
...THE VERSION OF YOU I LIKE BEST.
HUH!?

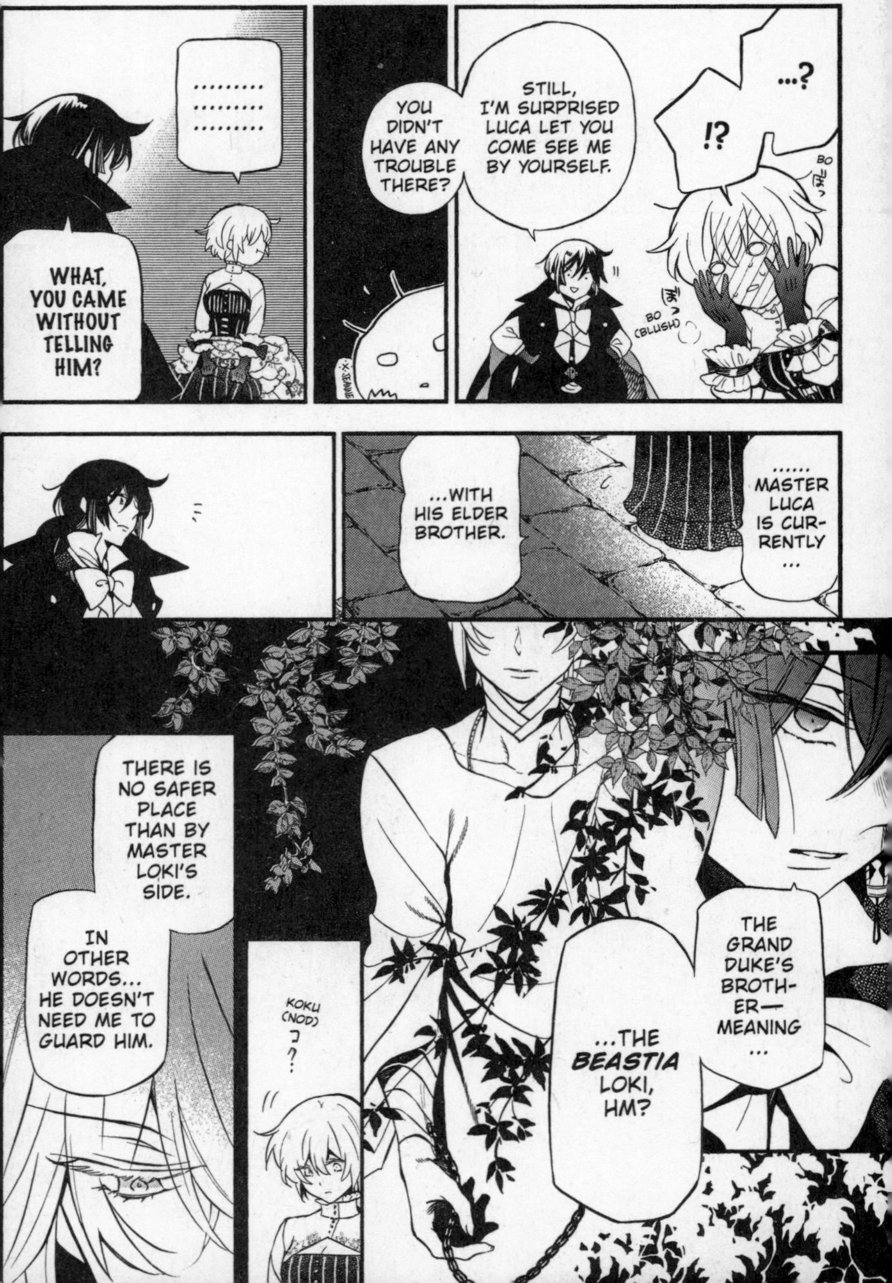
...?
!?
BO ぼっ
STILL, I'M SURPRISED LUCA LET YOU COME SEE ME BY YOURSELF.
YOU DIDN'T HAVE ANY TROUBLE THERE?
BO (BLUSH) ぼっ
....
....
....
WHAT, YOU CAME WITHOUT TELLING HIM?
...... MASTER LUCA IS CUR-RENTLY ...
...WITH HIS ELDER BROTHER.
THE GRAND DUKE'S BROTHER—MEANING ...
...THE *BEASTIA* LOKI, HM?
THERE IS NO SAFER PLACE THAN BY MASTER LOKI'S SIDE.
IN OTHER WORDS... HE DOESN'T NEED ME TO GUARD HIM.
KOKU (NOD) コク

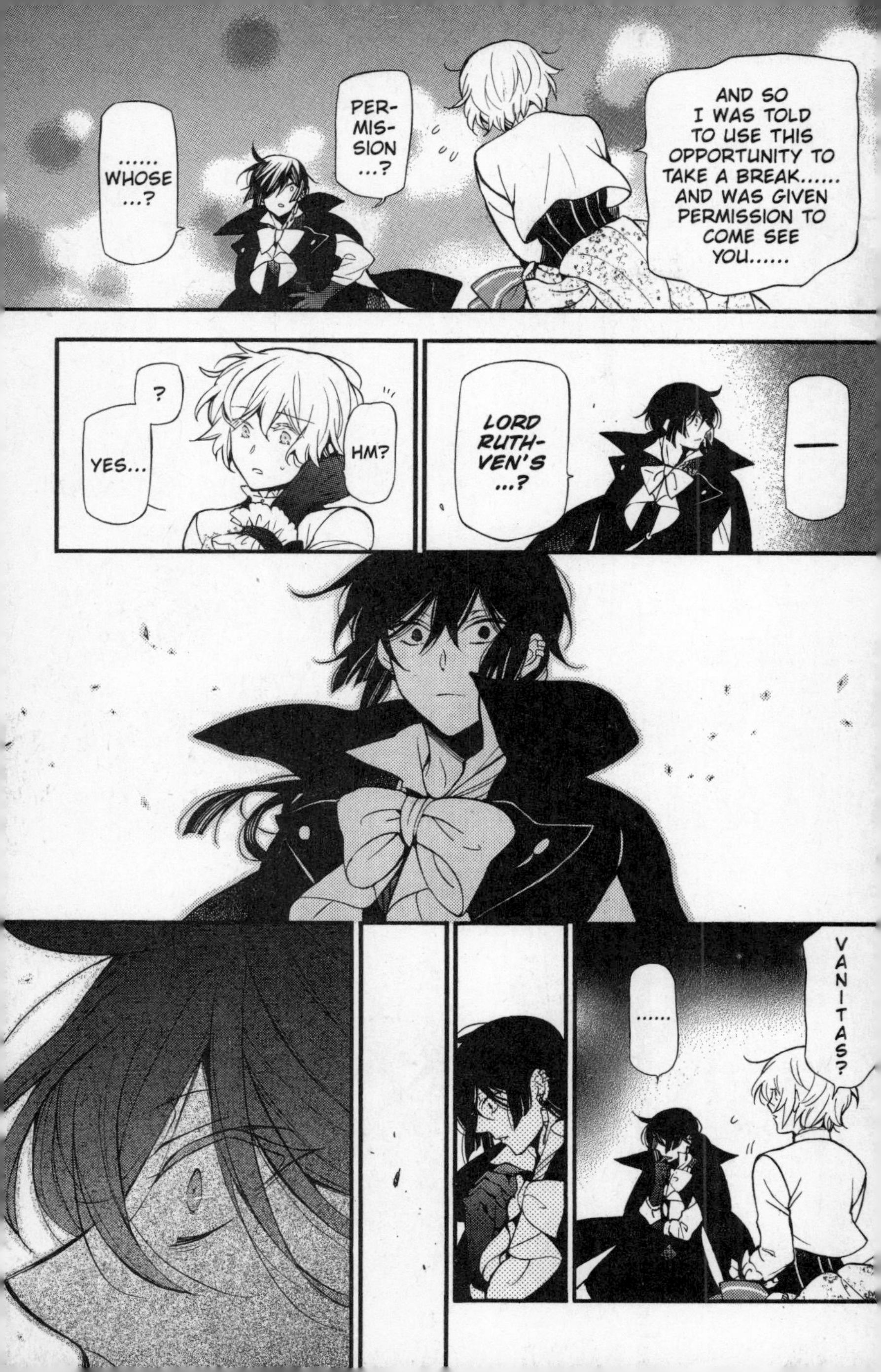
AND SO I WAS TOLD TO USE THIS OPPORTUNITY TO TAKE A BREAK...... AND WAS GIVEN PERMISSION TO COME SEE YOU......
PER-MIS-SION ...?
......WHOSE ...?
—
LORD RUTH-VEN'S ...?
HM?
?
YES...
VANITAS?
......

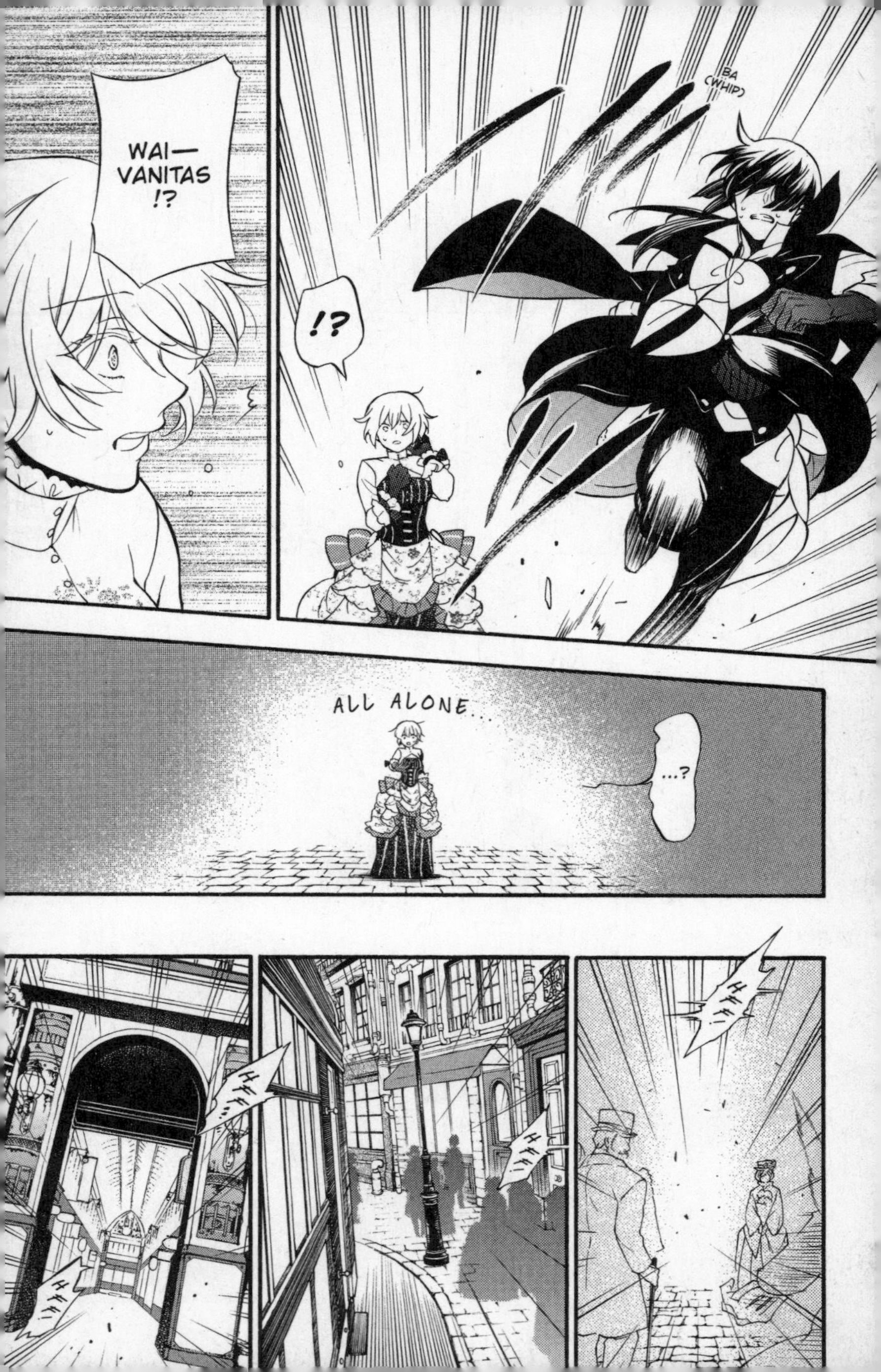
BA (WHIP)
!?
WAI— VANITAS !?
ALL ALONE...
...?
HEE!
HEE!
HEE...
HEE!

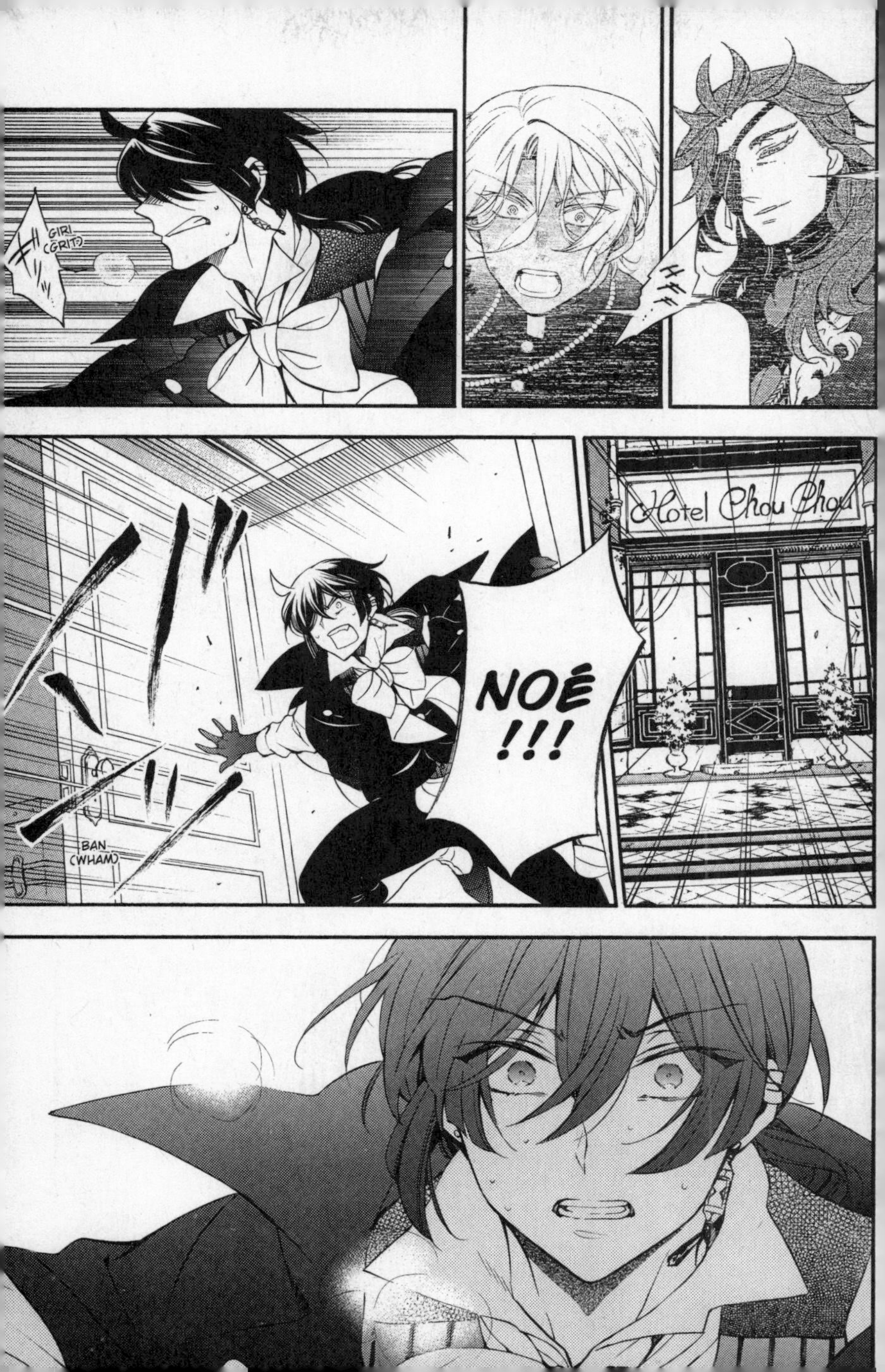
GIRI
(GRIT)
Hotel Chou Chou
NOÉ
!!!
BAN
(WHAM)

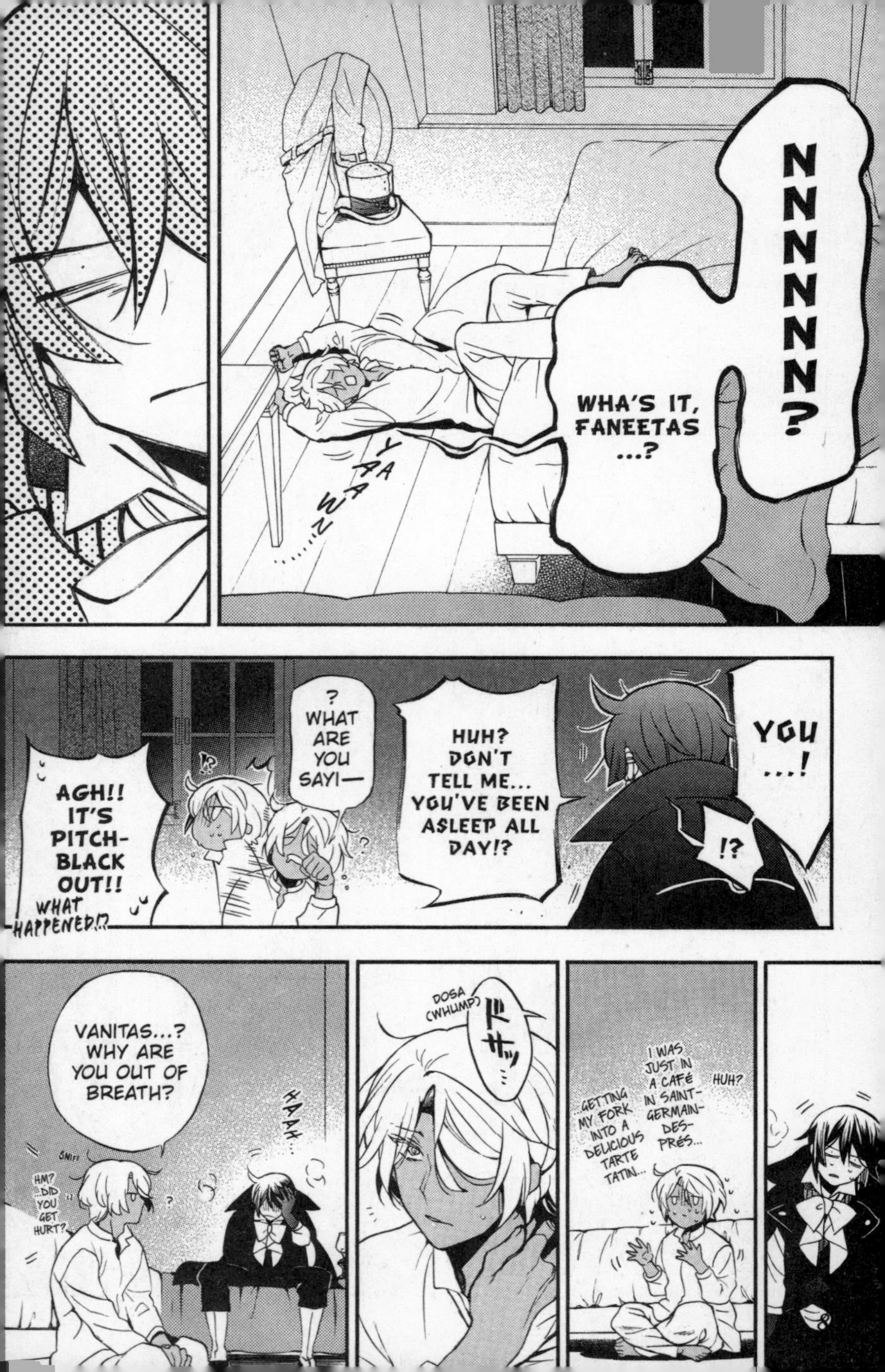
NNNNNN?
WHA'S IT, FANEETAS...?
YAAAWN......
YOU...!
!?
HUH? DON'T TELL ME... YOU'VE BEEN ASLEEP ALL DAY!?
? WHAT ARE YOU SAYI—
!?
AGH!! IT'S PITCH-BLACK OUT!!
WHAT HAPPENED!?
HUH?
I WAS JUST IN A CAFÉ IN SAINT-GERMAIN-DES-PRÉS...
...GETTING MY FORK INTO A DELICIOUS TARTE TATIN...
DOSA (WHUMP)
ドサッ…
VANITAS...? WHY ARE YOU OUT OF BREATH?
HAAH...
SNIFF
HM? ...DID YOU GET HURT?

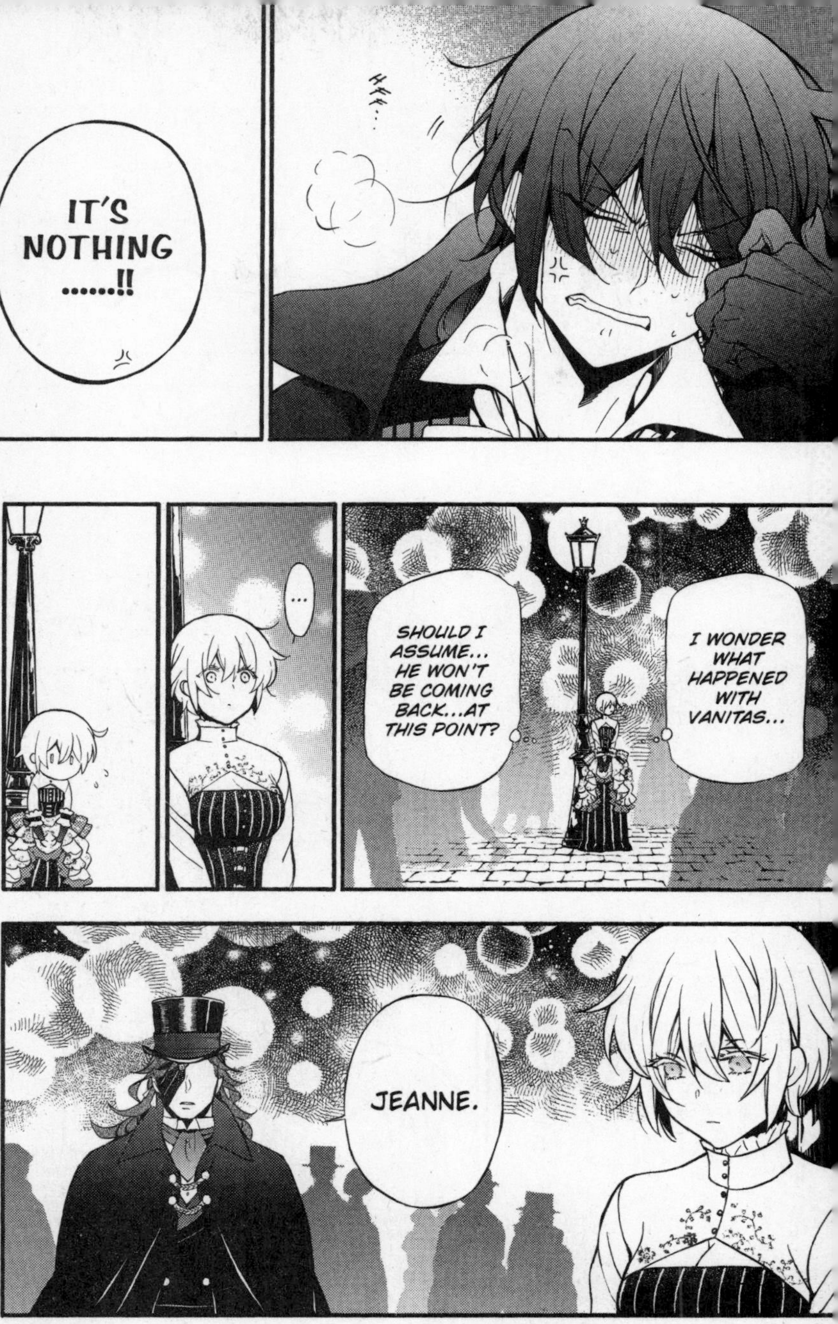
HFF...
IT'S NOTHING ......!!
I WONDER WHAT HAPPENED WITH VANITAS...
SHOULD I ASSUME... HE WON'T BE COMING BACK...AT THIS POINT?
...
JEANNE.

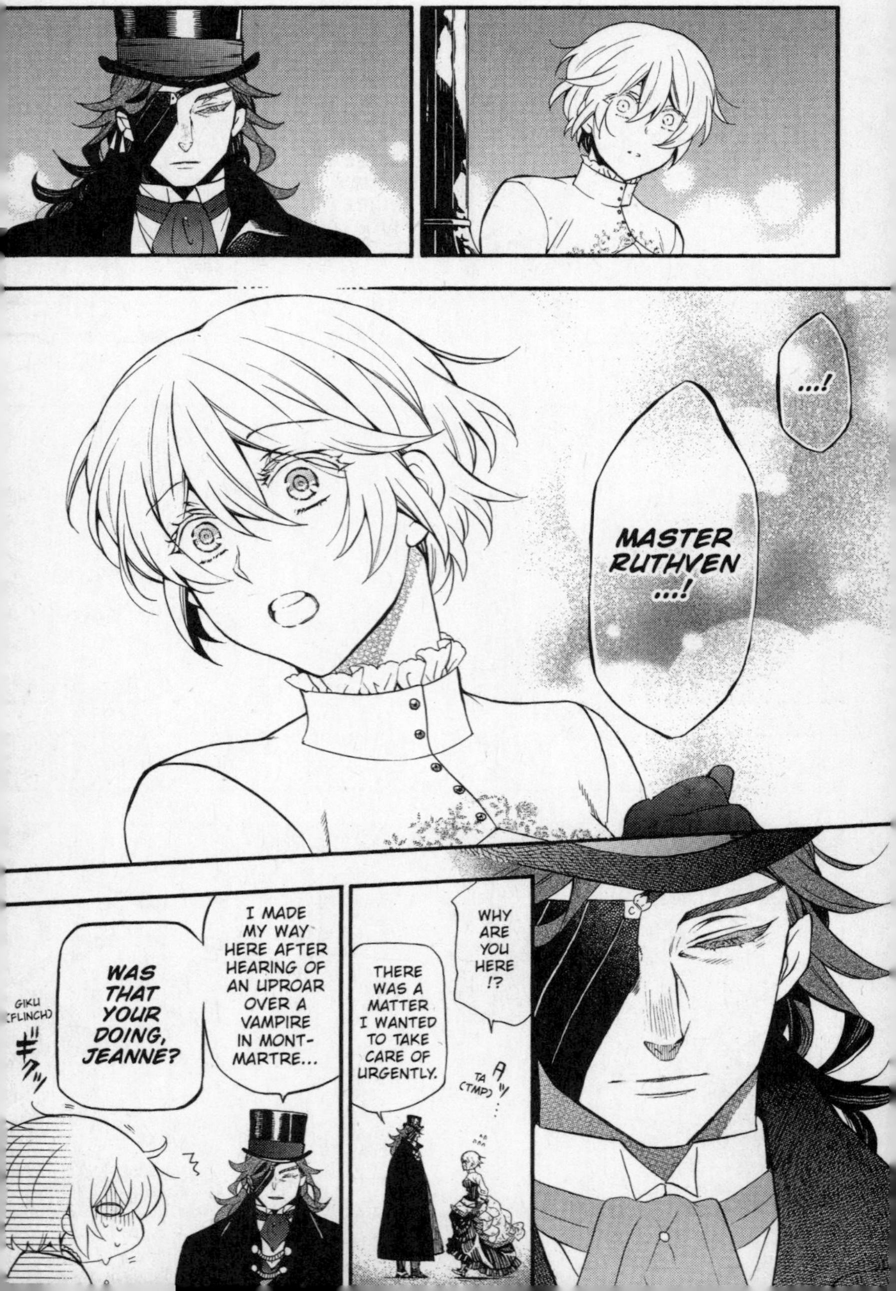
...!
MASTER RUTHVEN ...!
WHY ARE YOU HERE !?
TA (TMP)
THERE WAS A MATTER I WANTED TO TAKE CARE OF URGENTLY.
I MADE MY WAY HERE AFTER HEARING OF AN UPROAR OVER A VAMPIRE IN MONT-MARTRE...
WAS THAT YOUR DOING, JEANNE?
GIKU (FLINCH)

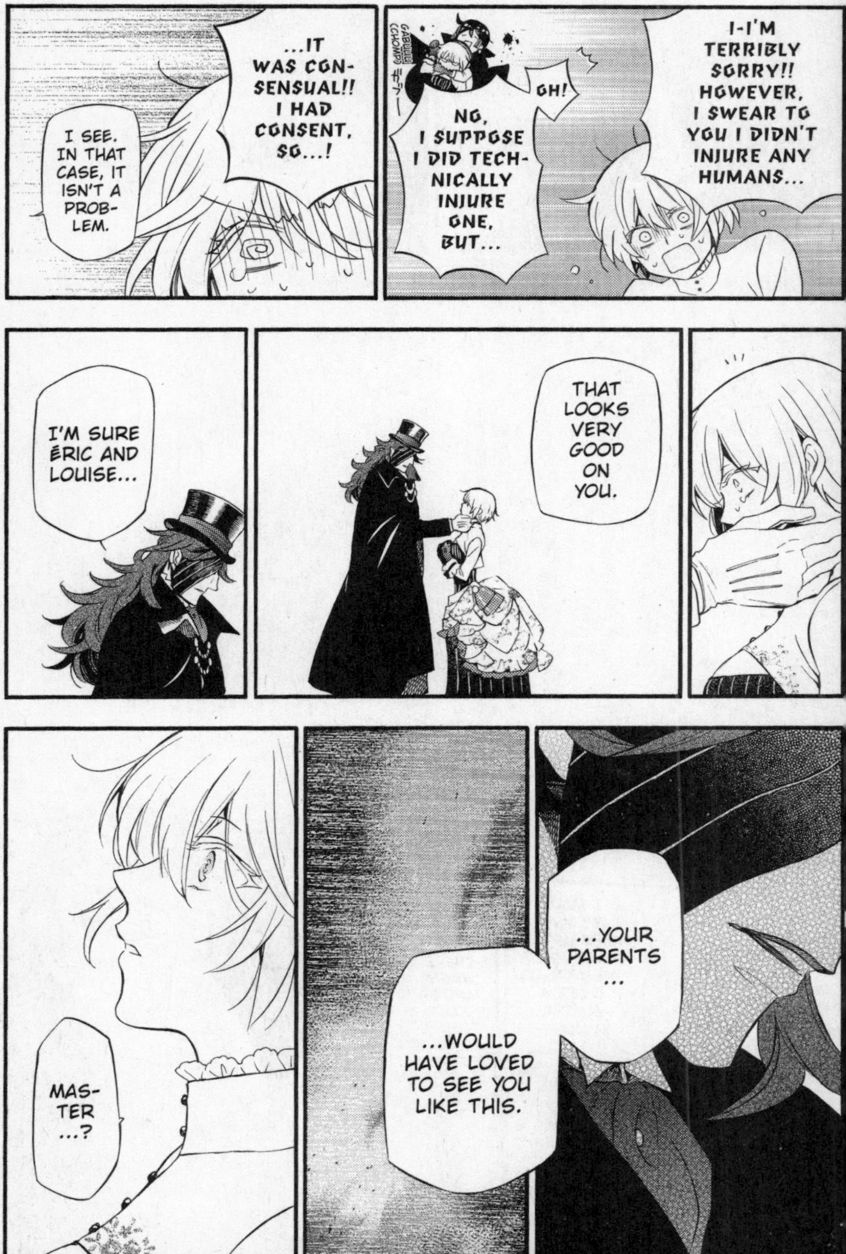
I-I'M TERRIBLY SORRY!! HOWEVER, I SWEAR TO YOU I DIDN'T INJURE ANY HUMANS...
OH!
NO, I SUPPOSE I DID TECHNICALLY INJURE ONE, BUT...
GABUUU (CHOMP)
...IT WAS CONSENSUAL!! I HAD CONSENT, SO...!
I SEE. IN THAT CASE, IT ISN'T A PROBLEM.
THAT LOOKS VERY GOOD ON YOU.
I'M SURE ÉRIC AND LOUISE...
...YOUR PARENTS ...
...WOULD HAVE LOVED TO SEE YOU LIKE THIS.
MASTER...?

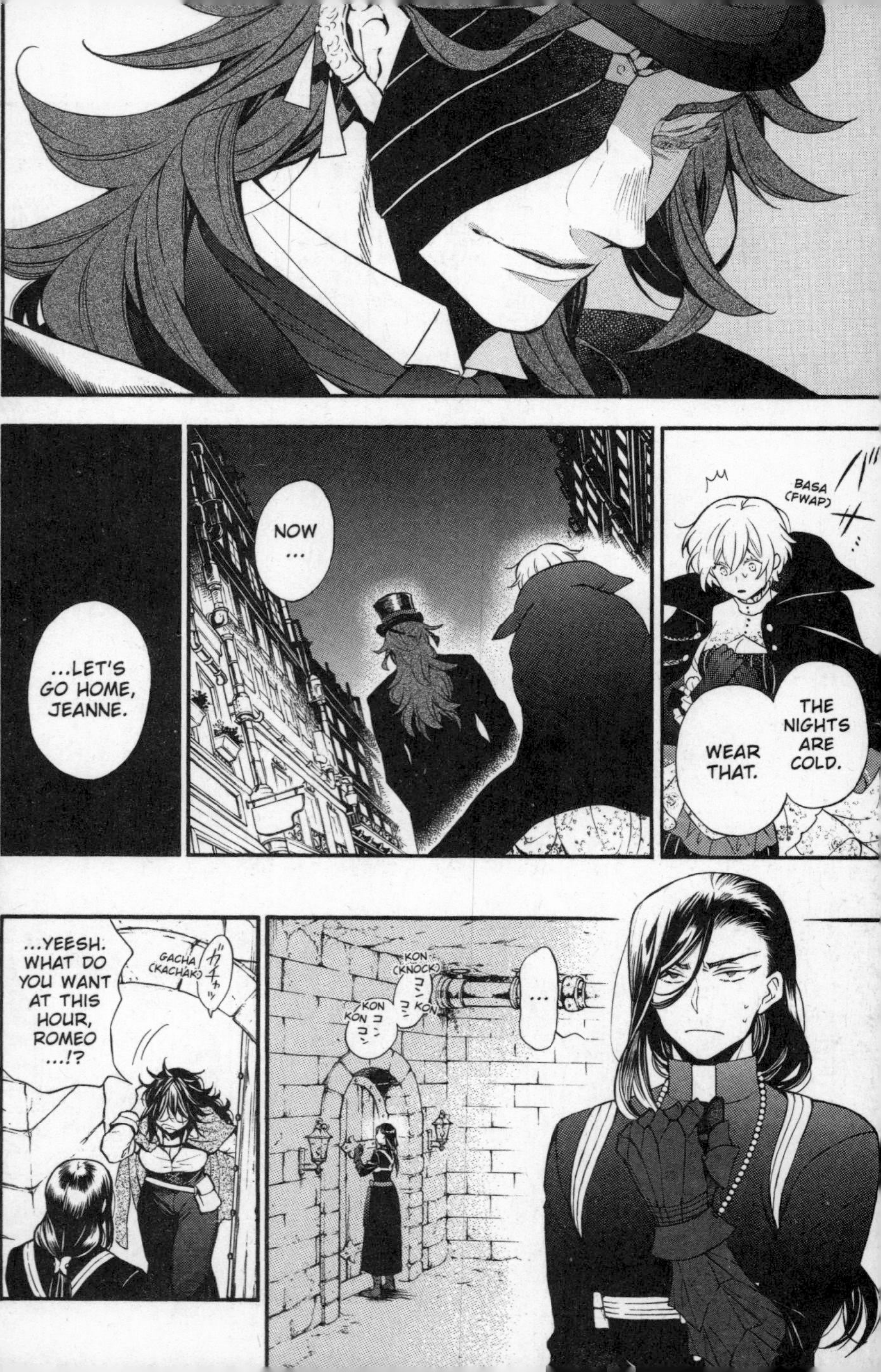

BASA (FWAP)
THE NIGHTS ARE COLD.
WEAR THAT.
NOW...
...LET'S GO HOME, JEANNE.
...
KON (KNOCK) KON
KON KON
GACHA (KACHAK)
...YEESH. WHAT DO YOU WANT AT THIS HOUR, ROMEO ...!?

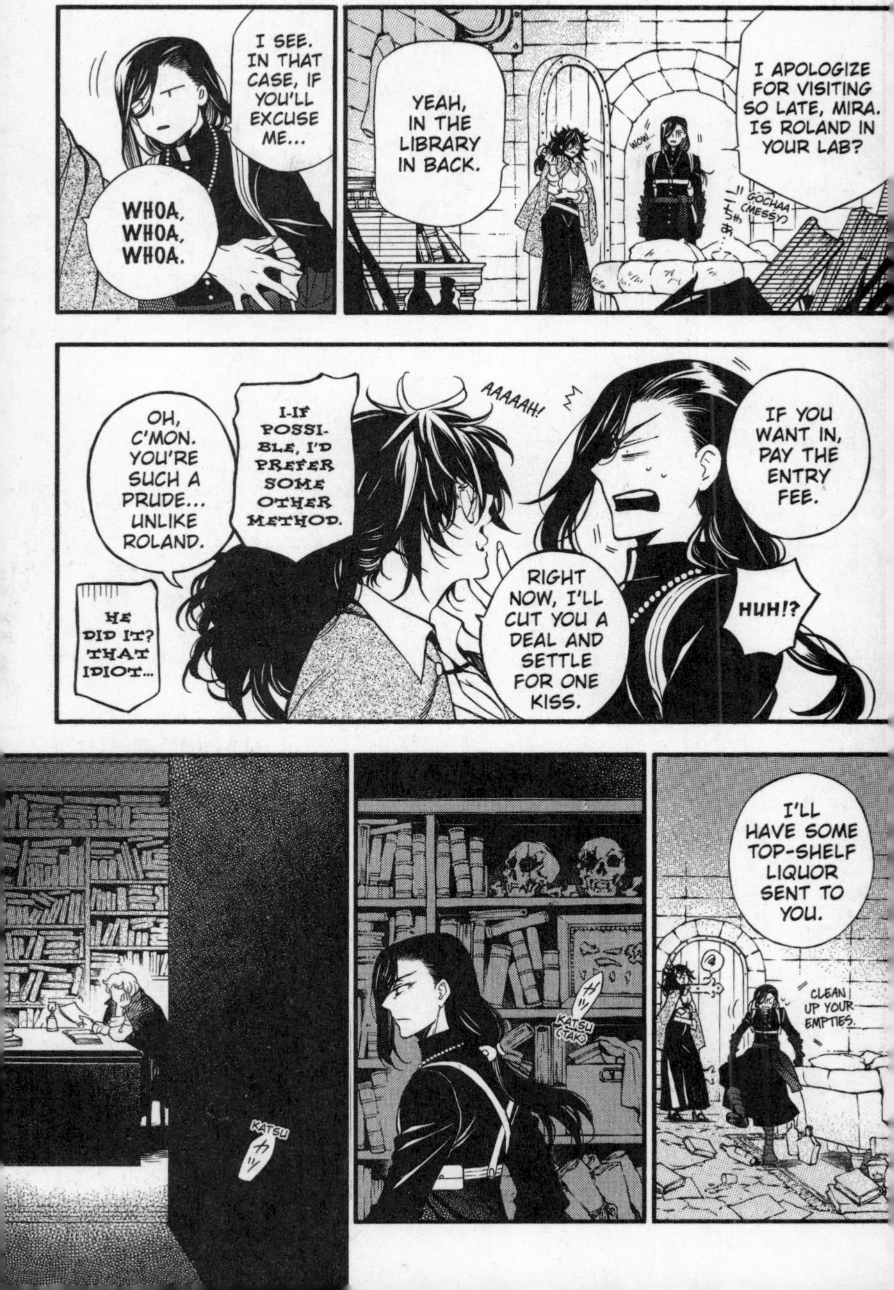
I APOLOGIZE FOR VISITING SO LATE, MIRA. IS ROLAND IN YOUR LAB?
WOW...
GOCHAA (MESSY)
YEAH, IN THE LIBRARY IN BACK.
I SEE. IN THAT CASE, IF YOU'LL EXCUSE ME...
WHOA, WHOA, WHOA.
IF YOU WANT IN, PAY THE ENTRY FEE.
AAAAAH!
HUH!?
RIGHT NOW, I'LL CUT YOU A DEAL AND SETTLE FOR ONE KISS.
I-IF POSSIBLE, I'D PREFER SOME OTHER METHOD.
OH, C'MON. YOU'RE SUCH A PRUDE... UNLIKE ROLAND.
HE DID IT? THAT IDIOT...
I'LL HAVE SOME TOP-SHELF LIQUOR SENT TO YOU.
CLEAN UP YOUR EMPTIES.
KATSU (TAK)
KATSU

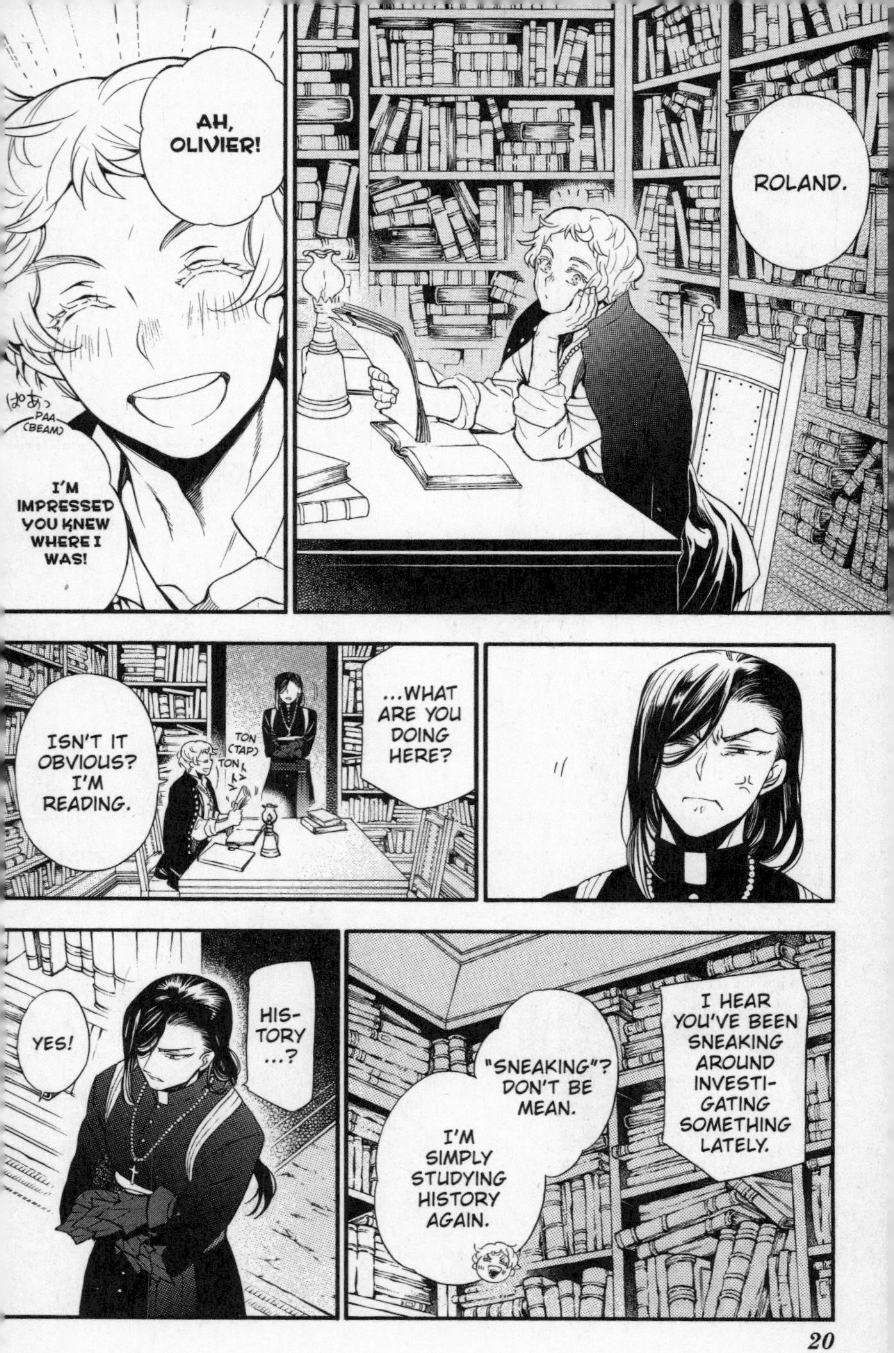
ROLAND.
AH, OLIVIER!
ぱあっ
PAA (BEAM)
I'M IMPRESSED YOU KNEW WHERE I WAS!
...WHAT ARE YOU DOING HERE?
TON (TAP) TON
ISN'T IT OBVIOUS? I'M READING.
I HEAR YOU'VE BEEN SNEAKING AROUND INVESTI-GATING SOMETHING LATELY.
"SNEAKING"? DON'T BE MEAN.
I'M SIMPLY STUDYING HISTORY AGAIN.
HIS-TORY ...?
YES!

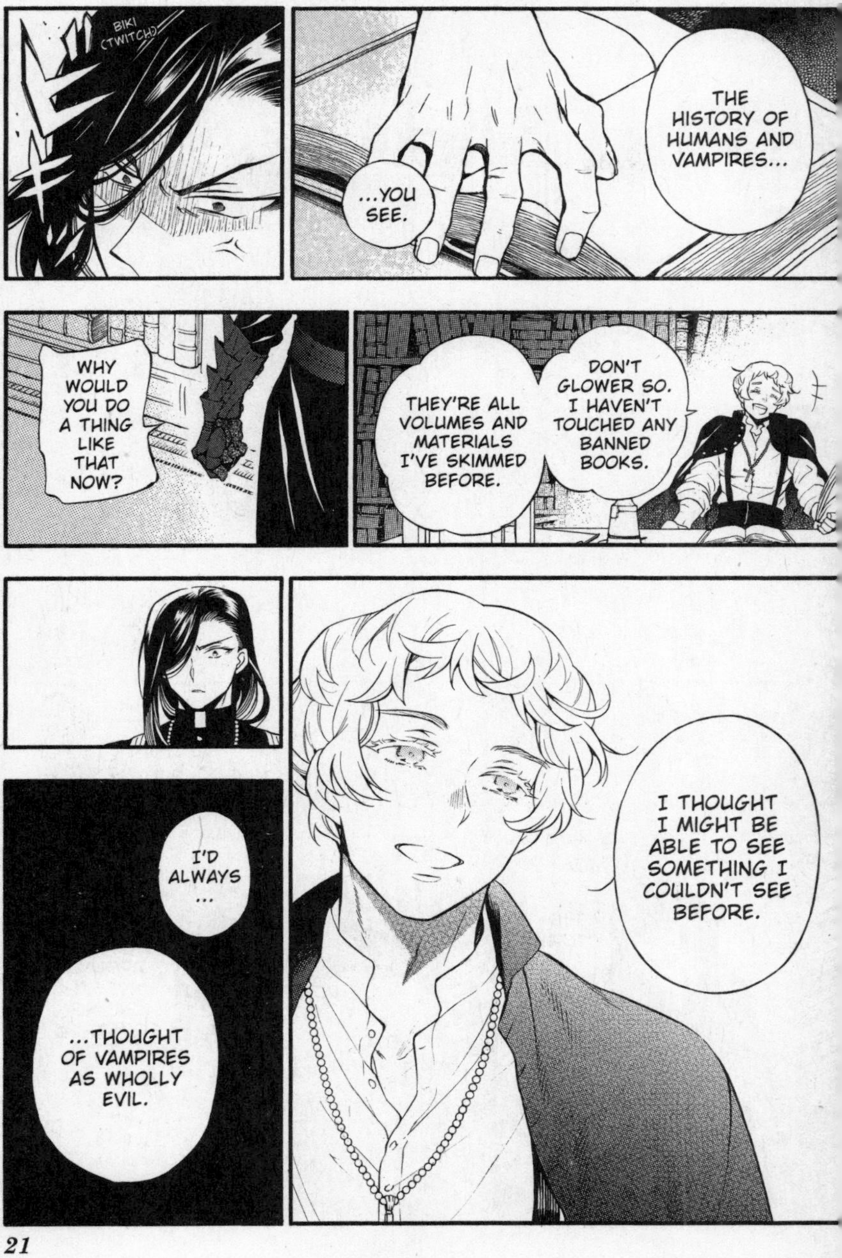
THE HISTORY OF HUMANS AND VAMPIRES...
...YOU SEE.
BIKI (TWITCH)
DON'T GLOWER SO. I HAVEN'T TOUCHED ANY BANNED BOOKS.
THEY'RE ALL VOLUMES AND MATERIALS I'VE SKIMMED BEFORE.
WHY WOULD YOU DO A THING LIKE THAT NOW?
I THOUGHT I MIGHT BE ABLE TO SEE SOMETHING I COULDN'T SEE BEFORE.
I'D ALWAYS ...
...THOUGHT OF VAMPIRES AS WHOLLY EVIL.

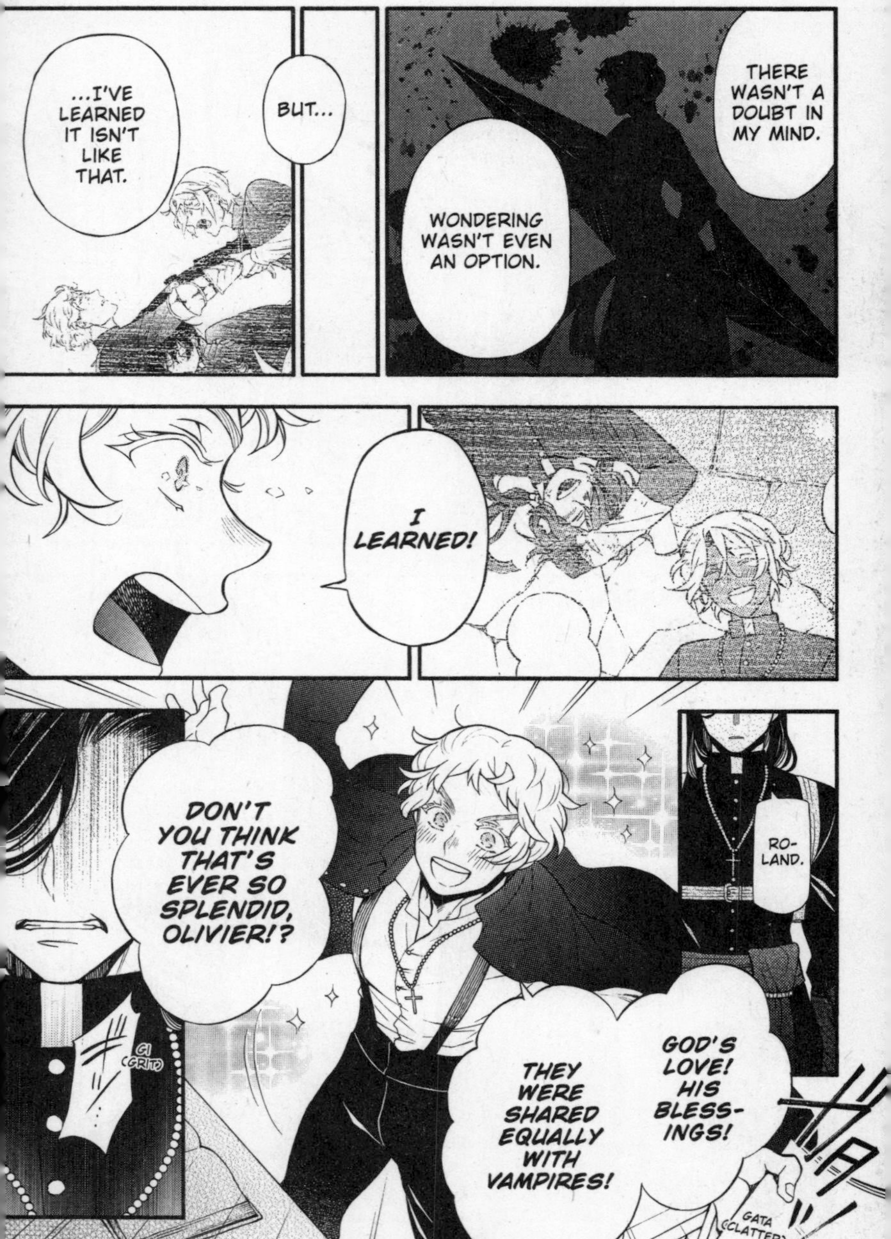
THERE WASN'T A DOUBT IN MY MIND.
WONDERING WASN'T EVEN AN OPTION.
BUT...
...I'VE LEARNED IT ISN'T LIKE THAT.
I LEARNED!
RO-LAND.
DON'T YOU THINK THAT'S EVER SO SPLENDID, OLIVIER!?
GOD'S LOVE! HIS BLESS-INGS!
THEY WERE SHARED EQUALLY WITH VAMPIRES!
GATA (CLATTER)
GI (GRIT)

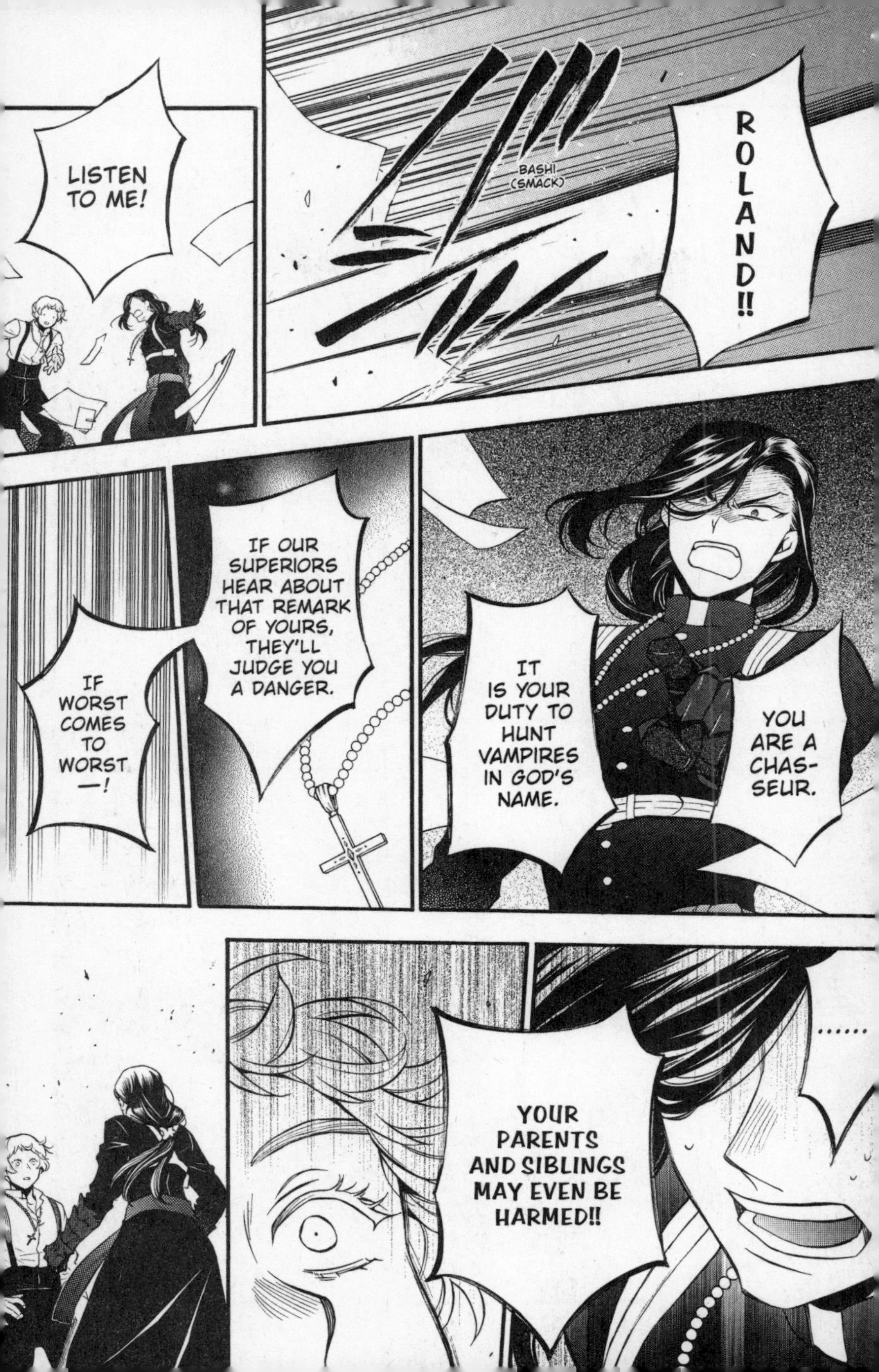
ROLAND!!
BASHI (SMACK)
LISTEN TO ME!
YOU ARE A CHASSEUR.
IT IS YOUR DUTY TO HUNT VAMPIRES IN GOD'S NAME.
IF OUR SUPERIORS HEAR ABOUT THAT REMARK OF YOURS, THEY'LL JUDGE YOU A DANGER.
IF WORST COMES TO WORST—!
......
YOUR PARENTS AND SIBLINGS MAY EVEN BE HARMED!!

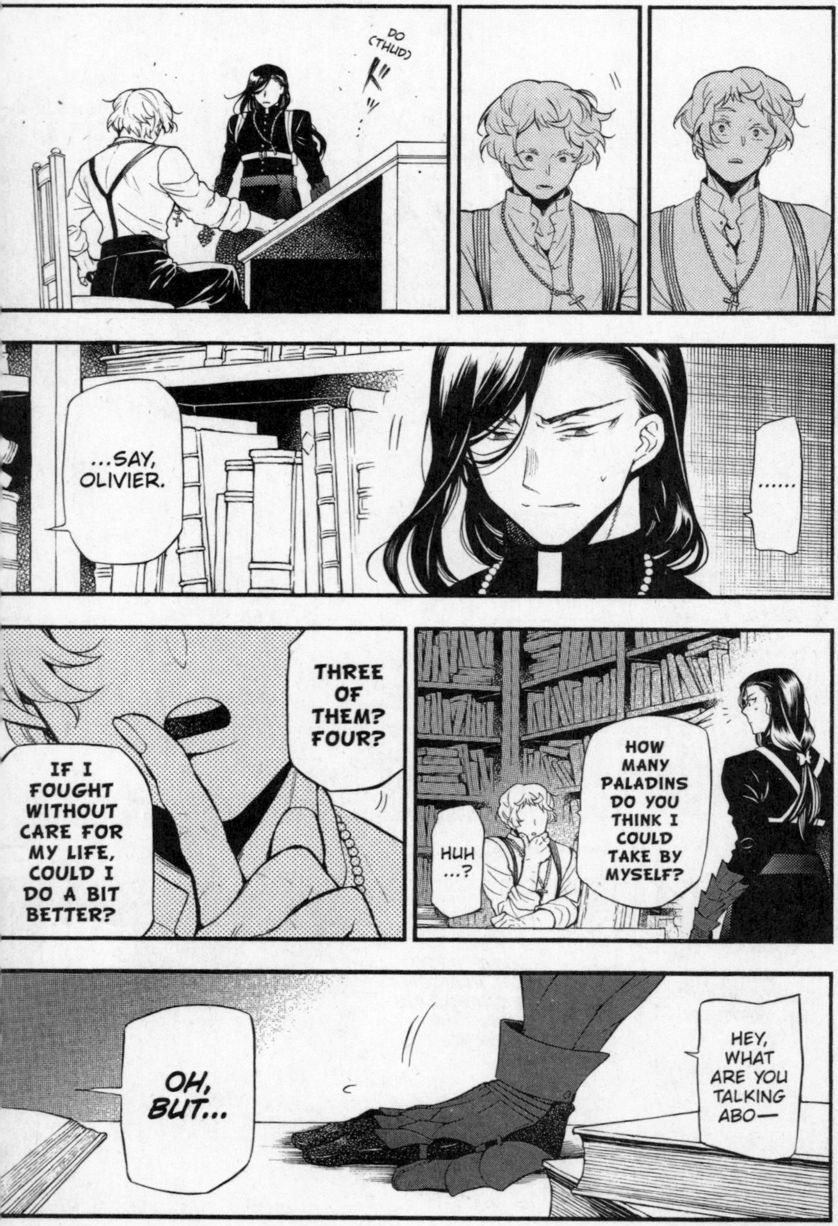
DO (THUD)
......
...SAY, OLIVIER.
HOW MANY PALADINS DO YOU THINK I COULD TAKE BY MYSELF?
HUH ...?
THREE OF THEM? FOUR?
IF I FOUGHT WITHOUT CARE FOR MY LIFE, COULD I DO A BIT BETTER?
HEY, WHAT ARE YOU TALKING ABO—
OH, BUT...

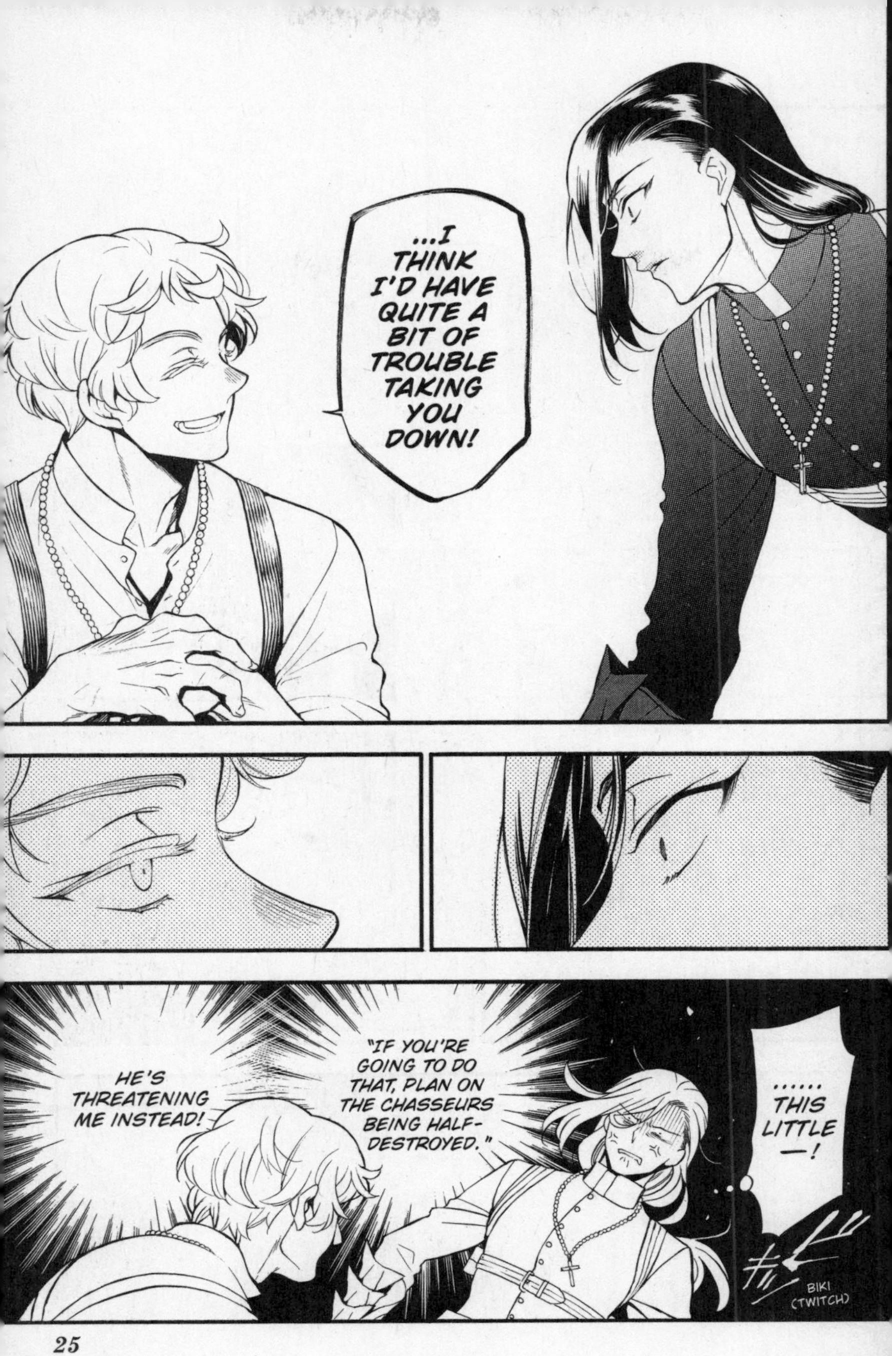
...I THINK I'D HAVE QUITE A BIT OF TROUBLE TAKING YOU DOWN!
...... THIS LITTLE—!
BIKI (TWITCH)
"IF YOU'RE GOING TO DO THAT, PLAN ON THE CHASSEURS BEING HALF-DESTROYED."
HE'S THREATENING ME INSTEAD!

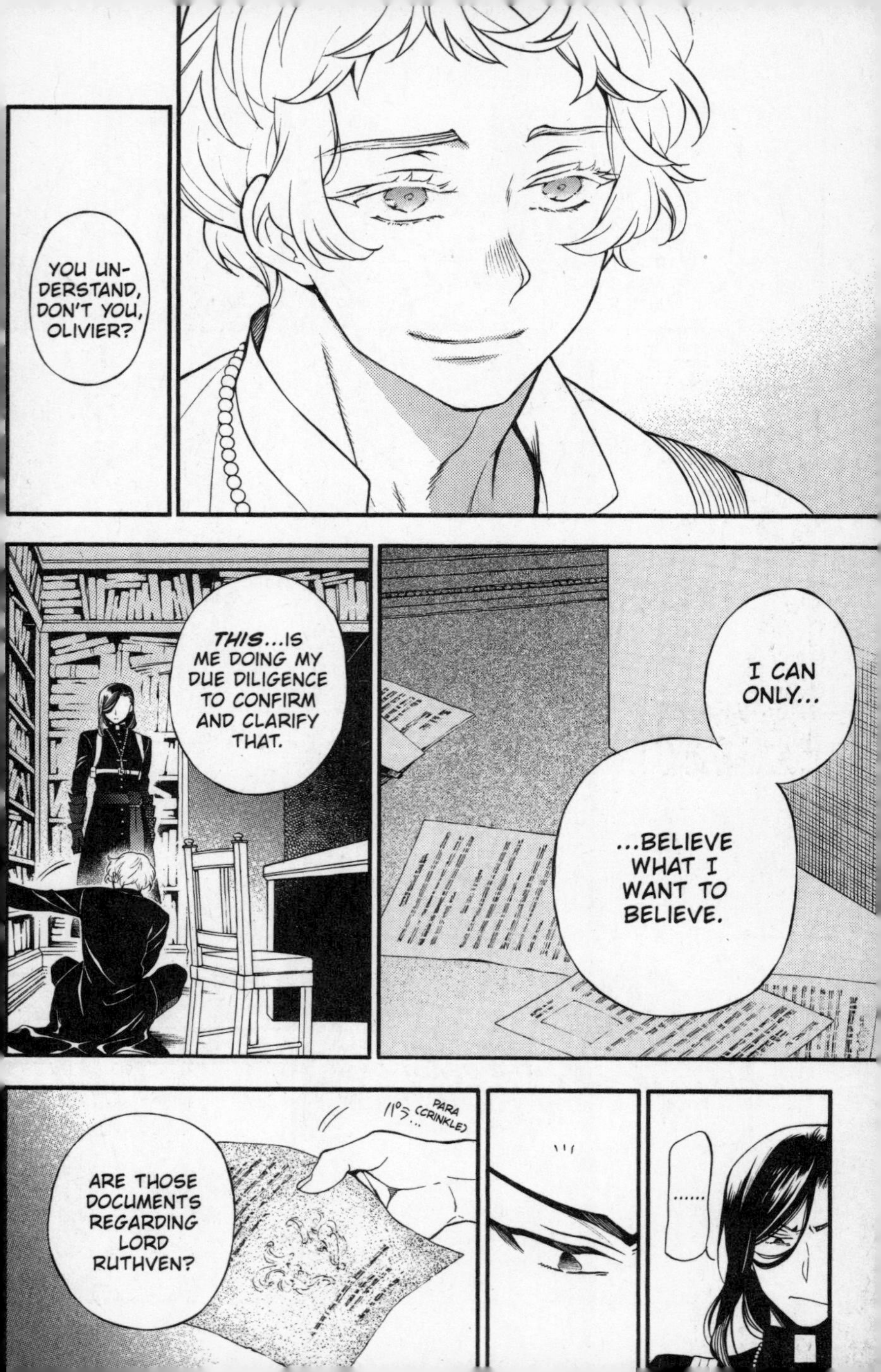
YOU UNDERSTAND, DON'T YOU, OLIVIER?
I CAN ONLY...
...BELIEVE WHAT I WANT TO BELIEVE.
THIS...IS ME DOING MY DUE DILIGENCE TO CONFIRM AND CLARIFY THAT.
......
パラ... PARA (CRINKLE)
ARE THOSE DOCUMENTS REGARDING LORD RUTHVEN?

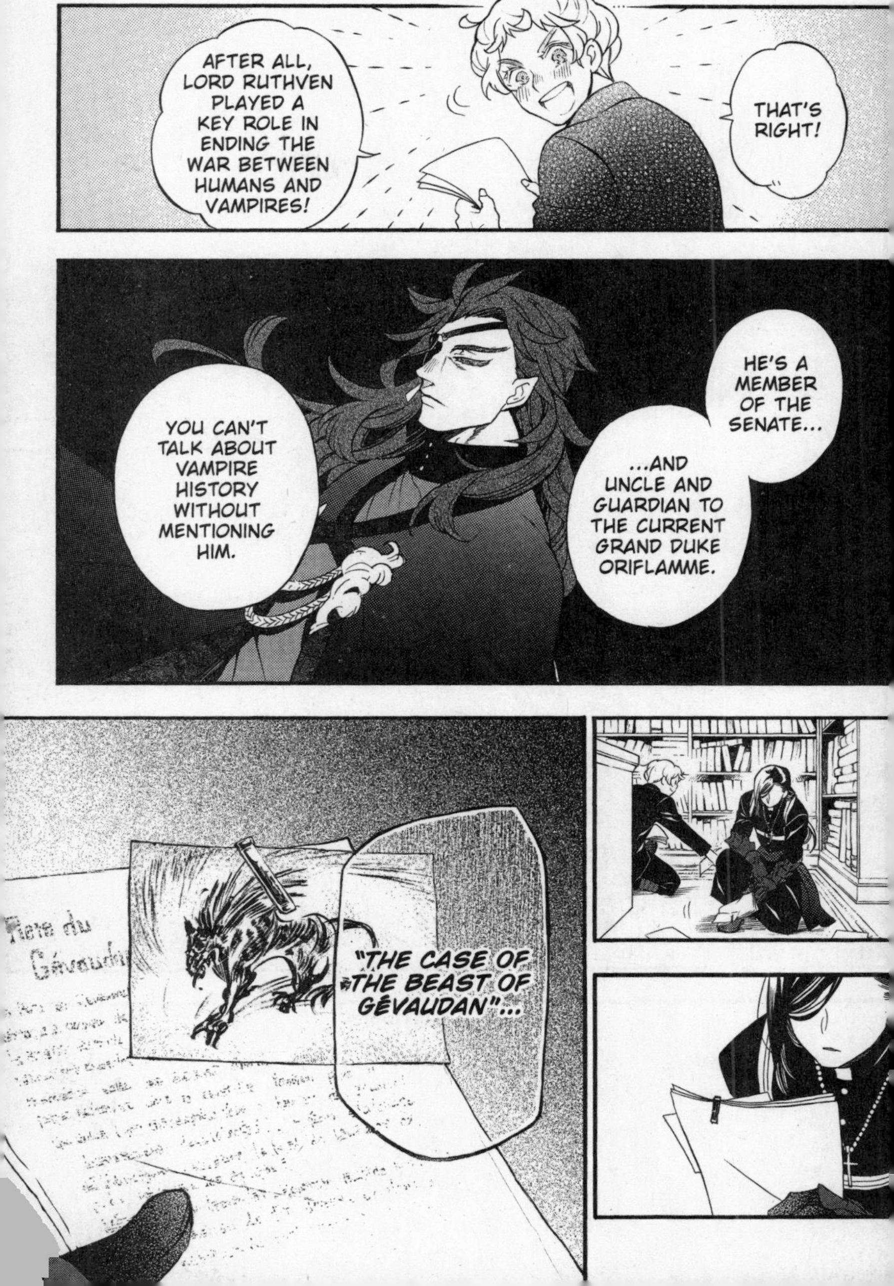
THAT'S RIGHT!
AFTER ALL, LORD RUTHVEN PLAYED A KEY ROLE IN ENDING THE WAR BETWEEN HUMANS AND VAMPIRES!
HE'S A MEMBER OF THE SENATE...
...AND UNCLE AND GUARDIAN TO THE CURRENT GRAND DUKE ORIFLAMME.
YOU CAN'T TALK ABOUT VAMPIRE HISTORY WITHOUT MENTIONING HIM.
"THE CASE OF THE BEAST OF GÉVAUDAN"...

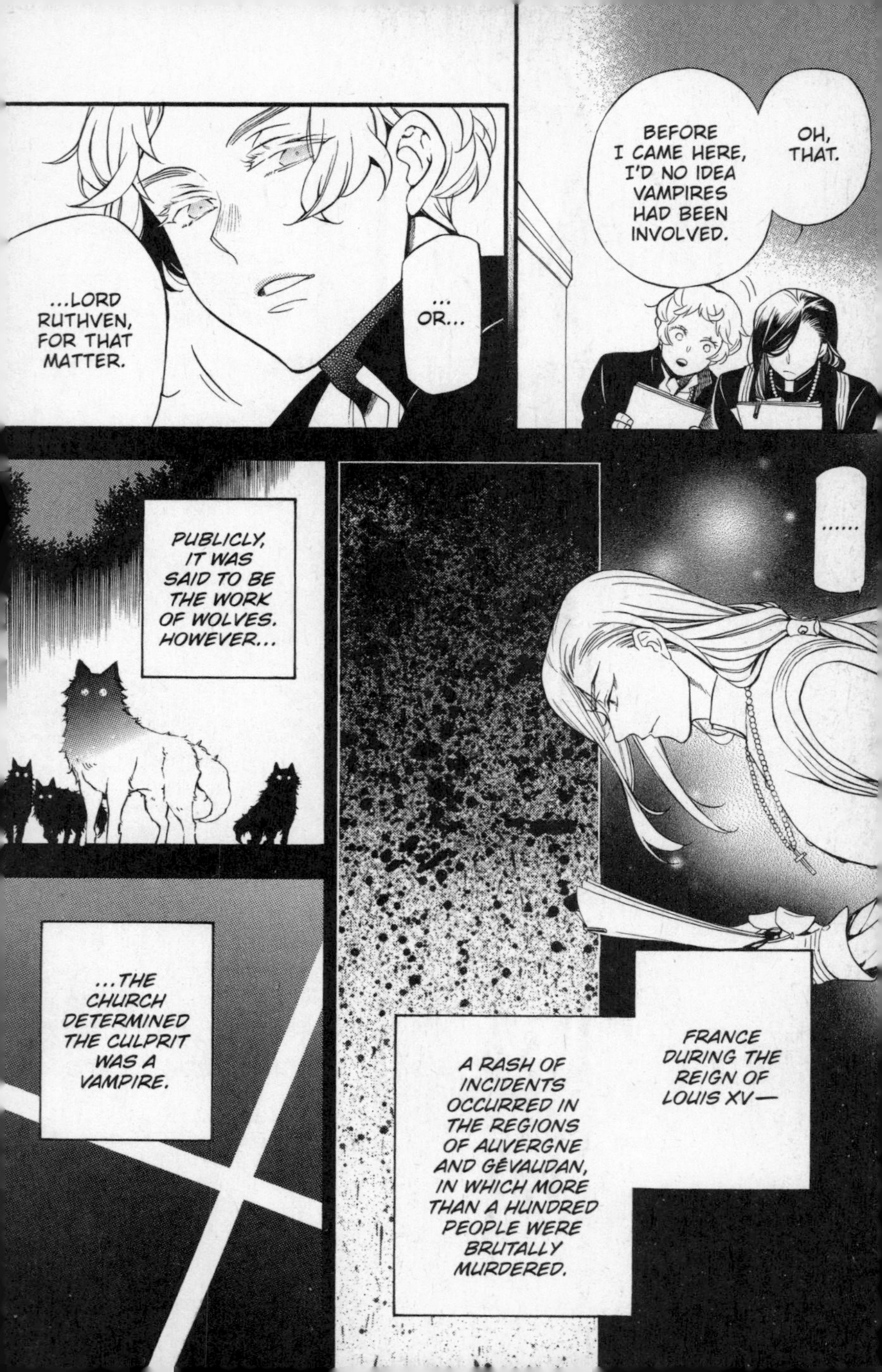
OH, THAT.
BEFORE I CAME HERE, I'D NO IDEA VAMPIRES HAD BEEN INVOLVED.
... OR...
...LORD RUTHVEN, FOR THAT MATTER.
......
FRANCE DURING THE REIGN OF LOUIS XV—
A RASH OF INCIDENTS OCCURRED IN THE REGIONS OF AUVERGNE AND GÉVAUDAN, IN WHICH MORE THAN A HUNDRED PEOPLE WERE BRUTALLY MURDERED.
PUBLICLY, IT WAS SAID TO BE THE WORK OF WOLVES. HOWEVER...
...THE CHURCH DETERMINED THE CULPRIT WAS A VAMPIRE.

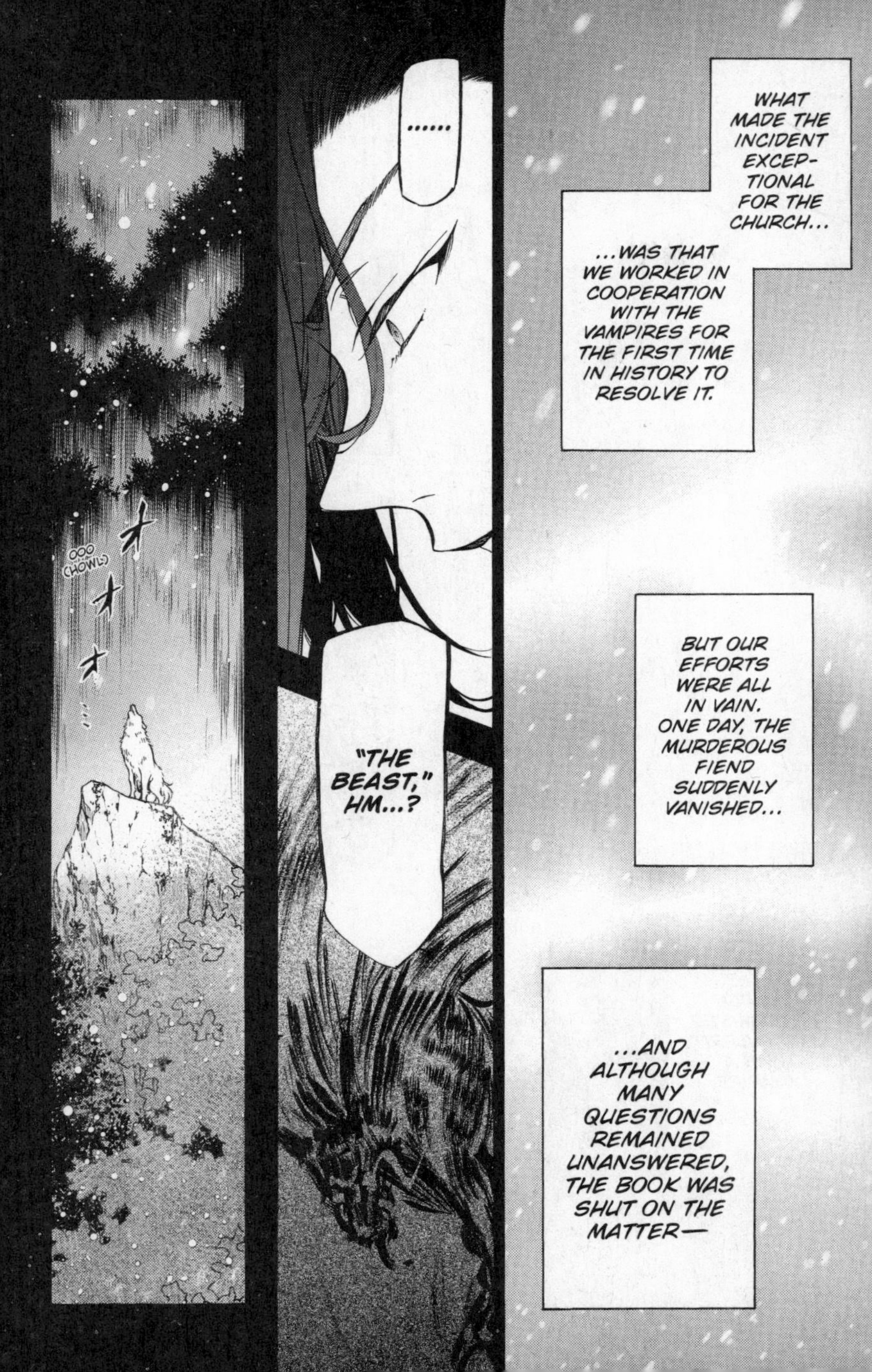
WHAT MADE THE INCIDENT EXCEPTIONAL FOR THE CHURCH...
...WAS THAT WE WORKED IN COOPERATION WITH THE VAMPIRES FOR THE FIRST TIME IN HISTORY TO RESOLVE IT.
BUT OUR EFFORTS WERE ALL IN VAIN. ONE DAY, THE MURDEROUS FIEND SUDDENLY VANISHED...
...AND ALTHOUGH MANY QUESTIONS REMAINED UNANSWERED, THE BOOK WAS SHUT ON THE MATTER—
......
"THE BEAST," HM...?
OOO (HOWL)

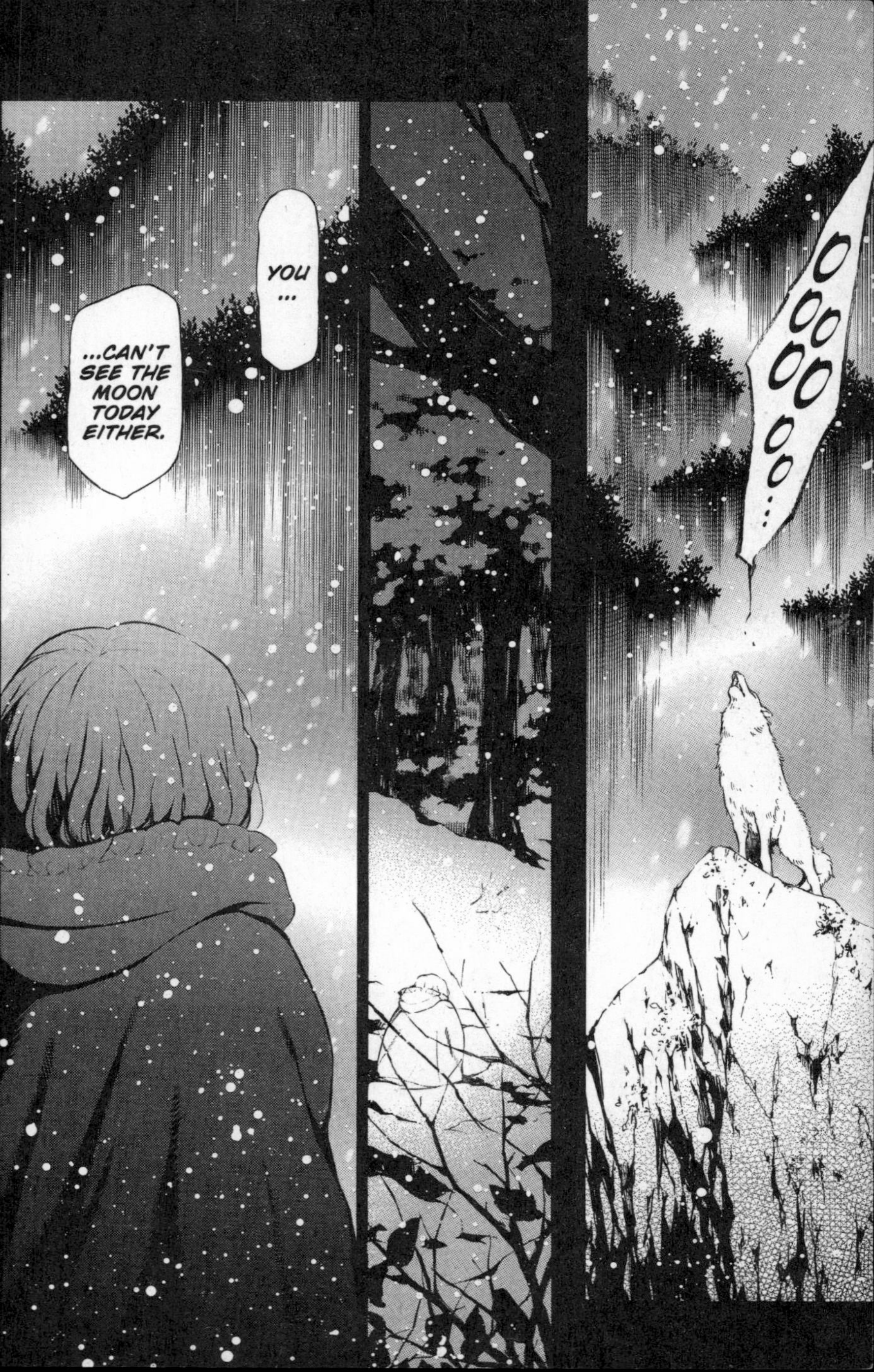
OOOOOOOOO...
YOU ...
...CAN'T SEE THE MOON TODAY EITHER.

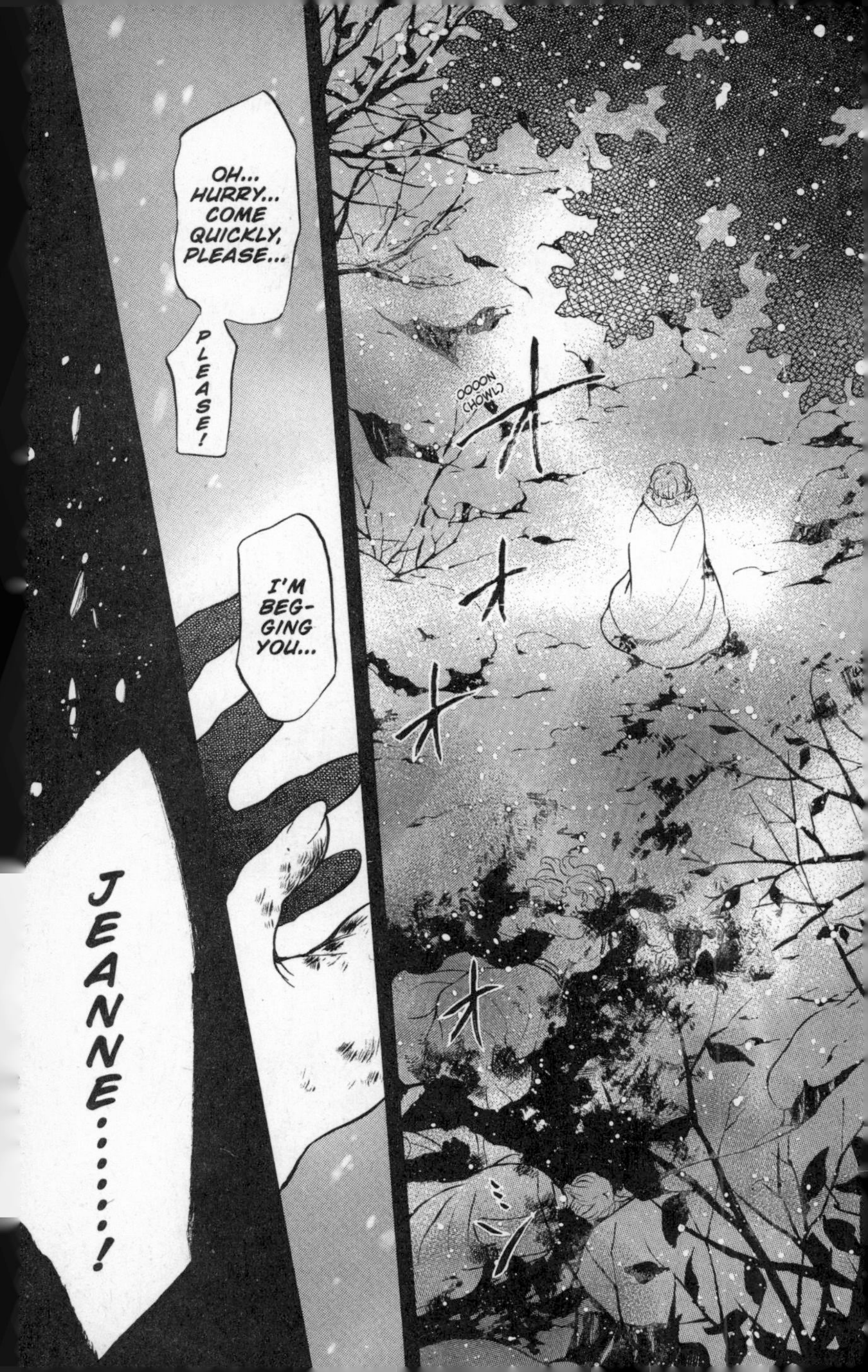
OOOON (HOWL)
OH... HURRY... COME QUICKLY, PLEASE...
PLEASE!
I'M BEG-GING YOU...
JEANNE......!

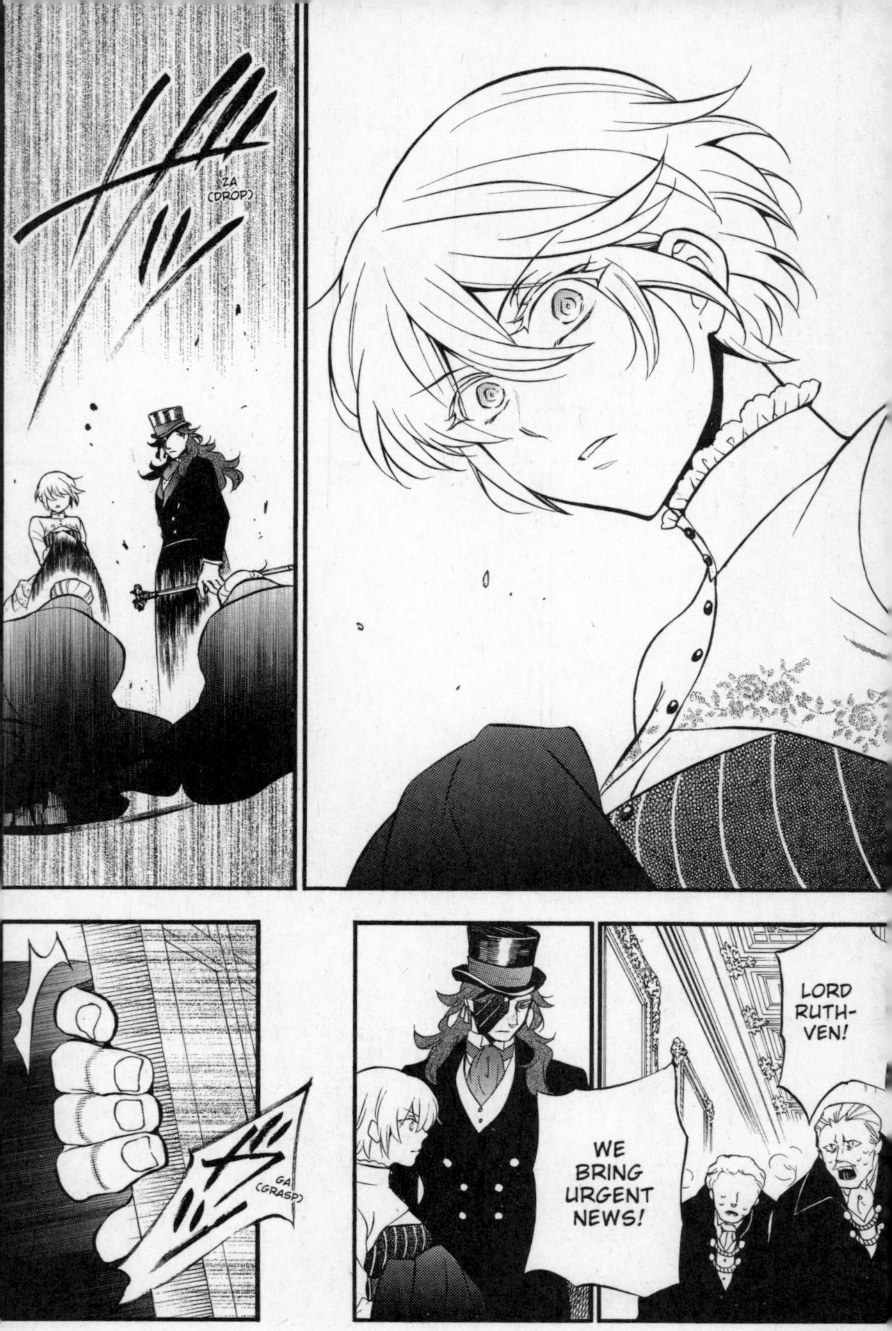
ZA (DROP)
LORD RUTH-VEN!
WE BRING URGENT NEWS!
GA (GRASP)

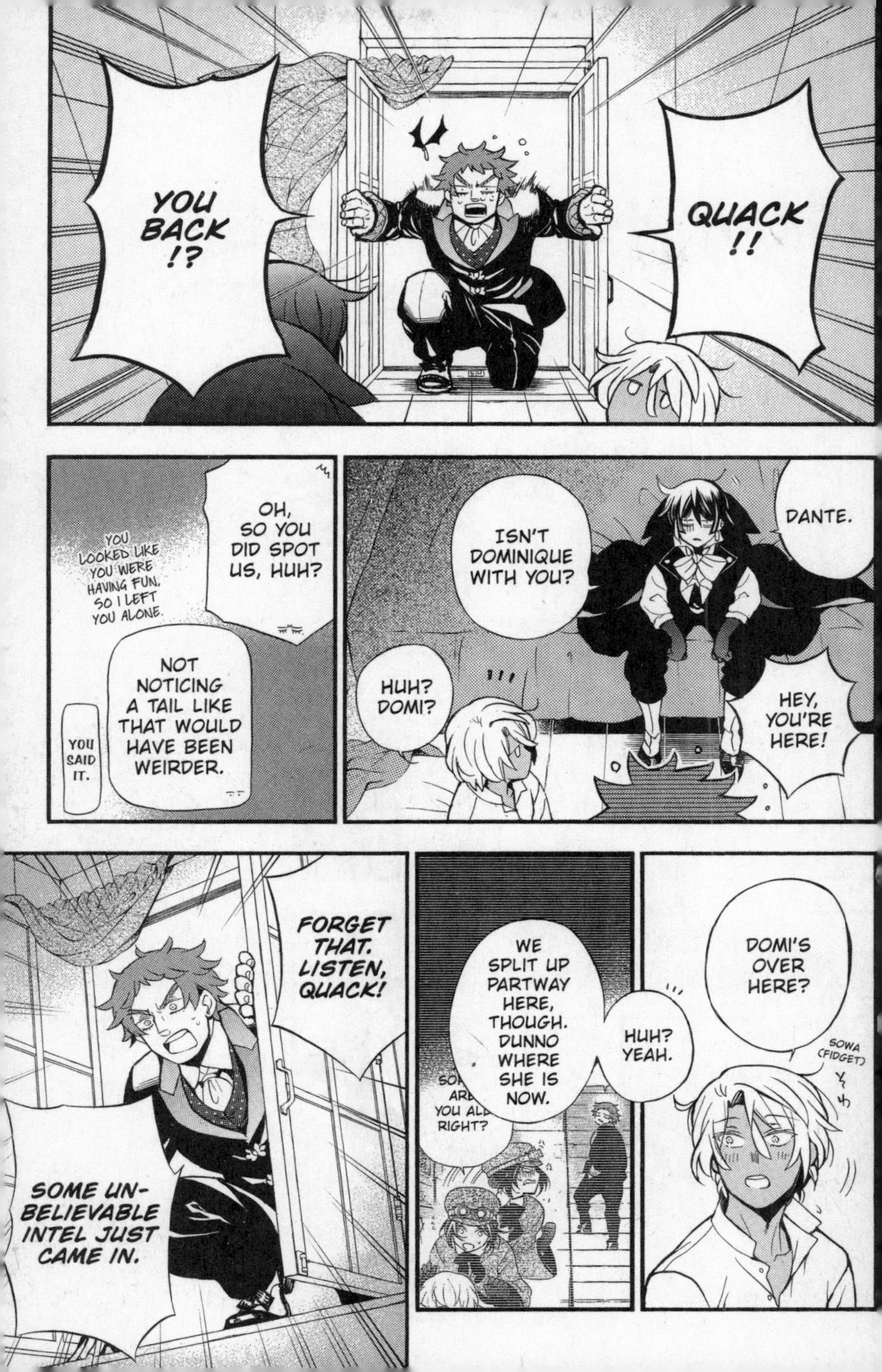
QUACK !!
YOU BACK !?
DANTE.
ISN'T DOMINIQUE WITH YOU?
HEY, YOU'RE HERE!
HUH? DOMI?
OH, SO YOU DID SPOT US, HUH?
YOU LOOKED LIKE YOU WERE HAVING FUN, SO I LEFT YOU ALONE.
NOT NOTICING A TAIL LIKE THAT WOULD HAVE BEEN WEIRDER.
YOU SAID IT.
DOMI'S OVER HERE?
SOWA (FIDGET)
HUH? YEAH.
WE SPLIT UP PARTWAY HERE, THOUGH. DUNNO WHERE SHE IS NOW.
ARE YOU ALL RIGHT?
FORGET THAT. LISTEN, QUACK!
SOME UN-BELIEVABLE INTEL JUST CAME IN.

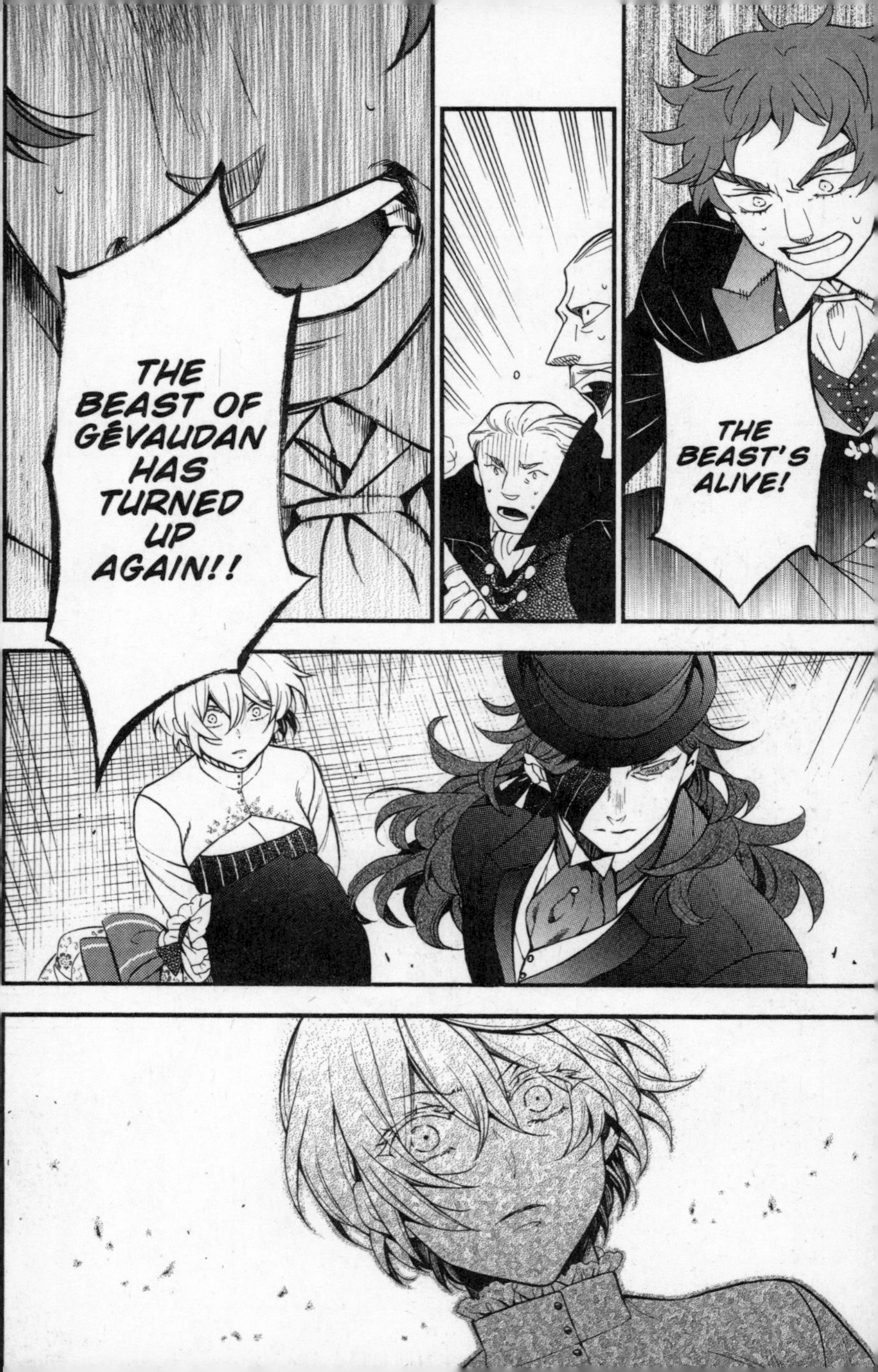
THE BEAST'S ALIVE!
THE BEAST OF GÊVAUDAN HAS TURNED UP AGAIN!!

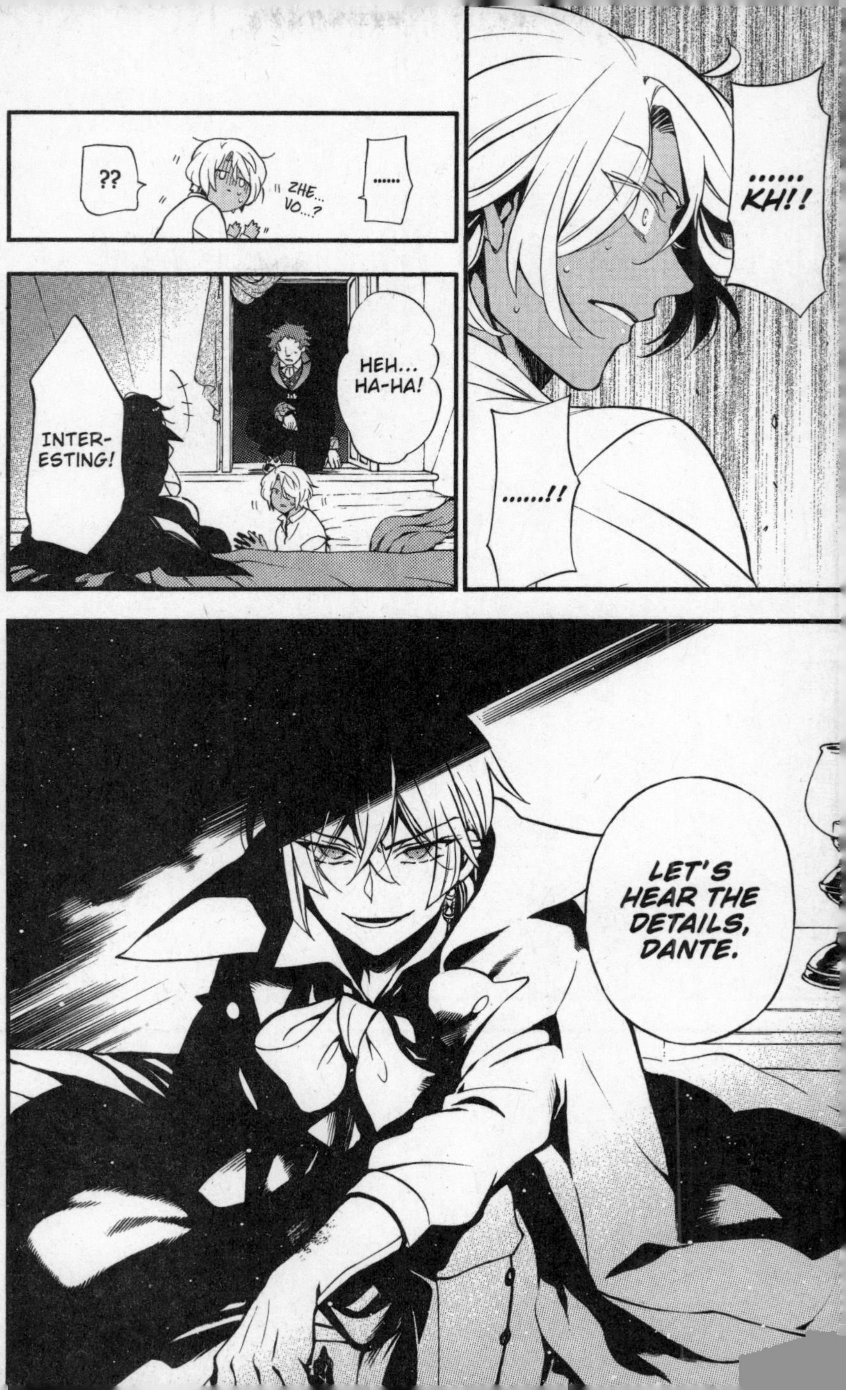
......KH!!
......!!
......
ZHE... VO...?
??
HEH... HA-HA!
INTER-ESTING!
LET'S HEAR THE DETAILS, DANTE.

Les Mémoires de Vanitas

THEY'VE KNOWN EACH OTHER FOR AGES, SO WHEN THEY'RE ALONE TOGETHER, HE SOMETIMES SLIPS INTO CASUAL SPEECH.

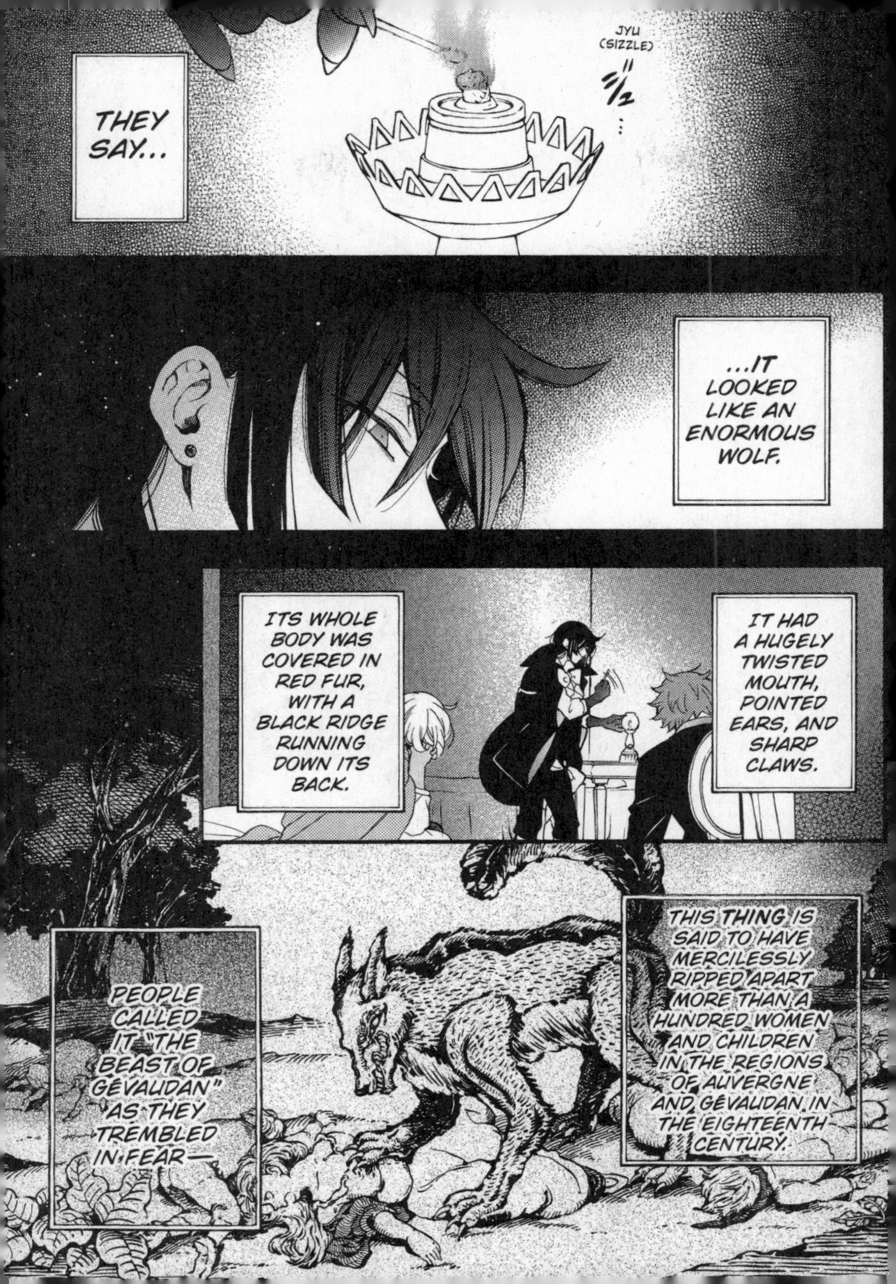
JYU (SIZZLE)
THEY SAY...
...IT LOOKED LIKE AN ENORMOUS WOLF.
IT HAD A HUGELY TWISTED MOUTH, POINTED EARS, AND SHARP CLAWS.
ITS WHOLE BODY WAS COVERED IN RED FUR, WITH A BLACK RIDGE RUNNING DOWN ITS BACK.
THIS THING IS SAID TO HAVE MERCILESSLY RIPPED APART MORE THAN A HUNDRED WOMEN AND CHILDREN IN THE REGIONS OF AUVERGNE AND GÉVAUDAN IN THE EIGHTEENTH CENTURY.
PEOPLE CALLED IT "THE BEAST OF GÉVAUDAN" AS THEY TREMBLED IN FEAR—

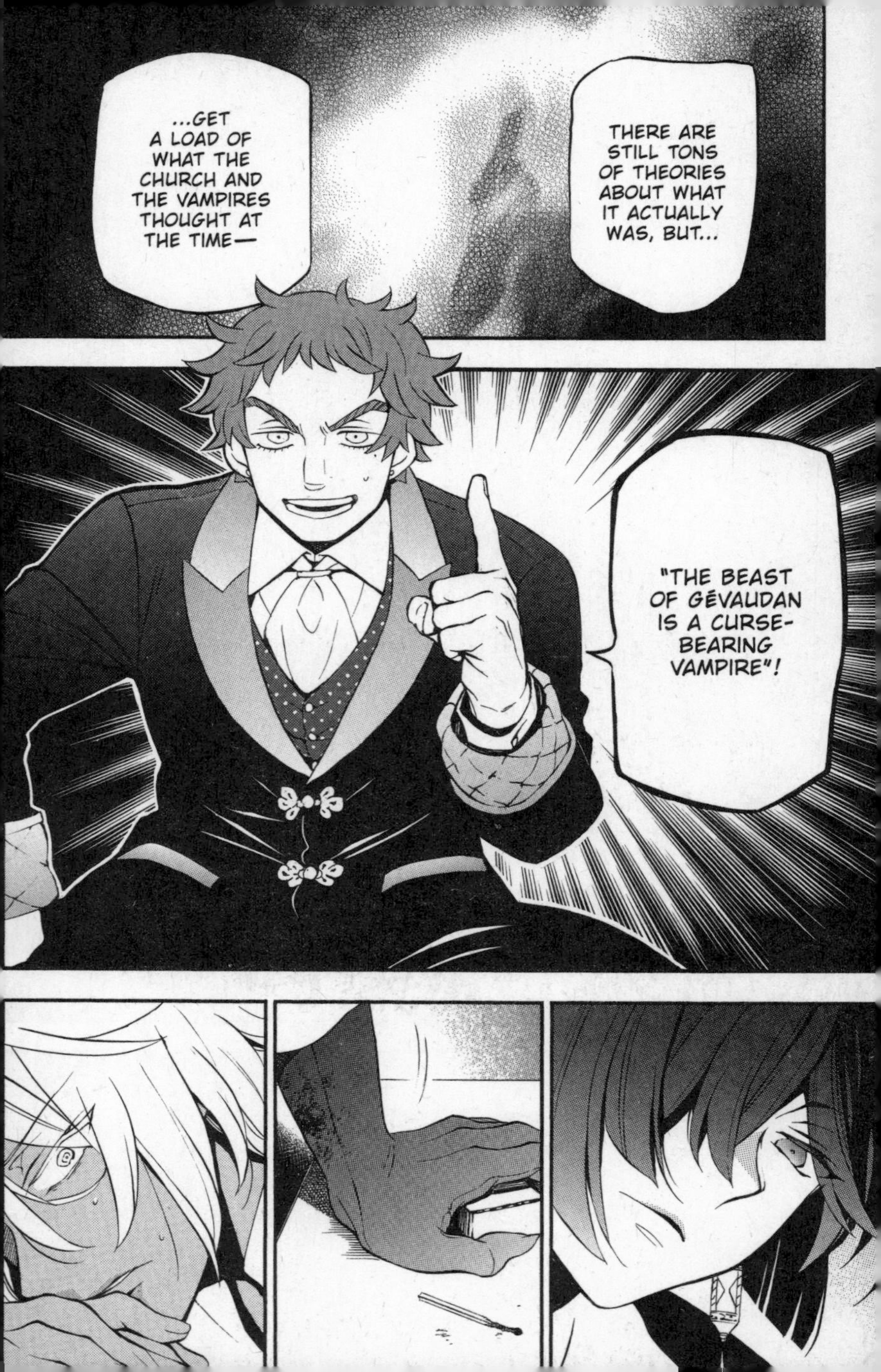
THERE ARE STILL TONS OF THEORIES ABOUT WHAT IT ACTUALLY WAS, BUT...
...GET A LOAD OF WHAT THE CHURCH AND THE VAMPIRES THOUGHT AT THE TIME—
"THE BEAST OF GÉVAUDAN IS A CURSE-BEARING VAMPIRE"!

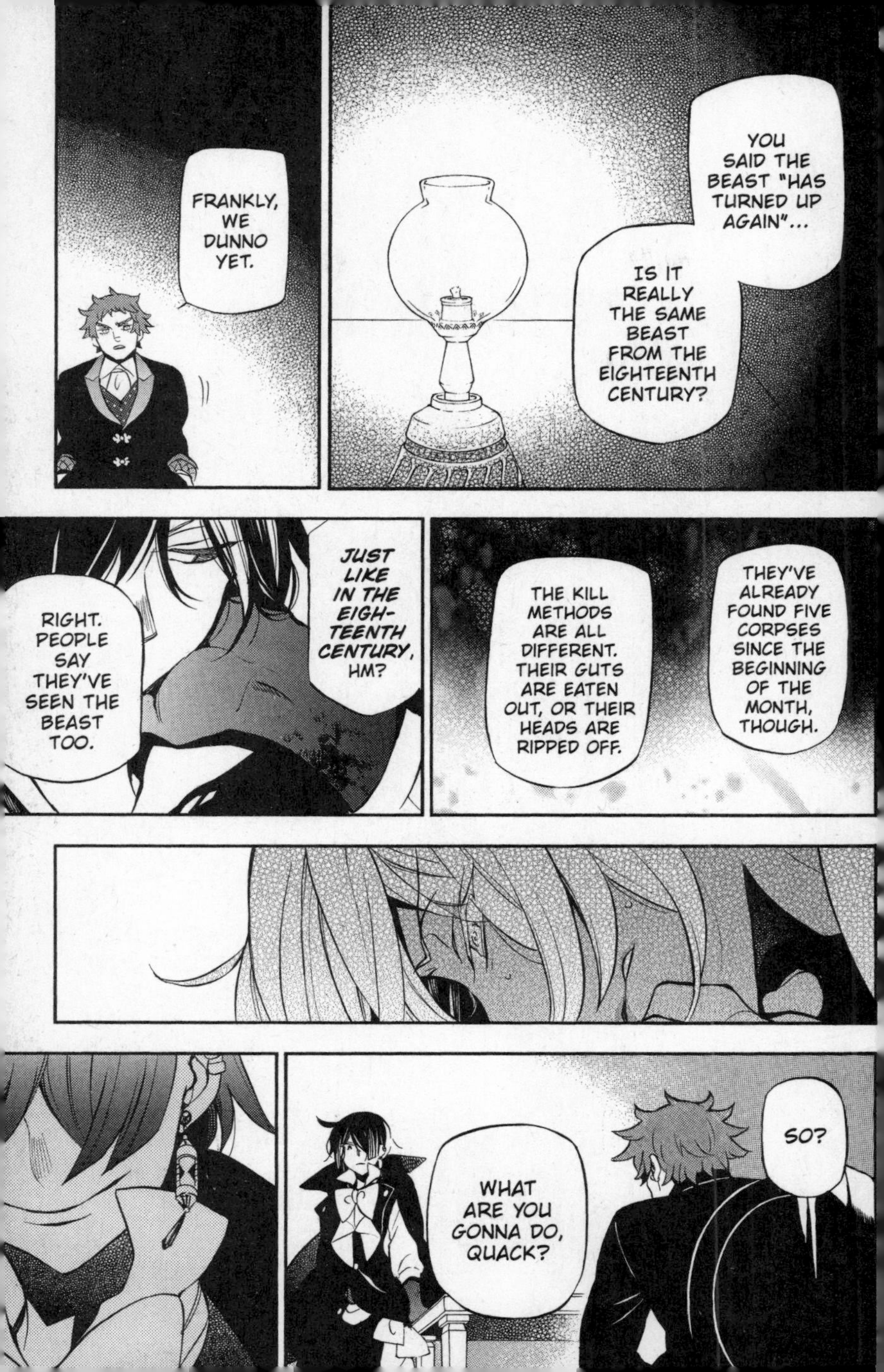
YOU SAID THE BEAST "HAS TURNED UP AGAIN"...
IS IT REALLY THE SAME BEAST FROM THE EIGHTEENTH CENTURY?
FRANKLY, WE DUNNO YET.
THEY'VE ALREADY FOUND FIVE CORPSES SINCE THE BEGINNING OF THE MONTH, THOUGH.
THE KILL METHODS ARE ALL DIFFERENT. THEIR GUTS ARE EATEN OUT, OR THEIR HEADS ARE RIPPED OFF.
JUST LIKE IN THE EIGH-TEENTH CENTURY, HM?
RIGHT. PEOPLE SAY THEY'VE SEEN THE BEAST TOO.
SO?
WHAT ARE YOU GONNA DO, QUACK?

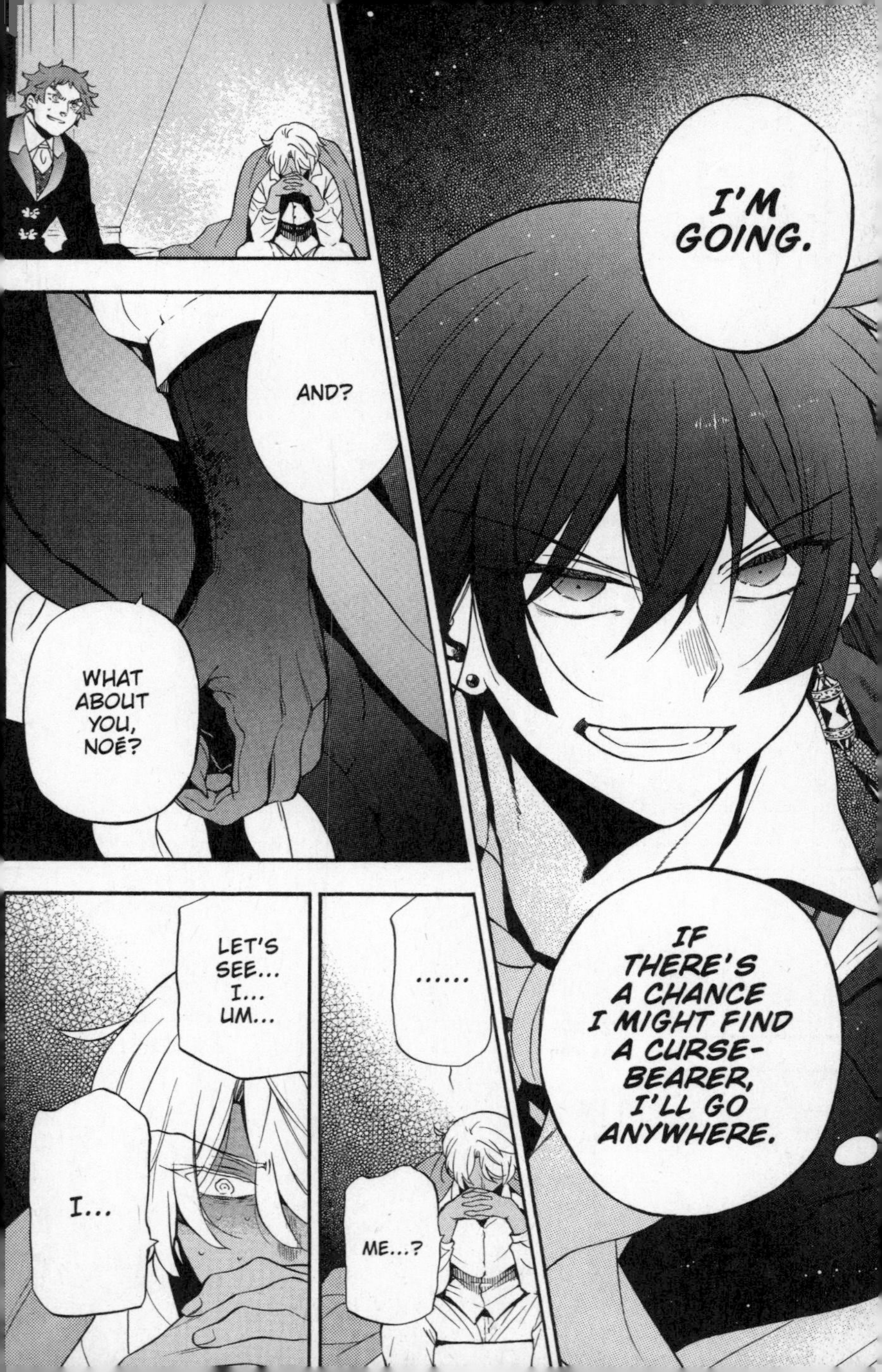
I'M GOING.
IF THERE'S A CHANCE I MIGHT FIND A CURSE-BEARER, I'LL GO ANYWHERE.
AND?
WHAT ABOUT YOU, NOÉ?
......
ME...?
LET'S SEE... I... UM...
I...

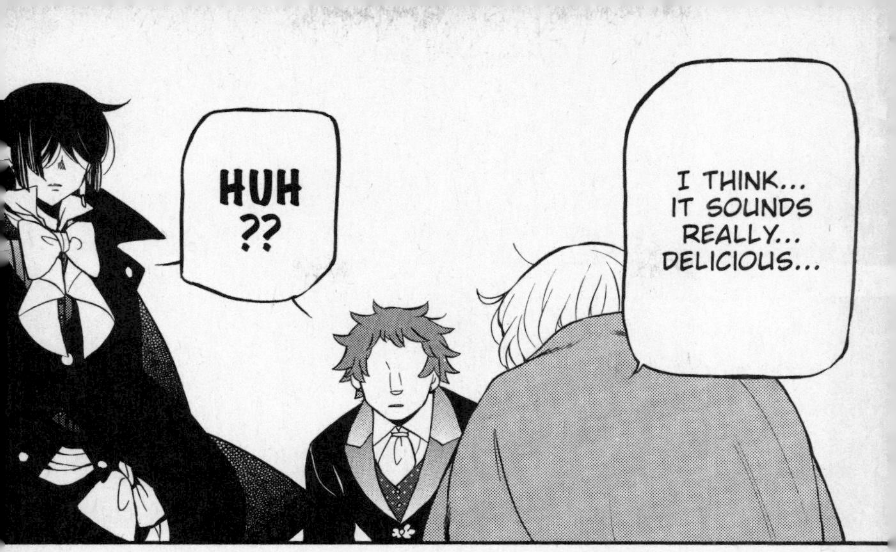
I THINK... IT SOUNDS REALLY... DELICIOUS...
HUH ??

Mémoire 23 Au Pas Camarade PACE

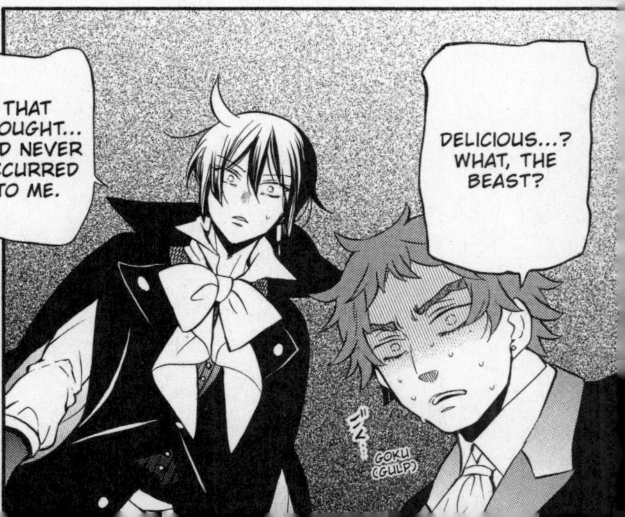
DELICIOUS...? WHAT, THE BEAST?
THAT THOUGHT... HAD NEVER OCCURRED TO ME.
GOKU (GULP)

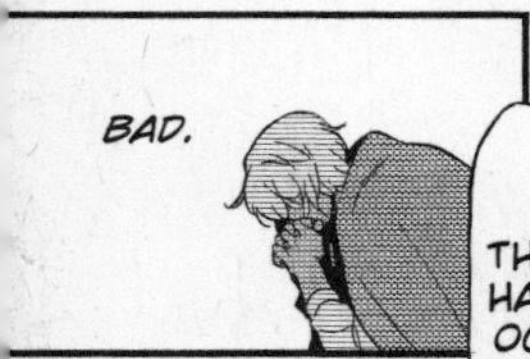
BAD.

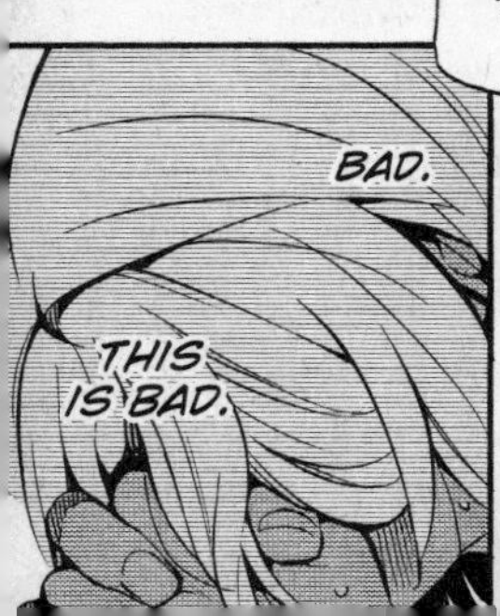
BAD.
THIS IS BAD.

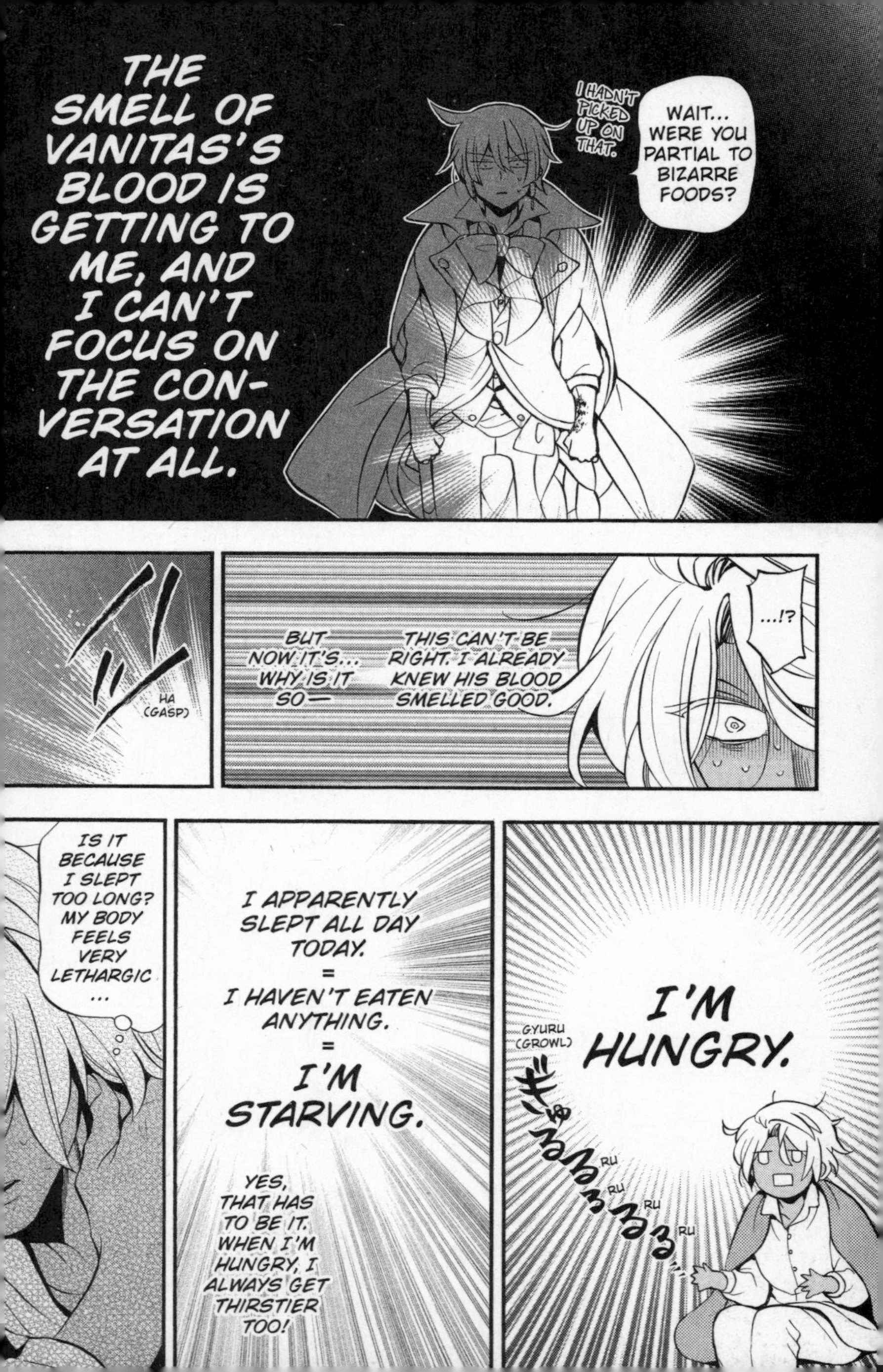
WAIT... WERE YOU PARTIAL TO BIZARRE FOODS?
I HADN'T PICKED UP ON THAT.
THE SMELL OF VANITAS'S BLOOD IS GETTING TO ME, AND I CAN'T FOCUS ON THE CON-VERSATION AT ALL.
...!?
THIS CAN'T BE RIGHT. I ALREADY KNEW HIS BLOOD SMELLED GOOD.
BUT NOW IT'S... WHY IS IT SO—
HA (GASP)
I'M HUNGRY.
GYURU (GROWL)
RU
RU
RU
RU
I APPARENTLY SLEPT ALL DAY TODAY.
=
I HAVEN'T EATEN ANYTHING.
=
I'M STARVING.
YES, THAT HAS TO BE IT. WHEN I'M HUNGRY, I ALWAYS GET THIRSTIER TOO!
IS IT BECAUSE I SLEPT TOO LONG? MY BODY FEELS VERY LETHARGIC...

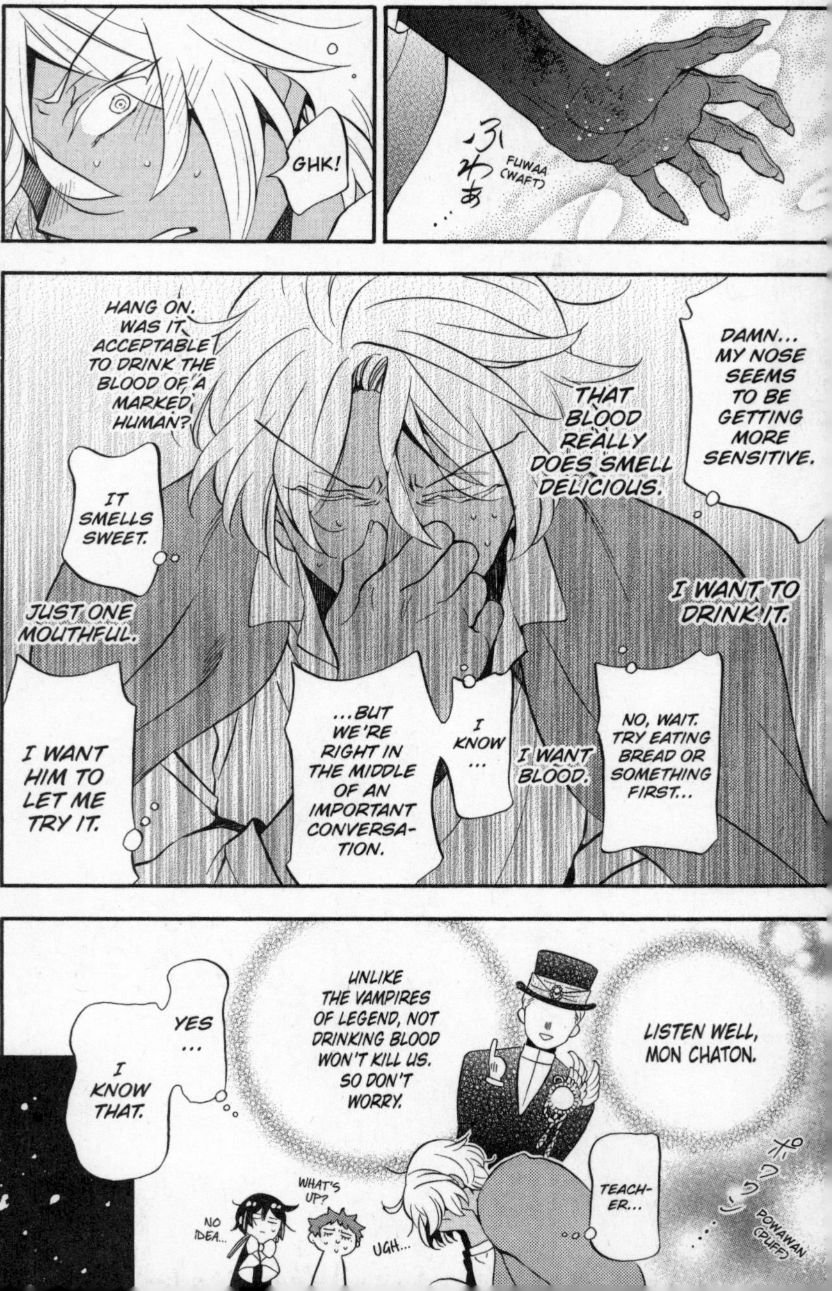
ふわぁ…
FUWAA (WAFT)
GHK!
DAMN... MY NOSE SEEMS TO BE GETTING MORE SENSITIVE.
THAT BLOOD REALLY DOES SMELL DELICIOUS.
HANG ON. WAS IT ACCEPTABLE TO DRINK THE BLOOD OF A MARKED HUMAN?
IT SMELLS SWEET.
I WANT TO DRINK IT.
JUST ONE MOUTHFUL.
NO, WAIT. TRY EATING BREAD OR SOMETHING FIRST...
I WANT BLOOD.
I KNOW...
...BUT WE'RE RIGHT IN THE MIDDLE OF AN IMPORTANT CONVERSATION.
I WANT HIM TO LET ME TRY IT.
LISTEN WELL, MON CHATON.
ポワワン
POWAWAN (PUFF)
UNLIKE THE VAMPIRES OF LEGEND, NOT DRINKING BLOOD WON'T KILL US. SO DON'T WORRY.
TEACHER...
YES... I KNOW THAT.
UGH...
WHAT'S UP?
NO IDEA...

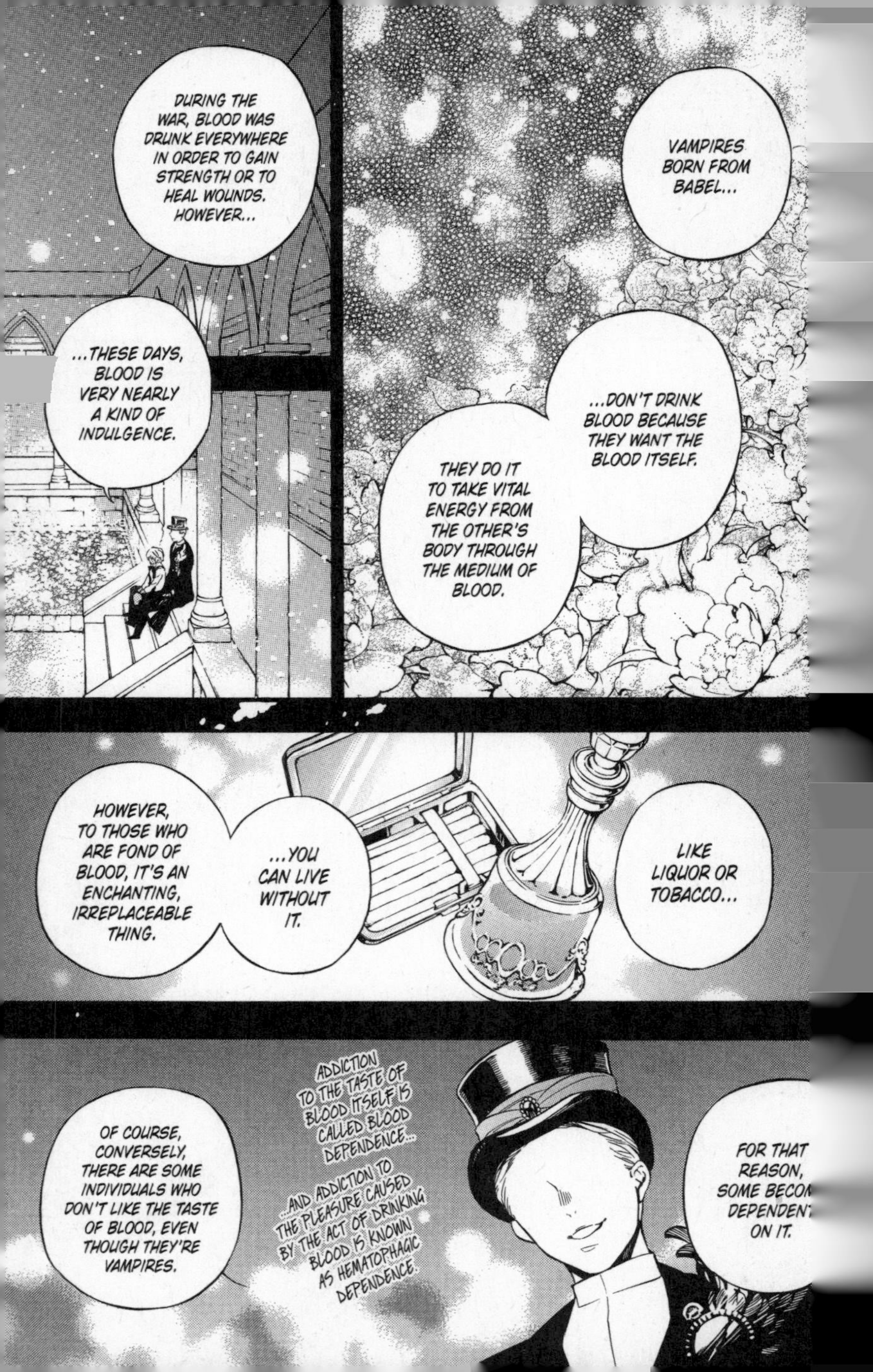
VAMPIRES BORN FROM BABEL...
...DON'T DRINK BLOOD BECAUSE THEY WANT THE BLOOD ITSELF.
THEY DO IT TO TAKE VITAL ENERGY FROM THE OTHER'S BODY THROUGH THE MEDIUM OF BLOOD.
DURING THE WAR, BLOOD WAS DRUNK EVERYWHERE IN ORDER TO GAIN STRENGTH OR TO HEAL WOUNDS. HOWEVER...
...THESE DAYS, BLOOD IS VERY NEARLY A KIND OF INDULGENCE.
LIKE LIQUOR OR TOBACCO...
...YOU CAN LIVE WITHOUT IT.
HOWEVER, TO THOSE WHO ARE FOND OF BLOOD, IT'S AN ENCHANTING, IRREPLACEABLE THING.
FOR THAT REASON, SOME BECOM DEPENDENT ON IT.
ADDICTION TO THE TASTE OF BLOOD ITSELF IS CALLED BLOOD DEPENDENCE...
...AND ADDICTION TO THE PLEASURE CAUSED BY THE ACT OF DRINKING BLOOD IS KNOWN AS HEMATOPHAGIC DEPENDENCE.
OF COURSE, CONVERSELY, THERE ARE SOME INDIVIDUALS WHO DON'T LIKE THE TASTE OF BLOOD, EVEN THOUGH THEY'RE VAMPIRES.

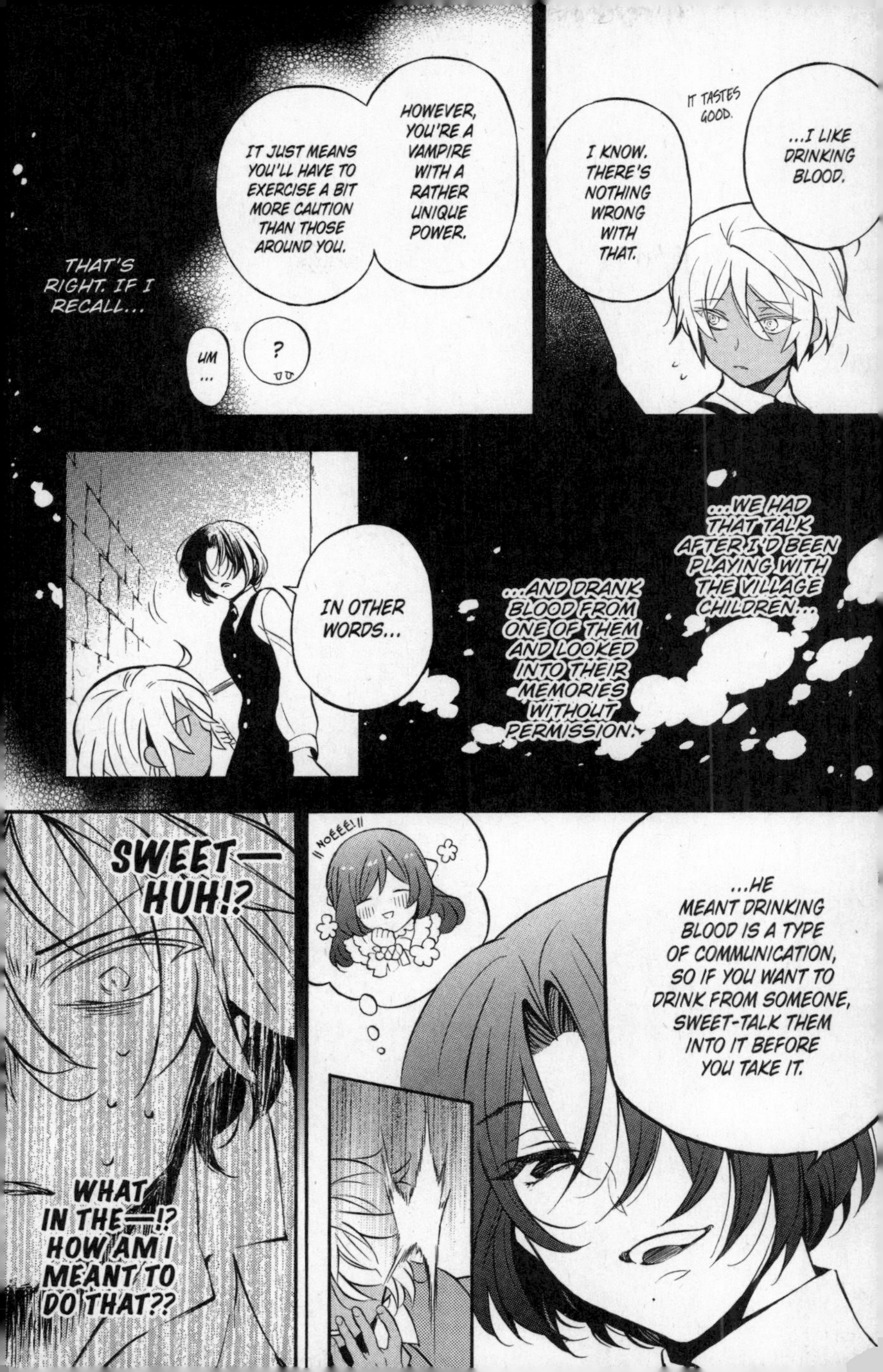
...I LIKE DRINKING BLOOD.
IT TASTES GOOD.
I KNOW. THERE'S NOTHING WRONG WITH THAT.
HOWEVER, YOU'RE A VAMPIRE WITH A RATHER UNIQUE POWER.
IT JUST MEANS YOU'LL HAVE TO EXERCISE A BIT MORE CAUTION THAN THOSE AROUND YOU.
?
UM...
THAT'S RIGHT. IF I RECALL...
...WE HAD THAT TALK AFTER I'D BEEN PLAYING WITH THE VILLAGE CHILDREN...
...AND DRANK BLOOD FROM ONE OF THEM AND LOOKED INTO THEIR MEMORIES WITHOUT PERMISSION.
IN OTHER WORDS...
...HE MEANT DRINKING BLOOD IS A TYPE OF COMMUNICATION, SO IF YOU WANT TO DRINK FROM SOMEONE, SWEET-TALK THEM INTO IT BEFORE YOU TAKE IT.
NOÉÉÉ!!
SWEET—HUH!?
WHAT IN THE—!? HOW AM I MEANT TO DO THAT??

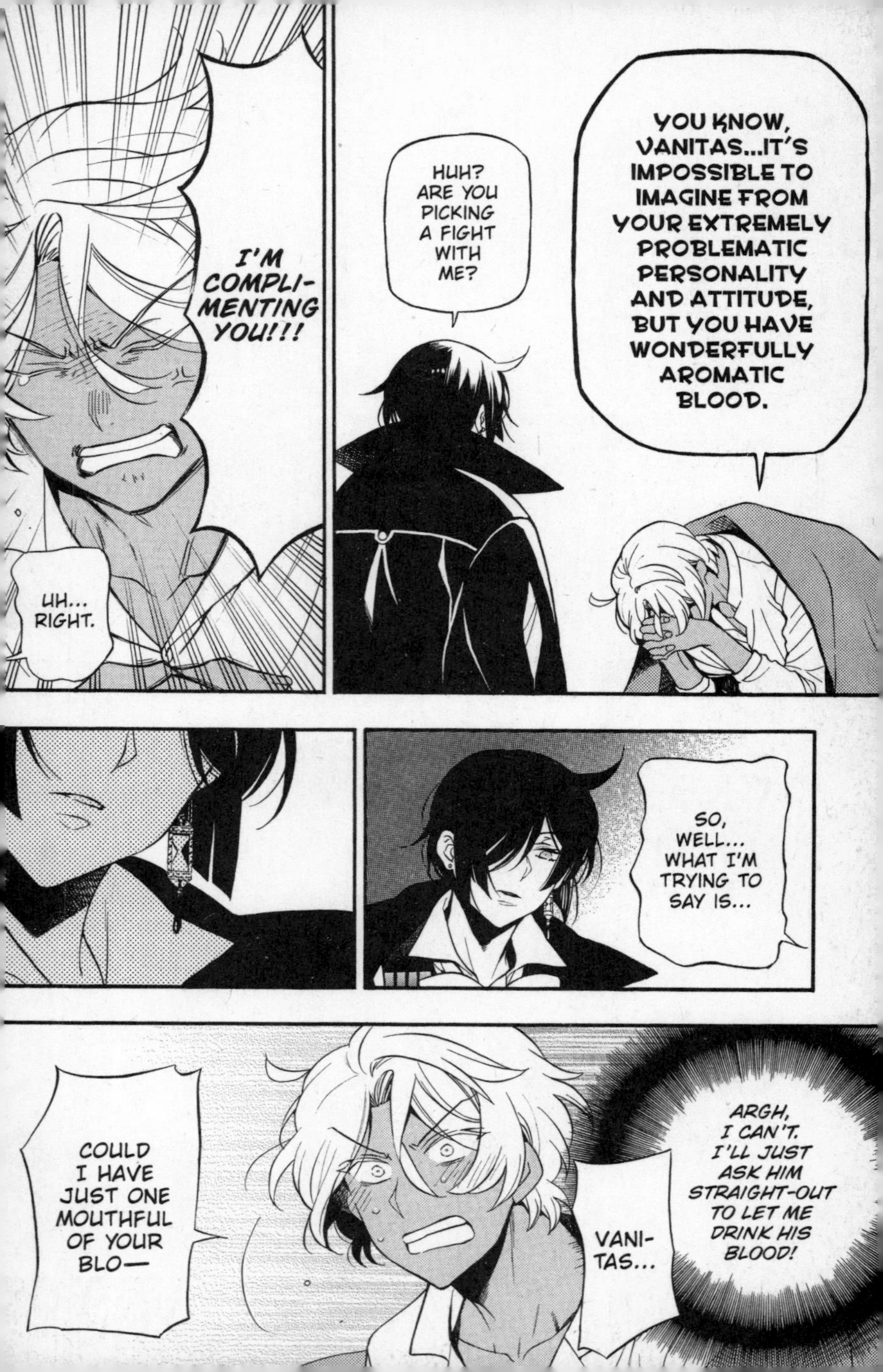
YOU KNOW, VANITAS...IT'S IMPOSSIBLE TO IMAGINE FROM YOUR EXTREMELY PROBLEMATIC PERSONALITY AND ATTITUDE, BUT YOU HAVE WONDERFULLY AROMATIC BLOOD.
HUH? ARE YOU PICKING A FIGHT WITH ME?
I'M COMPLI-MENTING YOU!!!
UH... RIGHT.
SO, WELL... WHAT I'M TRYING TO SAY IS...
ARGH, I CAN'T. I'LL JUST ASK HIM STRAIGHT-OUT TO LET ME DRINK HIS BLOOD!
VANI-TAS...
COULD I HAVE JUST ONE MOUTHFUL OF YOUR BLO—

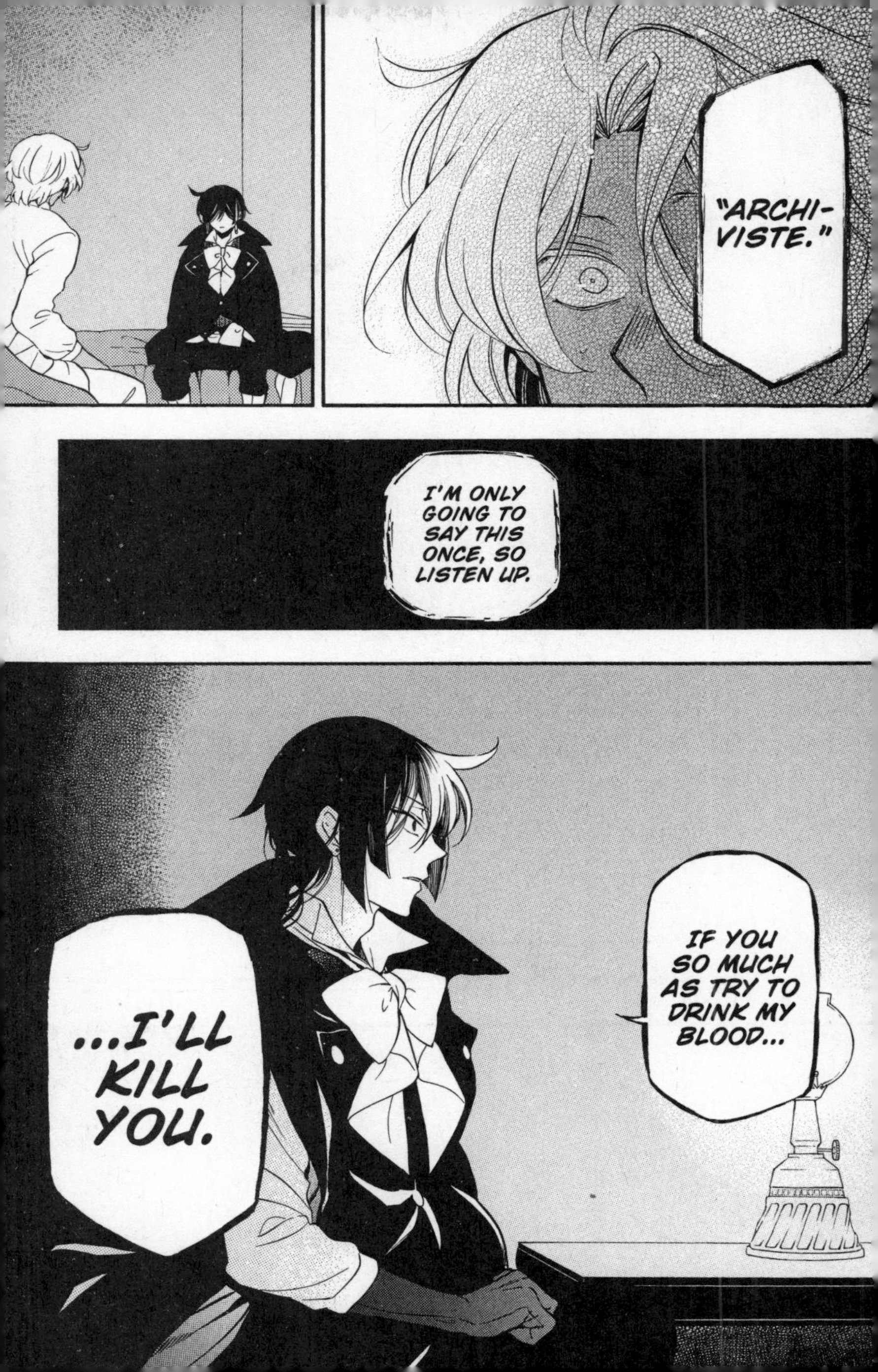
"ARCHIVISTE."
I'M ONLY GOING TO SAY THIS ONCE, SO LISTEN UP.
IF YOU SO MUCH AS TRY TO DRINK MY BLOOD...
...I'LL KILL YOU.

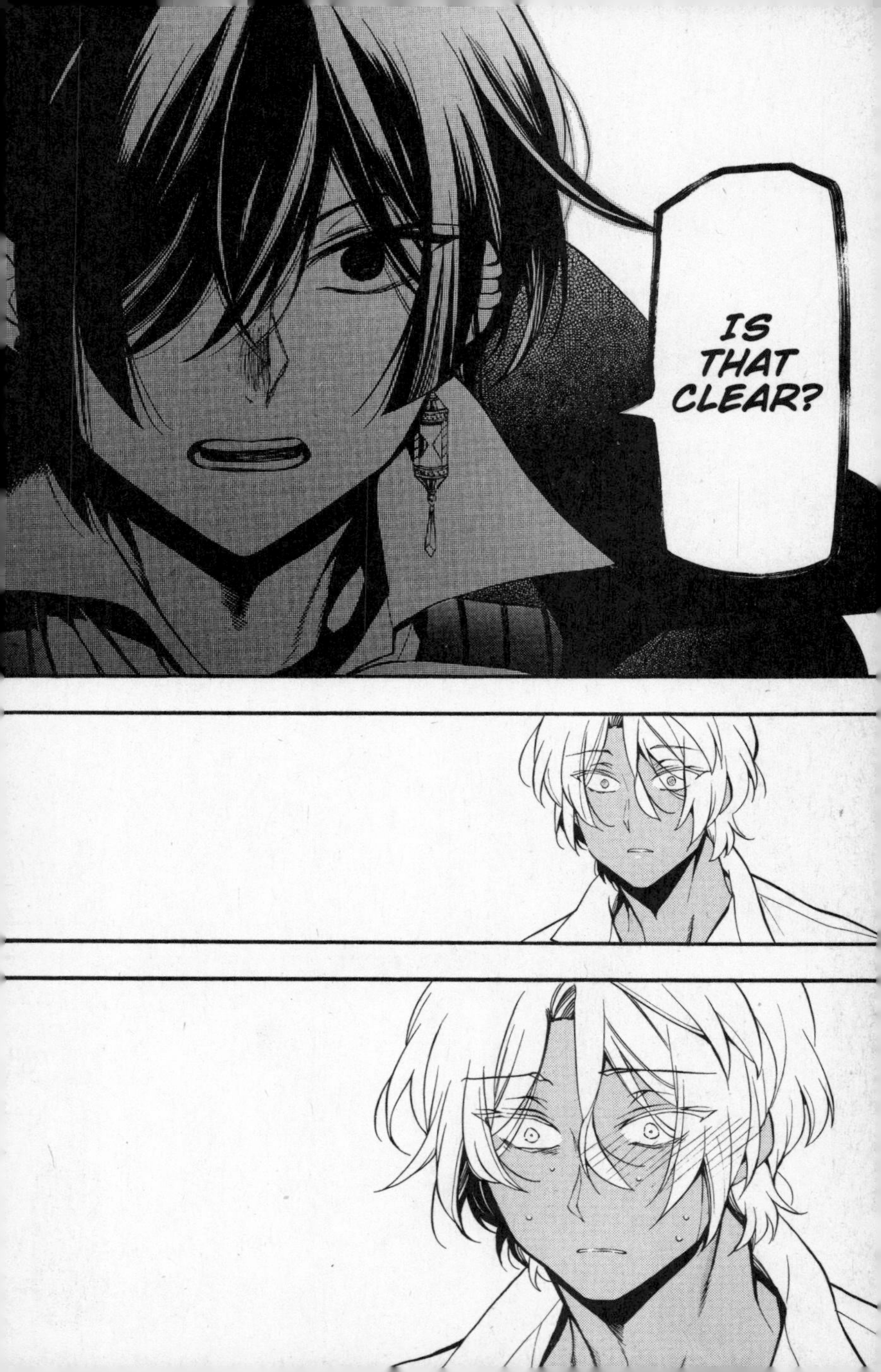
IS THAT CLEAR?

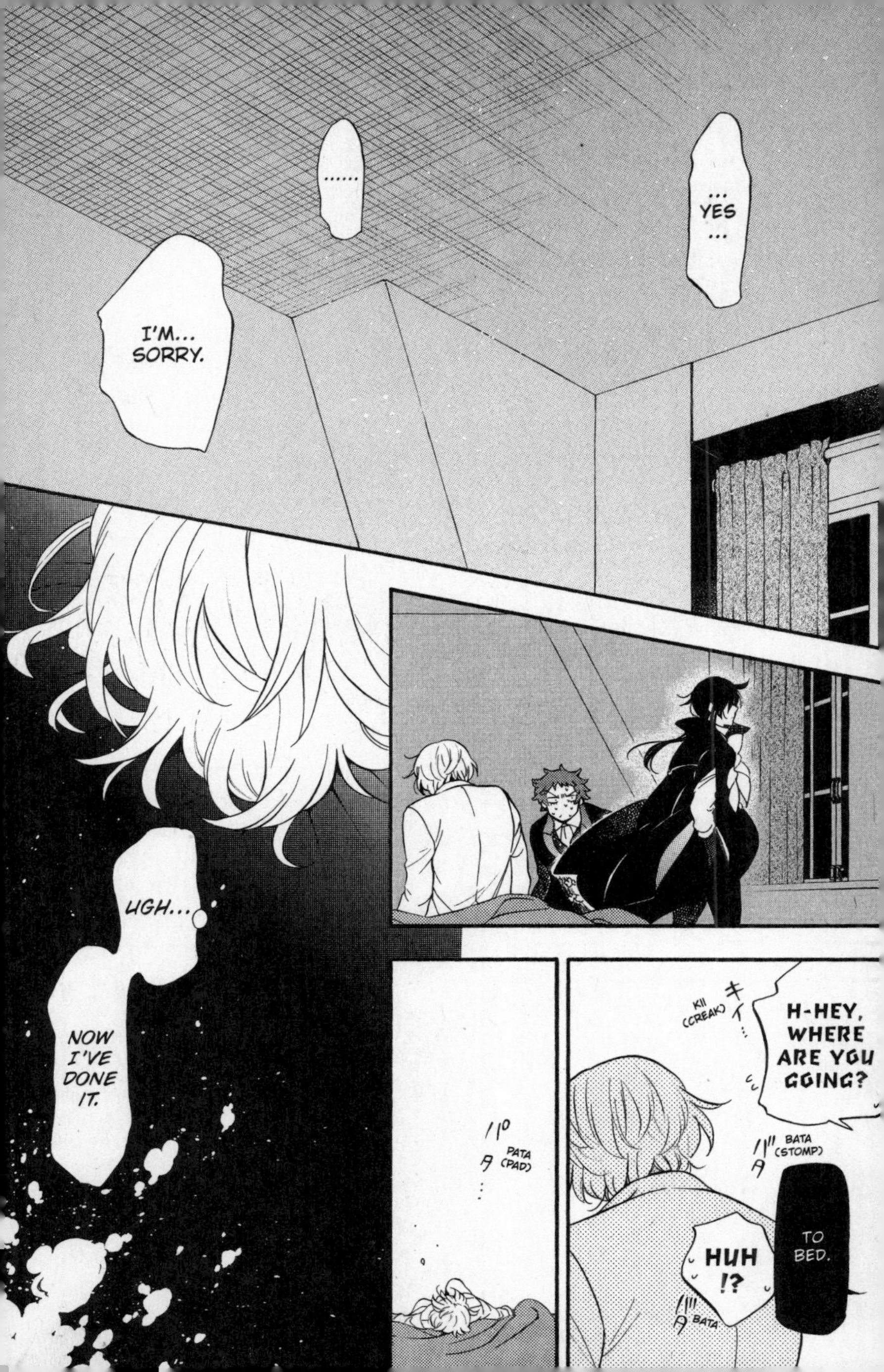
...YES...
......
I'M... SORRY.
キイ…
KII (CREAK)
H-HEY, WHERE ARE YOU GOING?
バタ
BATA (STOMP)
TO BED.
HUH!?
バタ
BATA
パタ…
PATA (PAD)
UGH...
NOW I'VE DONE IT.

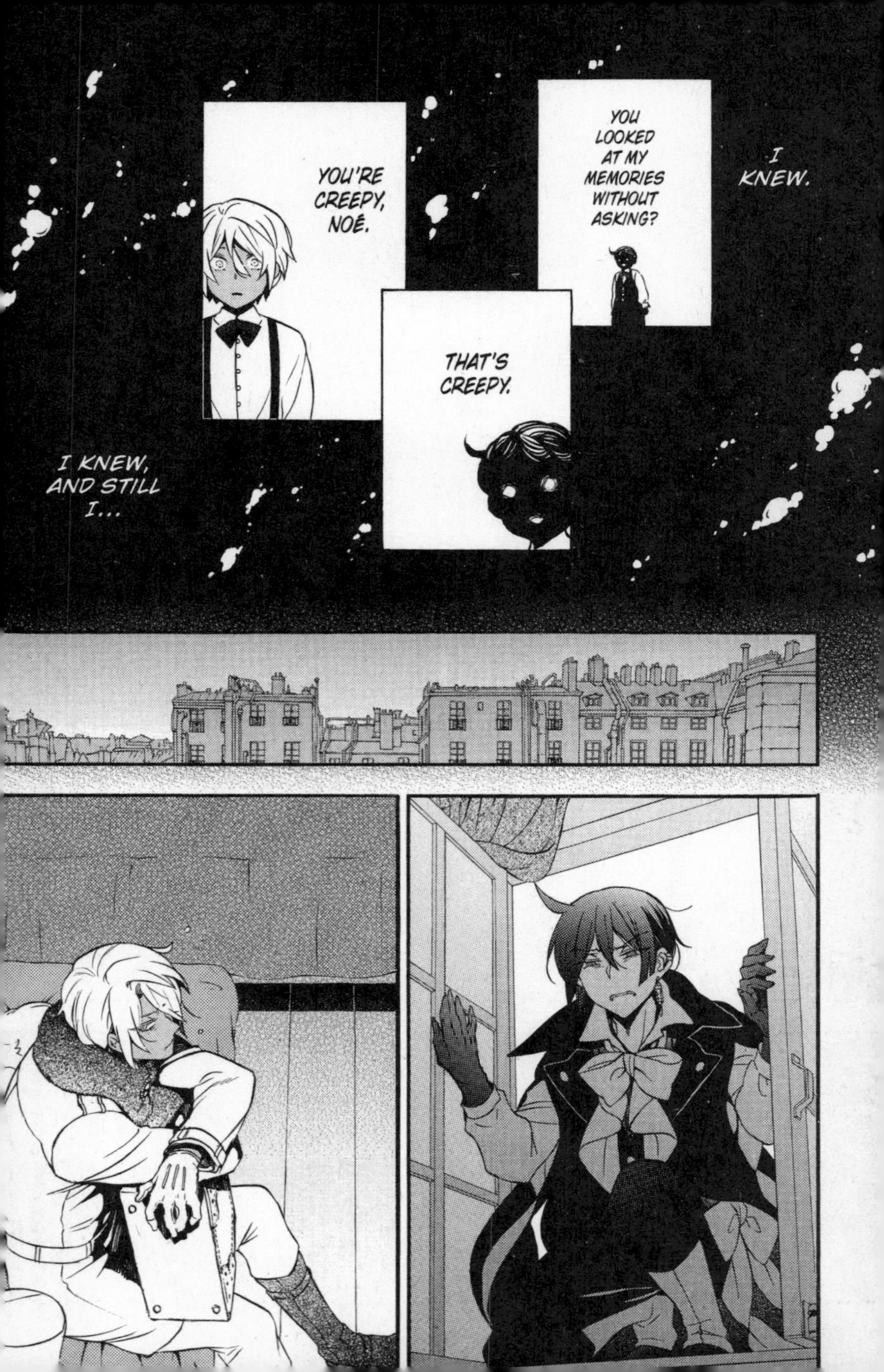
I KNEW.
YOU LOOKED AT MY MEMORIES WITHOUT ASKING?
YOU'RE CREEPY, NOÉ.
THAT'S CREEPY.
I KNEW, AND STILL I...

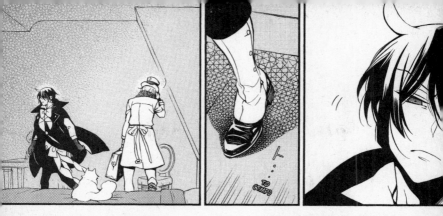

GA
(GRAB)

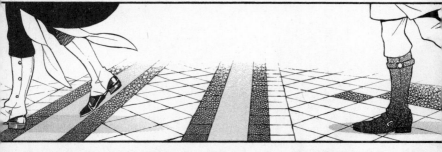

TOBO
(TOBO)

TAP
TAP
TAP

TOBO
(TRUDGE)

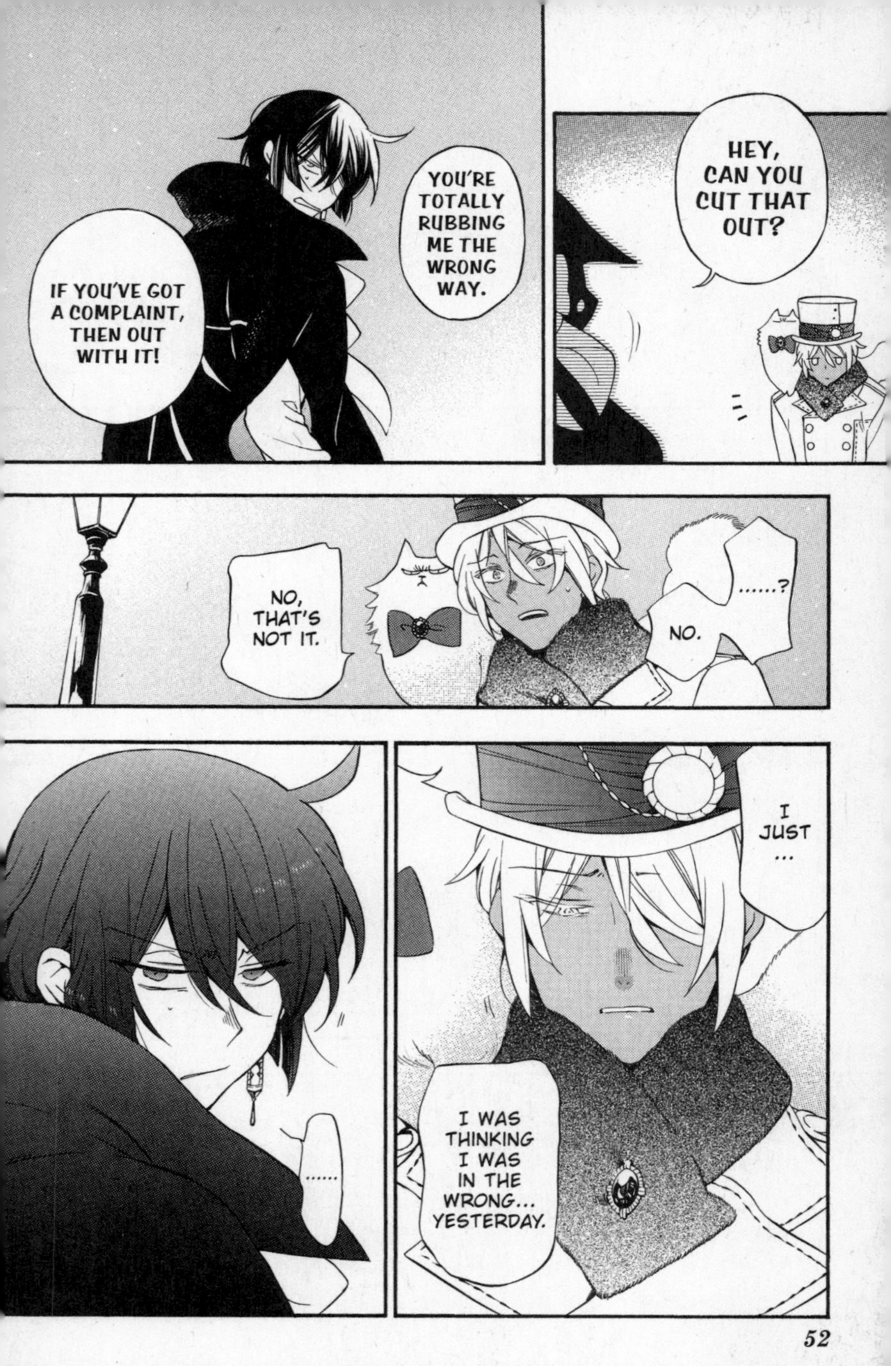
HEY, CAN YOU CUT THAT OUT?
YOU'RE TOTALLY RUBBING ME THE WRONG WAY.
IF YOU'VE GOT A COMPLAINT, THEN OUT WITH IT!
......?
NO.
NO, THAT'S NOT IT.
I JUST ...
I WAS THINKING I WAS IN THE WRONG... YESTERDAY.
......

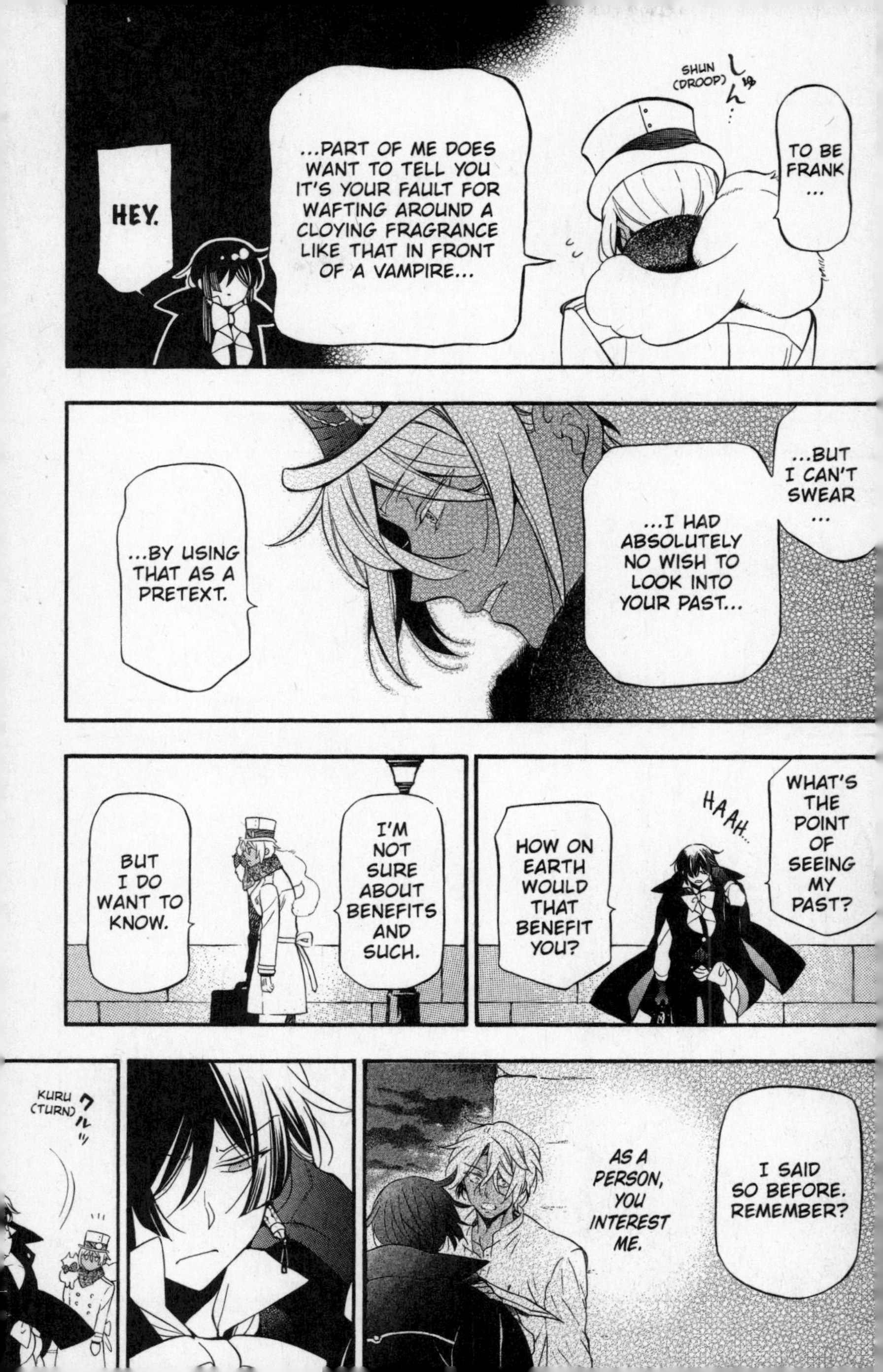
SHUN (DROOP)
TO BE FRANK...
...PART OF ME DOES WANT TO TELL YOU IT'S YOUR FAULT FOR WAFTING AROUND A CLOYING FRAGRANCE LIKE THAT IN FRONT OF A VAMPIRE...
HEY.
...BUT I CAN'T SWEAR...
...I HAD ABSOLUTELY NO WISH TO LOOK INTO YOUR PAST...
...BY USING THAT AS A PRETEXT.
WHAT'S THE POINT OF SEEING MY PAST?
HAAAH...
HOW ON EARTH WOULD THAT BENEFIT YOU?
I'M NOT SURE ABOUT BENEFITS AND SUCH.
BUT I DO WANT TO KNOW.
I SAID SO BEFORE. REMEMBER?
AS A PERSON, YOU INTEREST ME.
KURU (TURN)

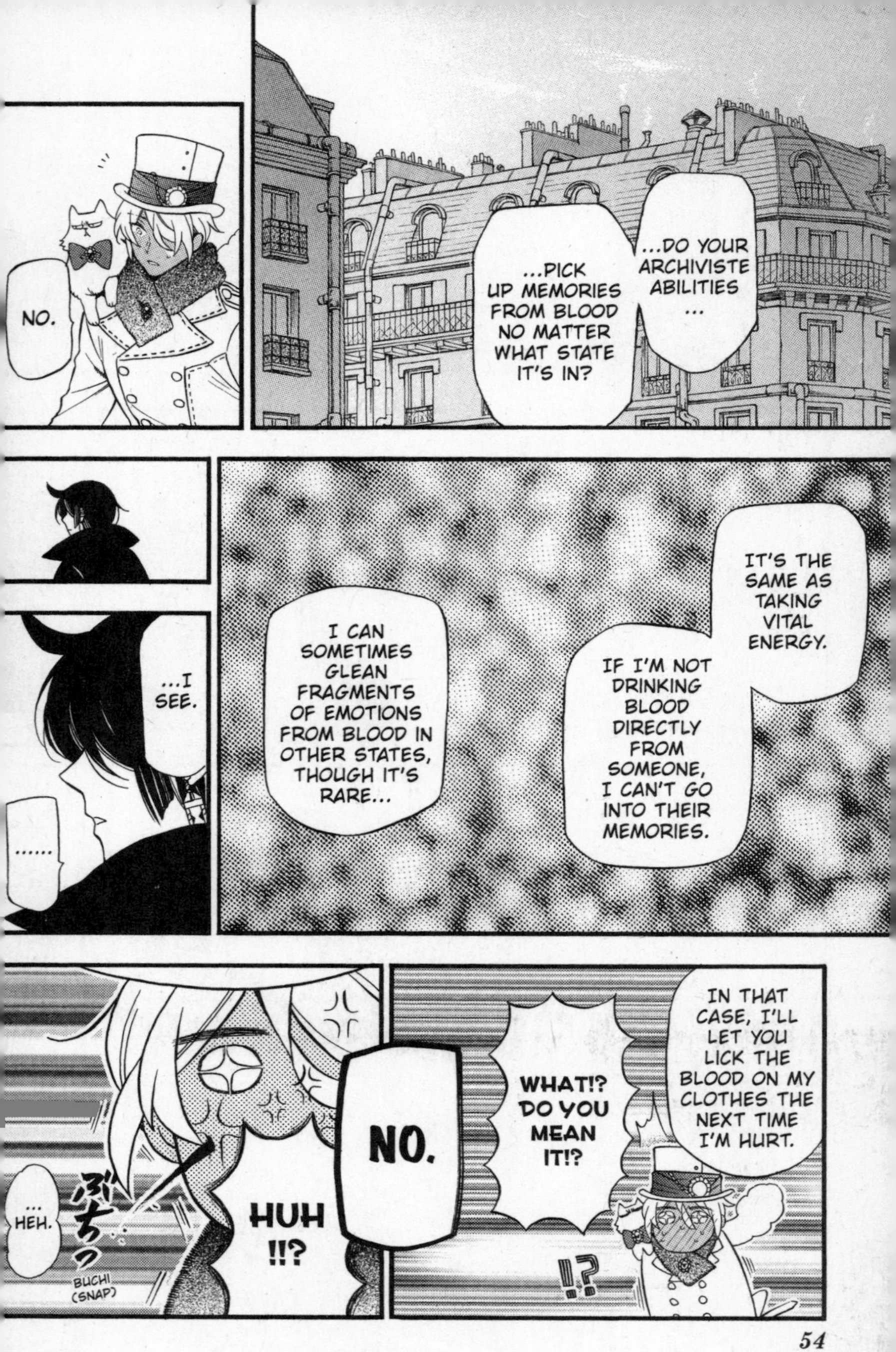
...DO YOUR ARCHIVISTE ABILITIES ...
...PICK UP MEMORIES FROM BLOOD NO MATTER WHAT STATE IT'S IN?
NO.
IT'S THE SAME AS TAKING VITAL ENERGY.
IF I'M NOT DRINKING BLOOD DIRECTLY FROM SOMEONE, I CAN'T GO INTO THEIR MEMORIES.
I CAN SOMETIMES GLEAN FRAGMENTS OF EMOTIONS FROM BLOOD IN OTHER STATES, THOUGH IT'S RARE...
...I SEE.
......
IN THAT CASE, I'LL LET YOU LICK THE BLOOD ON MY CLOTHES THE NEXT TIME I'M HURT.
WHAT!? DO YOU MEAN IT!?
!?
NO.
HUH !!?
ぶちっ
BUCHI (SNAP)
...HEH.

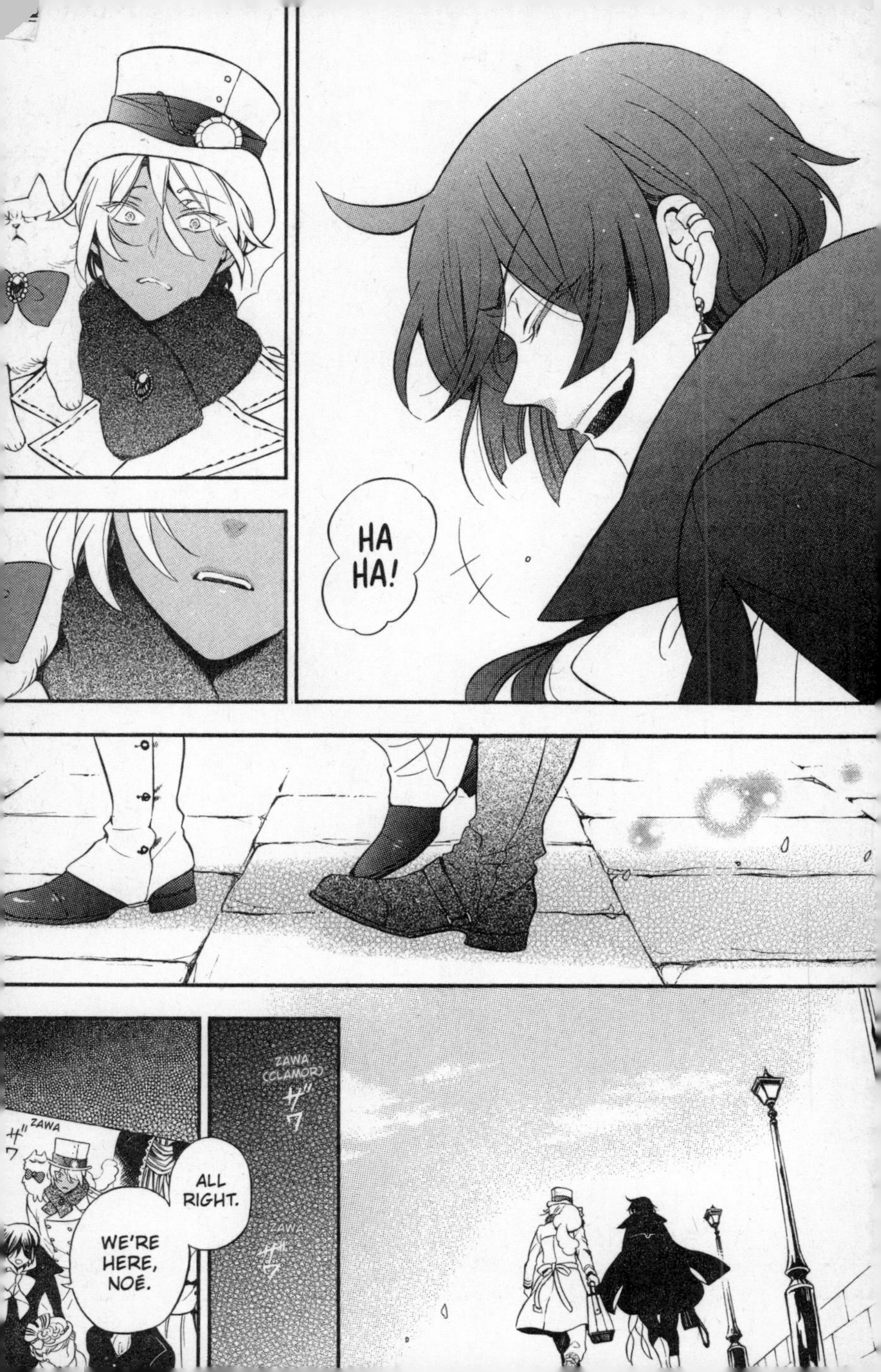
HA HA!
ZAWA (CLAMOR) ザワ
ZAWA ザワ
ALL RIGHT.
WE'RE HERE, NOÉ.
ZAWA ザワ

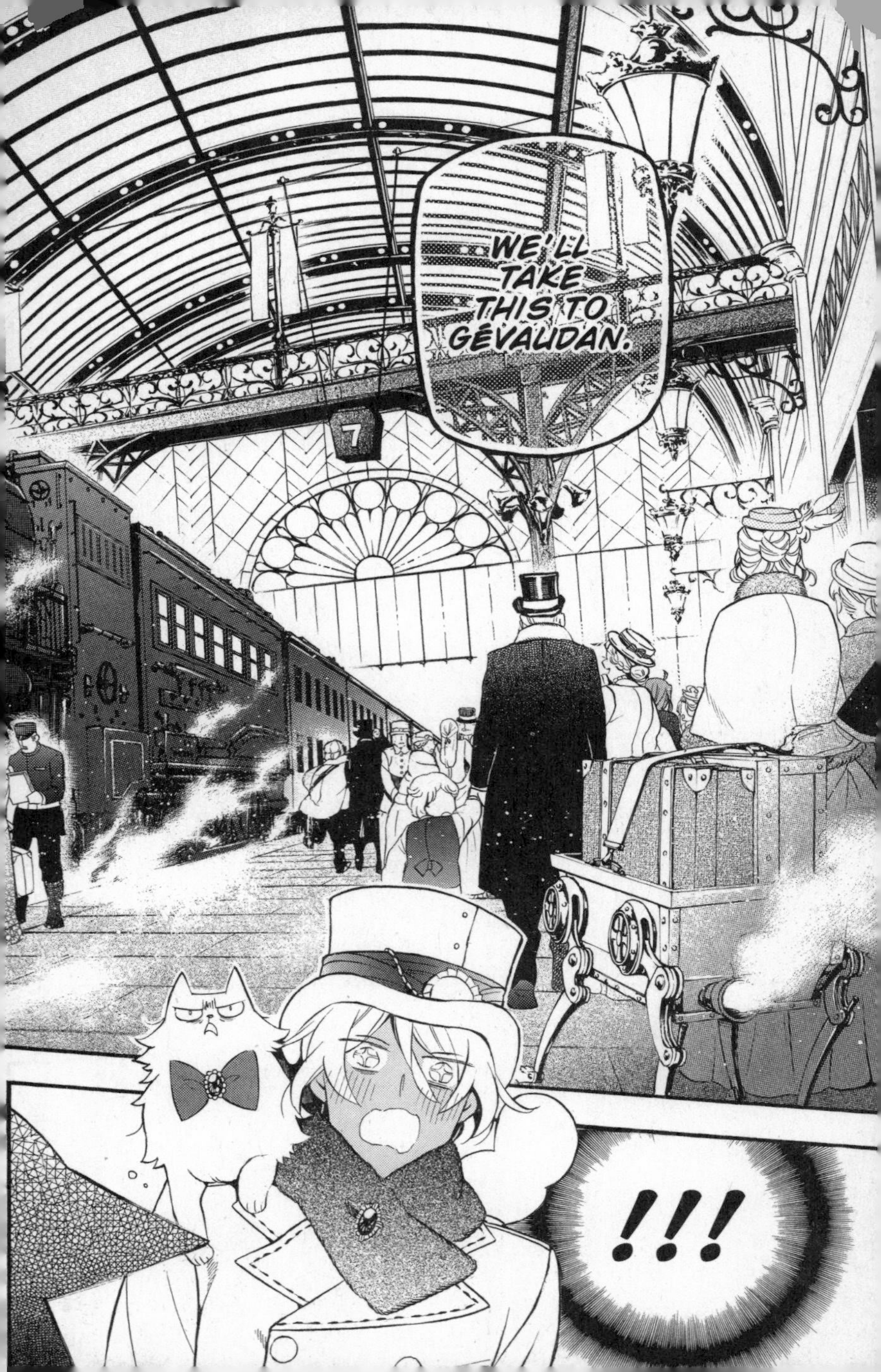
WE'LL TAKE THIS TO GÉVAUDAN.
7
!!!

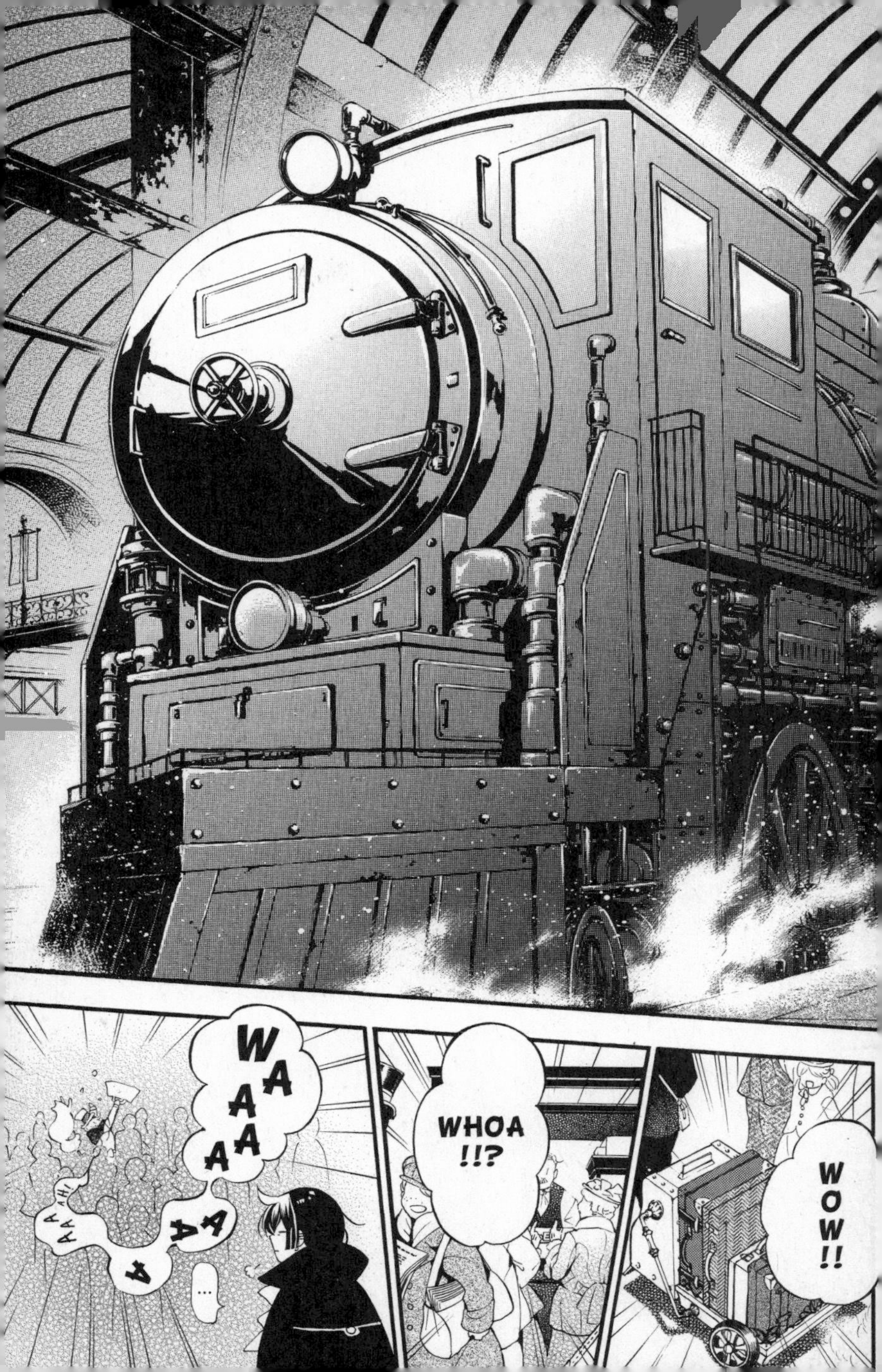
WOW!!
WHOA !!?
WAAAAAAAAAAAAH!
...

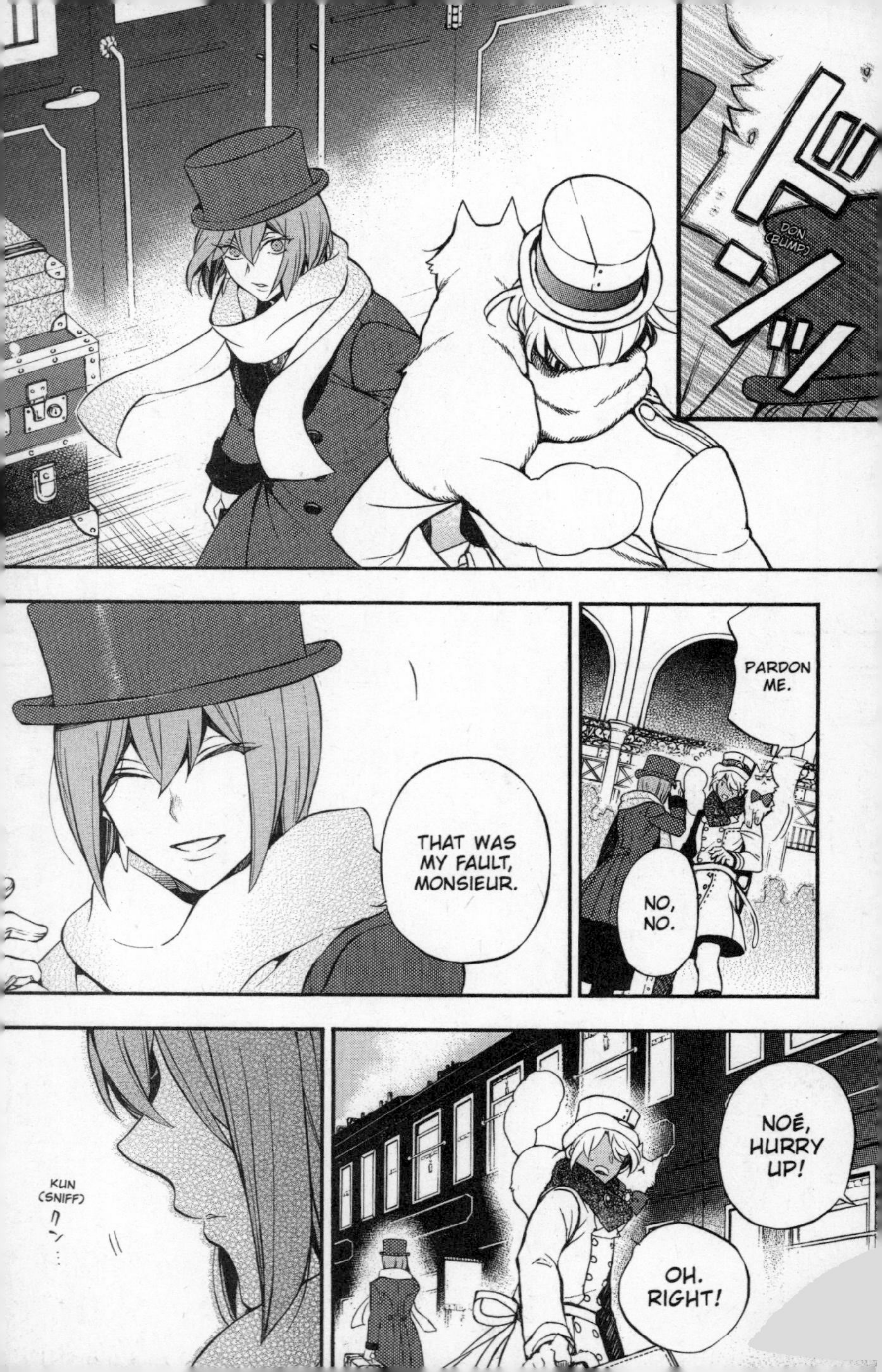
DON (BUMP)
PARDON ME.
NO, NO.
THAT WAS MY FAULT, MONSIEUR.
NOÉ, HURRY UP!
OH. RIGHT!
KUN (SNIFF)

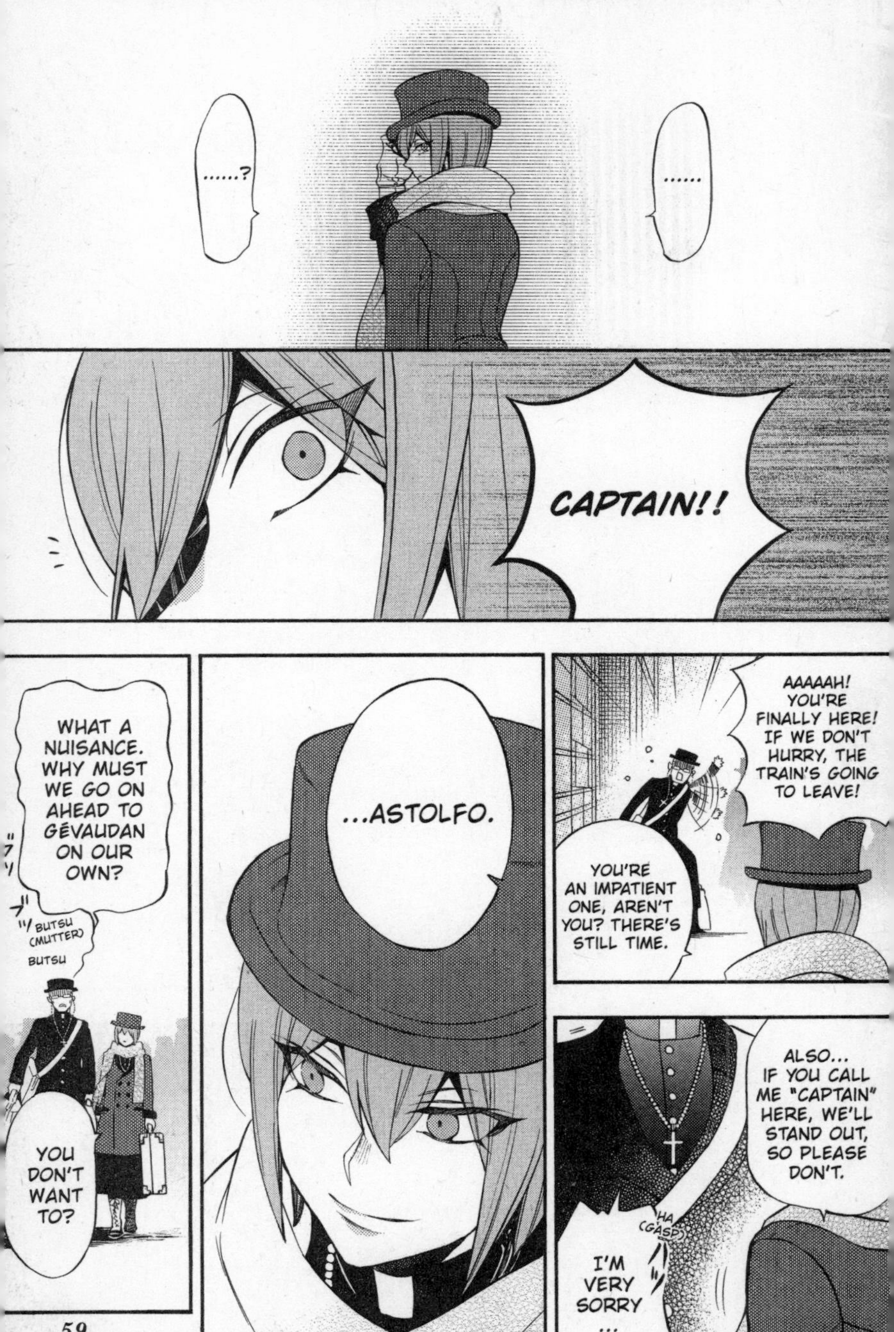
......
......?
CAPTAIN!!
AAAAAH! YOU'RE FINALLY HERE! IF WE DON'T HURRY, THE TRAIN'S GOING TO LEAVE!
YOU'RE AN IMPATIENT ONE, AREN'T YOU? THERE'S STILL TIME.
ALSO... IF YOU CALL ME "CAPTAIN" HERE, WE'LL STAND OUT, SO PLEASE DON'T.
HA (GASP)
I'M VERY SORRY ...
...ASTOLFO.
WHAT A NUISANCE. WHY MUST WE GO ON AHEAD TO GÉVAUDAN ON OUR OWN?
BUTSU (MUTTER) BUTSU
YOU DON'T WANT TO?

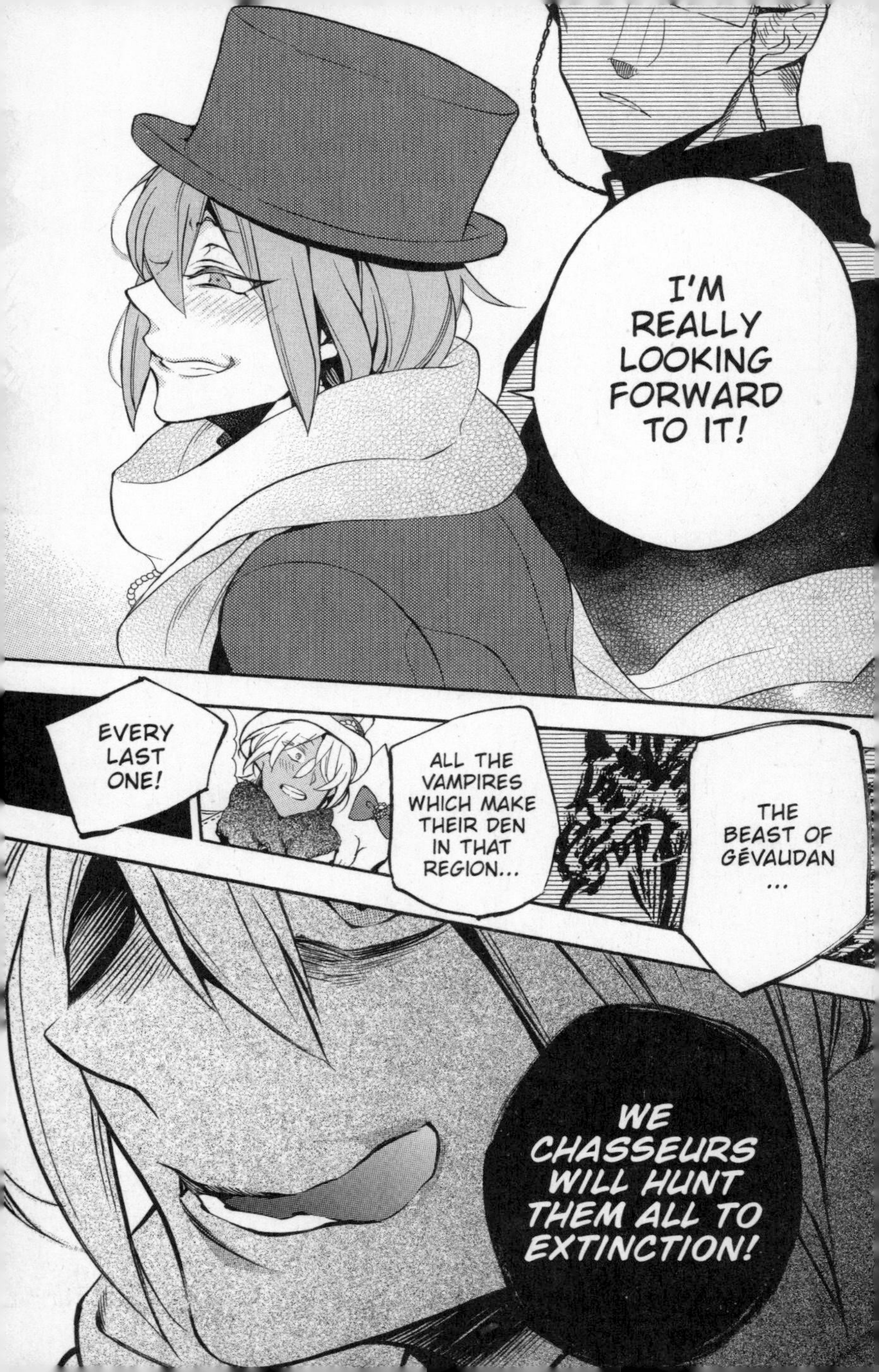
I'M REALLY LOOKING FORWARD TO IT!
THE BEAST OF GÉVAUDAN ...
ALL THE VAMPIRES WHICH MAKE THEIR DEN IN THAT REGION...
EVERY LAST ONE!
WE CHASSEURS WILL HUNT THEM ALL TO EXTINCTION!

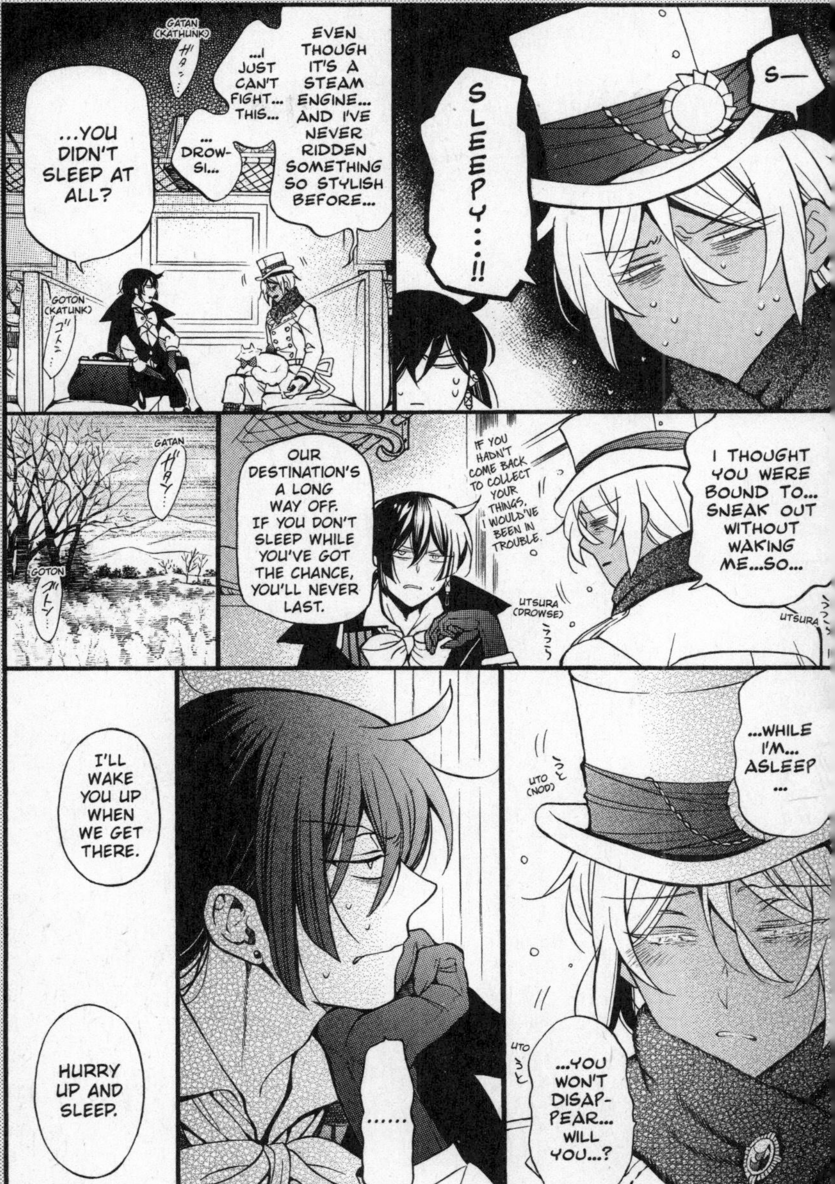
S—
SLEEPY...!!
EVEN THOUGH IT'S A STEAM ENGINE... AND I'VE NEVER RIDDEN SOMETHING SO STYLISH BEFORE...
...I JUST CAN'T FIGHT... THIS...
...DROWSI...
GATAN (KATHUNK)
...YOU DIDN'T SLEEP AT ALL?
GOTON (KATUNK)
I THOUGHT YOU WERE BOUND TO... SNEAK OUT WITHOUT WAKING ME...SO...
UTSURA
IF YOU HADN'T COME BACK TO COLLECT YOUR THINGS, I WOULD'VE BEEN IN TROUBLE.
UTSURA (DROWSE)
OUR DESTINATION'S A LONG WAY OFF. IF YOU DON'T SLEEP WHILE YOU'VE GOT THE CHANCE, YOU'LL NEVER LAST.
GATAN
GOTON
...WHILE I'M... ASLEEP...
UTO (NOD)
...YOU WON'T DISAPPEAR... WILL YOU...?
UTO
......
I'LL WAKE YOU UP WHEN WE GET THERE.
HURRY UP AND SLEEP.

Les Mémoires de Vanitas

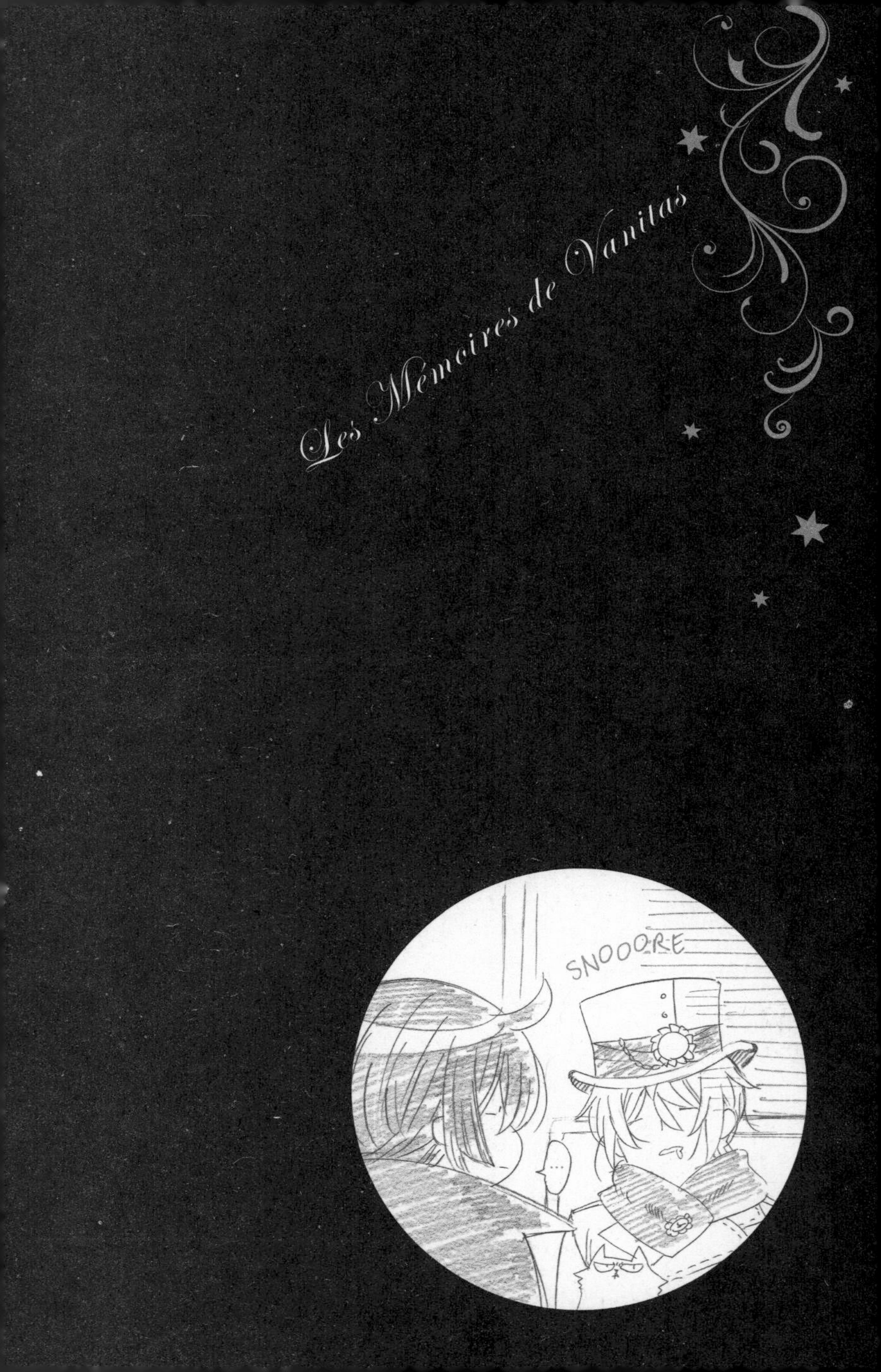
SNOOORE
...

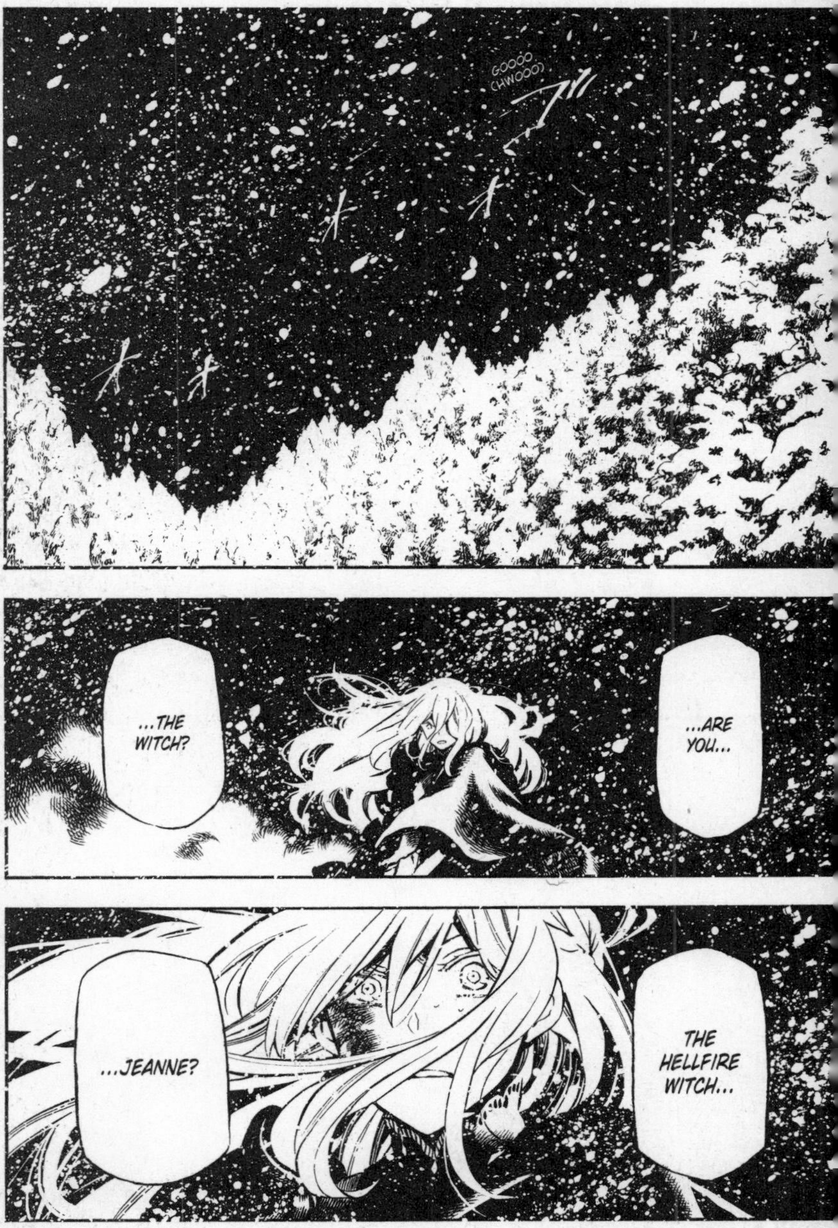
GOOOO (HWOOO)
...ARE YOU...
...THE WITCH?
THE HELLFIRE WITCH...
...JEANNE?

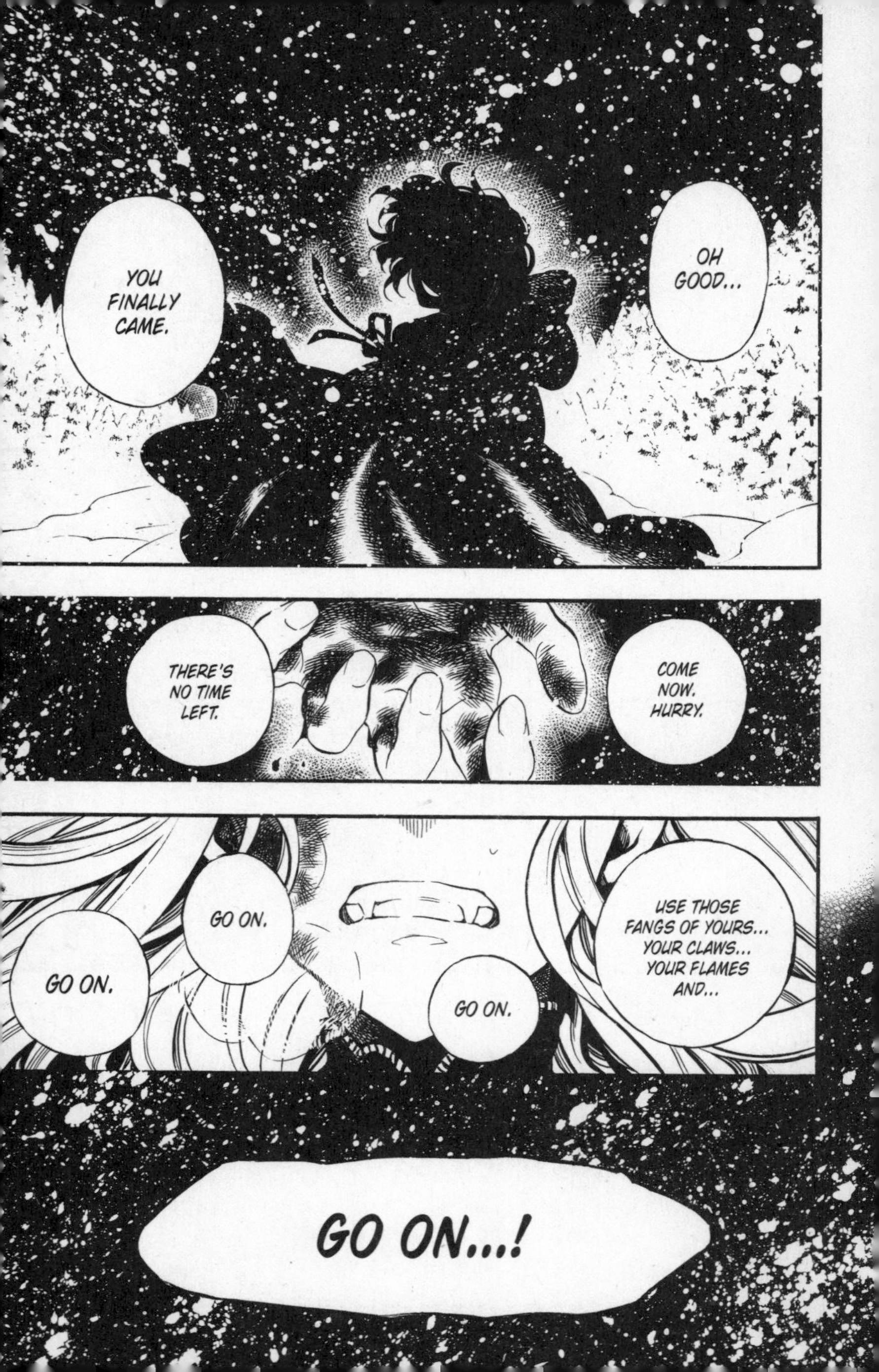
OH GOOD...
YOU FINALLY CAME.
COME NOW. HURRY.
THERE'S NO TIME LEFT.
USE THOSE FANGS OF YOURS... YOUR CLAWS... YOUR FLAMES AND...
GO ON.
GO ON.
GO ON.
GO ON...!

MÉMOIRE 24

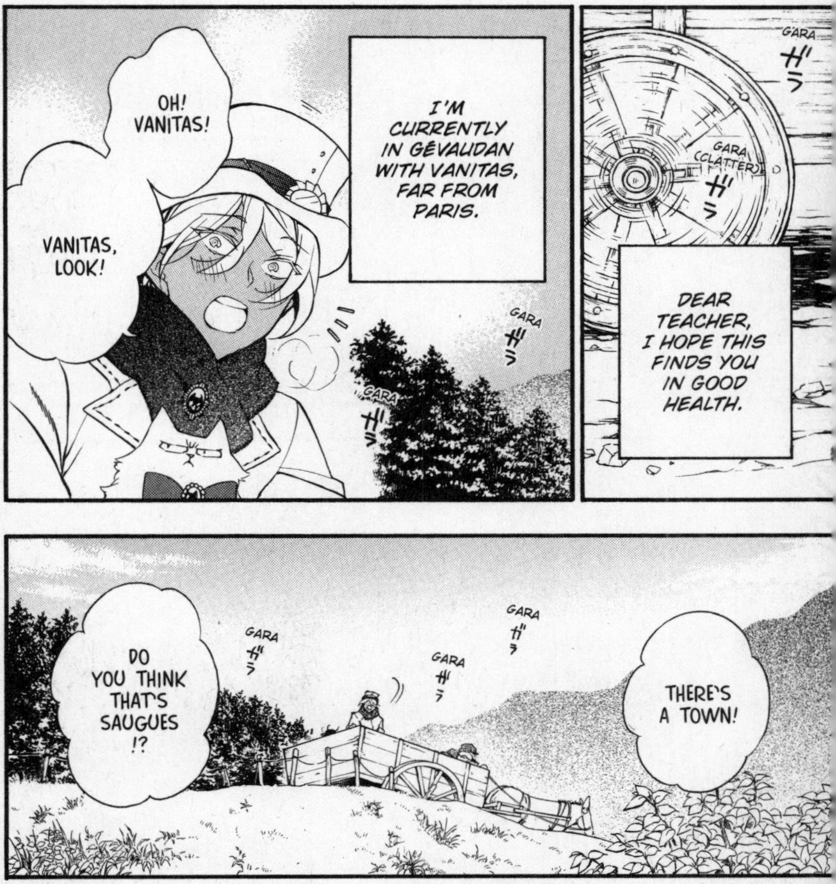

GARA ガラ
GARA (CLATTER) ガラ
DEAR TEACHER, I HOPE THIS FINDS YOU IN GOOD HEALTH.
I'M CURRENTLY IN GÉVAUDAN WITH VANITAS, FAR FROM PARIS.
GARA ガラ
OH! VANITAS!
VANITAS, LOOK!
GARA ガラ
THERE'S A TOWN!
GARA ガラ
GARA ガラ
GARA ガラ
DO YOU THINK THAT'S SAUGUES !?

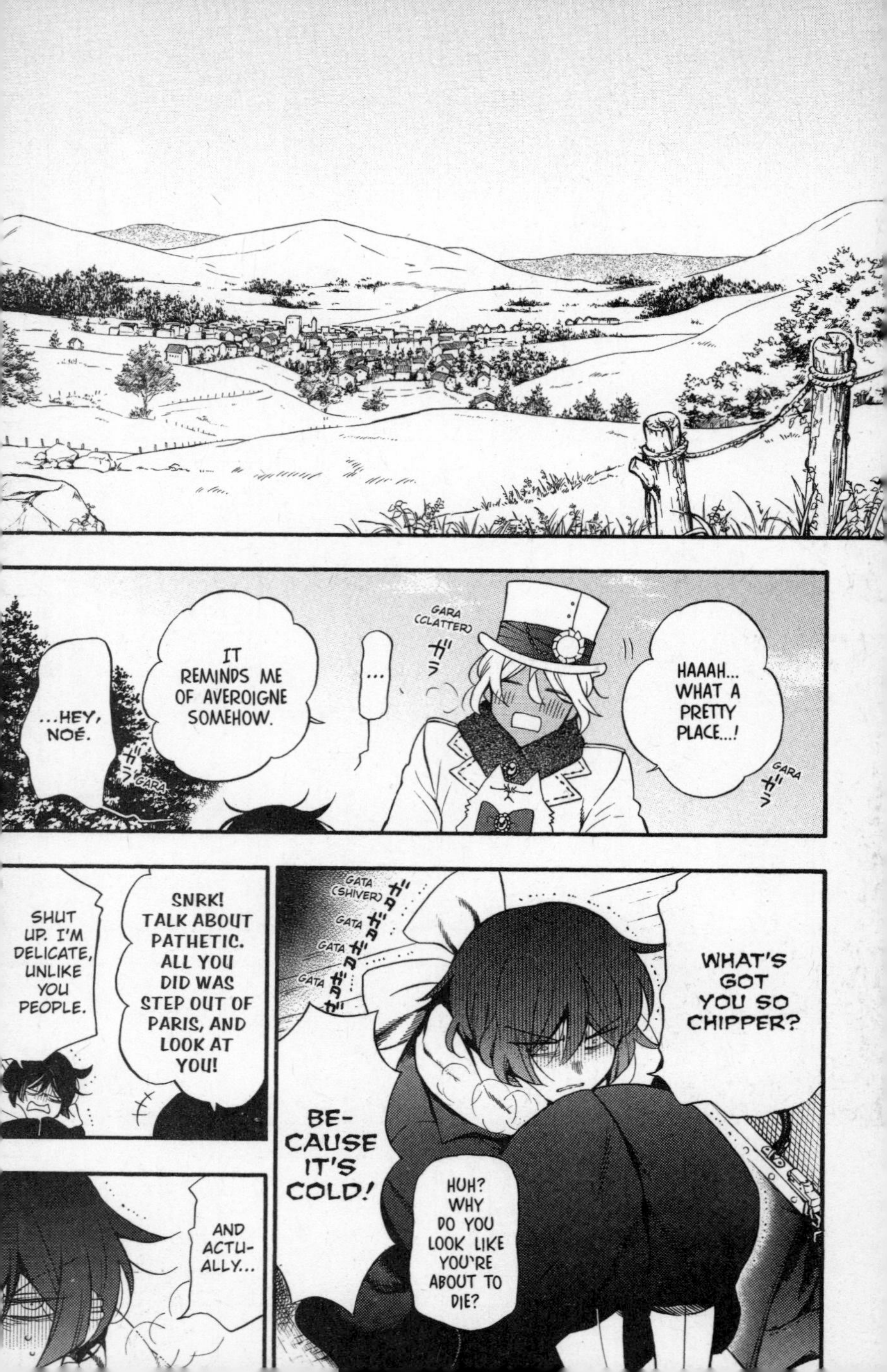
HAAAH... WHAT A PRETTY PLACE...!
GARA
GARA (CLATTER)
...
IT REMINDS ME OF AVEROIGNE SOMEHOW.
GARA
...HEY, NOÉ.
WHAT'S GOT YOU SO CHIPPER?
GATA (SHIVER) GATA GATA GATA
BE-CAUSE IT'S COLD!
HUH? WHY DO YOU LOOK LIKE YOU'RE ABOUT TO DIE?
SNRK! TALK ABOUT PATHETIC. ALL YOU DID WAS STEP OUT OF PARIS, AND LOOK AT YOU!
SHUT UP. I'M DELICATE, UNLIKE YOU PEOPLE.
AND ACTUALLY...

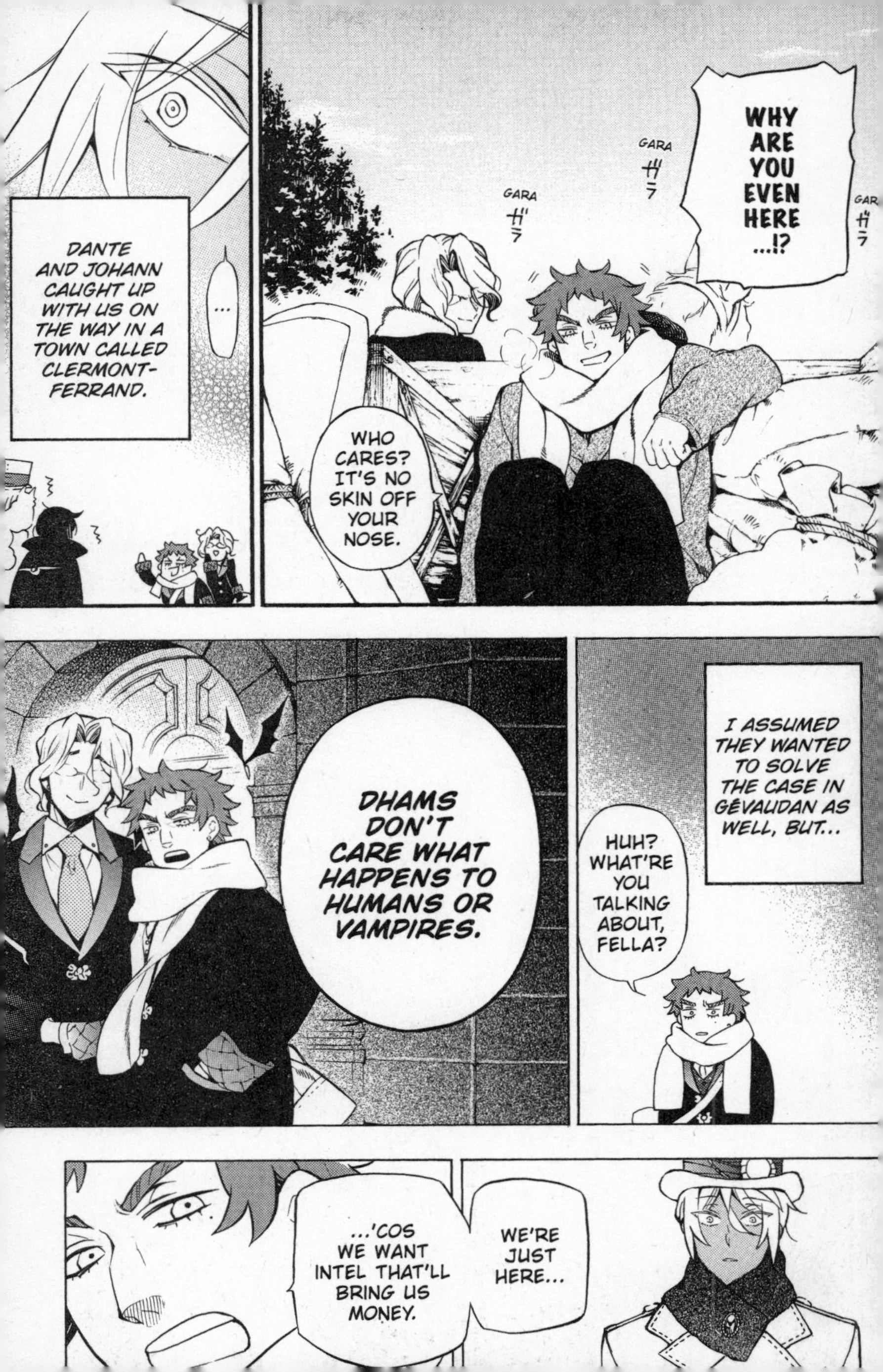
WHY ARE YOU EVEN HERE ...!?
GAR ガラ
GARA ガラ
GARA ガラ
WHO CARES? IT'S NO SKIN OFF YOUR NOSE.
...
DANTE AND JOHANN CAUGHT UP WITH US ON THE WAY IN A TOWN CALLED CLERMONT-FERRAND.
I ASSUMED THEY WANTED TO SOLVE THE CASE IN GÉVAUDAN AS WELL, BUT...
HUH? WHAT'RE YOU TALKING ABOUT, FELLA?
DHAMS DON'T CARE WHAT HAPPENS TO HUMANS OR VAMPIRES.
WE'RE JUST HERE...
...'COS WE WANT INTEL THAT'LL BRING US MONEY.

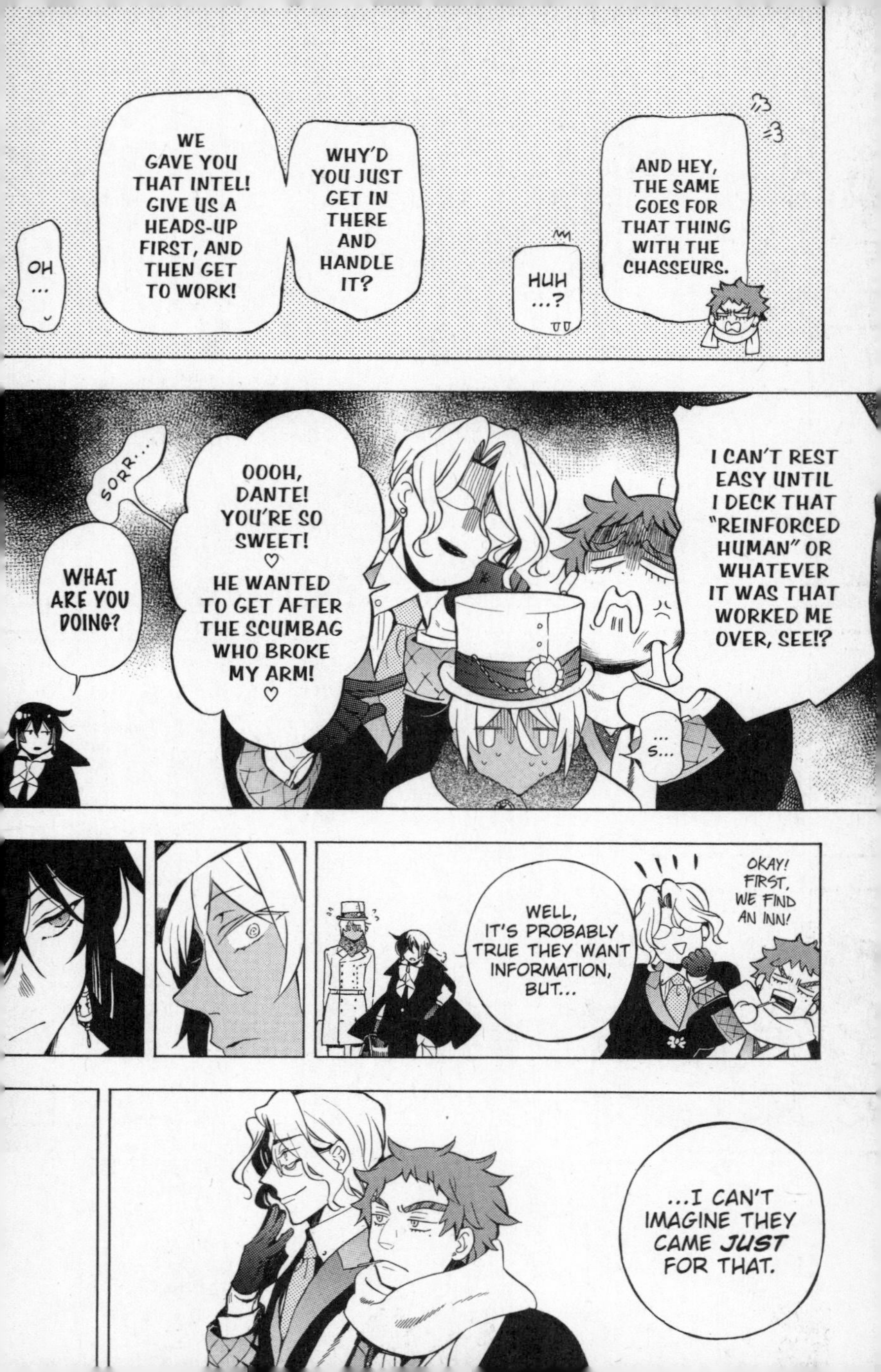
AND HEY, THE SAME GOES FOR THAT THING WITH THE CHASSEURS.
HUH ...?
WHY'D YOU JUST GET IN THERE AND HANDLE IT?
WE GAVE YOU THAT INTEL! GIVE US A HEADS-UP FIRST, AND THEN GET TO WORK!
OH ...
I CAN'T REST EASY UNTIL I DECK THAT "REINFORCED HUMAN" OR WHATEVER IT WAS THAT WORKED ME OVER, SEE!?
... S...
OOOH, DANTE! YOU'RE SO SWEET! ♡ HE WANTED TO GET AFTER THE SCUMBAG WHO BROKE MY ARM! ♡
SORR...
WHAT ARE YOU DOING?
OKAY! FIRST, WE FIND AN INN!
WELL, IT'S PROBABLY TRUE THEY WANT INFORMATION, BUT...
...I CAN'T IMAGINE THEY CAME *JUST* FOR THAT.

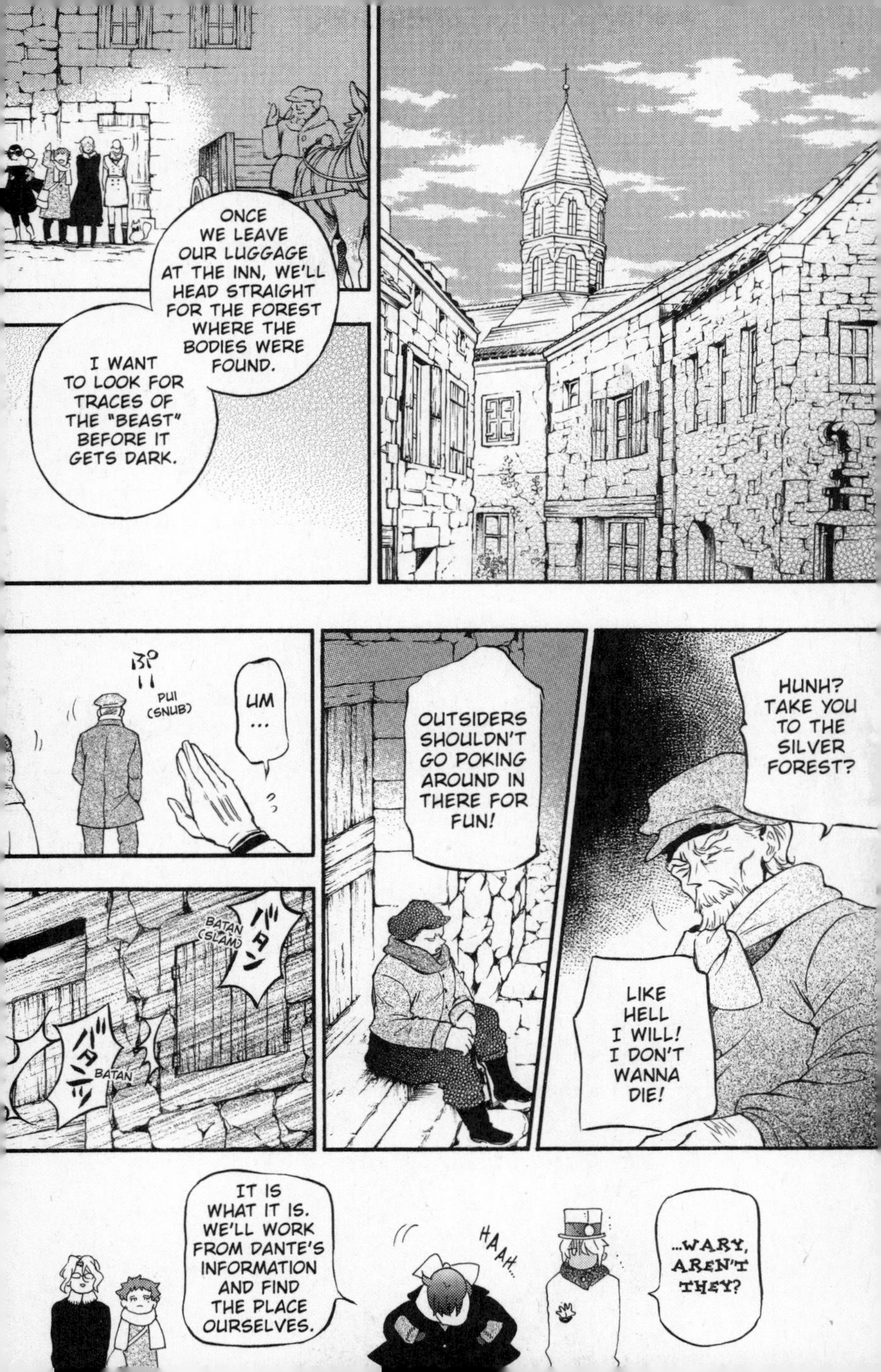
ONCE WE LEAVE OUR LUGGAGE AT THE INN, WE'LL HEAD STRAIGHT FOR THE FOREST WHERE THE BODIES WERE FOUND.
I WANT TO LOOK FOR TRACES OF THE "BEAST" BEFORE IT GETS DARK.
HUNH? TAKE YOU TO THE SILVER FOREST?
LIKE HELL I WILL! I DON'T WANNA DIE!
OUTSIDERS SHOULDN'T GO POKING AROUND IN THERE FOR FUN!
ぷい
PUI (SNUB)
UM ...
バタン
BATAN (SLAM)
バタンッ
BATAN
...WARY, AREN'T THEY?
HAAAH...
IT IS WHAT IT IS. WE'LL WORK FROM DANTE'S INFORMATION AND FIND THE PLACE OURSELVES.

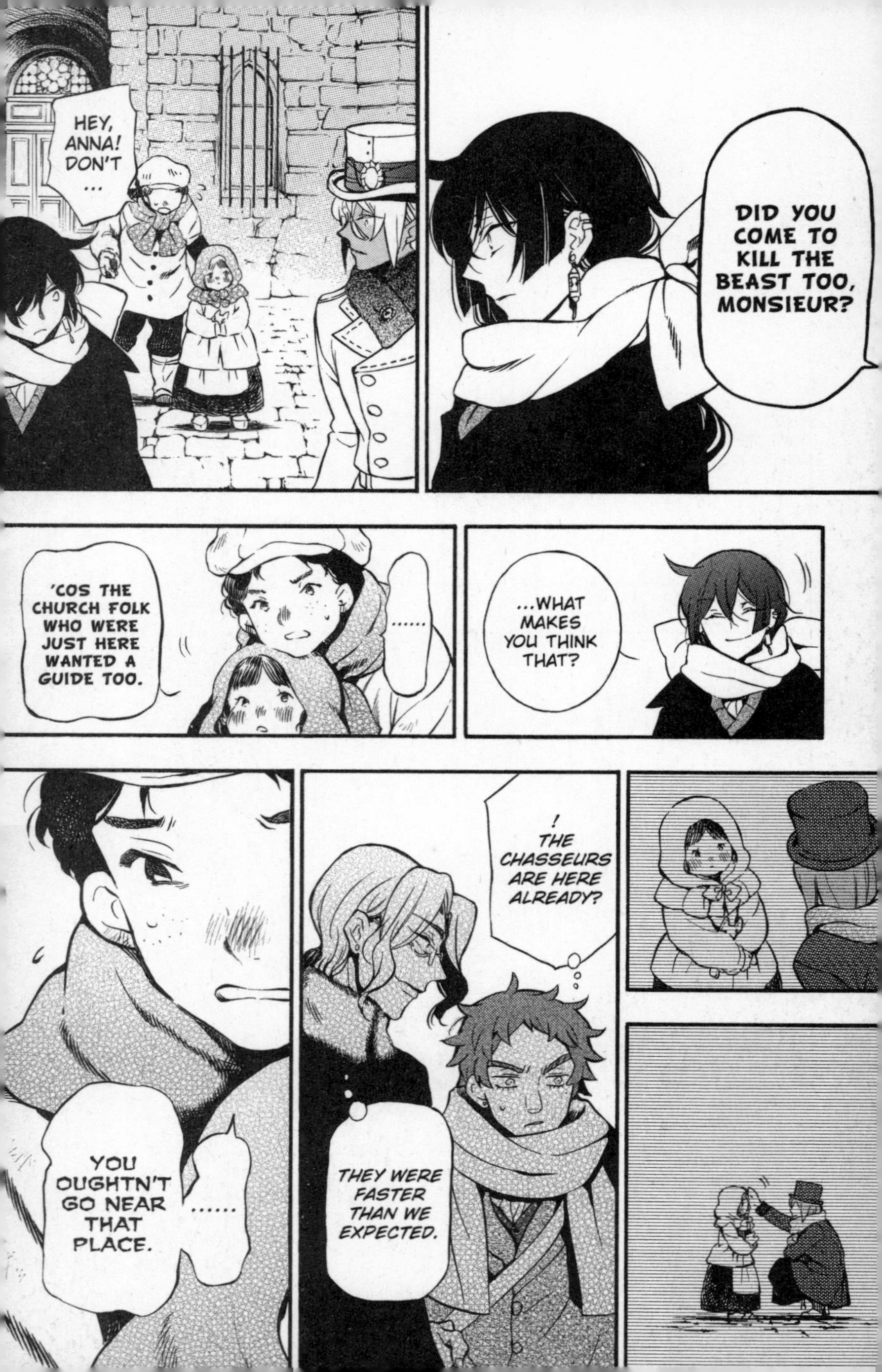
DID YOU COME TO KILL THE BEAST TOO, MONSIEUR?
HEY, ANNA! DON'T ...
...WHAT MAKES YOU THINK THAT?
......
'COS THE CHURCH FOLK WHO WERE JUST HERE WANTED A GUIDE TOO.
! THE CHASSEURS ARE HERE ALREADY?
THEY WERE FASTER THAN WE EXPECTED.
......
YOU OUGHTN'T GO NEAR THAT PLACE.

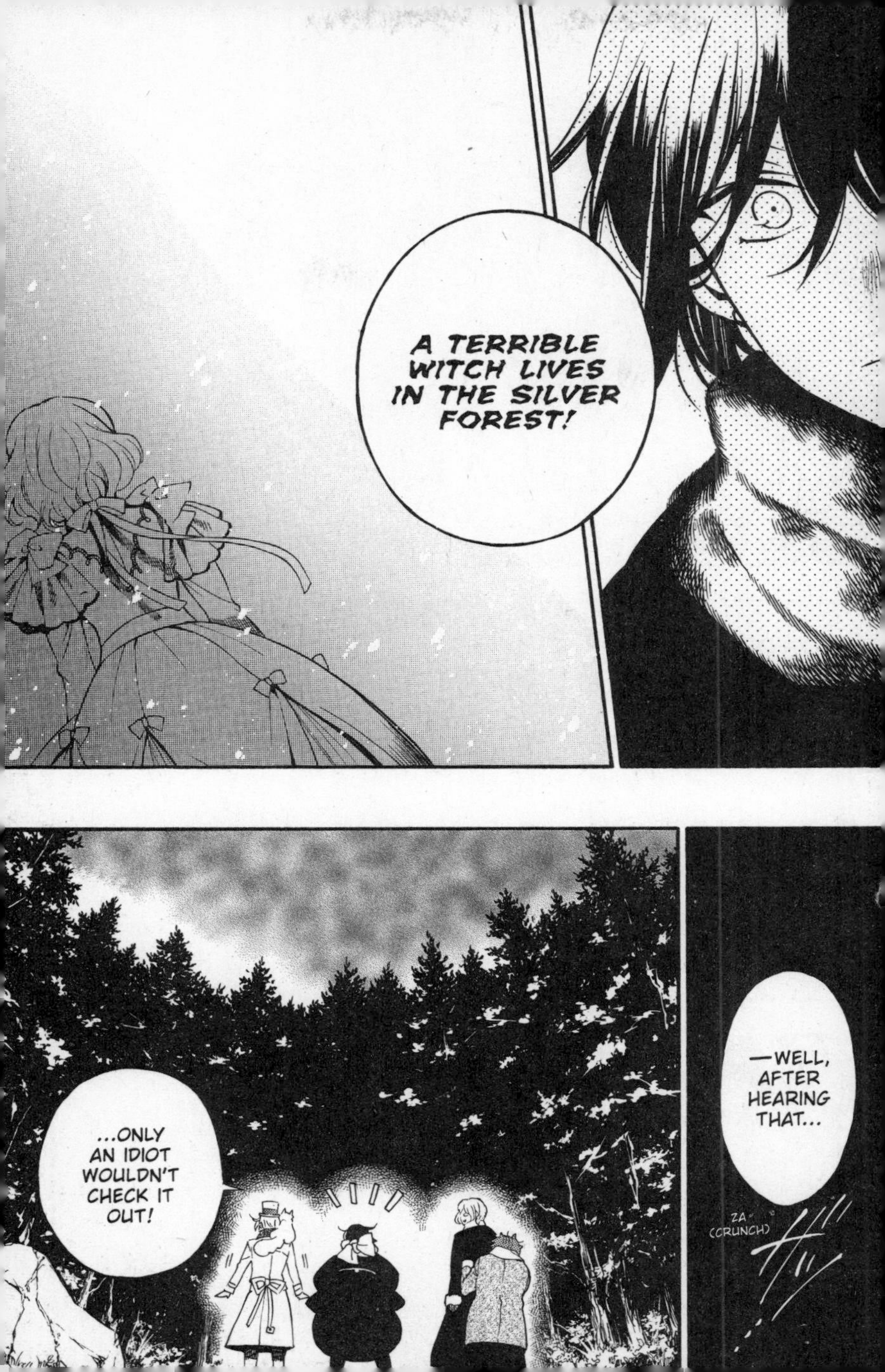
A TERRIBLE WITCH LIVES IN THE SILVER FOREST!
—WELL, AFTER HEARING THAT...
ZA (CRUNCH)
...ONLY AN IDIOT WOULDN'T CHECK IT OUT!

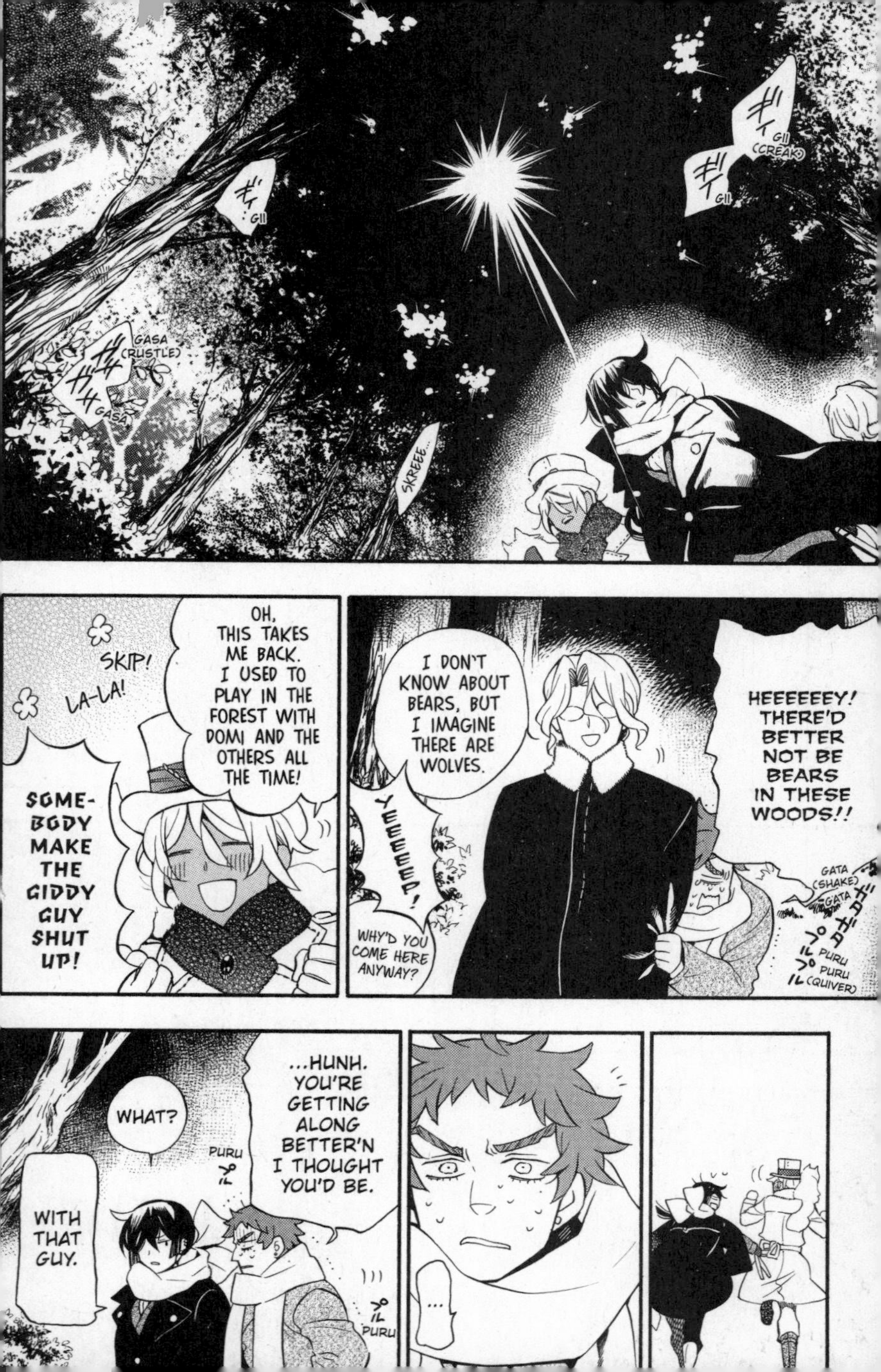
GII (CREAK)
GII
GII
GASA (RUSTLE)
GASA
SKREEE...
HEEEEEEY! THERE'D BETTER NOT BE BEARS IN THESE WOODS!!
GATA (SHAKE) GATA
PURU PURU (QUIVER)
I DON'T KNOW ABOUT BEARS, BUT I IMAGINE THERE ARE WOLVES.
YEEEEEP!
WHY'D YOU COME HERE ANYWAY?
OH, THIS TAKES ME BACK. I USED TO PLAY IN THE FOREST WITH DOMI AND THE OTHERS ALL THE TIME!
SKIP!
LA-LA!
SOME-BODY MAKE THE GIDDY GUY SHUT UP!
...
...HUNH. YOU'RE GETTING ALONG BETTER'N I THOUGHT YOU'D BE.
PURU
WHAT?
WITH THAT GUY.
PURU

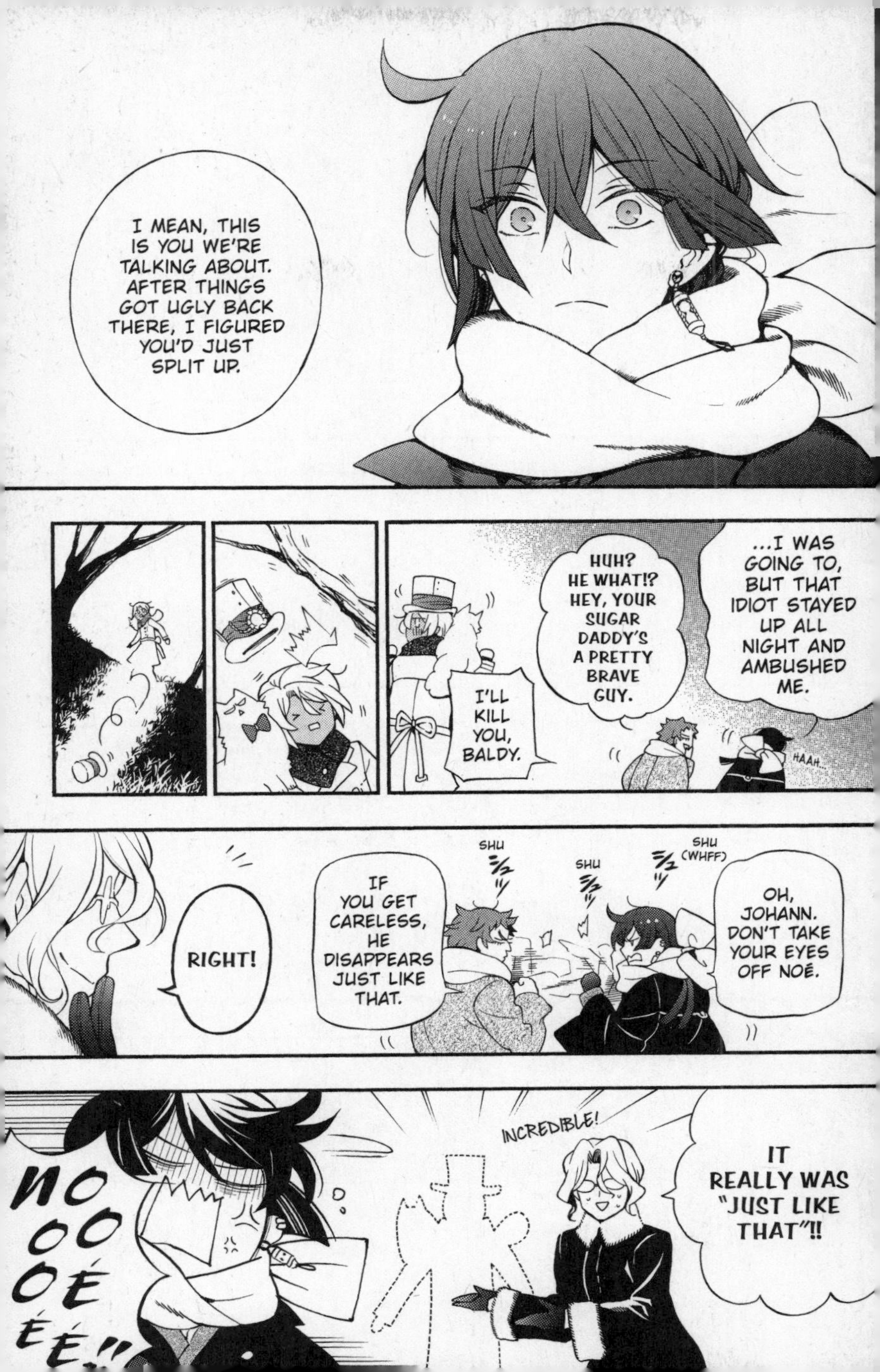
I MEAN, THIS IS YOU WE'RE TALKING ABOUT. AFTER THINGS GOT UGLY BACK THERE, I FIGURED YOU'D JUST SPLIT UP.
...I WAS GOING TO, BUT THAT IDIOT STAYED UP ALL NIGHT AND AMBUSHED ME.
HAAH...
HUH? HE WHAT!? HEY, YOUR SUGAR DADDY'S A PRETTY BRAVE GUY.
I'LL KILL YOU, BALDY.
OH, JOHANN. DON'T TAKE YOUR EYES OFF NOÉ.
SHU (WHFF)
SHU
SHU
IF YOU GET CARELESS, HE DISAPPEARS JUST LIKE THAT.
RIGHT!
IT REALLY WAS "JUST LIKE THAT"!!
INCREDIBLE!
NOOOOOÉÉÉ!!

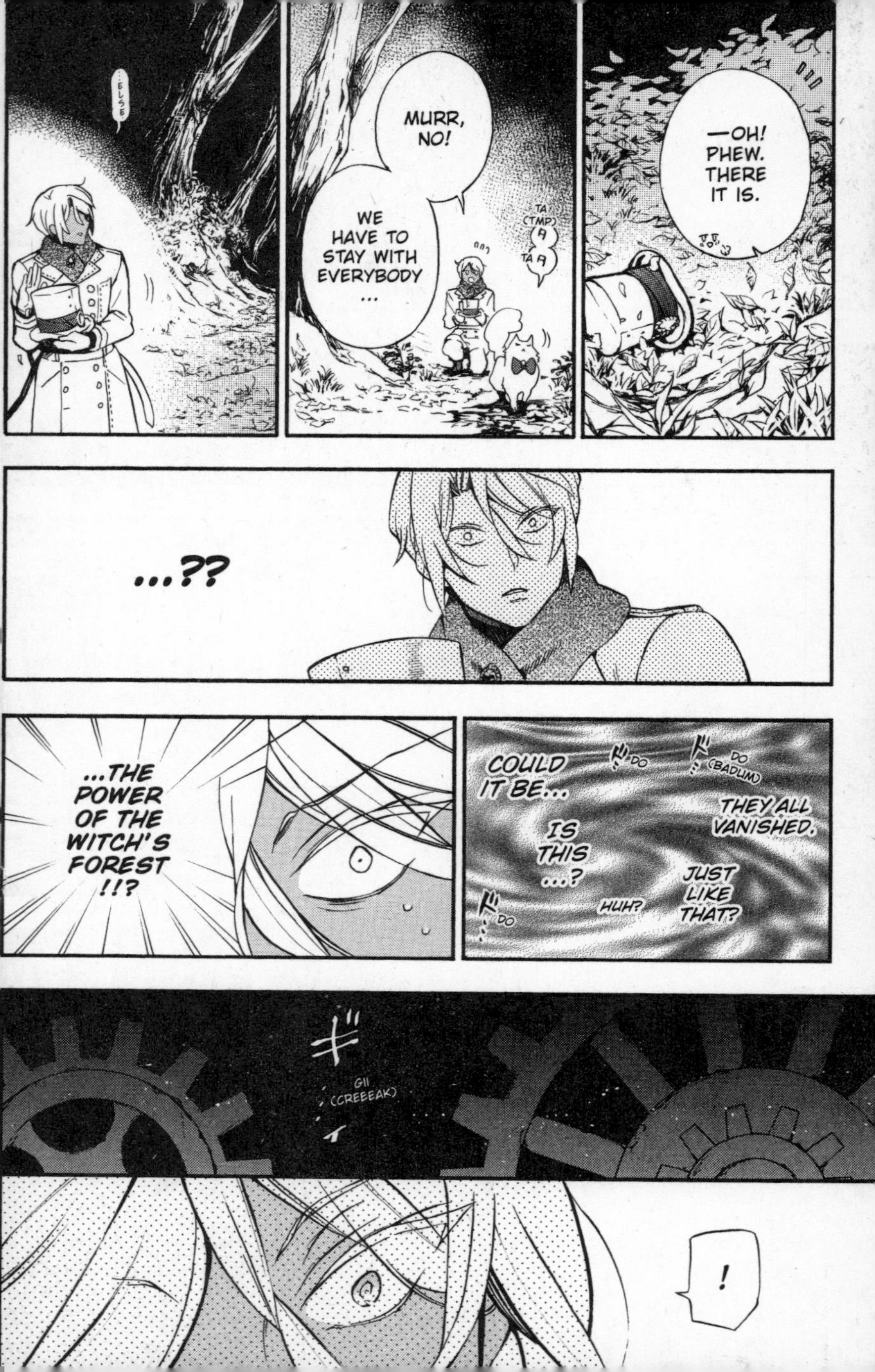
—OH! PHEW. THERE IT IS.
MURR, NO!
WE HAVE TO STAY WITH EVERYBODY ...
TA (TMP)
TA
...ELSE.
...??
COULD IT BE...
DO
DO (BADUM)
THEY ALL VANISHED.
IS THIS ...?
JUST LIKE THAT?
HUH?
DO
...THE POWER OF THE WITCH'S FOREST!!?
GII (CREEEAK)
!

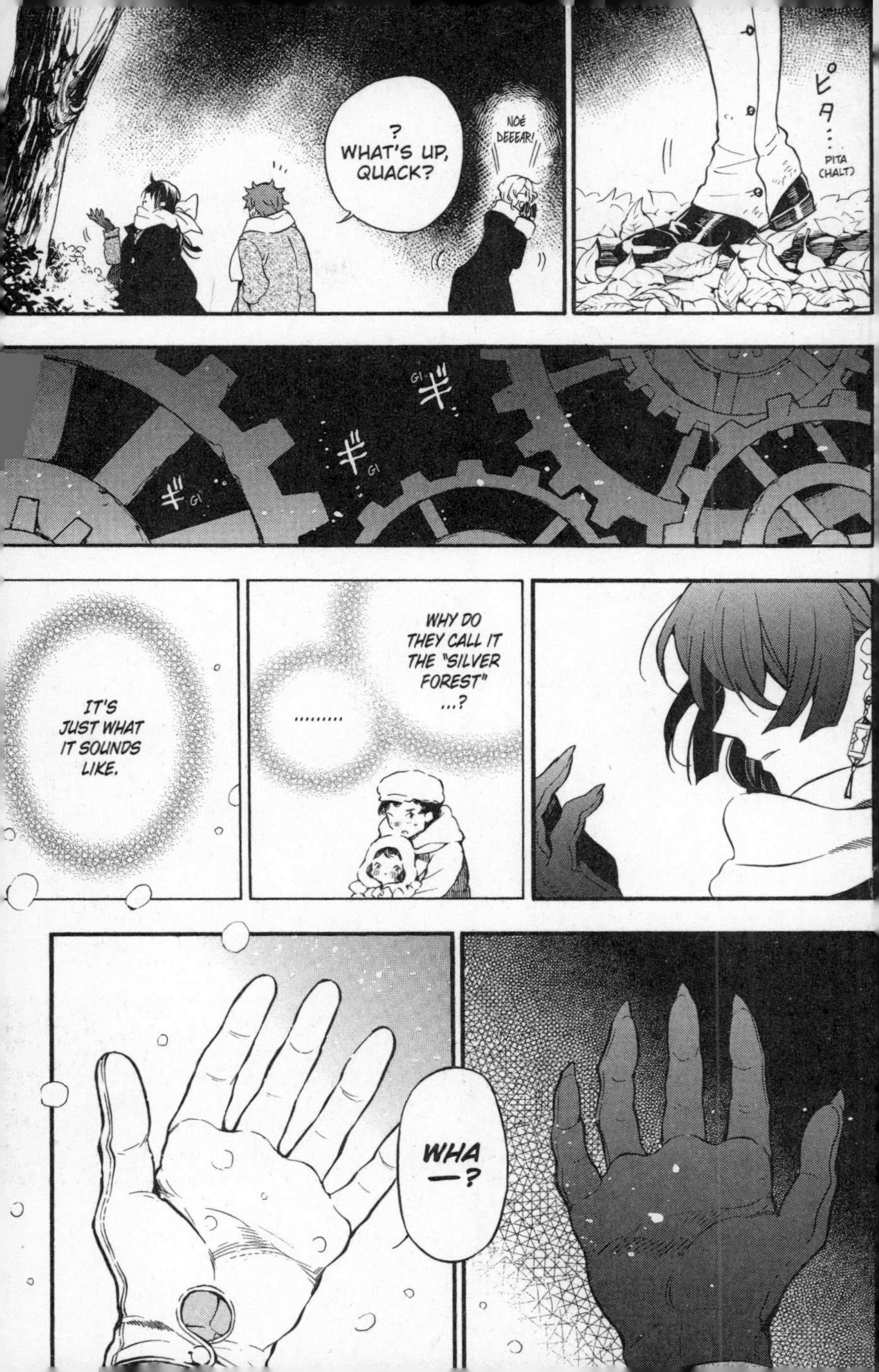
ピタ…
PITA (HALT)
NOÉ DEEEAR!
? WHAT'S UP, QUACK?
ギ GI
ギ GI
ギ GI
WHY DO THEY CALL IT THE "SILVER FOREST" ...?
....
IT'S JUST WHAT IT SOUNDS LIKE.
WHA—?

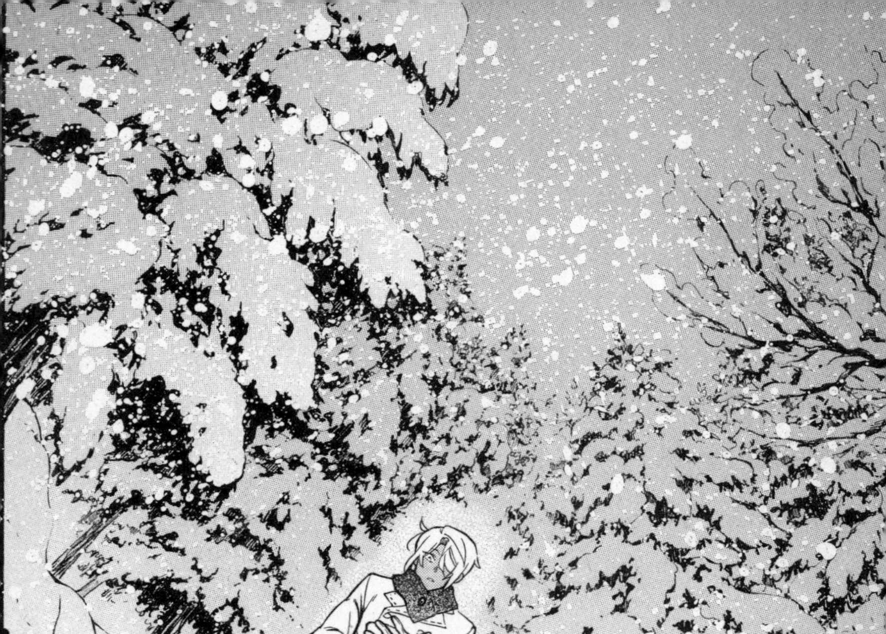
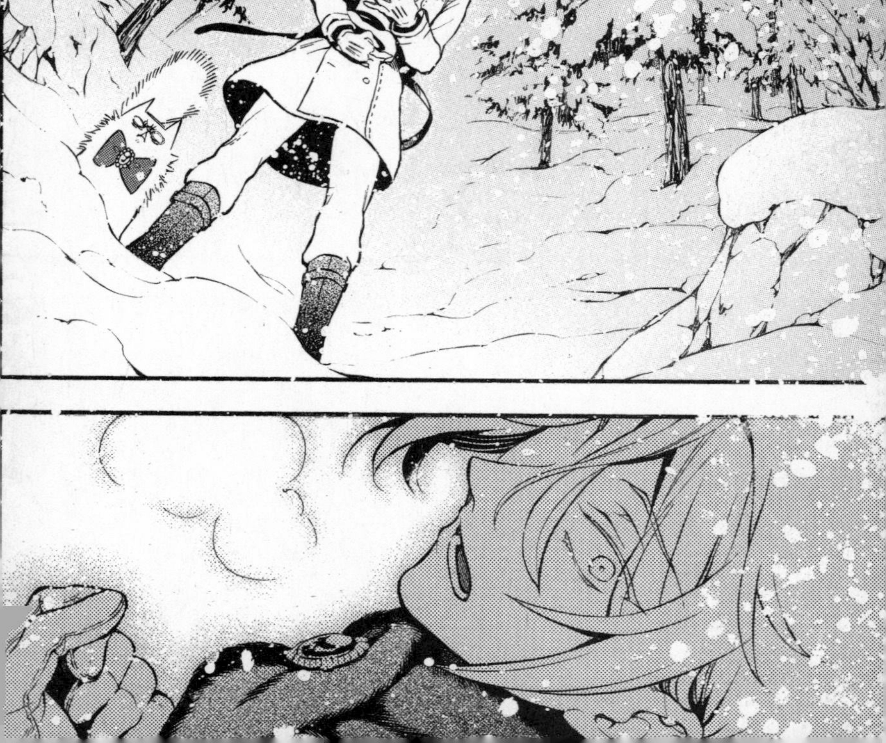

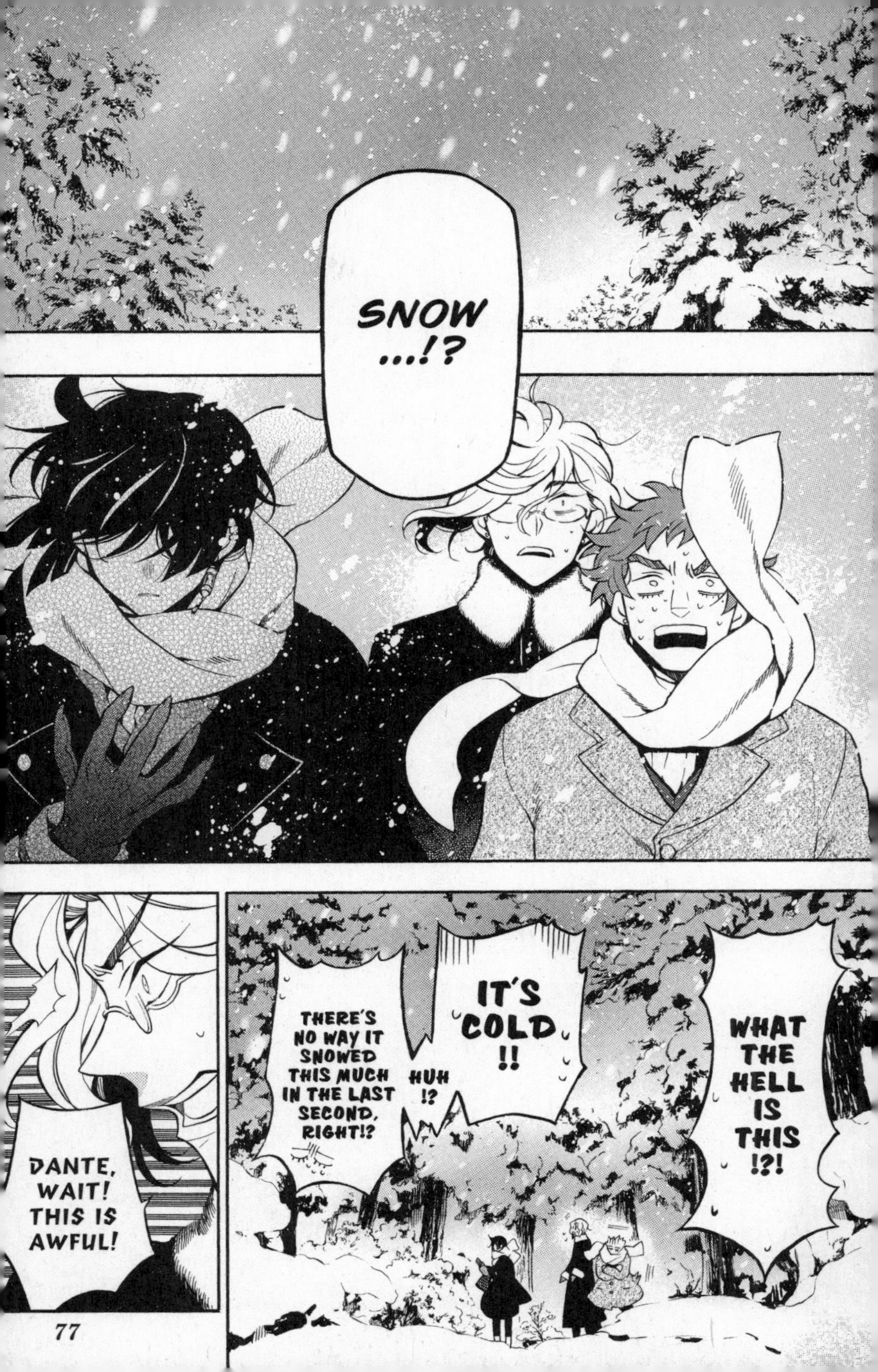
SNOW ...!?
WHAT THE HELL IS THIS !?!
IT'S COLD !!
HUH !?
THERE'S NO WAY IT SNOWED THIS MUCH IN THE LAST SECOND, RIGHT!?
DANTE, WAIT! THIS IS AWFUL!

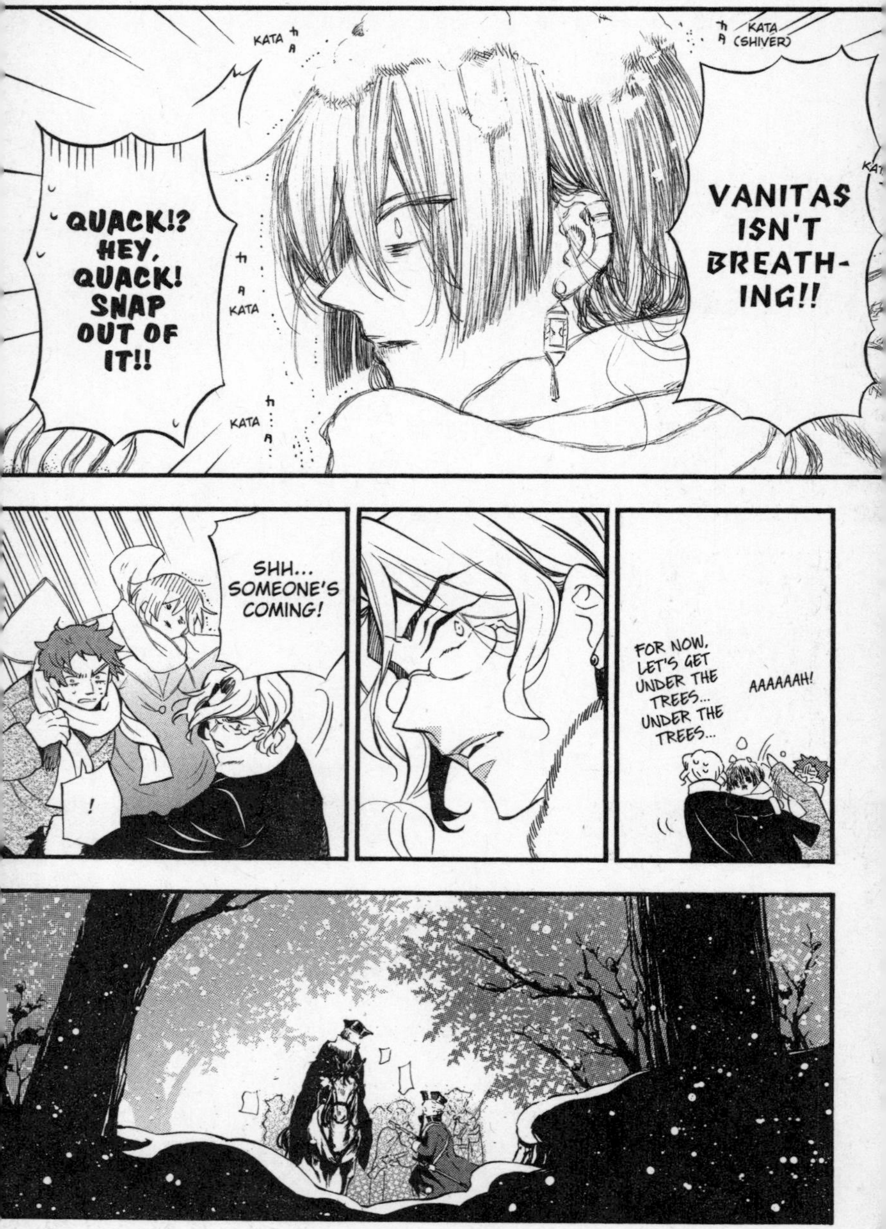
KATA (SHIVER)
KATA
VANITAS ISN'T BREATHING!!
KATA
KATA
QUACK!? HEY, QUACK! SNAP OUT OF IT!!
KATA
FOR NOW, LET'S GET UNDER THE TREES... UNDER THE TREES...
AAAAAAH!
SHH... SOMEONE'S COMING!
!

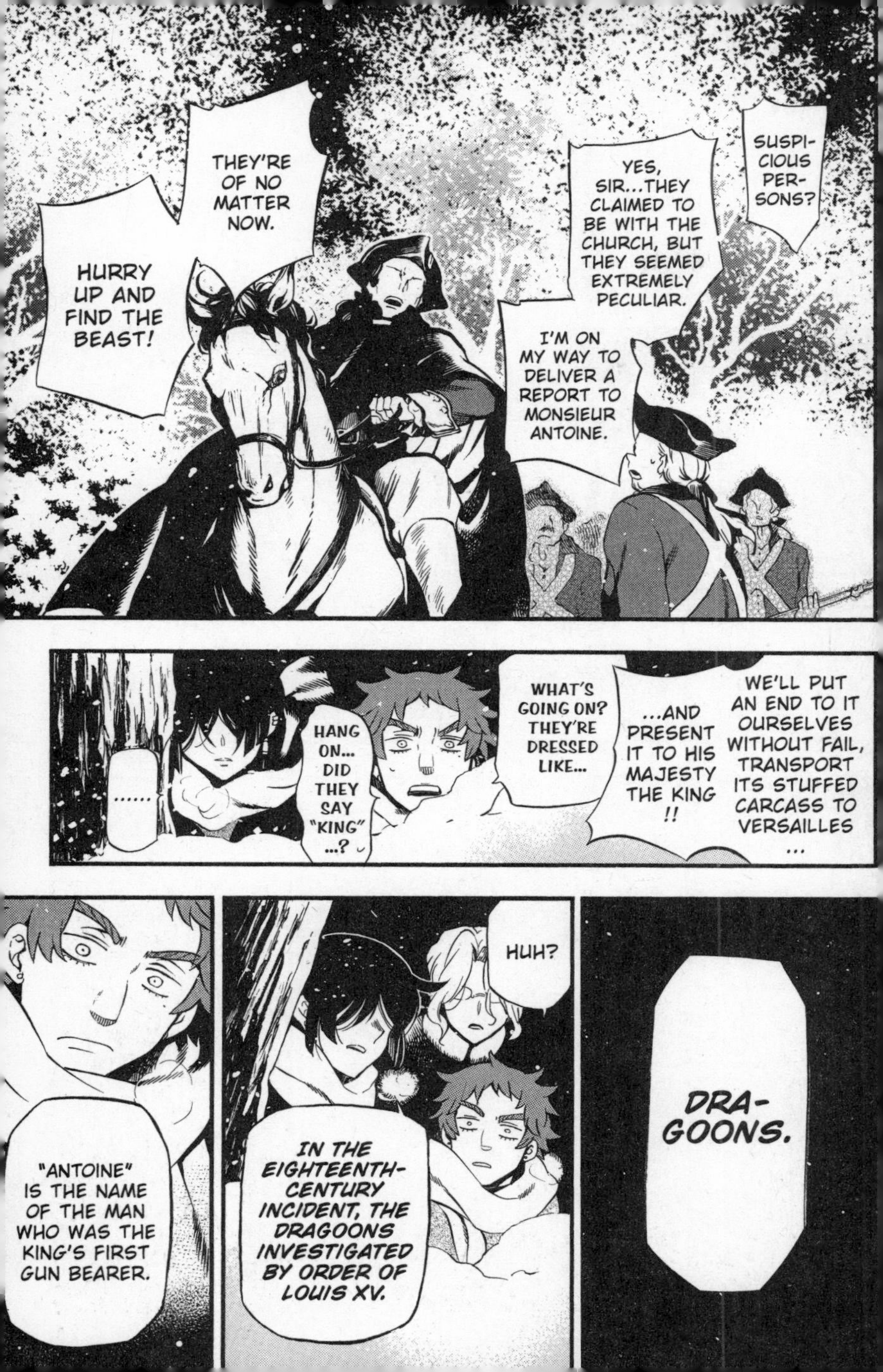
SUSPICIOUS PERSONS?
YES, SIR...THEY CLAIMED TO BE WITH THE CHURCH, BUT THEY SEEMED EXTREMELY PECULIAR.
I'M ON MY WAY TO DELIVER A REPORT TO MONSIEUR ANTOINE.
THEY'RE OF NO MATTER NOW.
HURRY UP AND FIND THE BEAST!
WE'LL PUT AN END TO IT OURSELVES WITHOUT FAIL, TRANSPORT ITS STUFFED CARCASS TO VERSAILLES...
...AND PRESENT IT TO HIS MAJESTY THE KING!!
WHAT'S GOING ON? THEY'RE DRESSED LIKE...
HANG ON... DID THEY SAY "KING"...?
......
DRAGOONS.
HUH?
IN THE EIGHTEENTH-CENTURY INCIDENT, THE DRAGOONS INVESTIGATED BY ORDER OF LOUIS XV.
"ANTOINE" IS THE NAME OF THE MAN WHO WAS THE KING'S FIRST GUN BEARER.

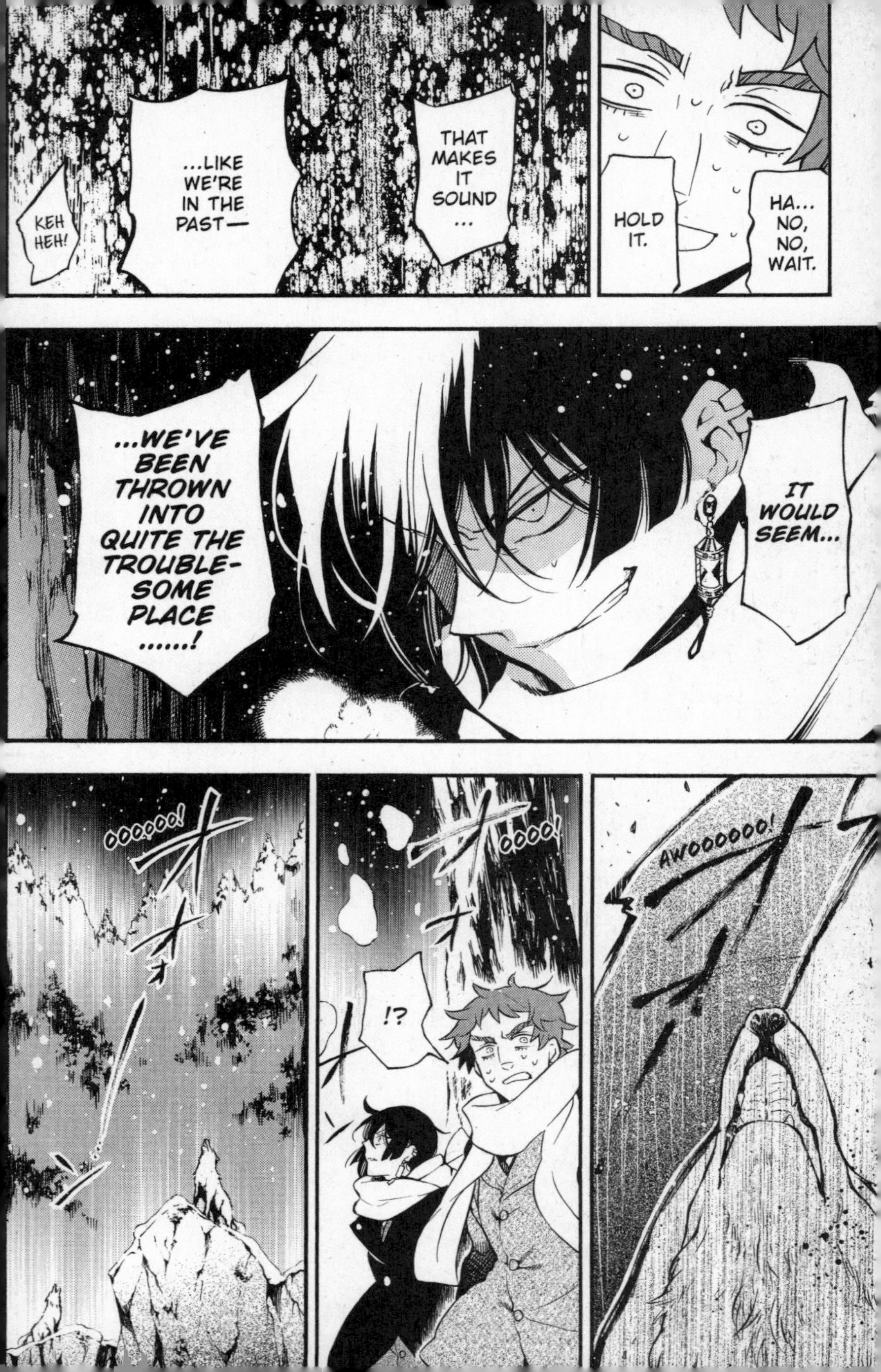
HA... NO, NO, WAIT.
HOLD IT.
THAT MAKES IT SOUND ...
...LIKE WE'RE IN THE PAST—
KEH HEH!
IT WOULD SEEM...
...WE'VE BEEN THROWN INTO QUITE THE TROUBLE-SOME PLACE......!
AWOOOOOO!
OOOO!
!?
OOOOOO!

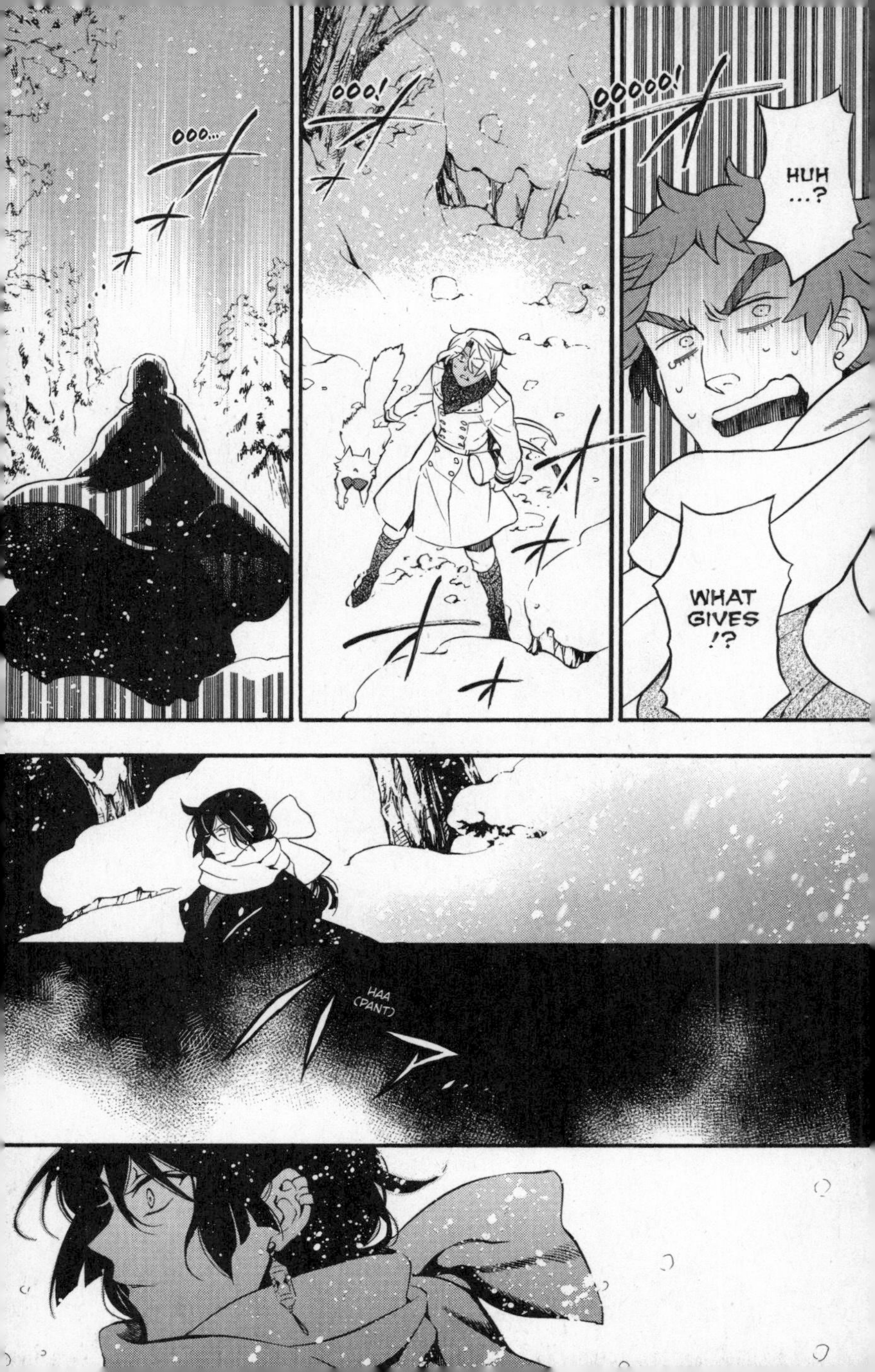
OOOOO!
HUH ...?
WHAT GIVES !?
OOO!
OOO...
HAA (PANT)

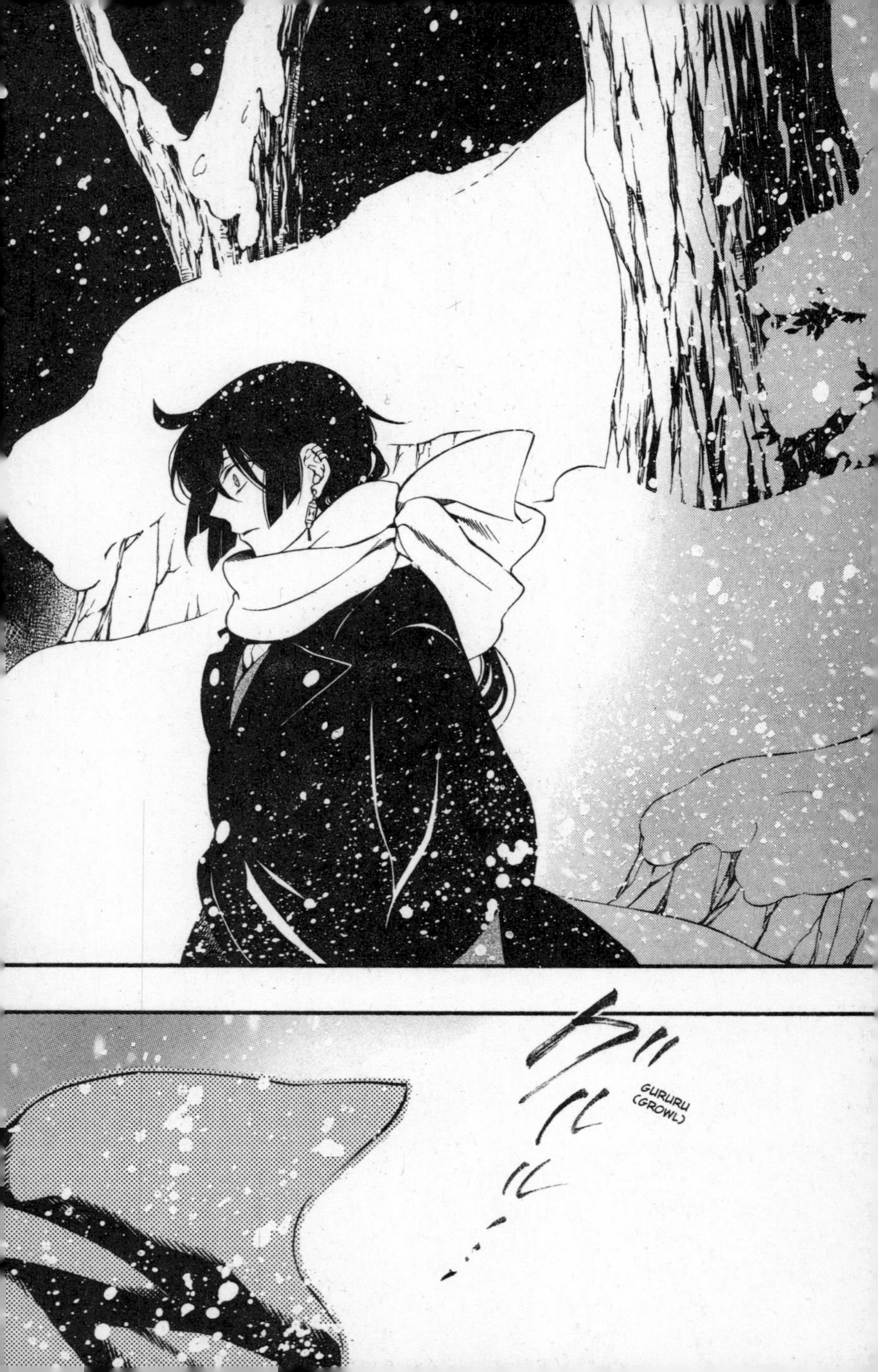
GURURU
(GROWL)

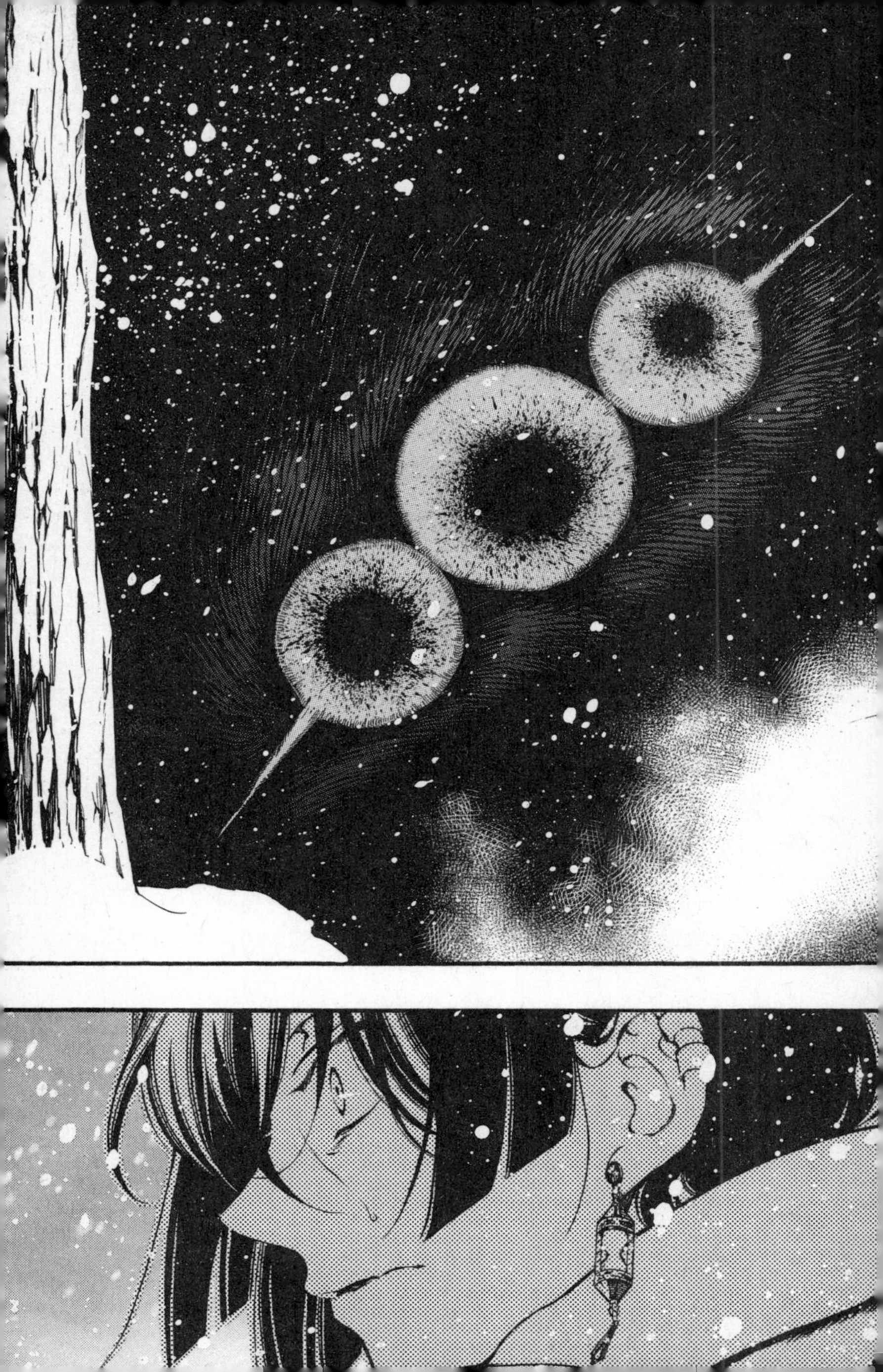

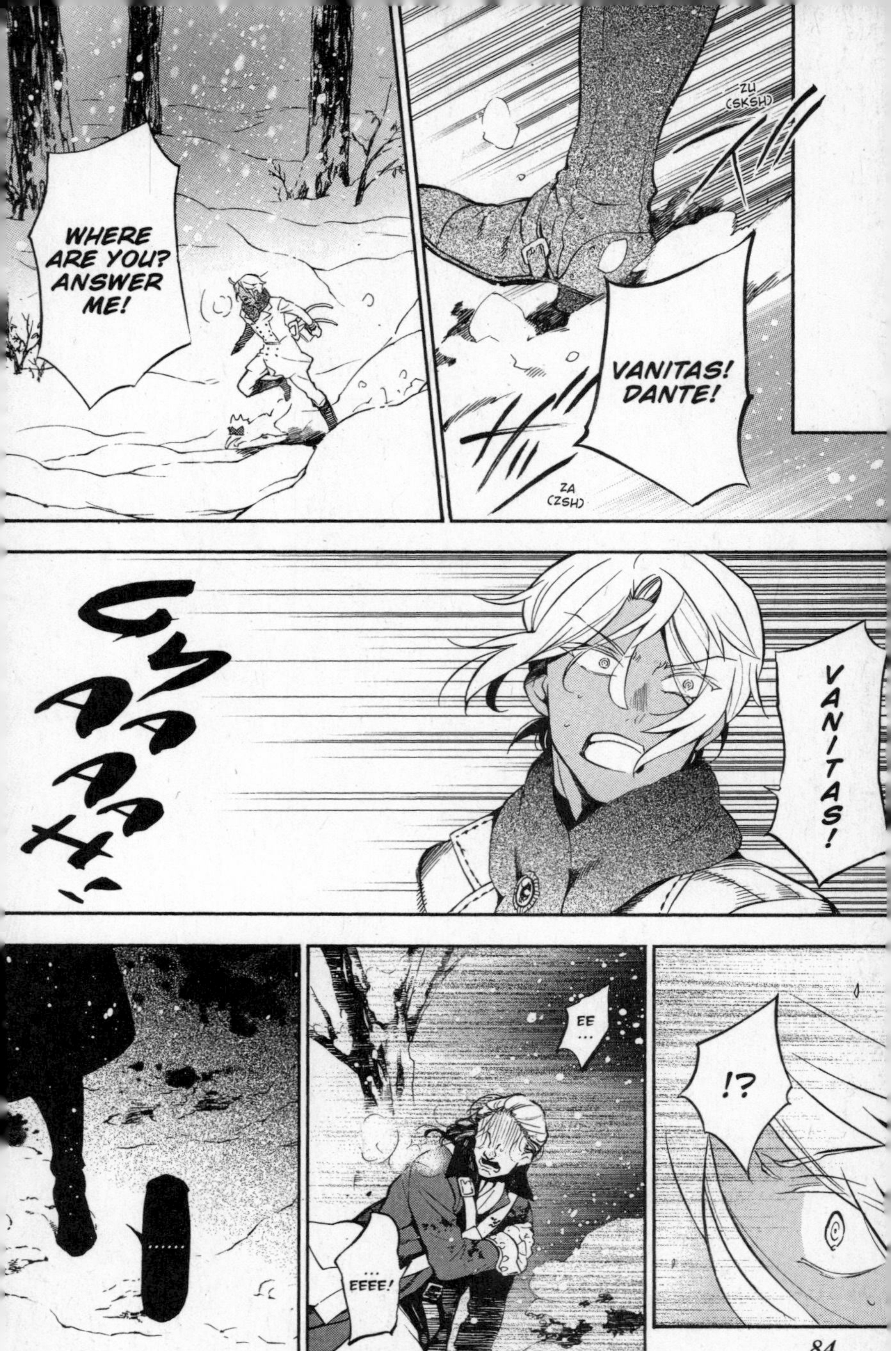
ZU (SKSH)
VANITAS! DANTE!
ZA (ZSH)
WHERE ARE YOU? ANSWER ME!
VANITAS!
GYAAAAH!
!?
EE...
...EEEE!
......

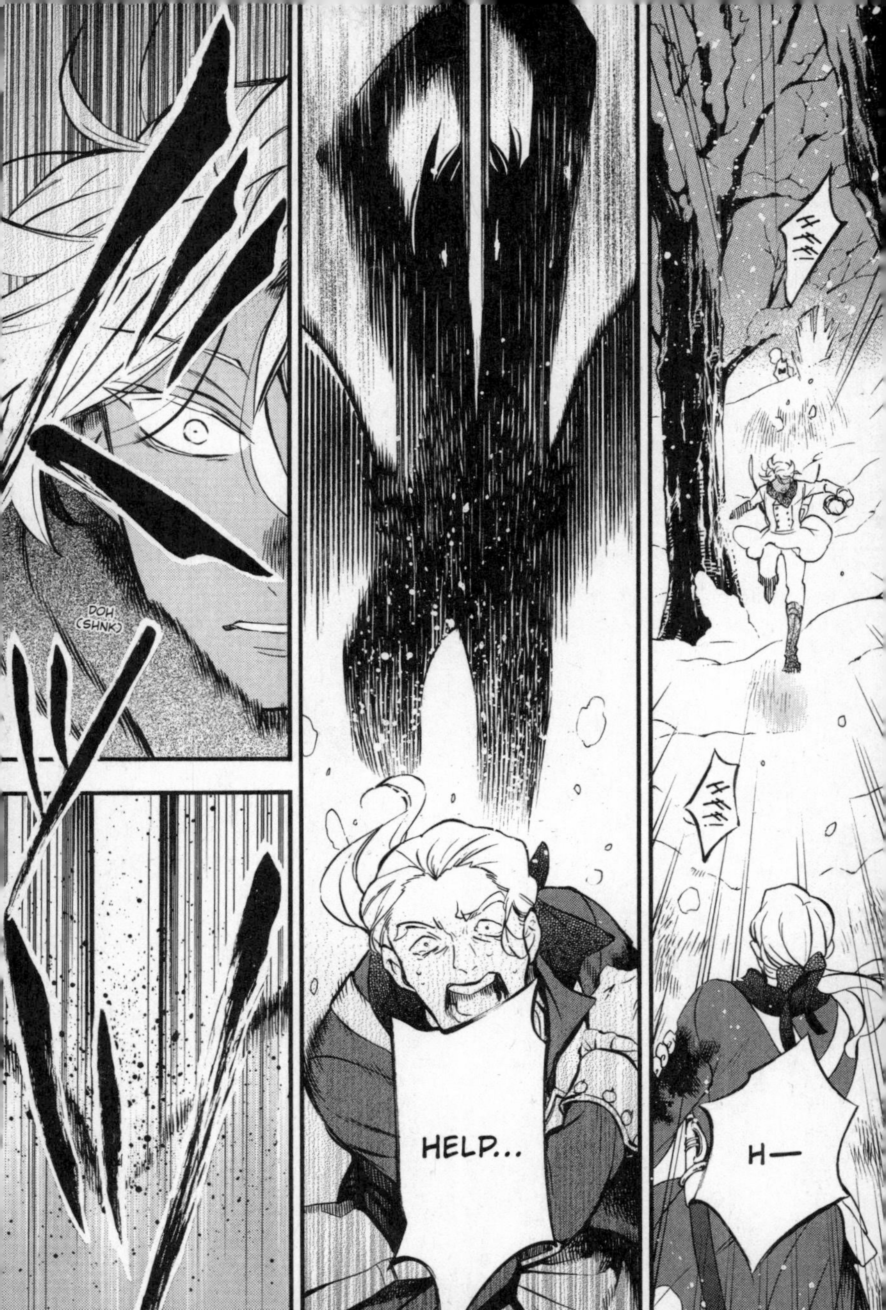
HFFF!
HFFF!
H—
HELP...
DOH
(SHNK)

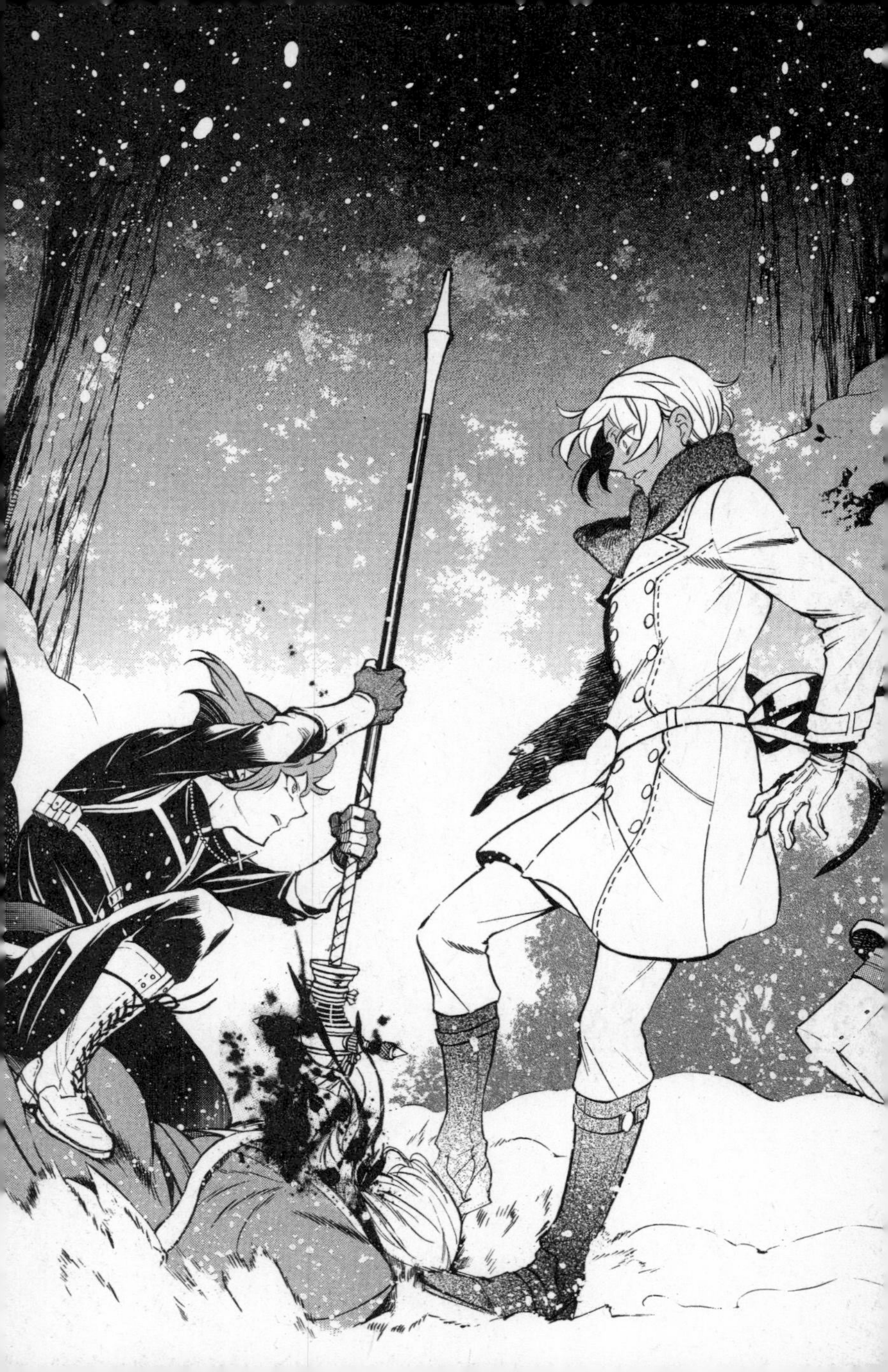

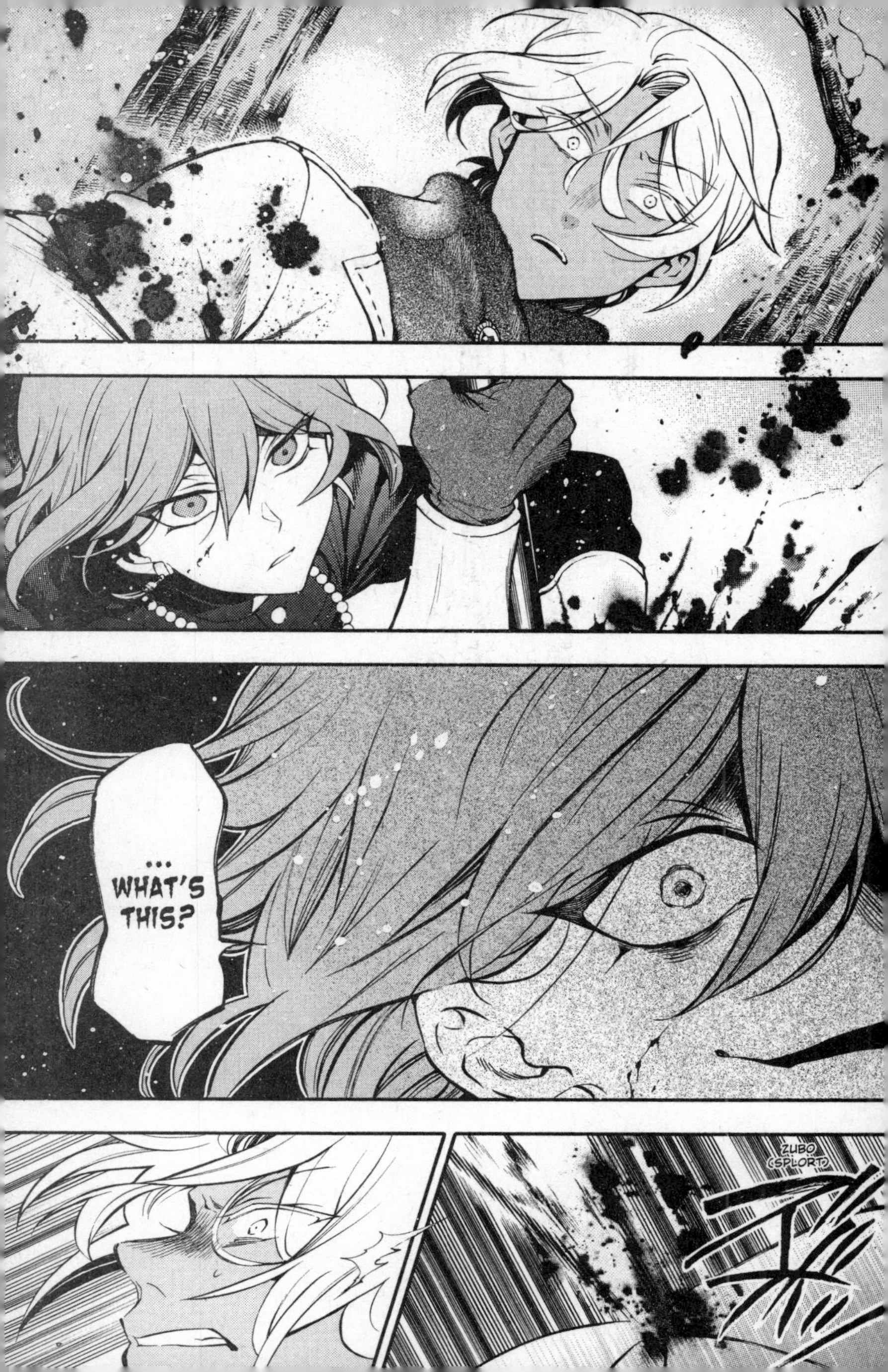
... WHAT'S THIS?
ZUBO (SPLORT)

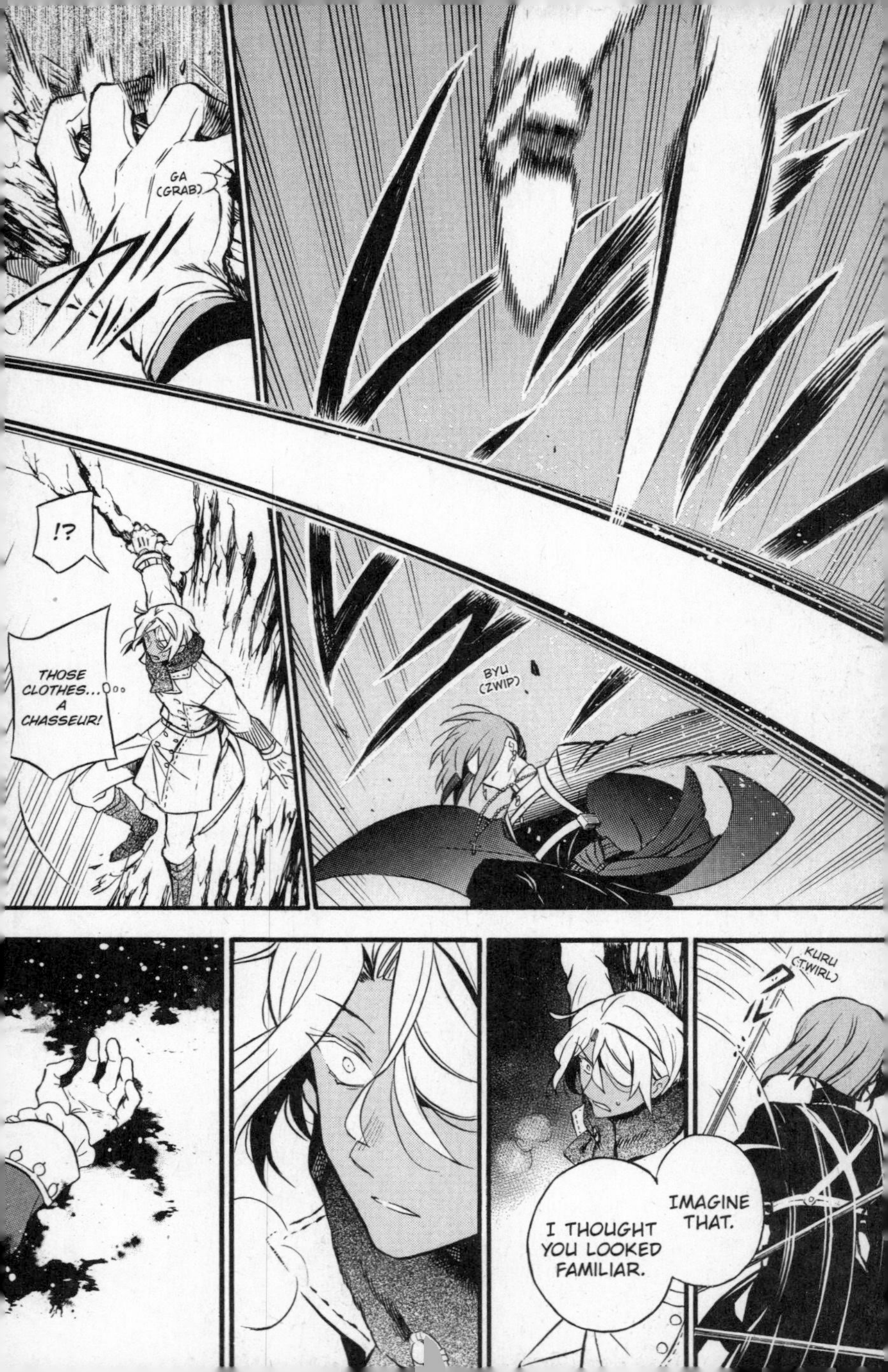
GA (GRAB)
BYU (ZWIP)
!?
THOSE CLOTHES... A CHASSEUR!
KURU (TWIRL)
IMAGINE THAT.
I THOUGHT YOU LOOKED FAMILIAR.

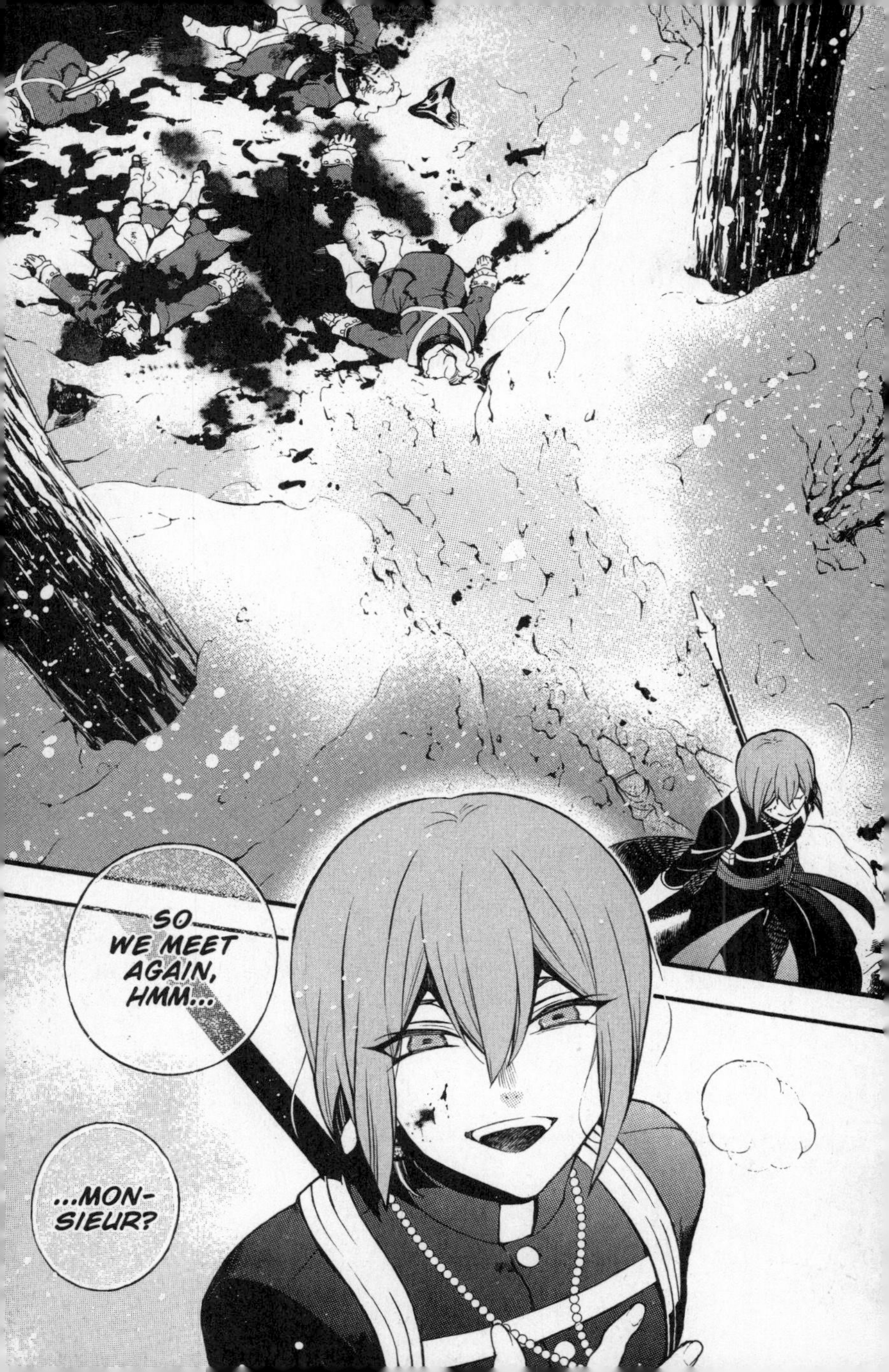
SO WE MEET AGAIN, HMM...
...MON-SIEUR?

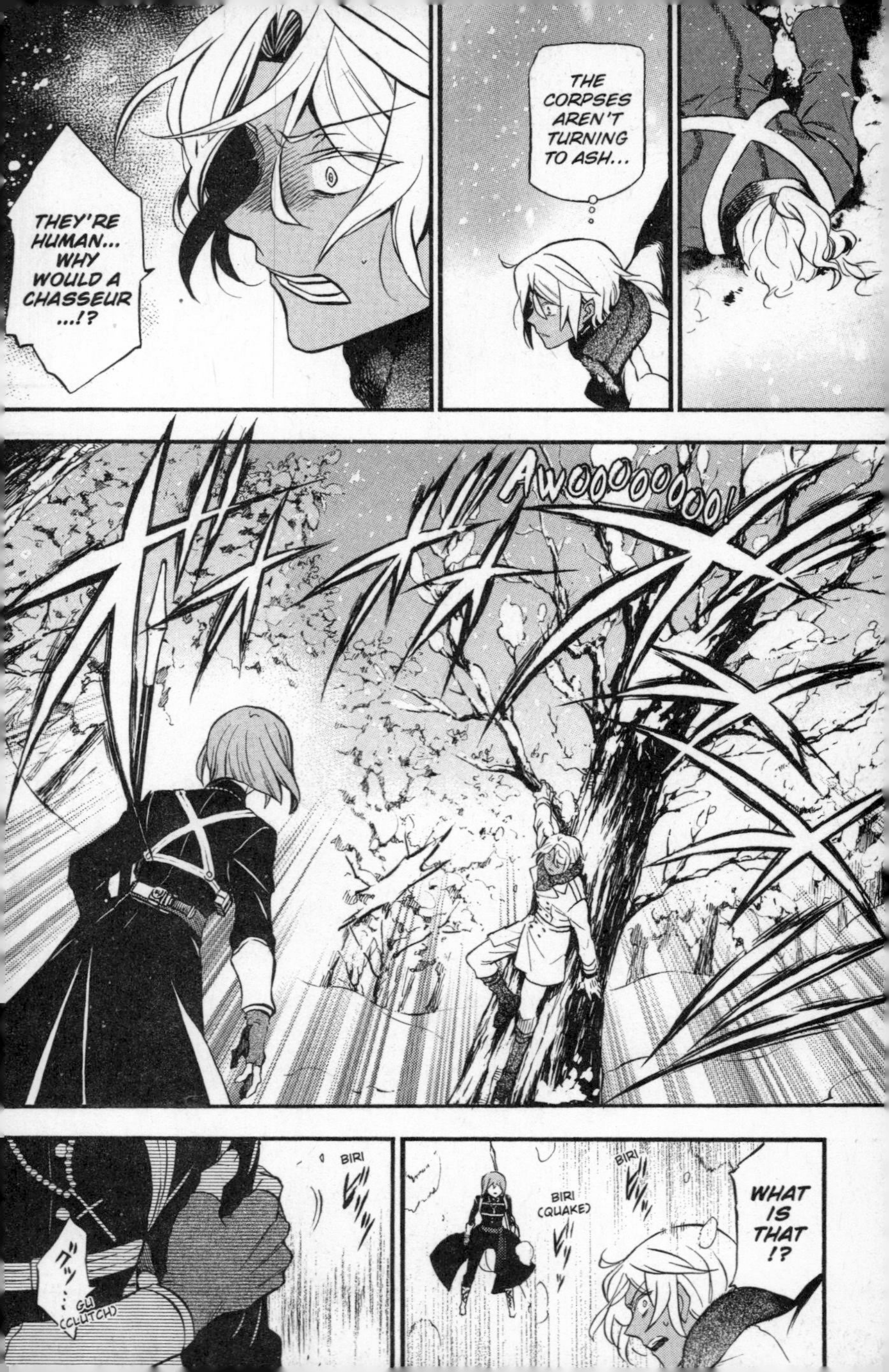
THE CORPSES AREN'T TURNING TO ASH...
THEY'RE HUMAN... WHY WOULD A CHASSEUR ...!?
AWOOOOOOOO!
WHAT IS THAT !?
BIRI
BIRI (QUAKE)
BIRI
GU (CLUTCH)

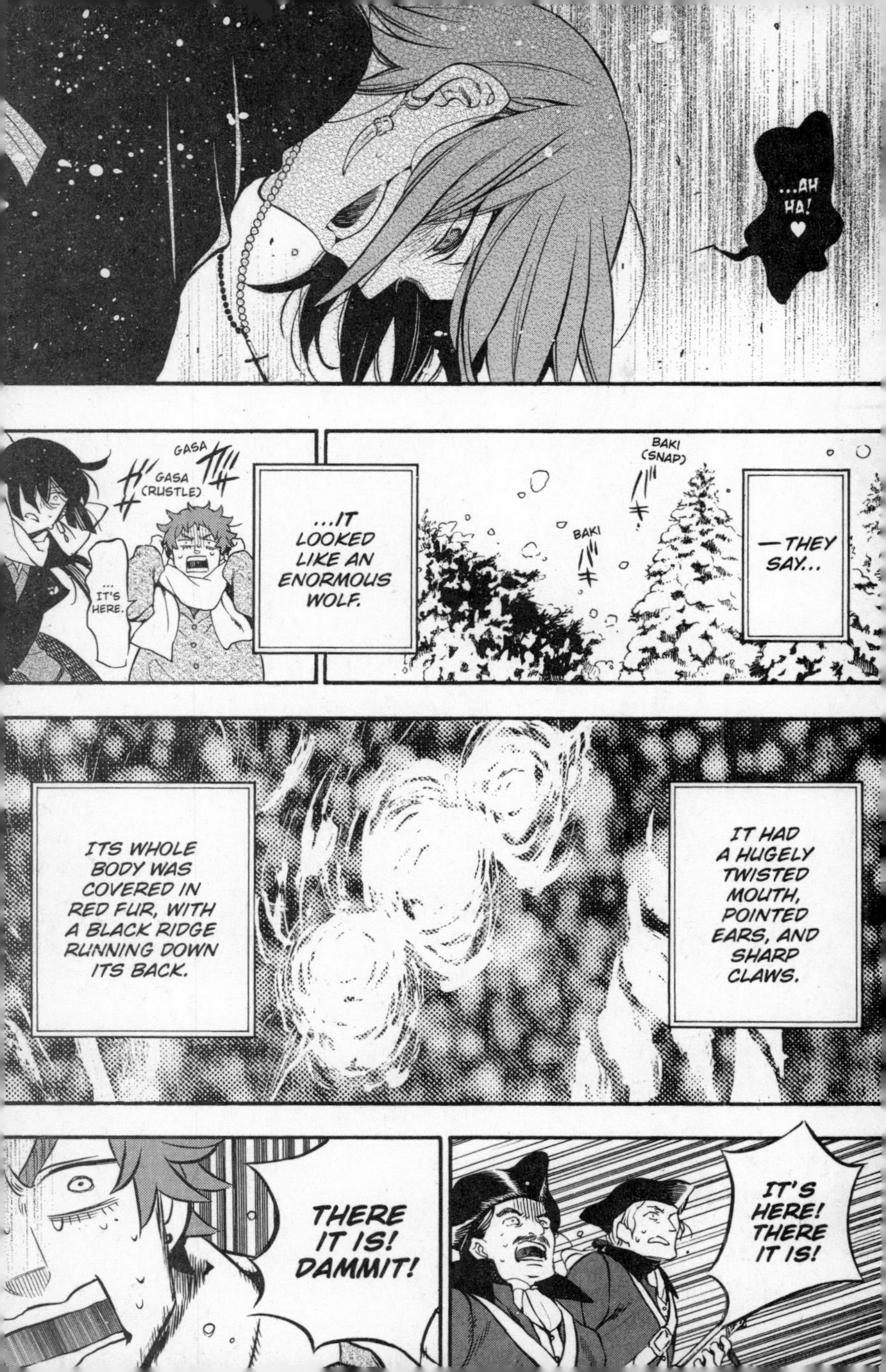
...AH HA! ♥
—THEY SAY...
BAKI (SNAP)
BAKI
...IT LOOKED LIKE AN ENORMOUS WOLF.
GASA
GASA (RUSTLE)
... IT'S HERE.
IT HAD A HUGELY TWISTED MOUTH, POINTED EARS, AND SHARP CLAWS.
ITS WHOLE BODY WAS COVERED IN RED FUR, WITH A BLACK RIDGE RUNNING DOWN ITS BACK.
IT'S HERE! THERE IT IS!
THERE IT IS! DAMMIT!

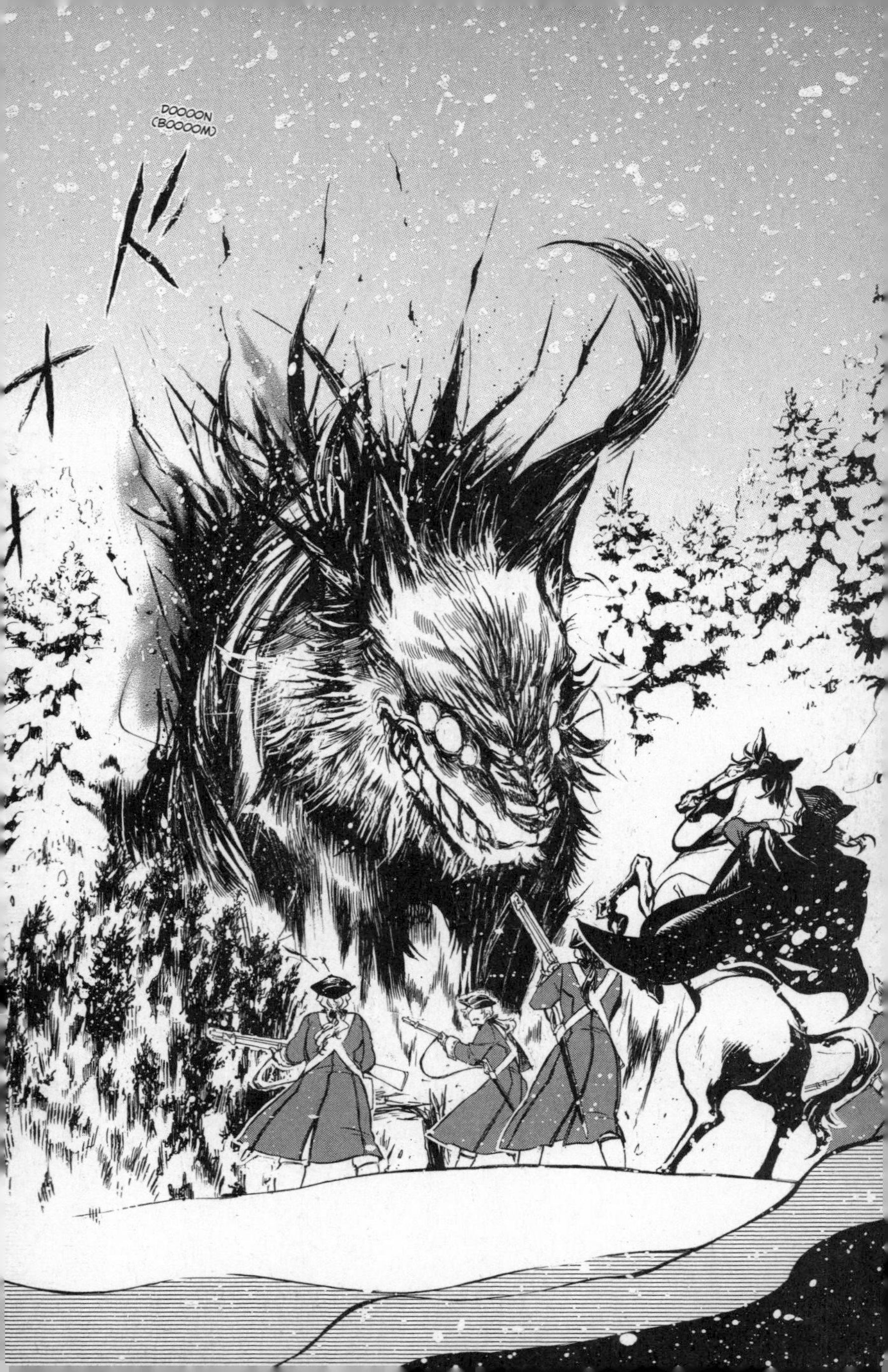
DOOOON
(BOOOOM)

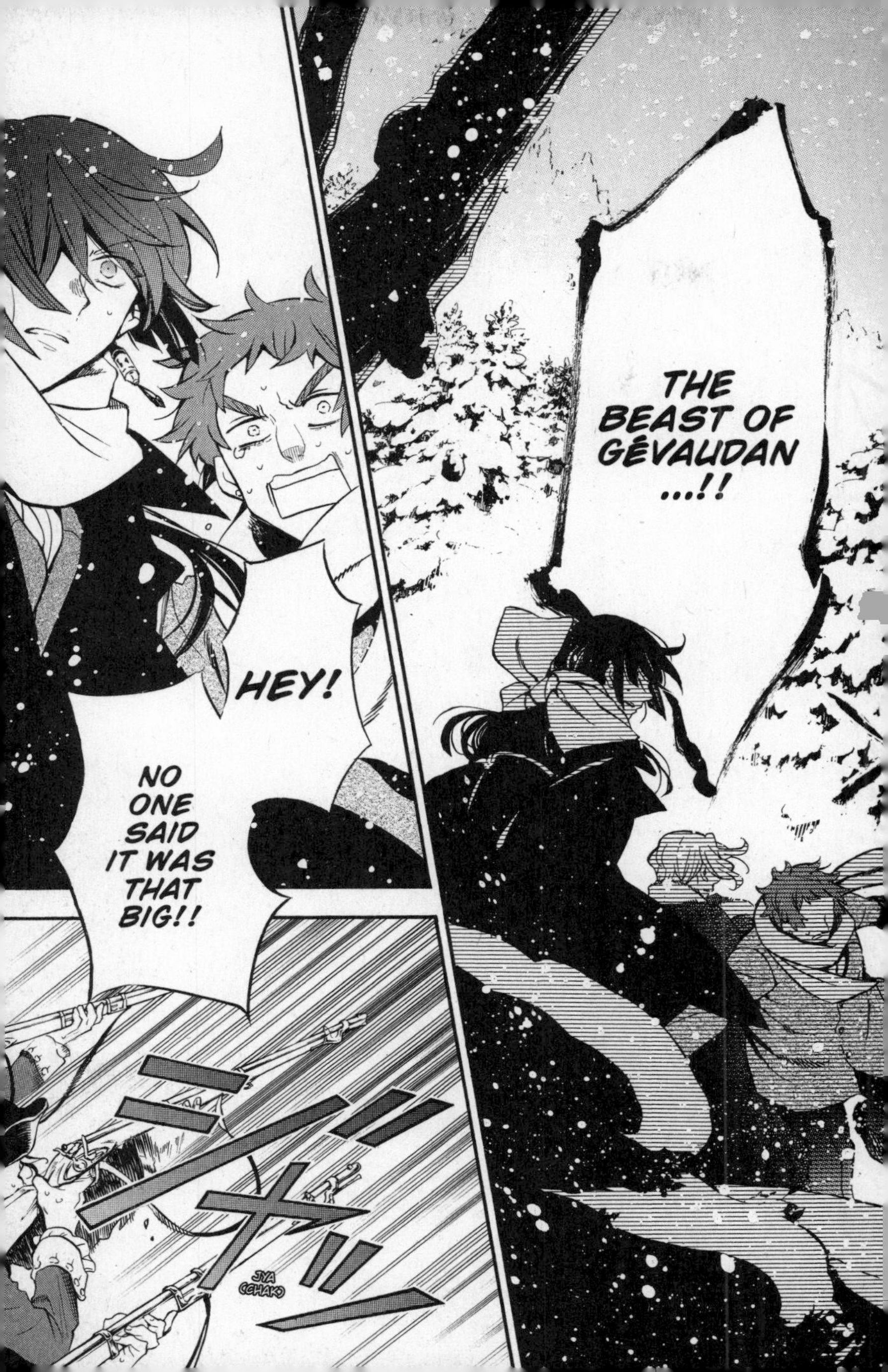
THE BEAST OF GÉVAUDAN ...!!
HEY!
NO ONE SAID IT WAS THAT BIG!!
JYA (CHAK)

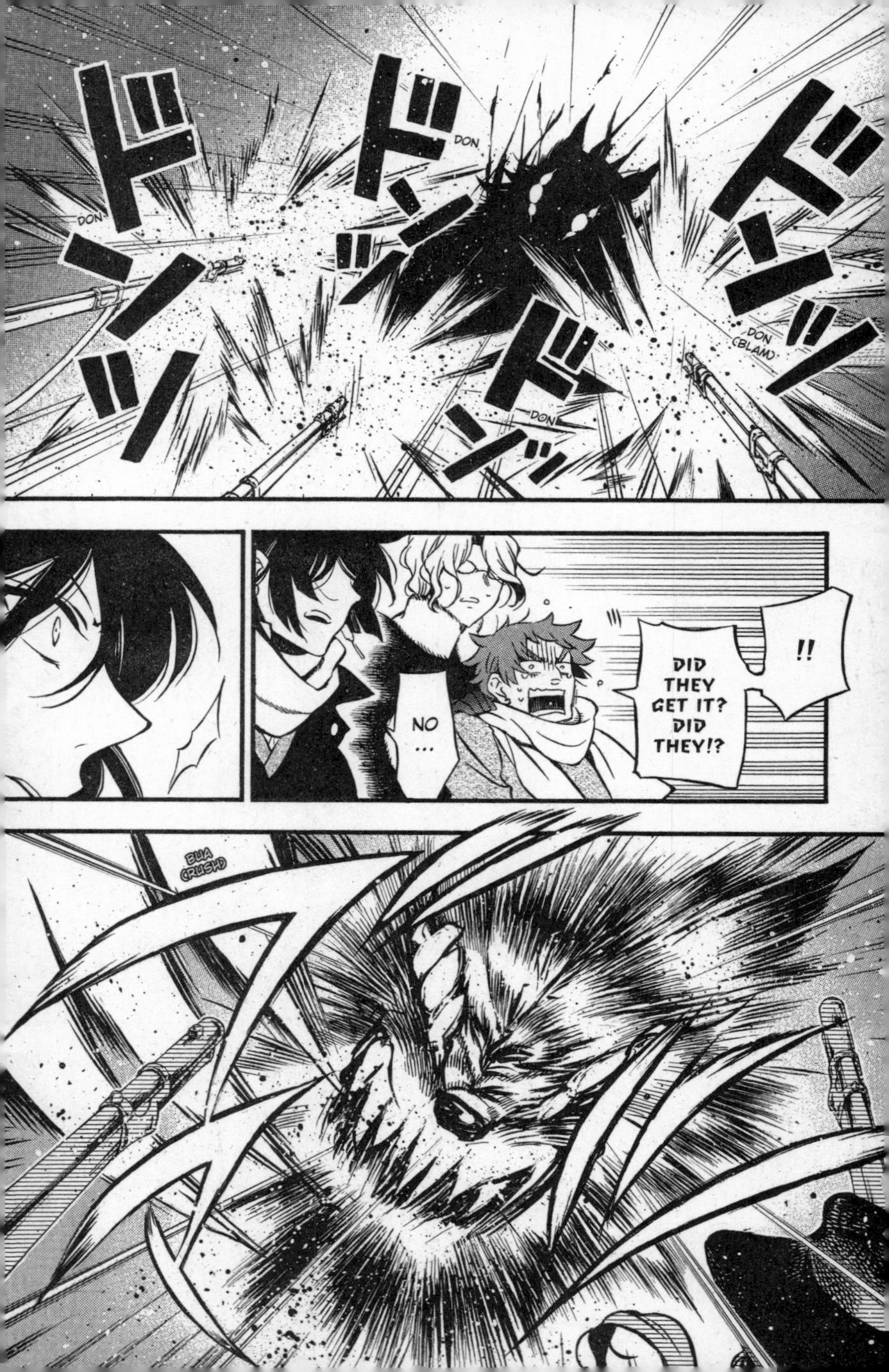
ドンッ
DON (BLAM)
ドンッ
DON
ドンッ
DON
ドンッ
DON
!!
DID THEY GET IT? DID THEY!?
NO ...
BUA (CRUSH)

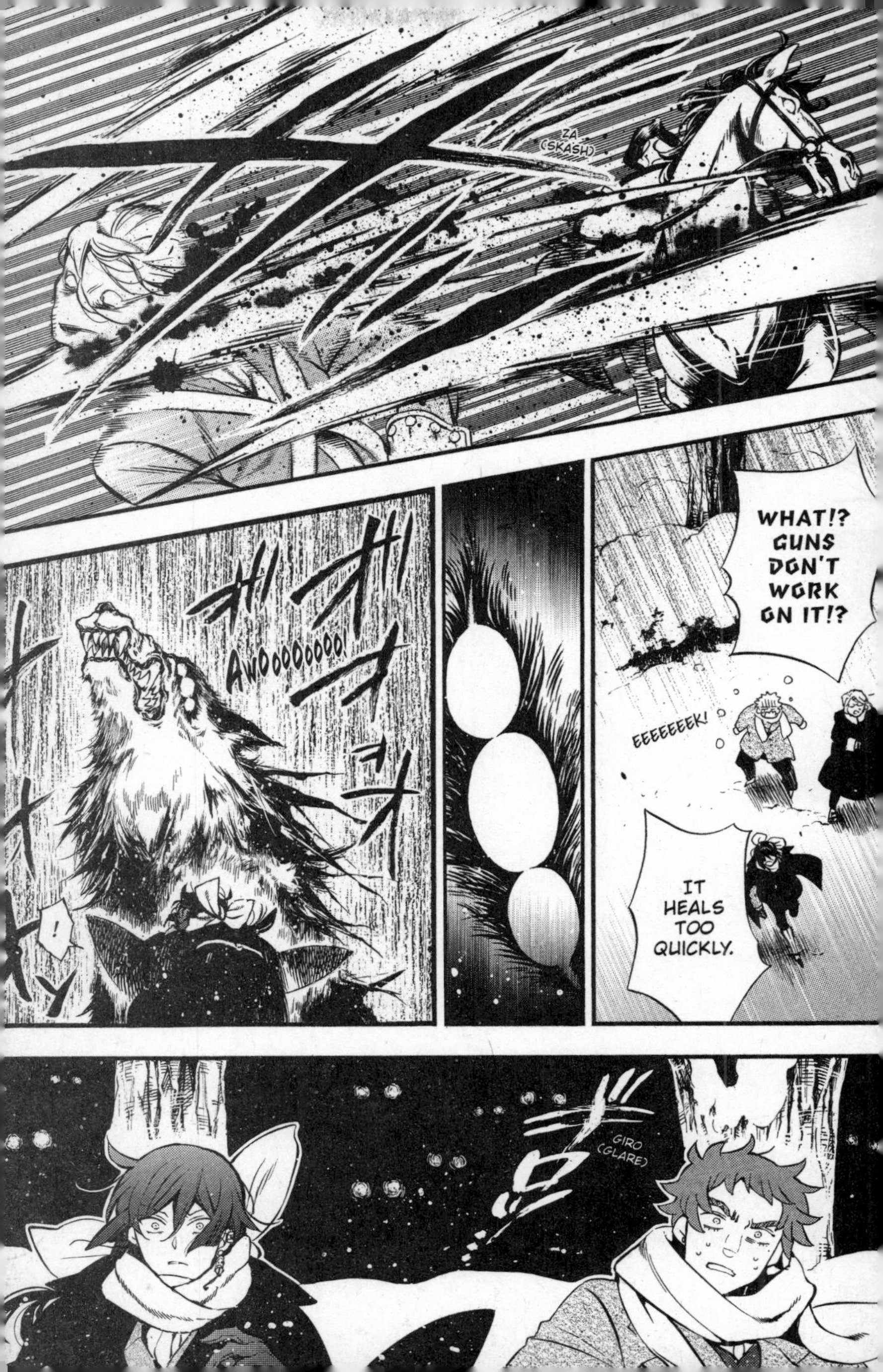
ZA
(SKASH)
WHAT!? GUNS DON'T WORK ON IT!?
EEEEEEEK!
IT HEALS TOO QUICKLY.
AWOOOOOOOO!
!
GIRO
(GLARE)

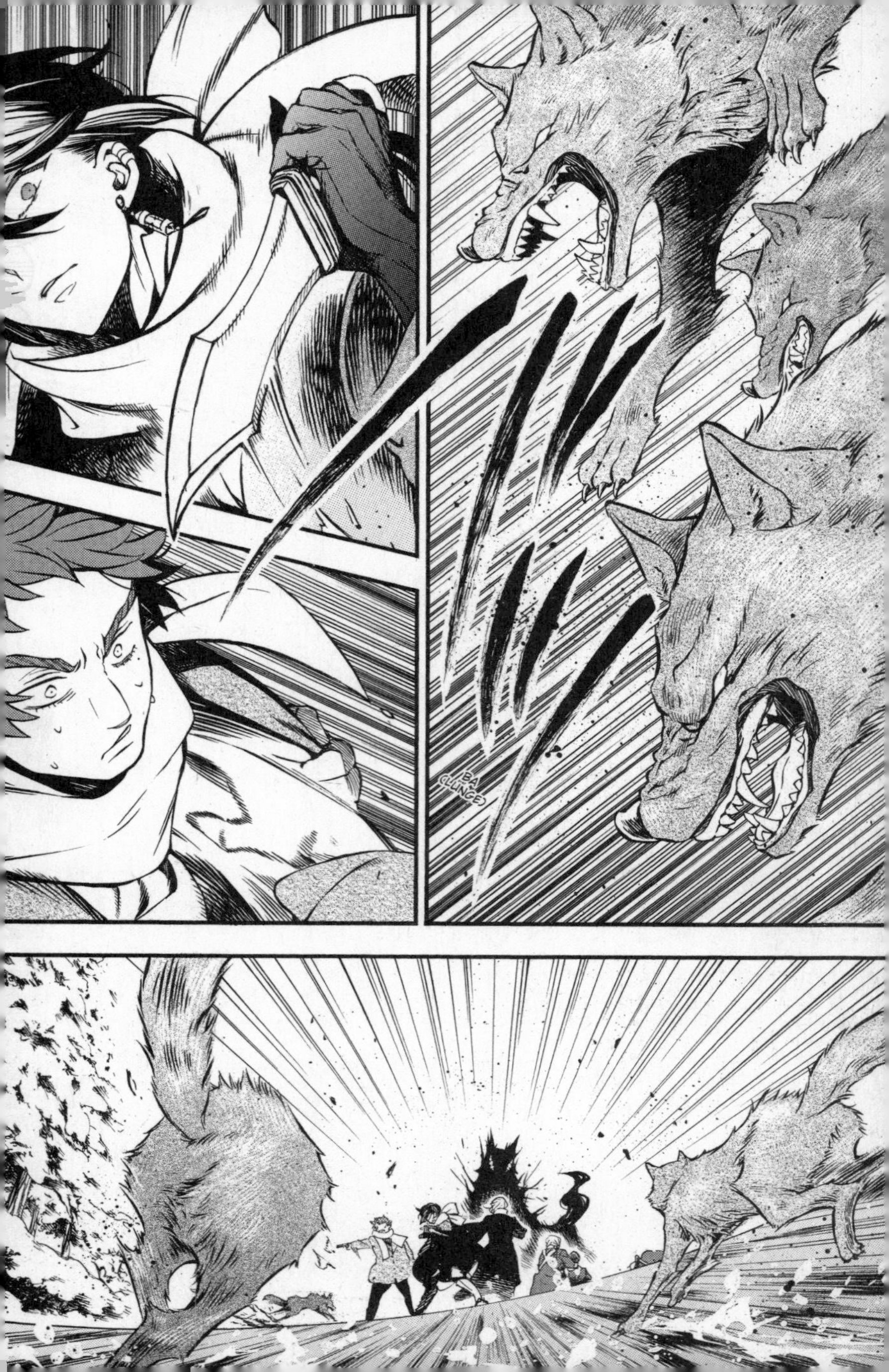
BA
(LUNGE)

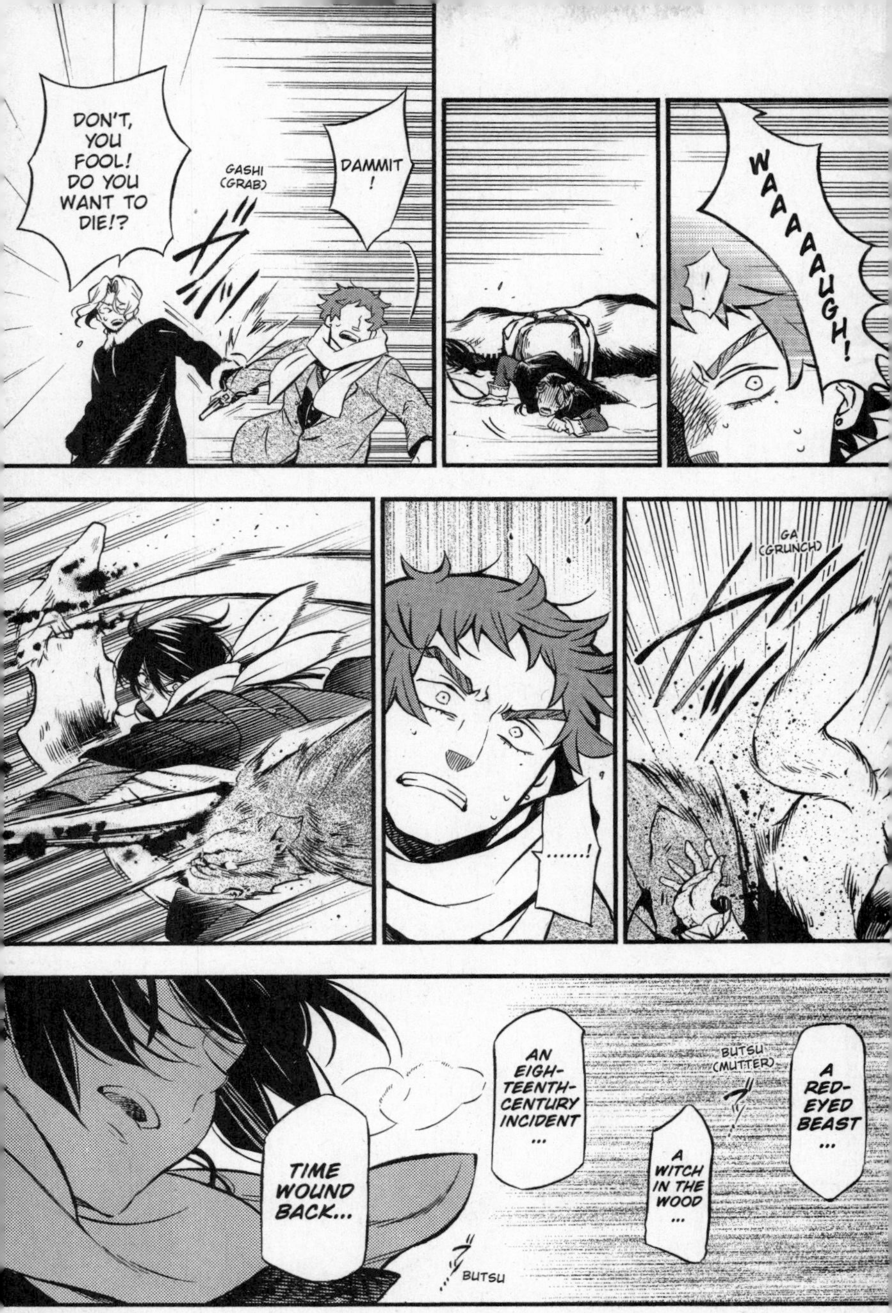
WAAAAAUGH!
!
DAMMIT!
GASHI (GRAB)
DON'T, YOU FOOL! DO YOU WANT TO DIE!?
GA (GRUNCH)
......!
A RED-EYED BEAST...
BUTSU (MUTTER)
A WITCH IN THE WOOD...
AN EIGHTEENTH-CENTURY INCIDENT...
BUTSU
TIME WOUND BACK...

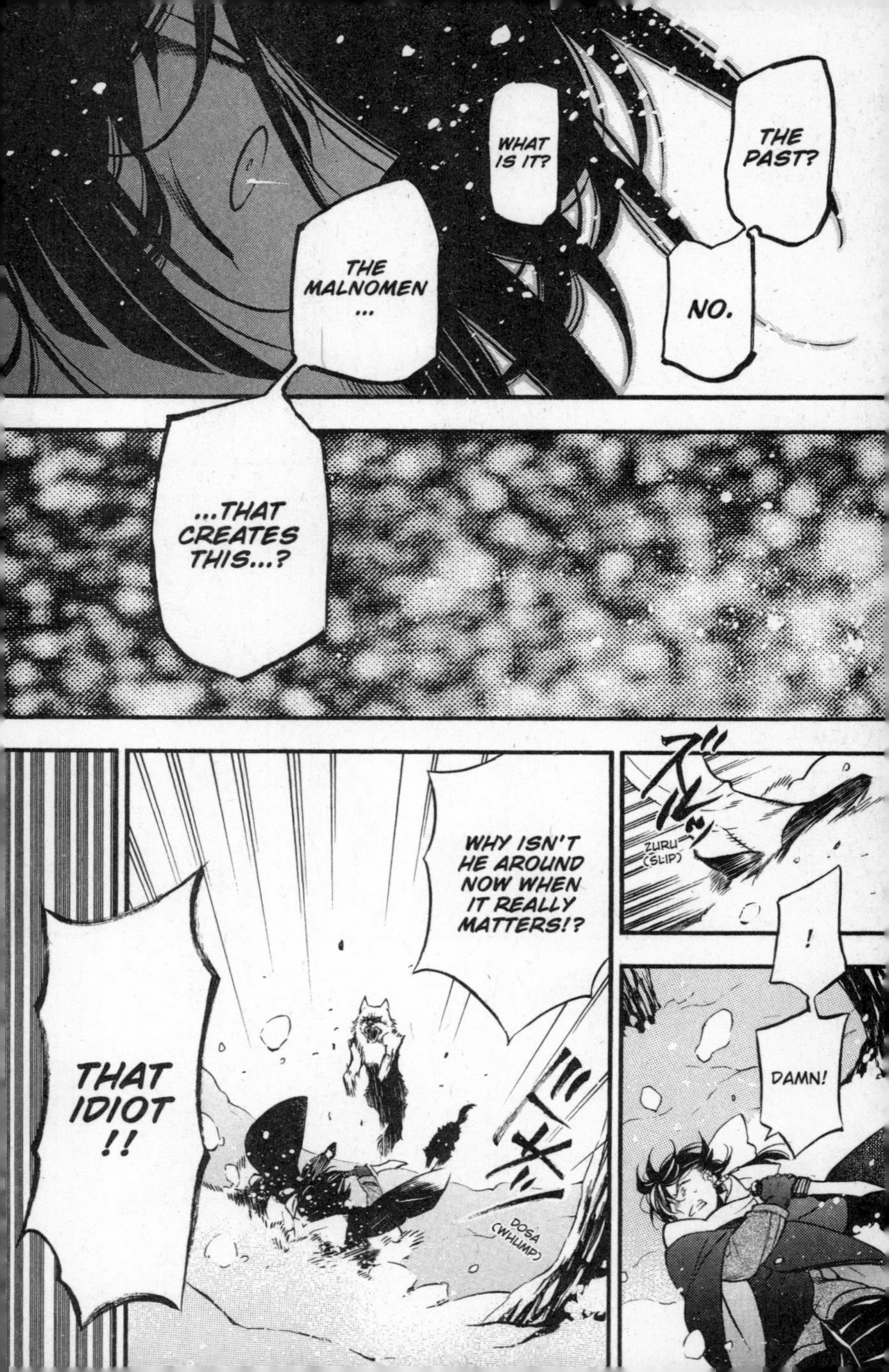
THE PAST?
NO.
WHAT IS IT?
THE MALNOMEN ...
...THAT CREATES THIS...?
ZURU (SLIP)
!
DAMN!
WHY ISN'T HE AROUND NOW WHEN IT REALLY MATTERS!?
DOSA (WHUMP)
THAT IDIOT !!

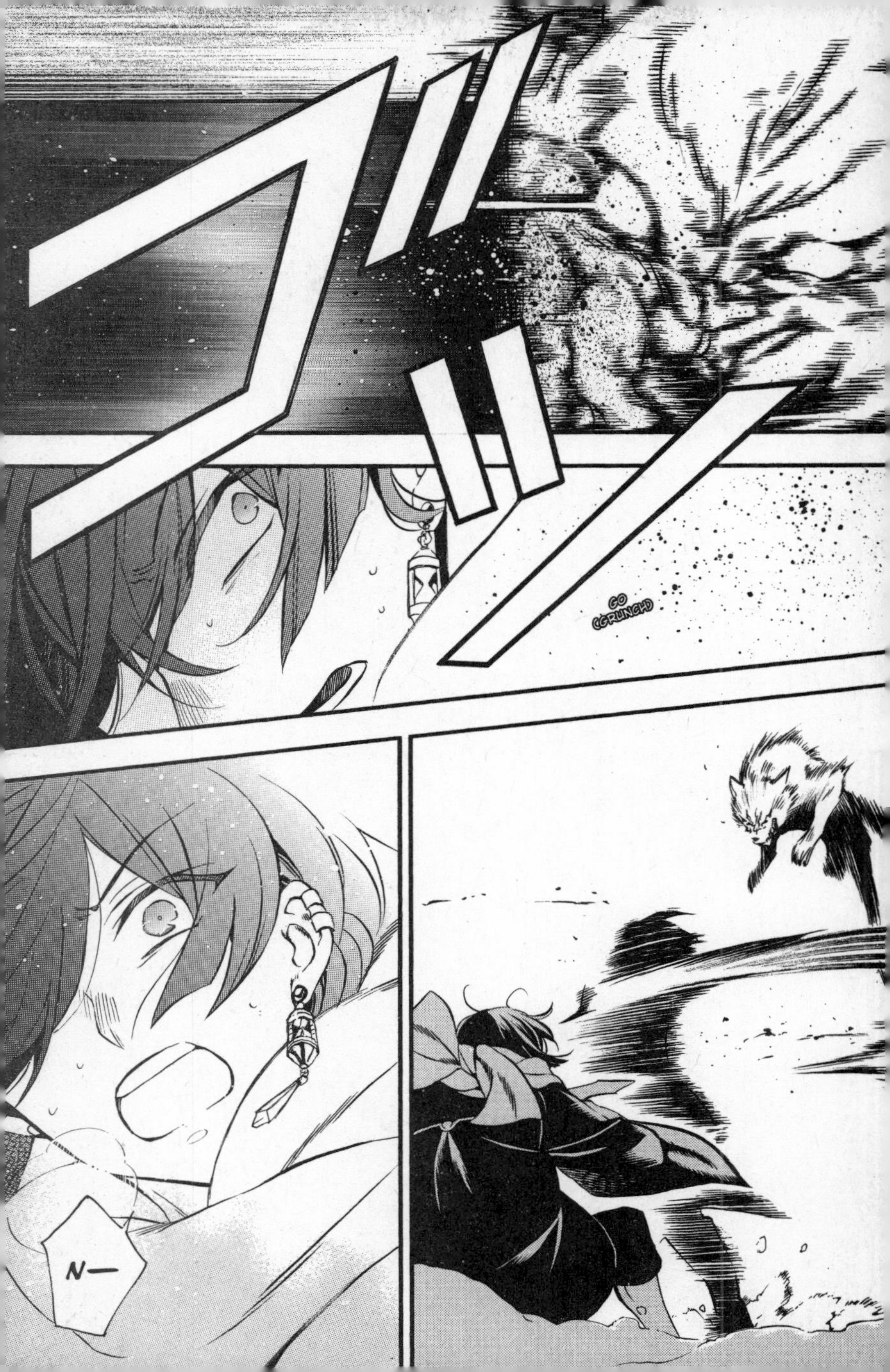
GO (CRUNCH)
N—

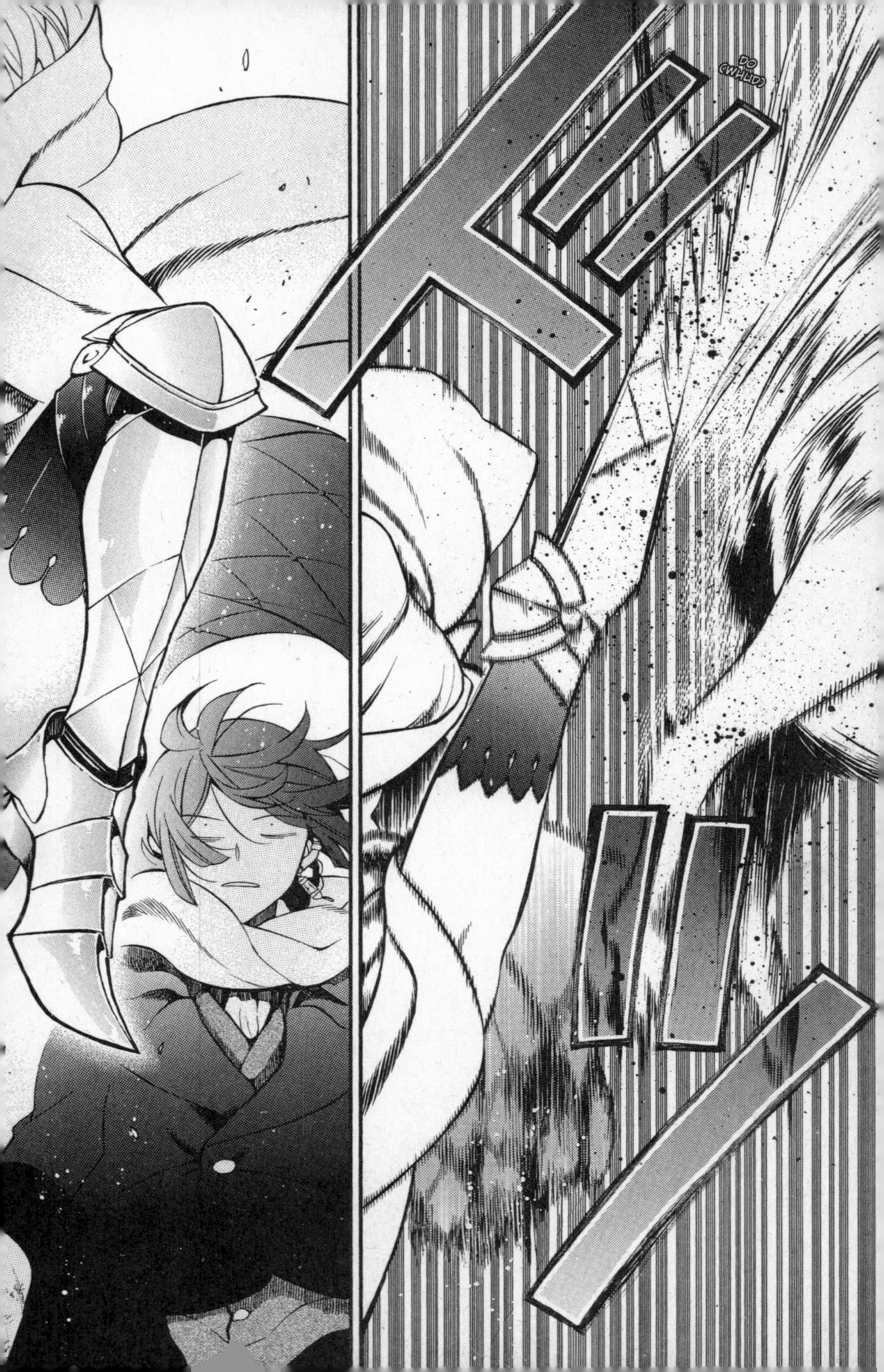
DO
(WHUD)

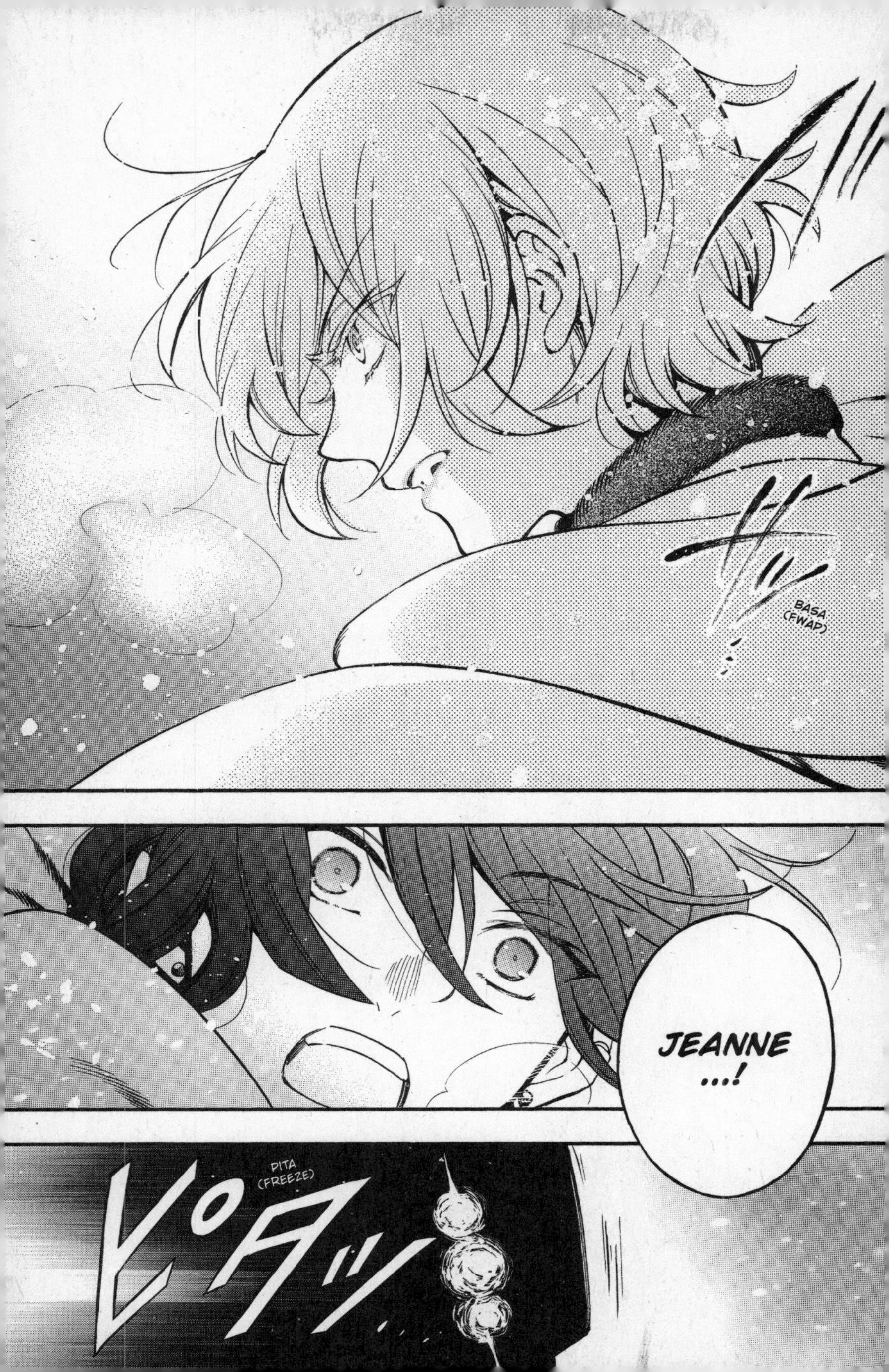
BASA (FWAP)
JEANNE ...!
PITA (FREEZE)
ピタッ

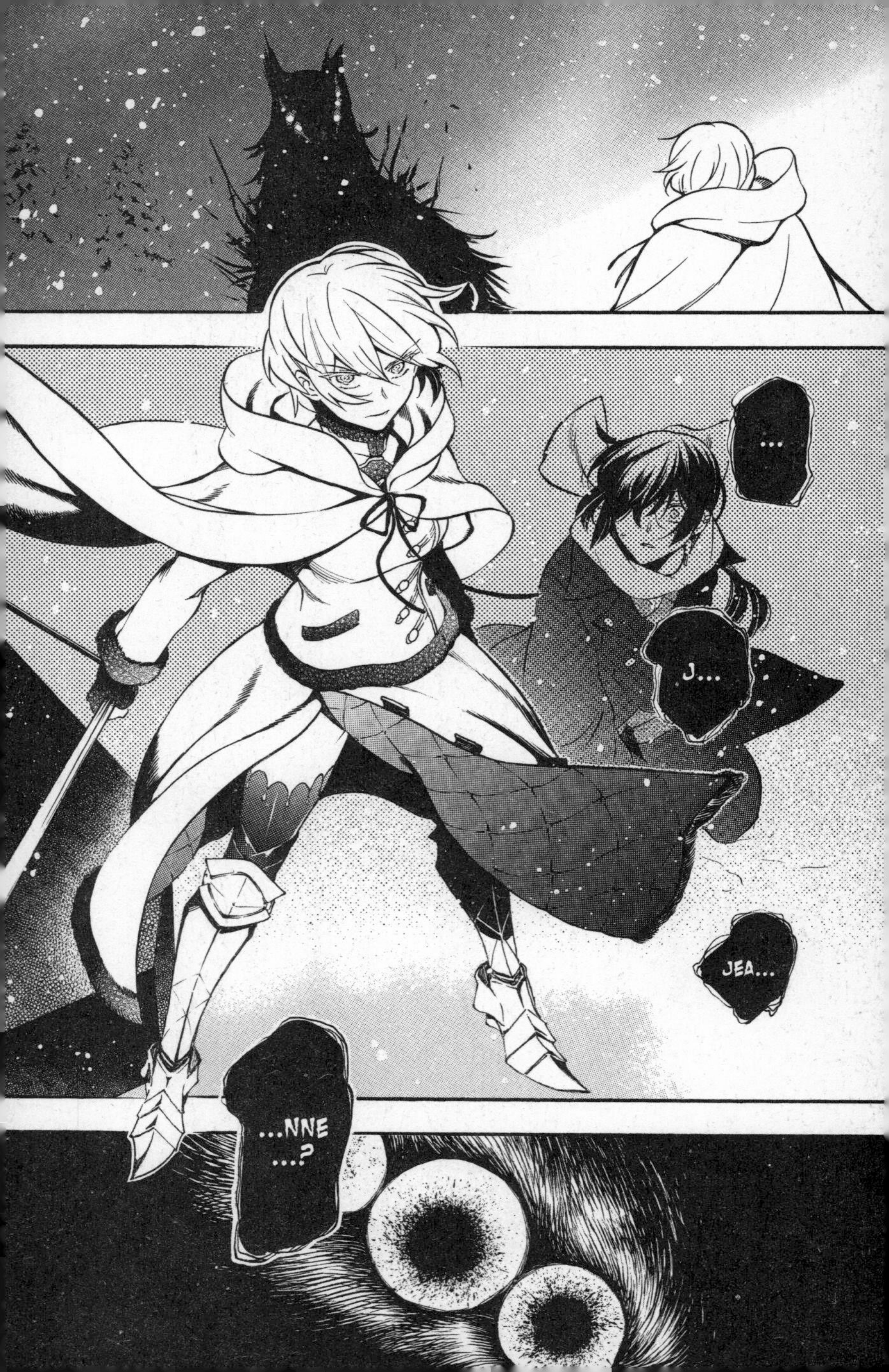
...
J...
JEA...
...NNE ...?

Mémoire 24 Forêt d'argent CHANCE ENCOUNTER

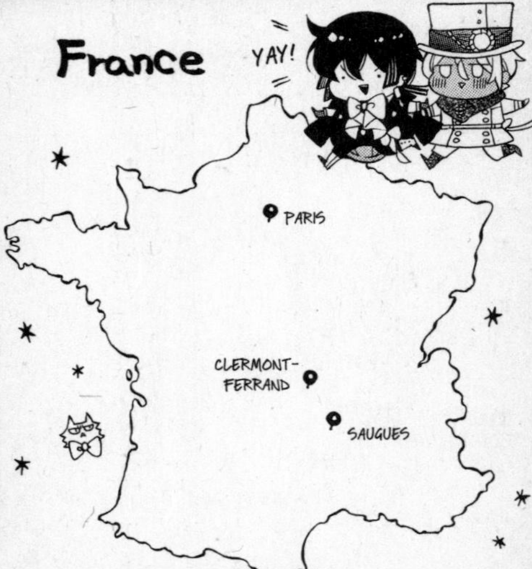
France
YAY!
PARIS
CLERMONT-
FERRAND
SAUGUES

TO BE COMPLETELY ACCURATE, THE VILLAGE OF SAUGUES APPARENTLY ISN'T CONSIDERED PART OF THE REGION OF GÉVAUDAN. BUT I WANTED TO AVOID ADDING MORE PLACE NAMES AND MAKING THINGS HARD TO UNDERSTAND, SO I'M WRITING ABOUT IT AS "(THE AREA OF DAMAGE INFLICTED BY THE BEAST OF) GÉVAUDAN."

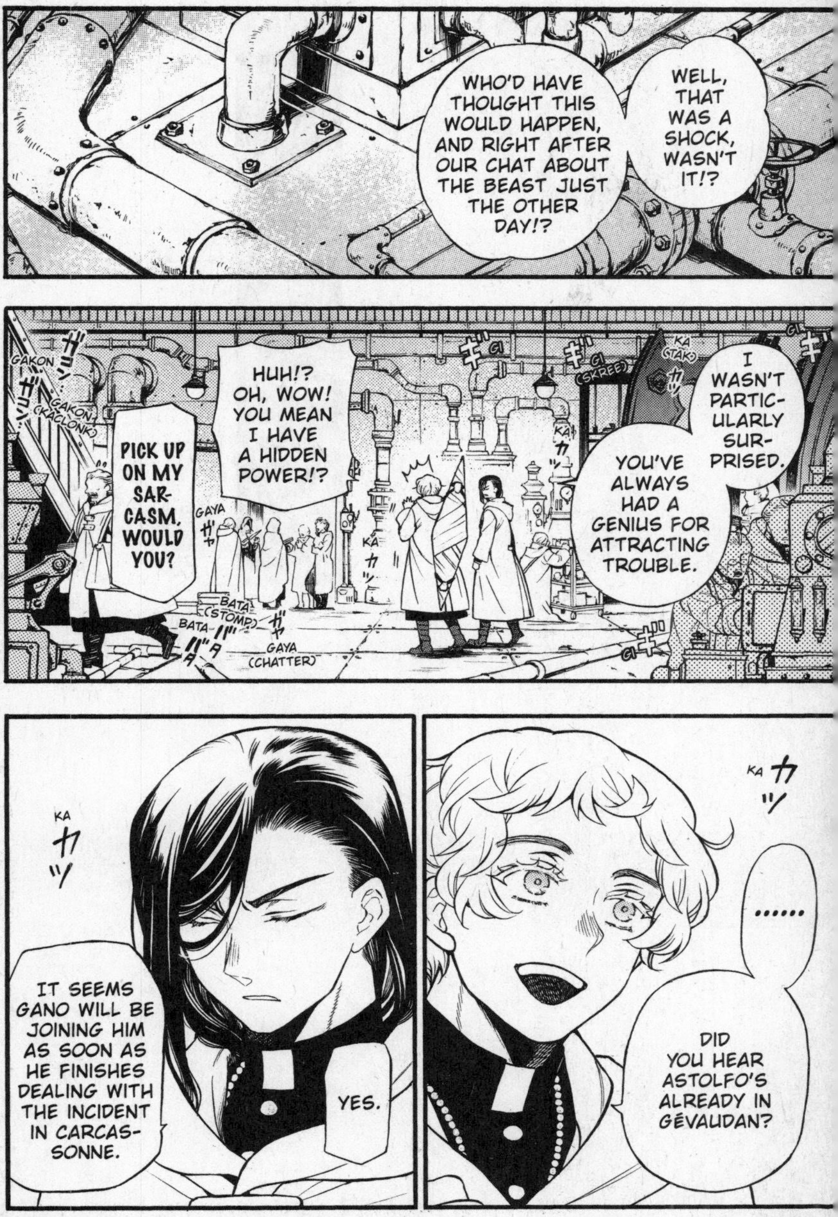
WELL, THAT WAS A SHOCK, WASN'T IT!?
WHO'D HAVE THOUGHT THIS WOULD HAPPEN, AND RIGHT AFTER OUR CHAT ABOUT THE BEAST JUST THE OTHER DAY!?
GI
KA (TAK)
GI (SKREE)
I WASN'T PARTICULARLY SURPRISED.
YOU'VE ALWAYS HAD A GENIUS FOR ATTRACTING TROUBLE.
KA
HUH!? OH, WOW! YOU MEAN I HAVE A HIDDEN POWER!?
KA
GAYA
PICK UP ON MY SARCASM, WOULD YOU?
GAKON
GAKON (KACLONK)
BATA (STOMP)
BATA
GAYA (CHATTER)
GI
KA
......
DID YOU HEAR ASTOLFO'S ALREADY IN GÉVAUDAN?
KA
YES.
IT SEEMS GANO WILL BE JOINING HIM AS SOON AS HE FINISHES DEALING WITH THE INCIDENT IN CARCASSONNE.

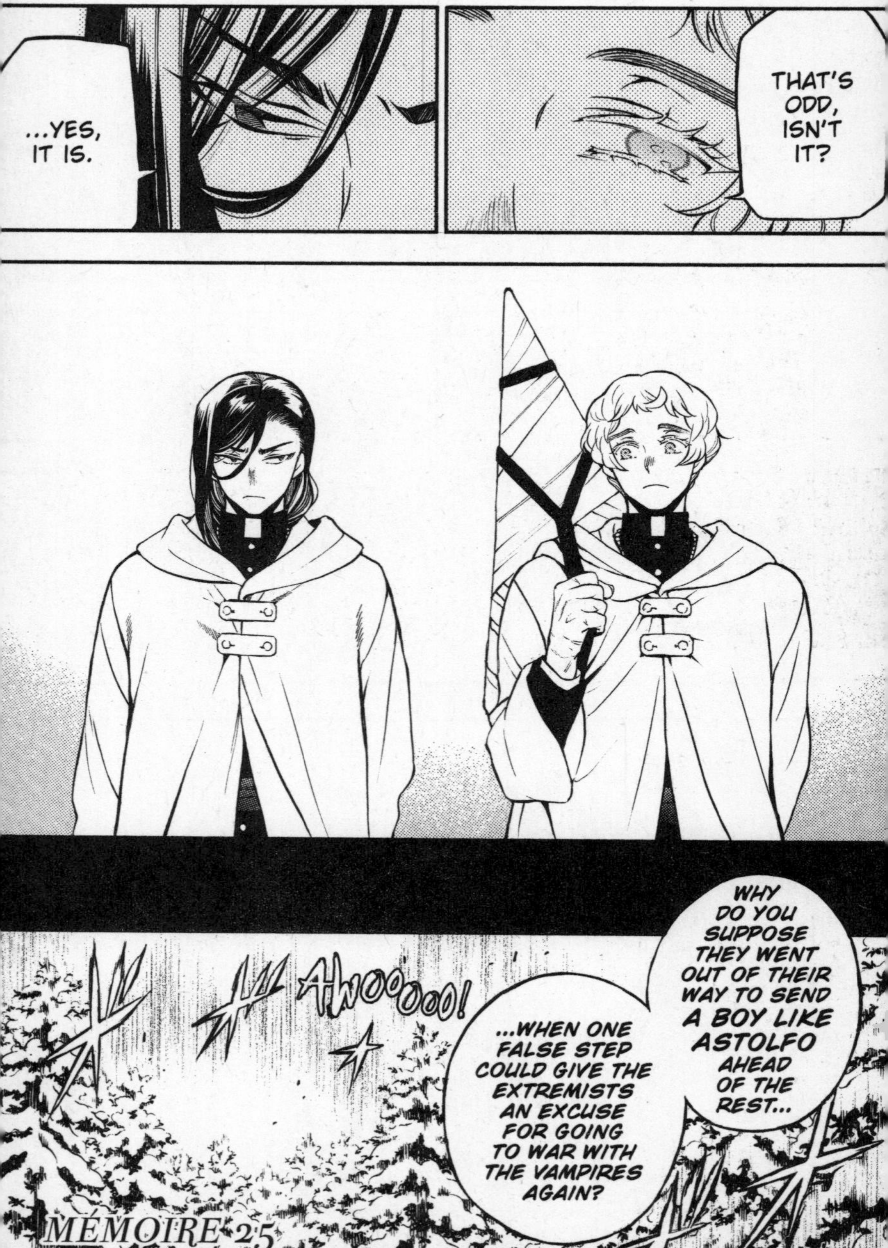
THAT'S ODD, ISN'T IT?
...YES, IT IS.
WHY DO YOU SUPPOSE THEY WENT OUT OF THEIR WAY TO SEND A BOY LIKE ASTOLFO AHEAD OF THE REST...
AWOOOOOO!
...WHEN ONE FALSE STEP COULD GIVE THE EXTREMISTS AN EXCUSE FOR GOING TO WAR WITH THE VAMPIRES AGAIN?
MÉMOIRE 25

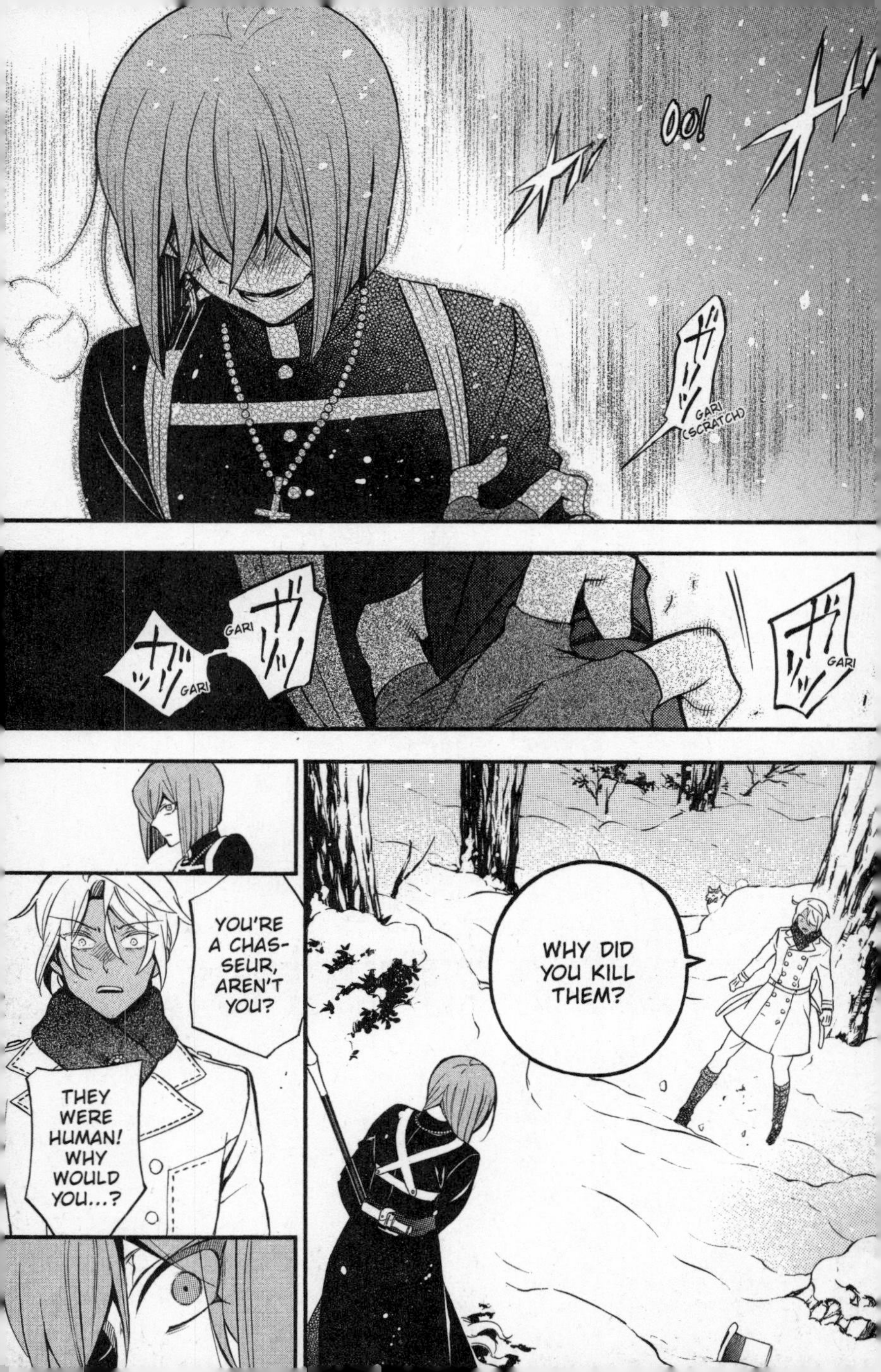
OO!
GARI (SCRATCH)
GARI
GARI
GARI
WHY DID YOU KILL THEM?
YOU'RE A CHASSEUR, AREN'T YOU?
THEY WERE HUMAN! WHY WOULD YOU...?

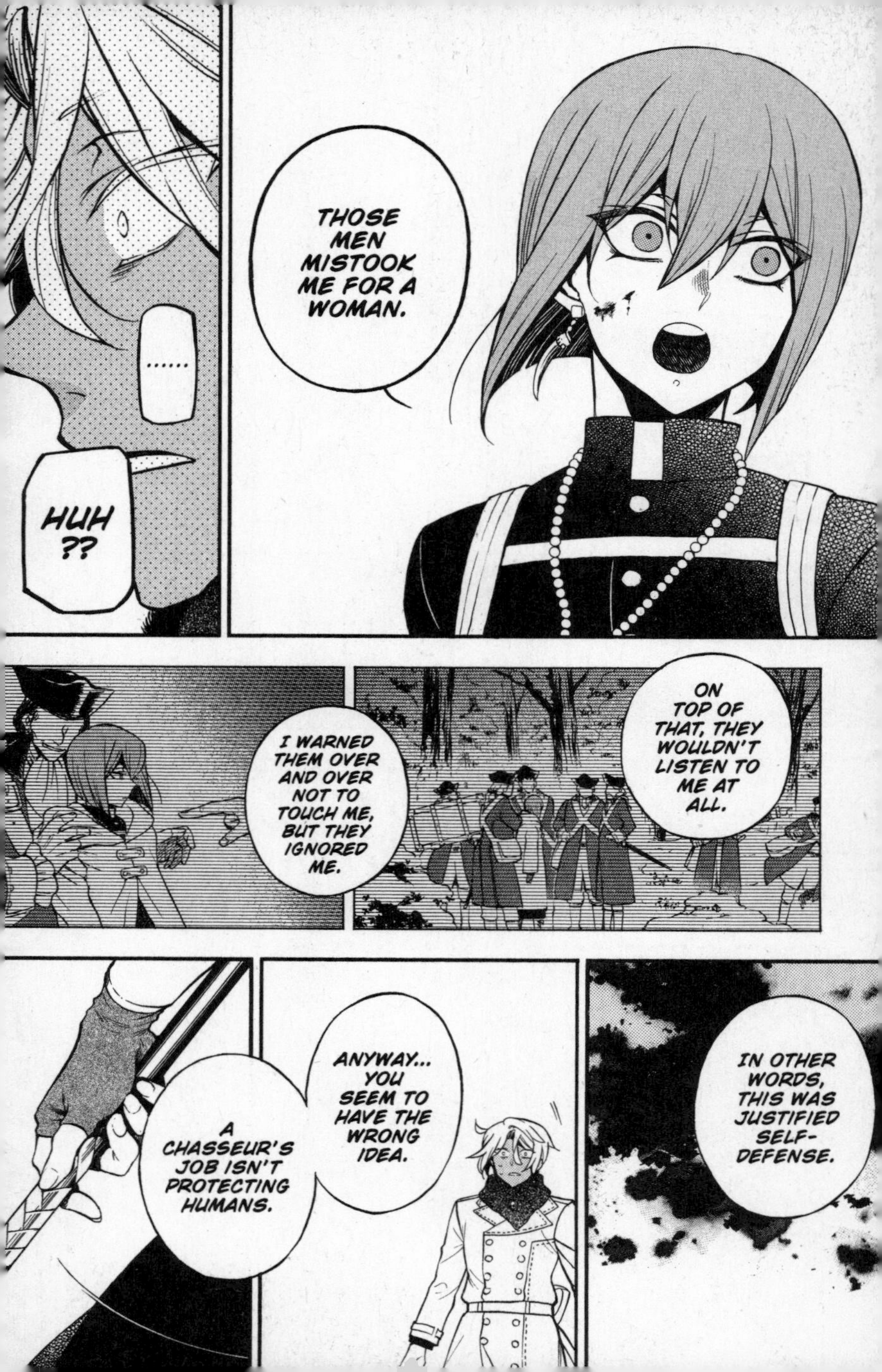
THOSE MEN MISTOOK ME FOR A WOMAN.
......
HUH ??
ON TOP OF THAT, THEY WOULDN'T LISTEN TO ME AT ALL.
I WARNED THEM OVER AND OVER NOT TO TOUCH ME, BUT THEY IGNORED ME.
IN OTHER WORDS, THIS WAS JUSTIFIED SELF-DEFENSE.
ANYWAY... YOU SEEM TO HAVE THE WRONG IDEA.
A CHASSEUR'S JOB ISN'T PROTECTING HUMANS.

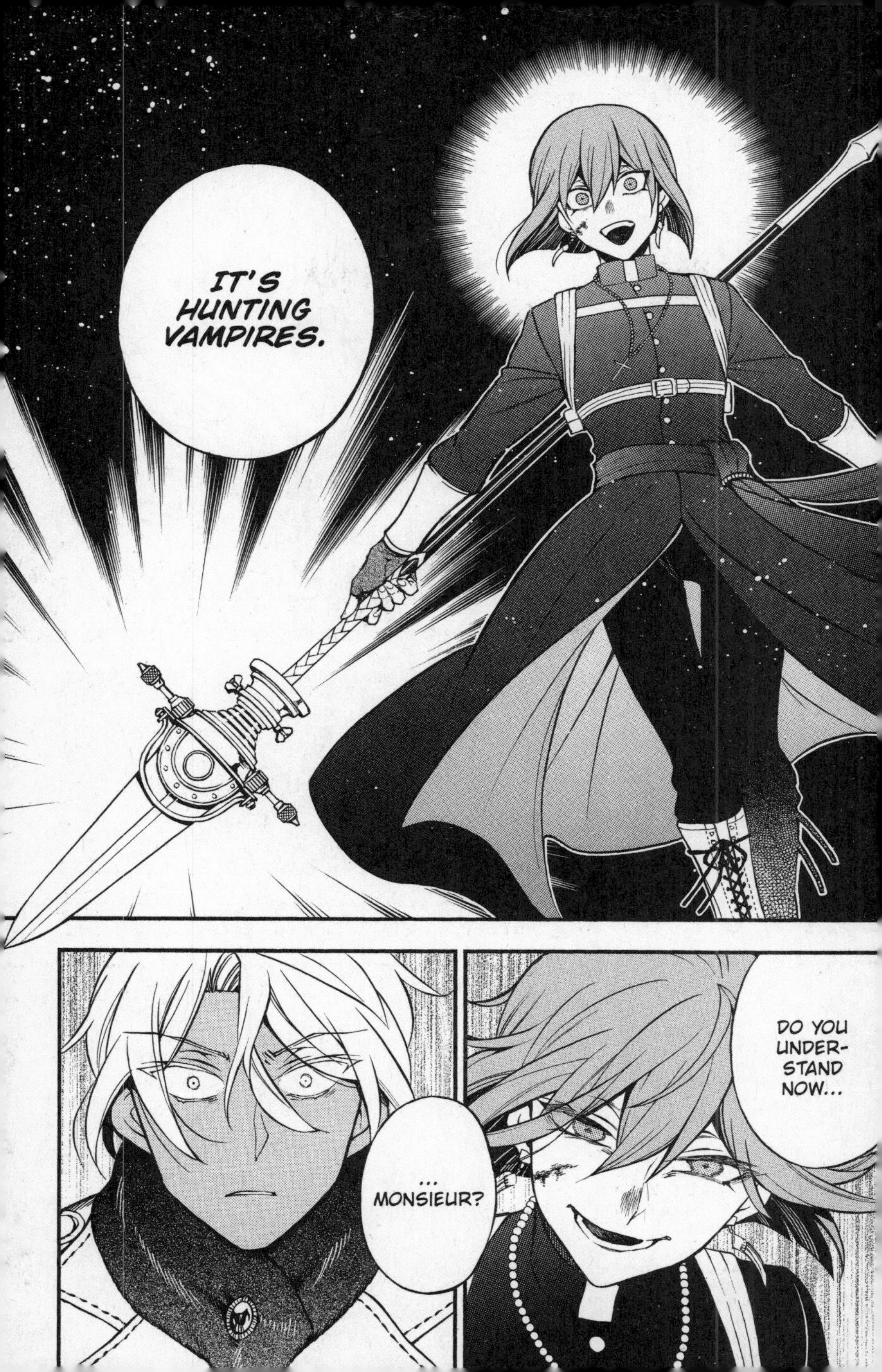
IT'S HUNTING VAMPIRES.
DO YOU UNDER-STAND NOW...
... MONSIEUR?

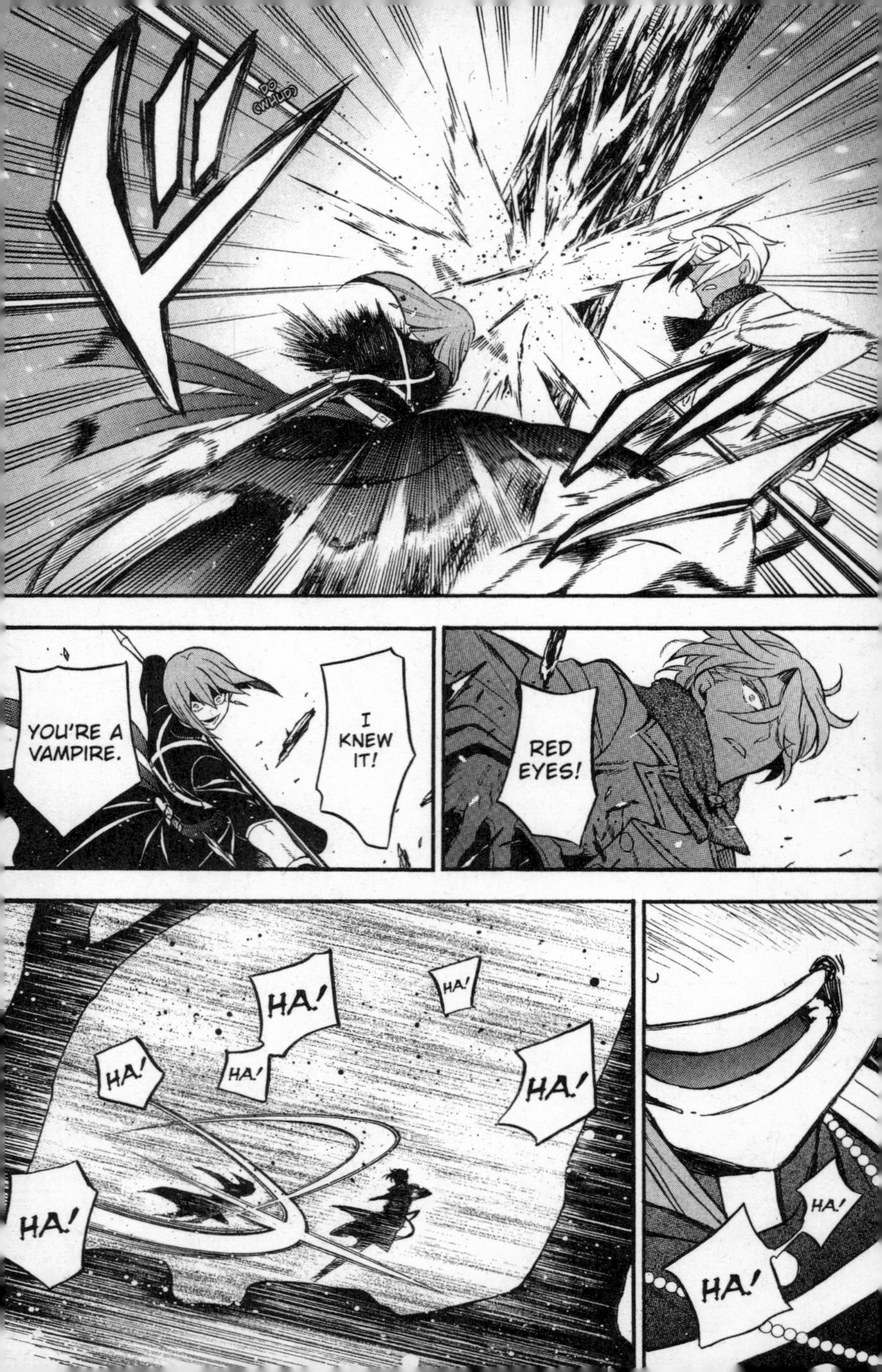
DO (WHUD)
RED EYES!
I KNEW IT!
YOU'RE A VAMPIRE.
HA!
HA!
HA!
HA!
HA!
HA!
HA!
HA!

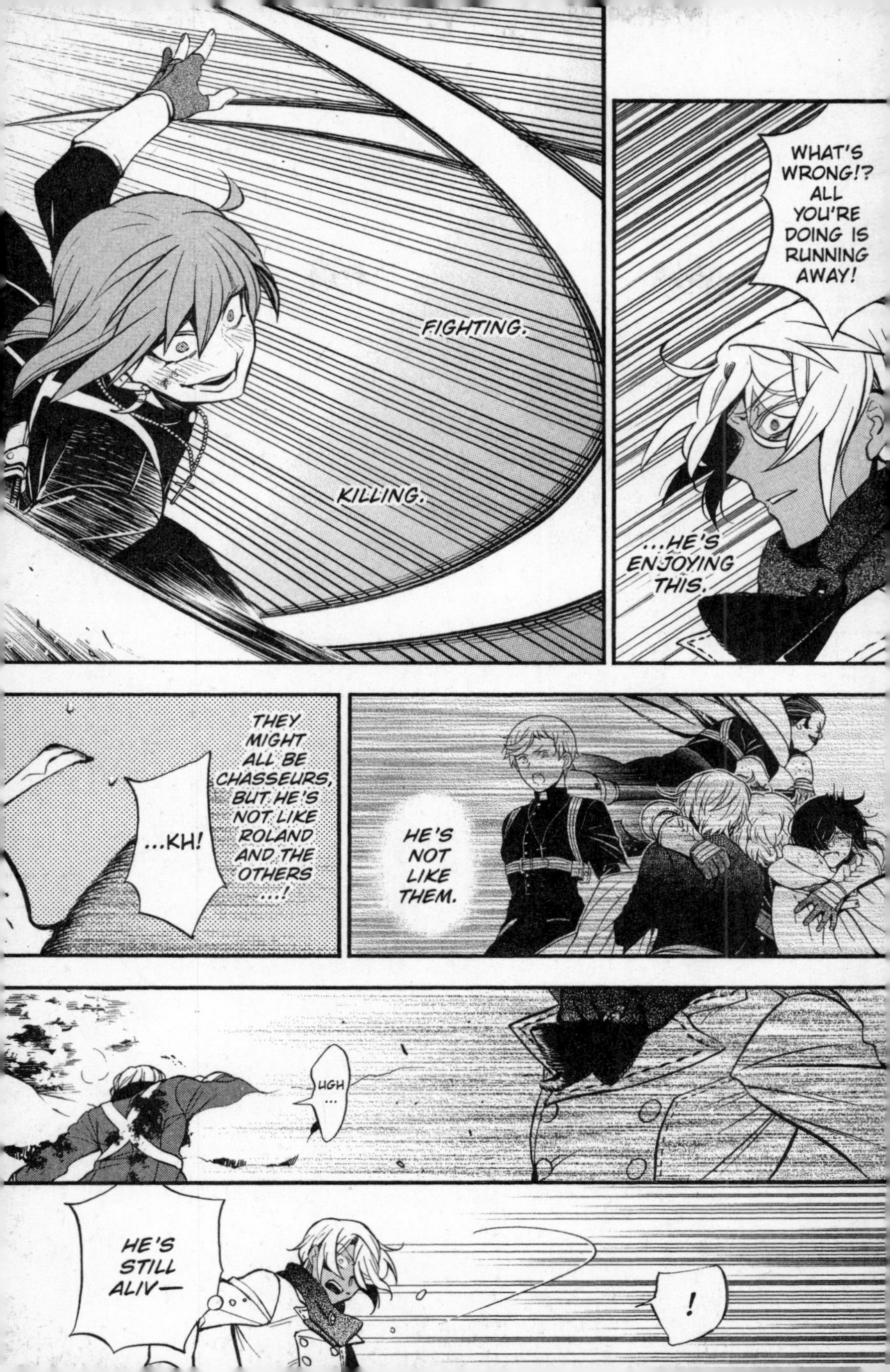
WHAT'S WRONG!? ALL YOU'RE DOING IS RUNNING AWAY!
...HE'S ENJOYING THIS.
FIGHTING.
KILLING.
HE'S NOT LIKE THEM.
THEY MIGHT ALL BE CHASSEURS, BUT HE'S NOT LIKE ROLAND AND THE OTHERS ...!
...KH!
UGH ...
HE'S STILL ALIV—
!

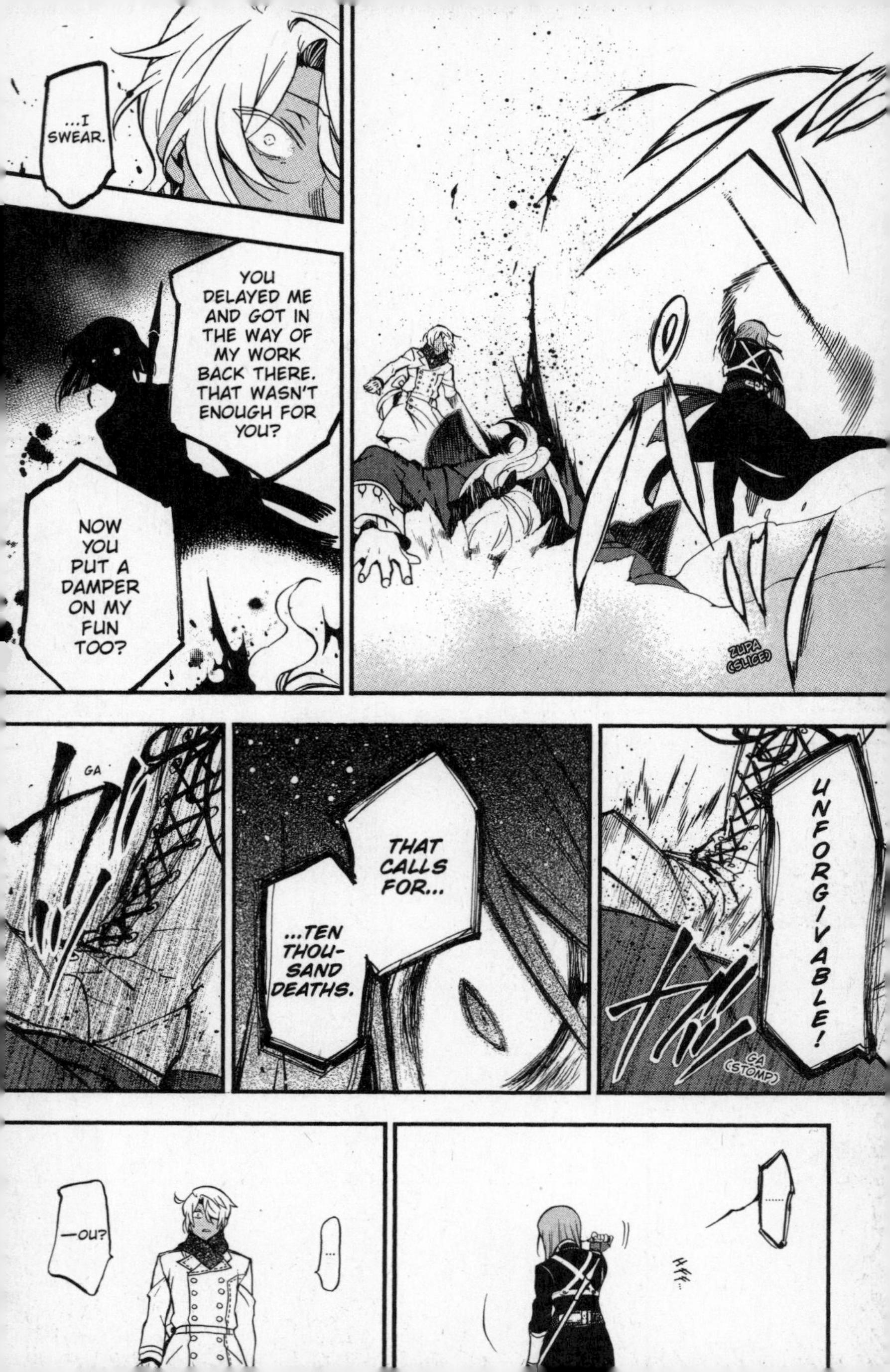

ZUPA (SLICE)
...I SWEAR.
YOU DELAYED ME AND GOT IN THE WAY OF MY WORK BACK THERE. THAT WASN'T ENOUGH FOR YOU?
NOW YOU PUT A DAMPER ON MY FUN TOO?
UNFORGIVABLE!
GA (STOMP)
THAT CALLS FOR...
...TEN THOU-SAND DEATHS.
GA
......
HFF...
—OU?
...

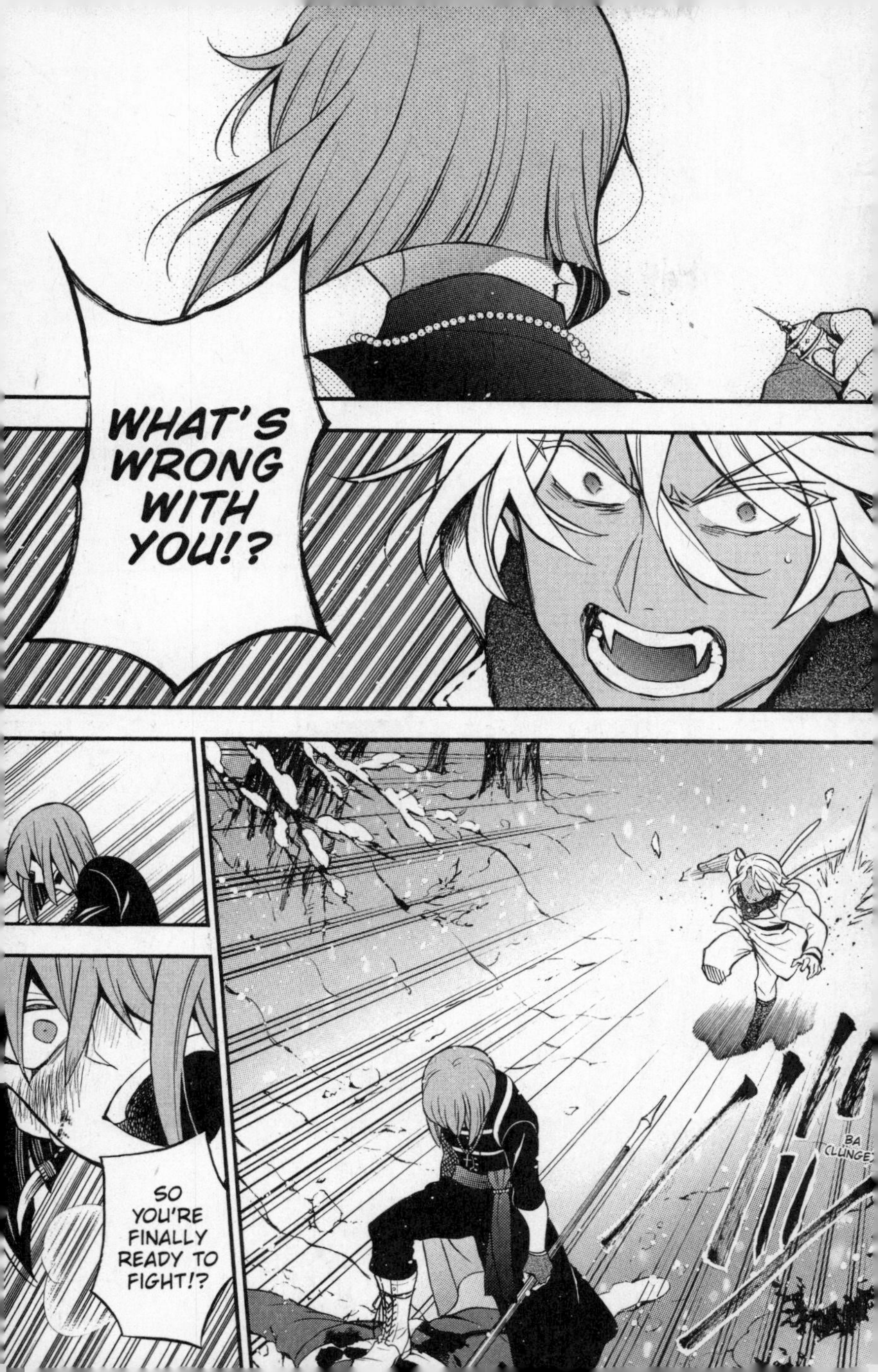
WHAT'S WRONG WITH YOU!?
BA CLUNGE
SO YOU'RE FINALLY READY TO FIGHT!?

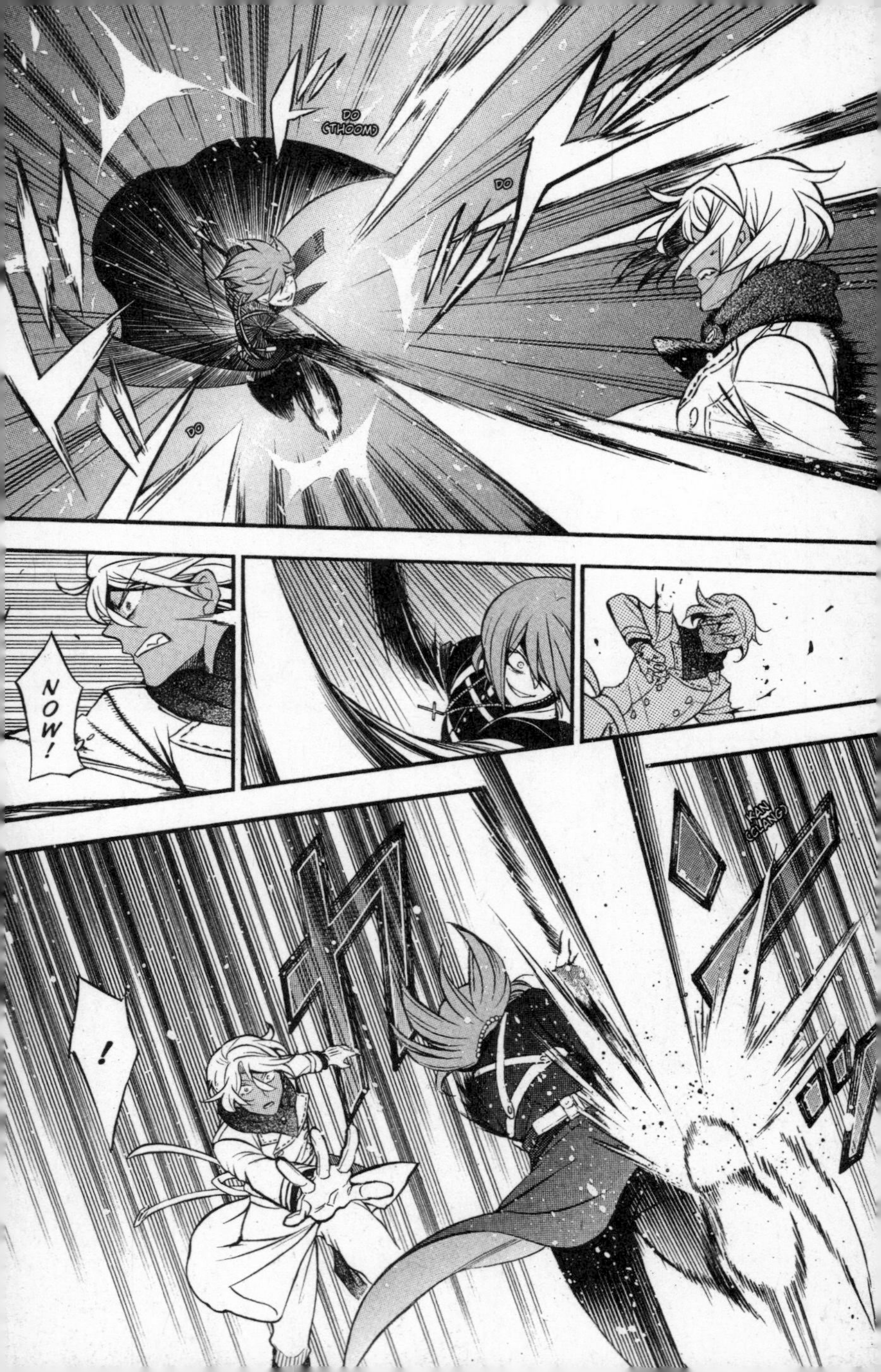
DO
(THOOM)
DO
DO
NOW!
KAN
(CLANG)
!

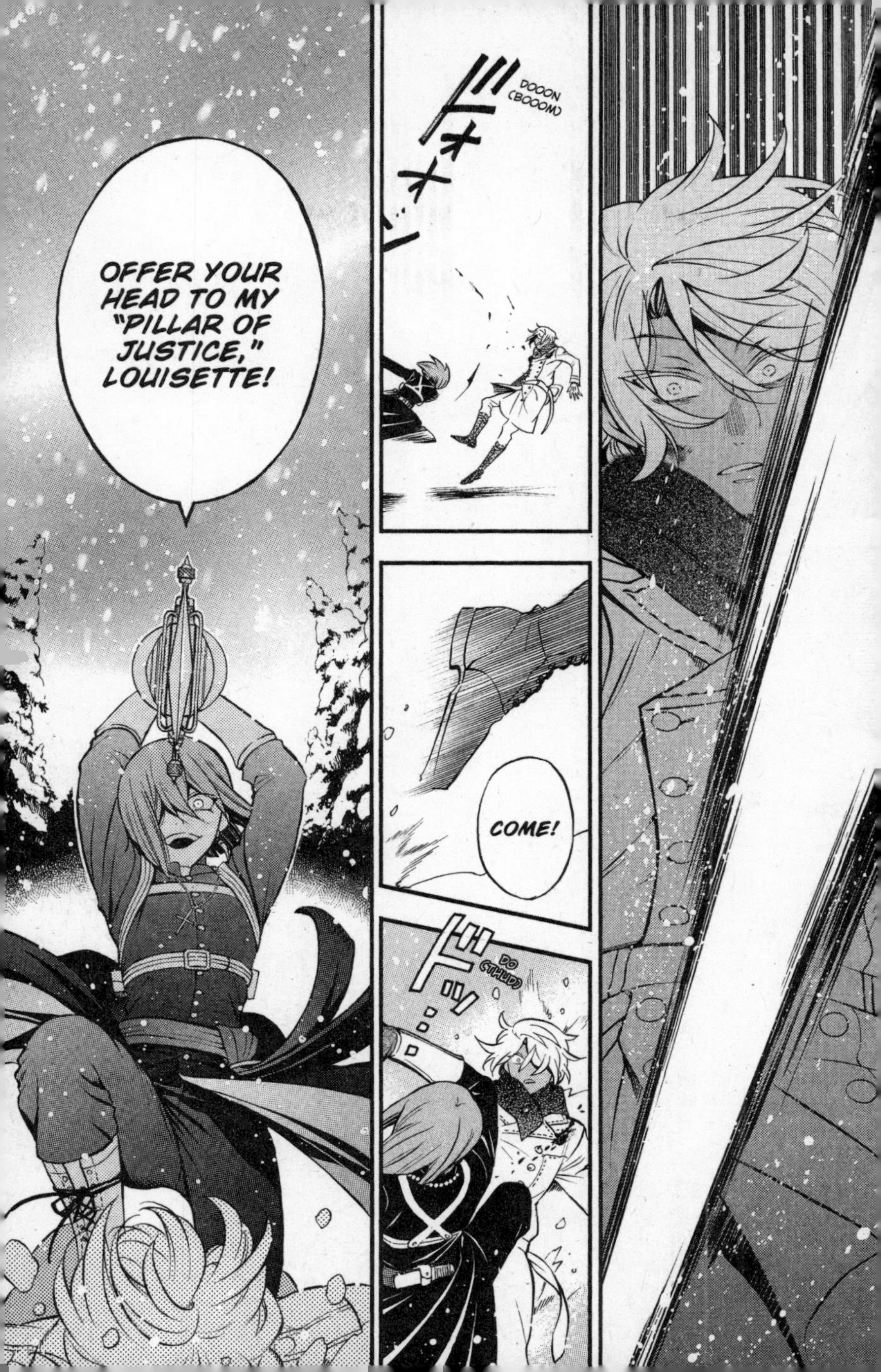
DOOON (BOOOM)
COME!
DO (THUD)
OFFER YOUR HEAD TO MY "PILLAR OF JUSTICE," LOUISETTE!

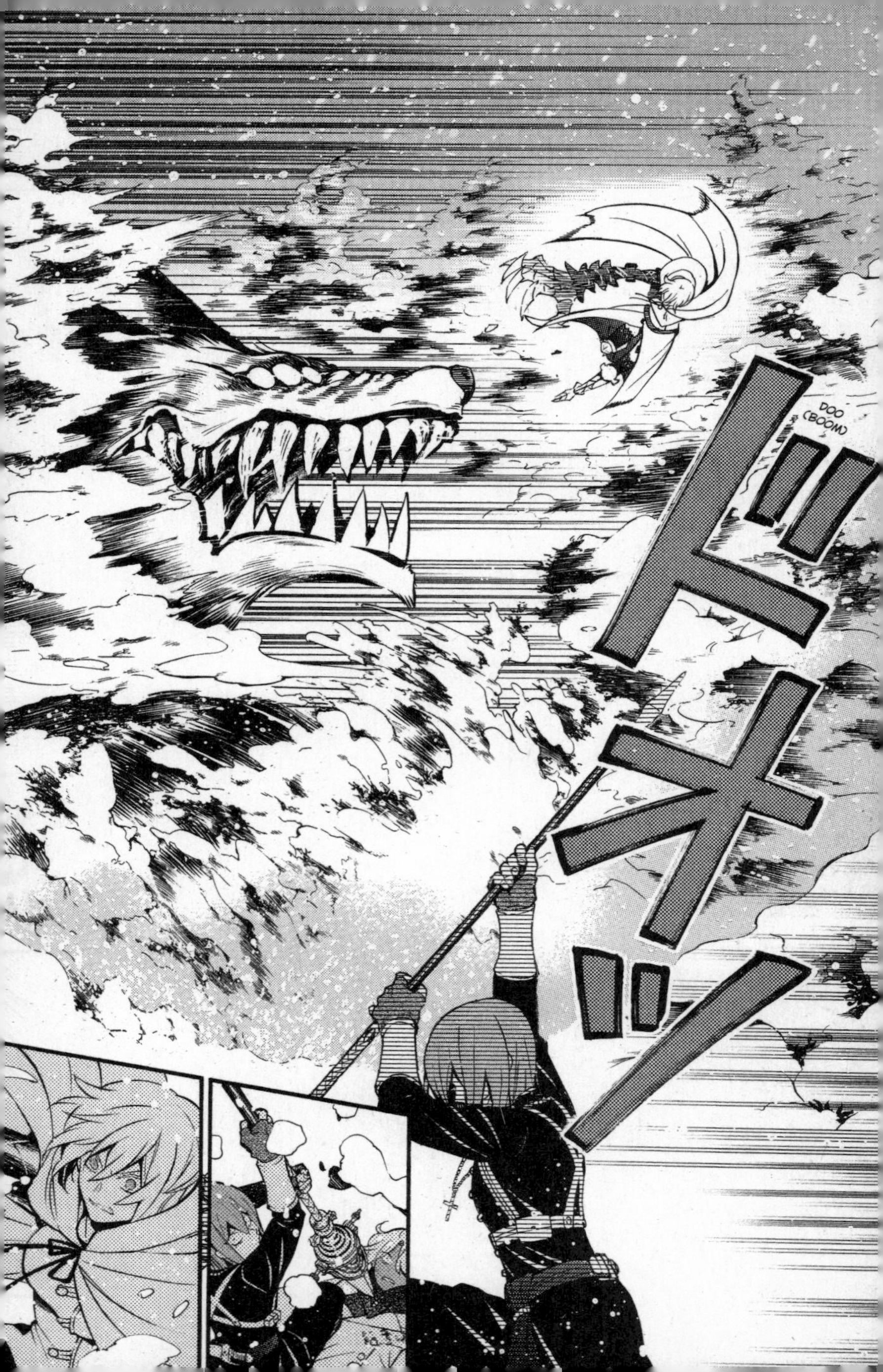
ドーン
DOO (BOOM)

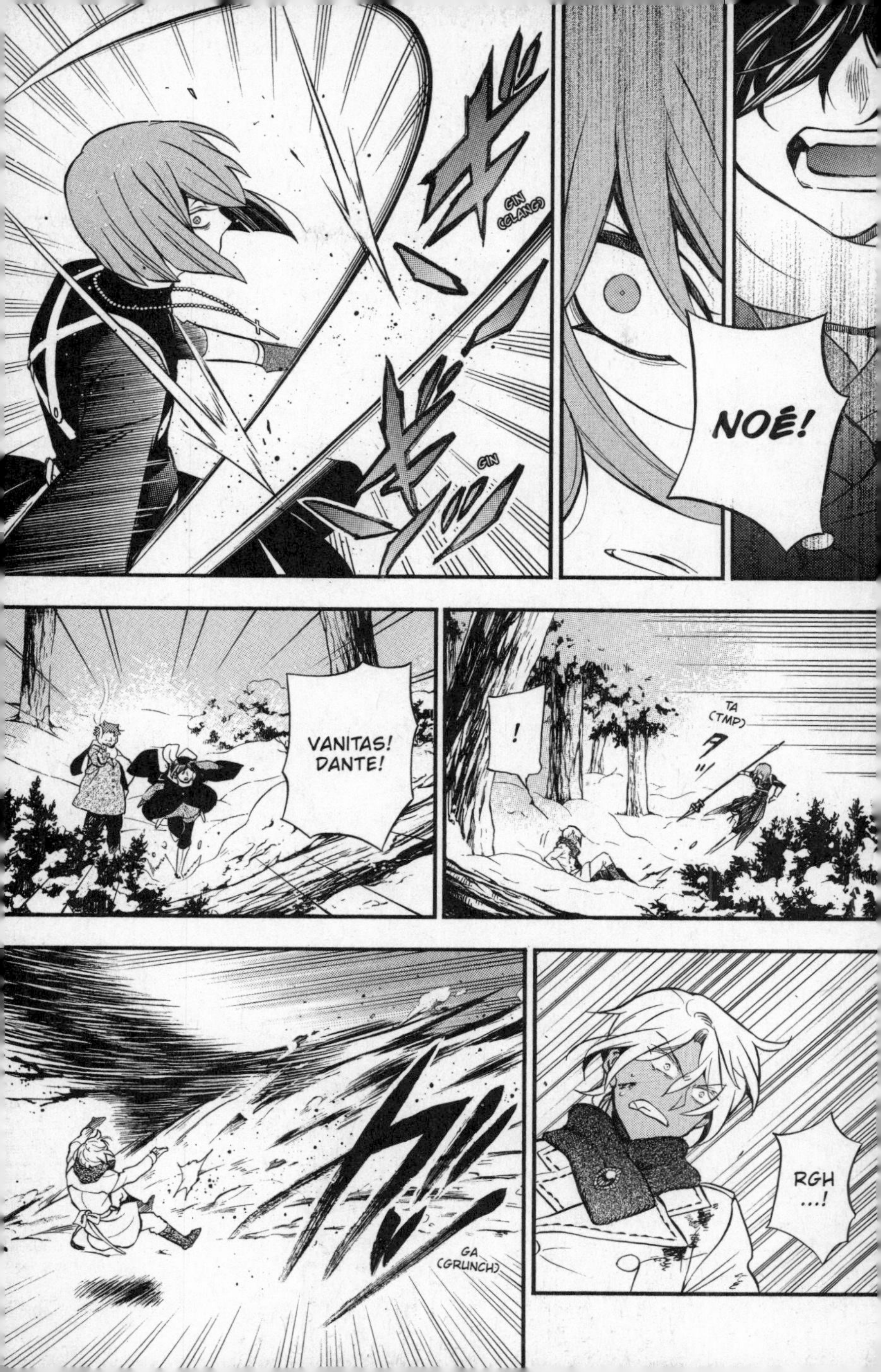
NOÉ!
GIN (CLANG)
GIN
!
TA (TMP)
VANITAS! DANTE!
RGH ...!
GA (GRUNCH)

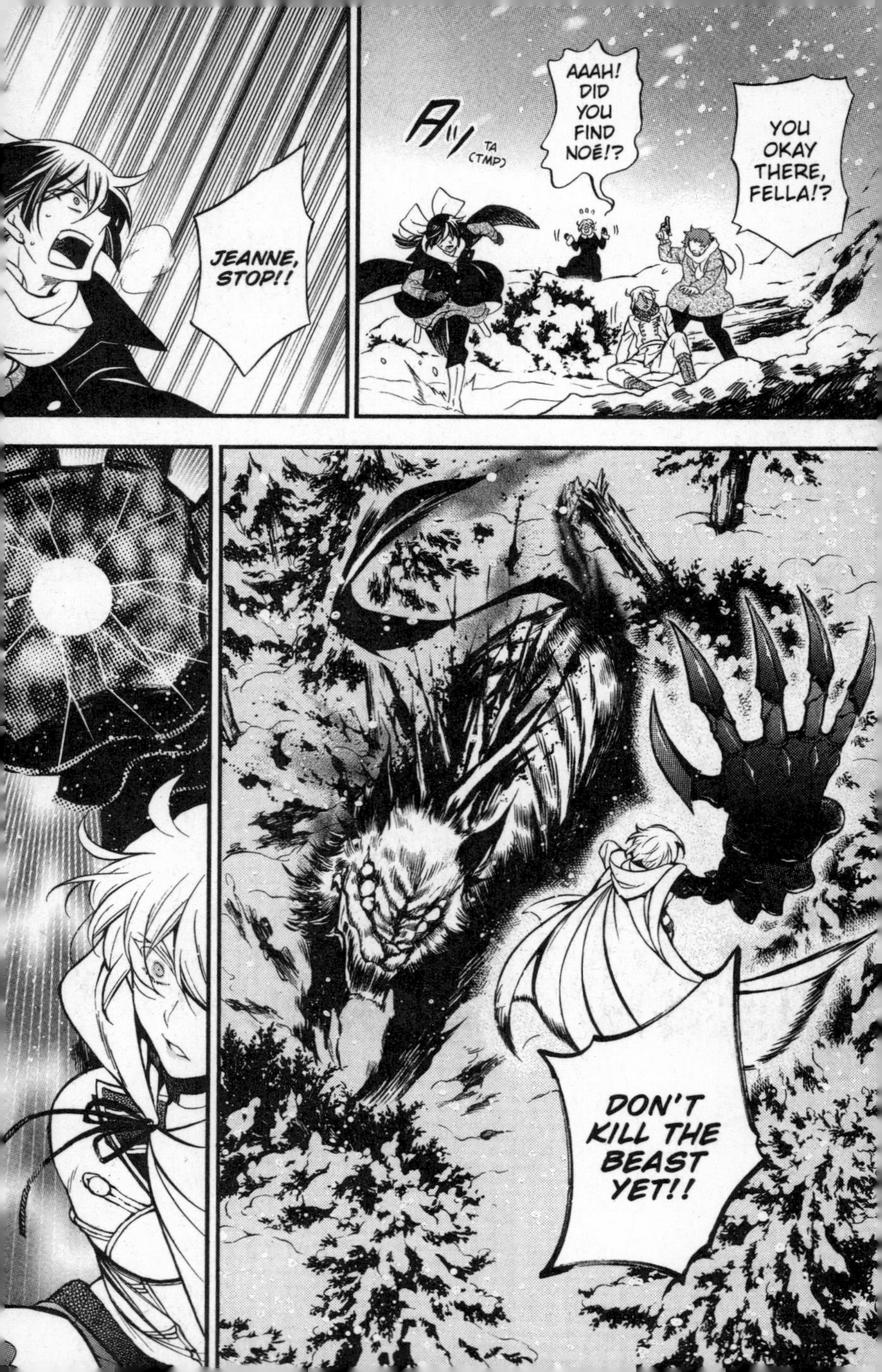
YOU OKAY THERE, FELLA!?
AAAH! DID YOU FIND NOÉ!?
TA (TMP)
JEANNE, STOP!!
DON'T KILL THE BEAST YET!!

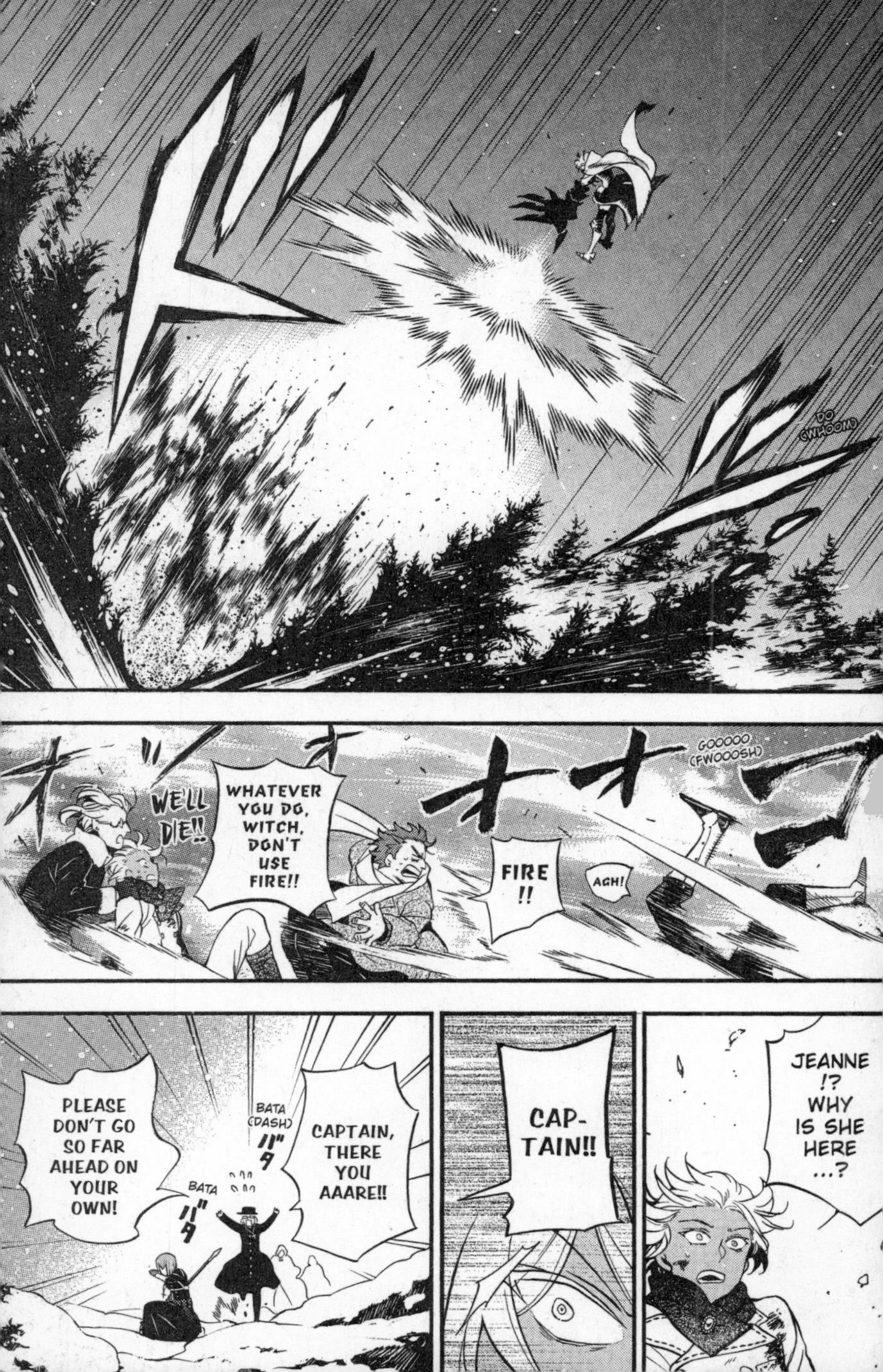
DO (WHOOM)
GOOOOO (FWOOOSH)
AGH!
FIRE!!
WHATEVER YOU DO, WITCH, DON'T USE FIRE!!
WE'LL DIE!!
JEANNE!? WHY IS SHE HERE...?
CAP-TAIN!!
CAPTAIN, THERE YOU AAARE!!
BATA (DASH)
BATA
PLEASE DON'T GO SO FAR AHEAD ON YOUR OWN!

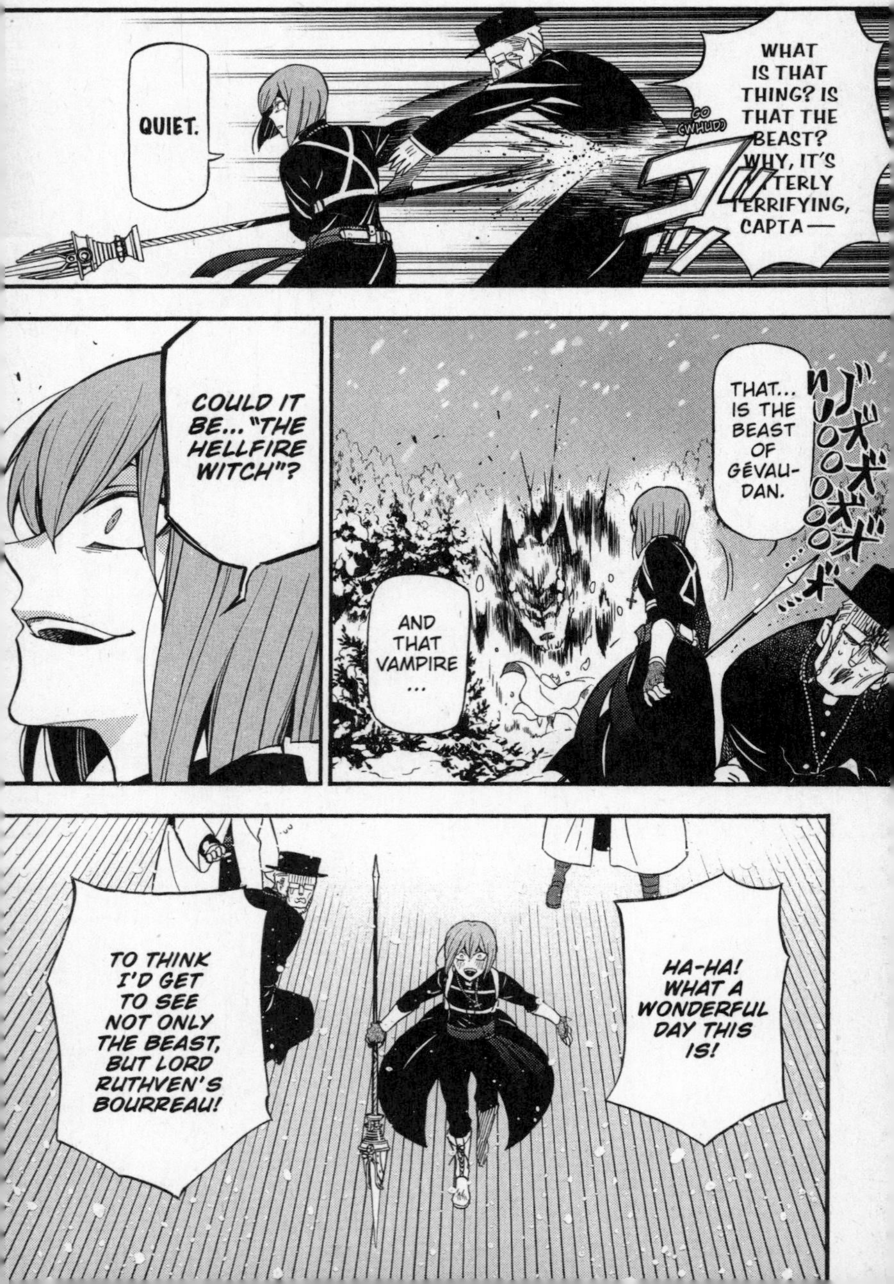
WHAT IS THAT THING? IS THAT THE BEAST? WHY, IT'S UTTERLY TERRIFYING, CAPTA—
GO (WHUD)
QUIET.
THAT... IS THE BEAST OF GÉVAUDAN.
AND THAT VAMPIRE...
COULD IT BE... "THE HELLFIRE WITCH"?
HA-HA! WHAT A WONDERFUL DAY THIS IS!
TO THINK I'D GET TO SEE NOT ONLY THE BEAST, BUT LORD RUTHVEN'S BOURREAU!

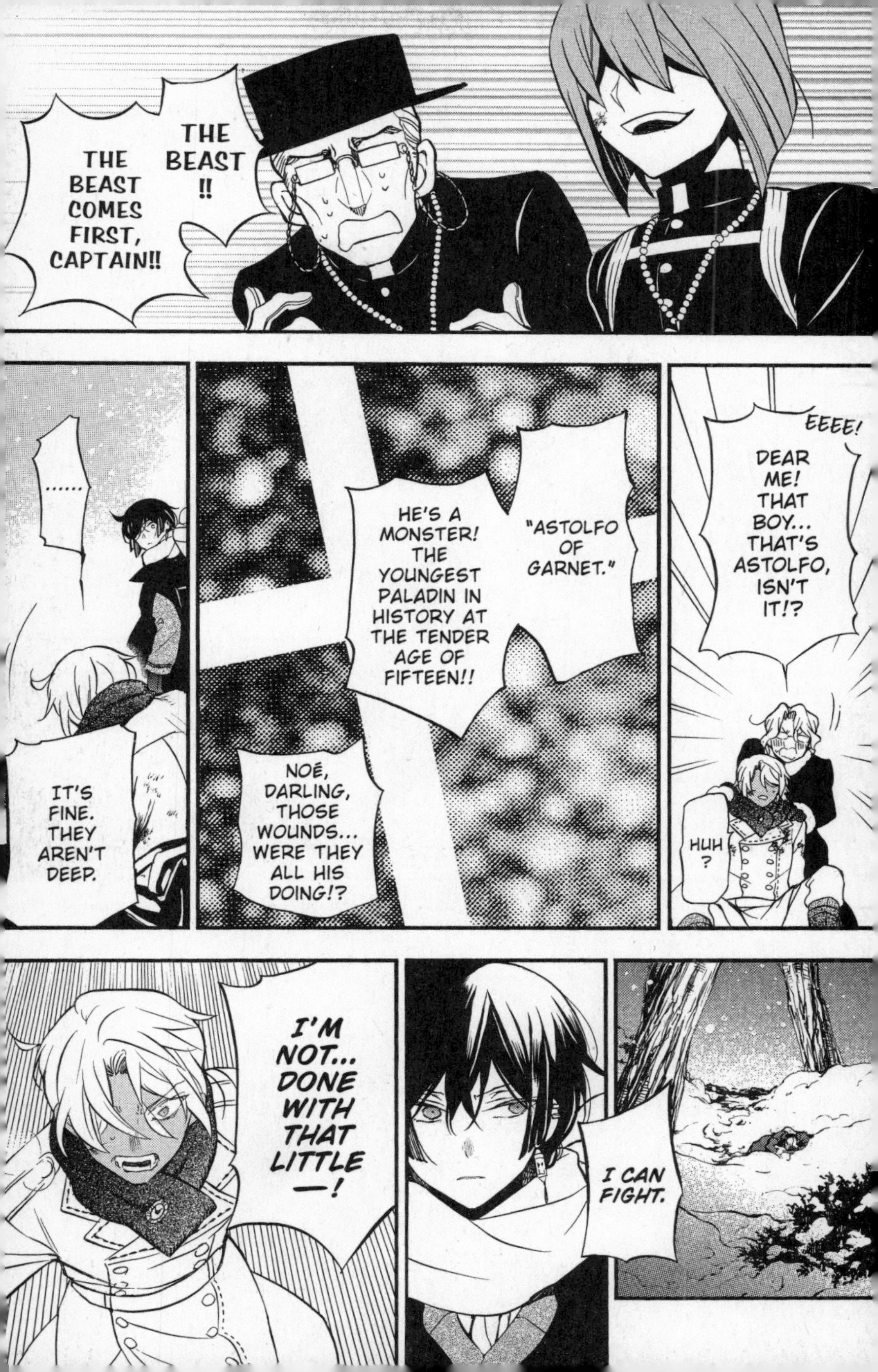
THE BEAST !!
THE BEAST COMES FIRST, CAPTAIN!!
EEEE!
DEAR ME! THAT BOY... THAT'S ASTOLFO, ISN'T IT!?
HUH ?
"ASTOLFO OF GARNET."
HE'S A MONSTER! THE YOUNGEST PALADIN IN HISTORY AT THE TENDER AGE OF FIFTEEN!!
NOÉ, DARLING, THOSE WOUNDS... WERE THEY ALL HIS DOING!?
......
IT'S FINE. THEY AREN'T DEEP.
I CAN FIGHT.
I'M NOT... DONE WITH THAT LITTLE—!

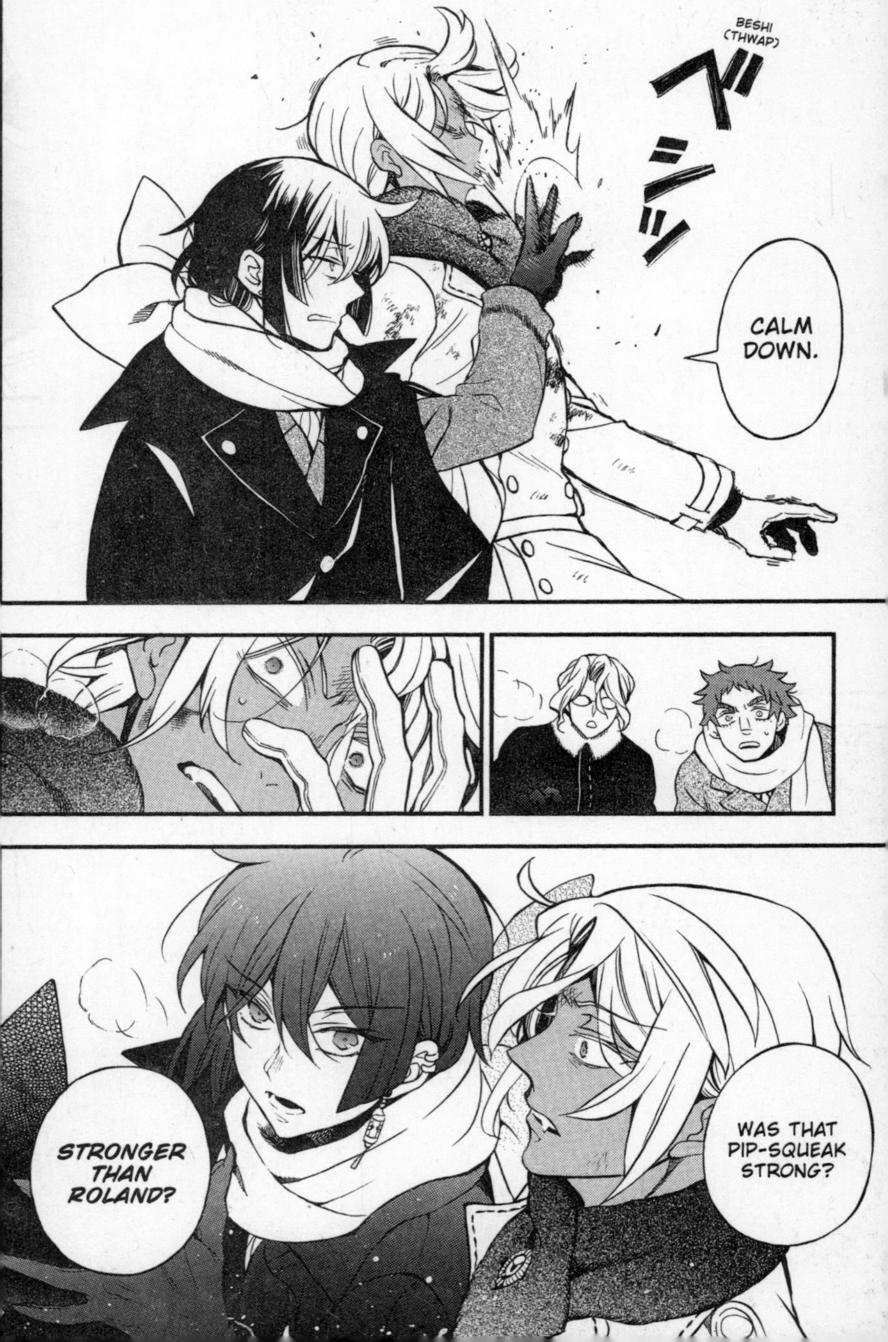
BESHI (THWAP)
CALM DOWN.
WAS THAT PIP-SQUEAK STRONG?
STRONGER THAN ROLAND?

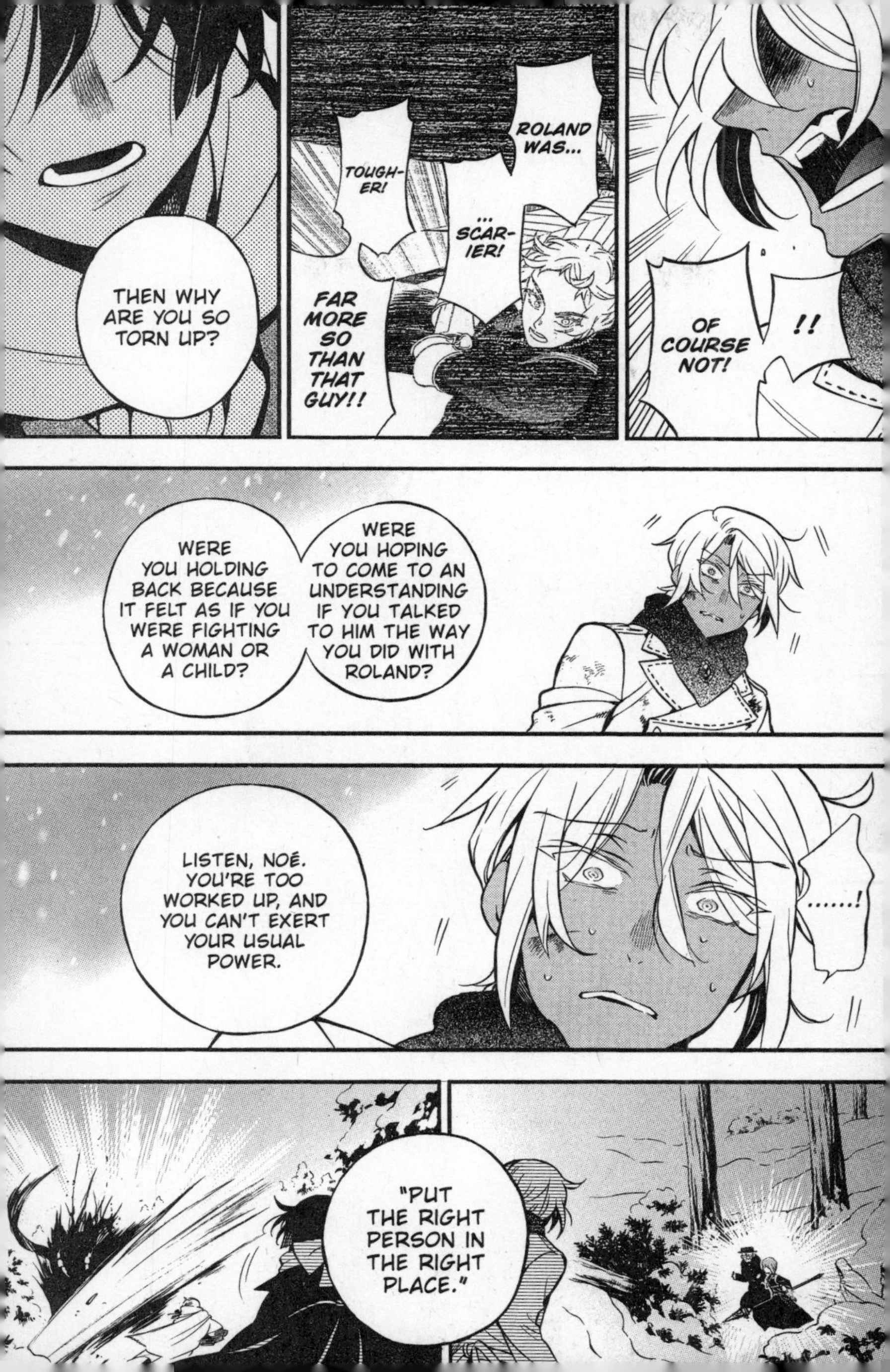
!!
OF COURSE NOT!
ROLAND WAS...
TOUGHER!
...SCARIER!
FAR MORE SO THAN THAT GUY!!
THEN WHY ARE YOU SO TORN UP?
WERE YOU HOPING TO COME TO AN UNDERSTANDING IF YOU TALKED TO HIM THE WAY YOU DID WITH ROLAND?
WERE YOU HOLDING BACK BECAUSE IT FELT AS IF YOU WERE FIGHTING A WOMAN OR A CHILD?
......!
LISTEN, NOÉ. YOU'RE TOO WORKED UP, AND YOU CAN'T EXERT YOUR USUAL POWER.
"PUT THE RIGHT PERSON IN THE RIGHT PLACE."

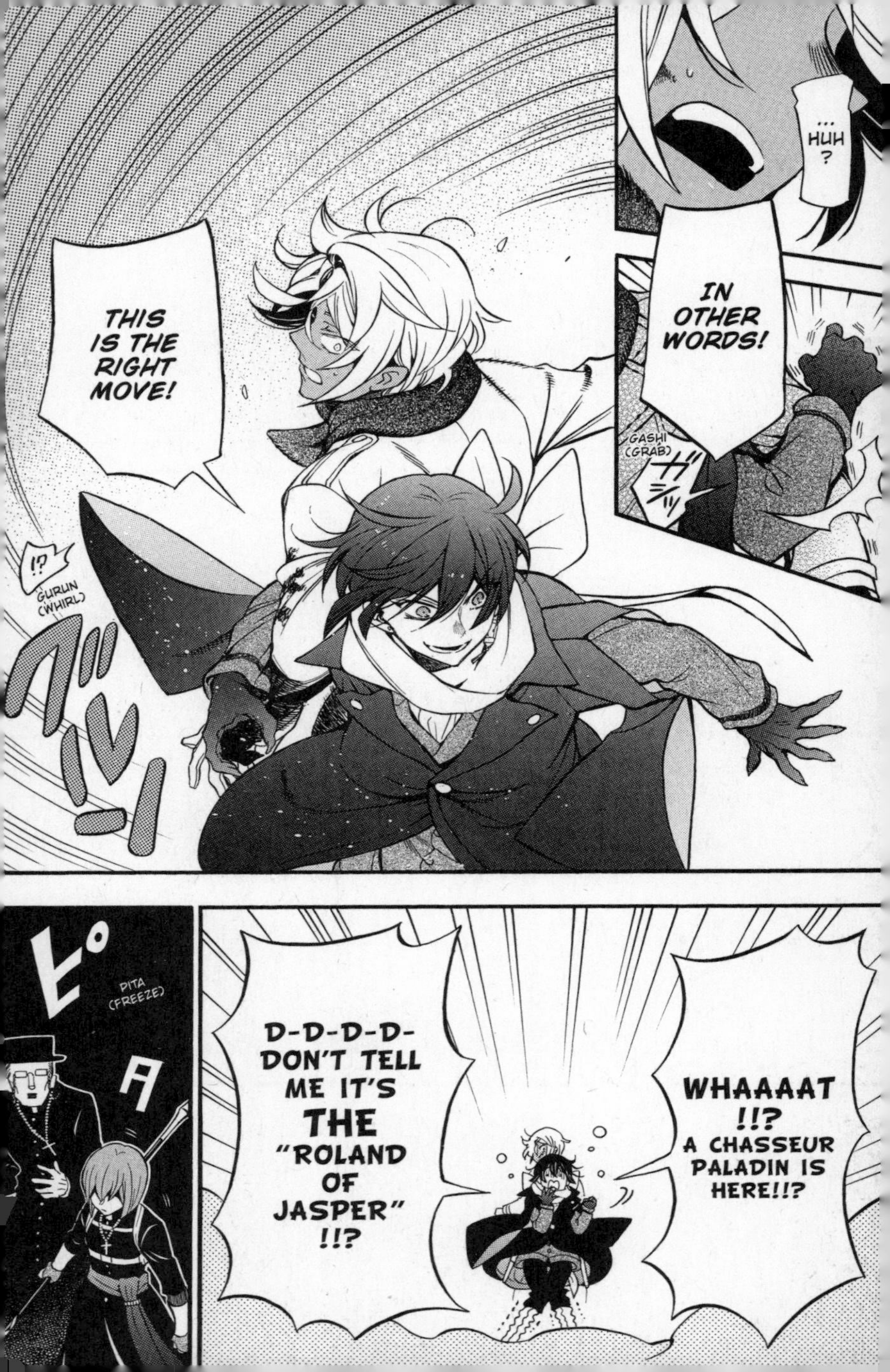
...HUH?
IN OTHER WORDS!
GASHI (GRAB)
THIS IS THE RIGHT MOVE!
!?
GURUN (WHIRL)
WHAAAAT!!? A CHASSEUR PALADIN IS HERE!!?
D-D-D-D-DON'T TELL ME IT'S THE "ROLAND OF JASPER"!!?
PITA (FREEZE)

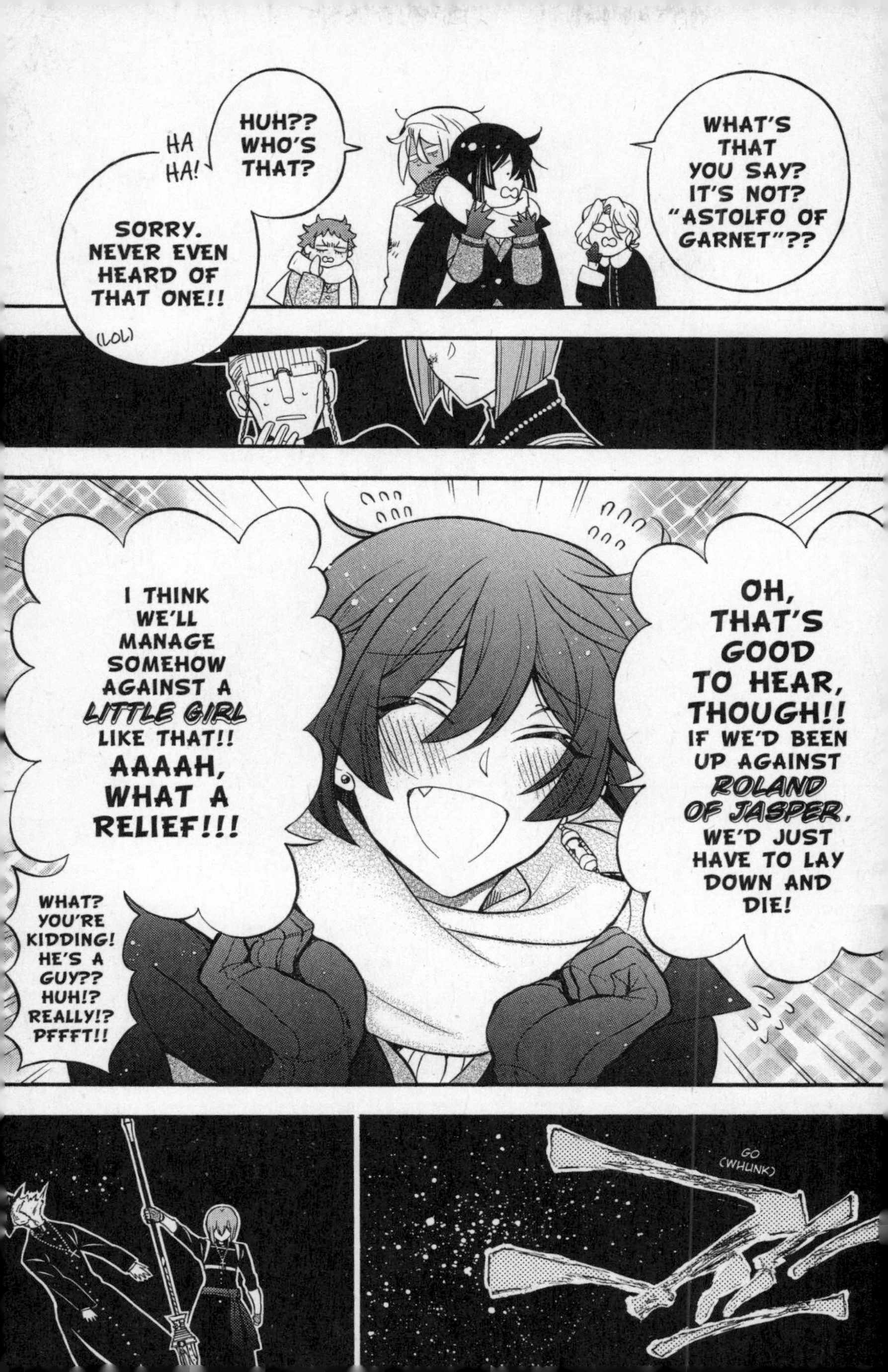
WHAT'S THAT YOU SAY? IT'S NOT? "ASTOLFO OF GARNET"??
HUH?? WHO'S THAT?
HA HA!
SORRY. NEVER EVEN HEARD OF THAT ONE!!
(LOL)
OH, THAT'S GOOD TO HEAR, THOUGH!! IF WE'D BEEN UP AGAINST ROLAND OF JASPER, WE'D JUST HAVE TO LAY DOWN AND DIE!
I THINK WE'LL MANAGE SOMEHOW AGAINST A LITTLE GIRL LIKE THAT!! AAAAH, WHAT A RELIEF!!!
WHAT? YOU'RE KIDDING! HE'S A GUY?? HUH!? REALLY!? PFFFT!!
GO (WHUNK)

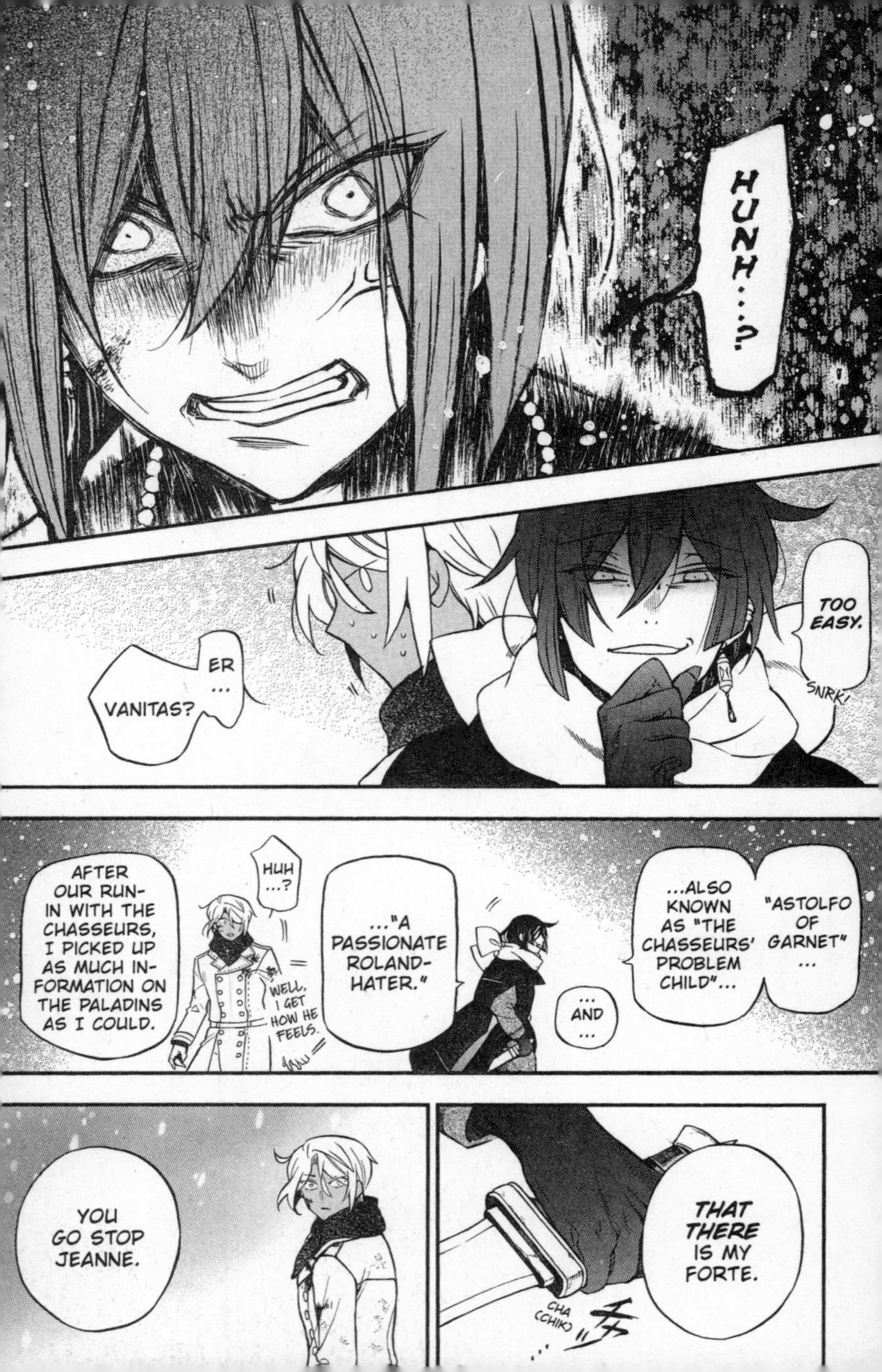
HUNH...?
TOO EASY.
SNRK!
ER ... VANITAS?
"ASTOLFO OF GARNET" ...
...ALSO KNOWN AS "THE CHASSEURS' PROBLEM CHILD"...
... AND ...
..."A PASSIONATE ROLAND-HATER."
HUH ...?
WELL, I GET HOW HE FEELS.
AFTER OUR RUN-IN WITH THE CHASSEURS, I PICKED UP AS MUCH INFORMATION ON THE PALADINS AS I COULD.
THAT THERE IS MY FORTE.
CHA (CHIK)
YOU GO STOP JEANNE.

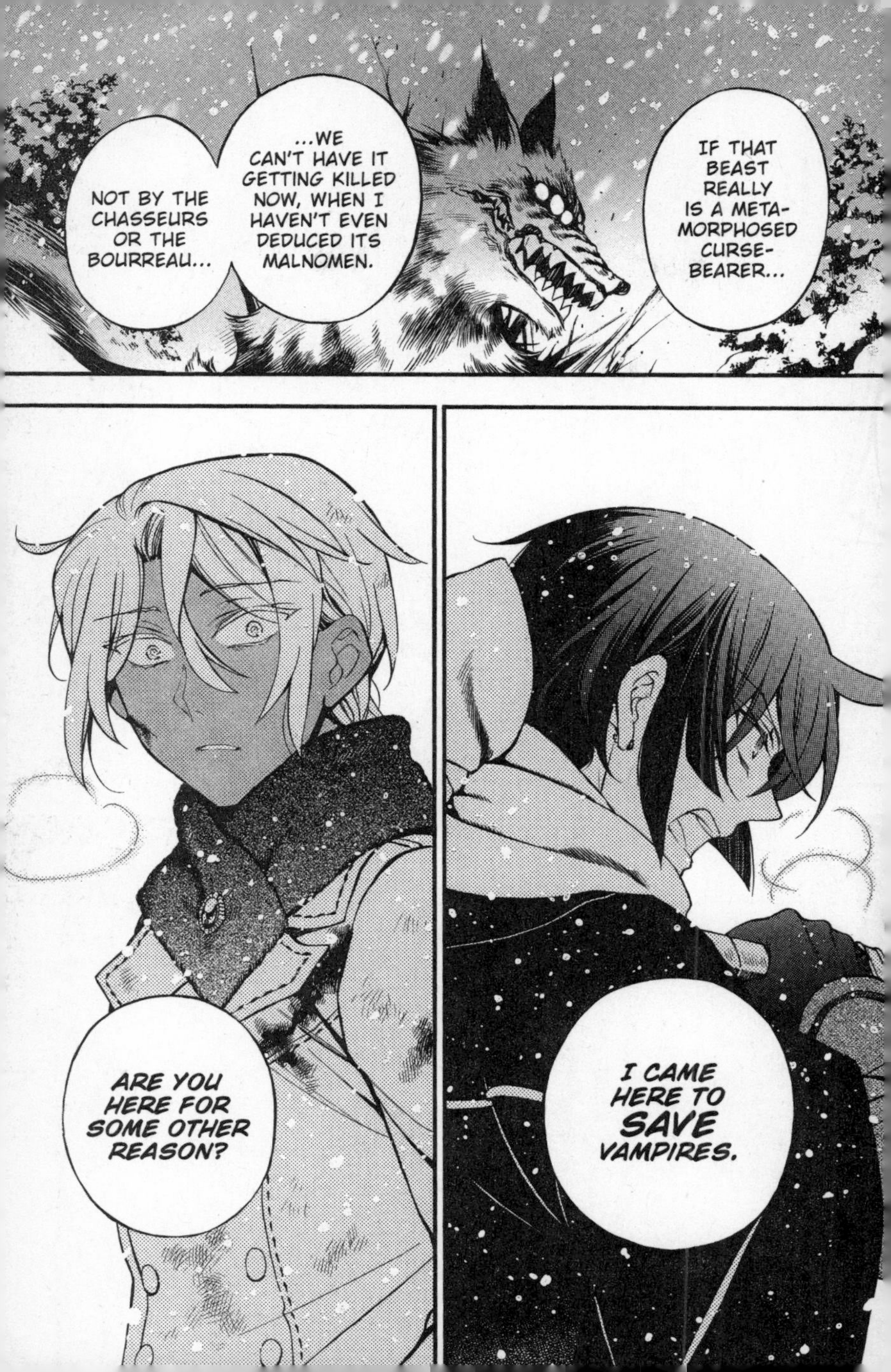
IF THAT BEAST REALLY IS A META-MORPHOSED CURSE-BEARER...
...WE CAN'T HAVE IT GETTING KILLED NOW, WHEN I HAVEN'T EVEN DEDUCED ITS MALNOMEN.
NOT BY THE CHASSEURS OR THE BOURREAU...
I CAME HERE TO SAVE VAMPIRES.
ARE YOU HERE FOR SOME OTHER REASON?

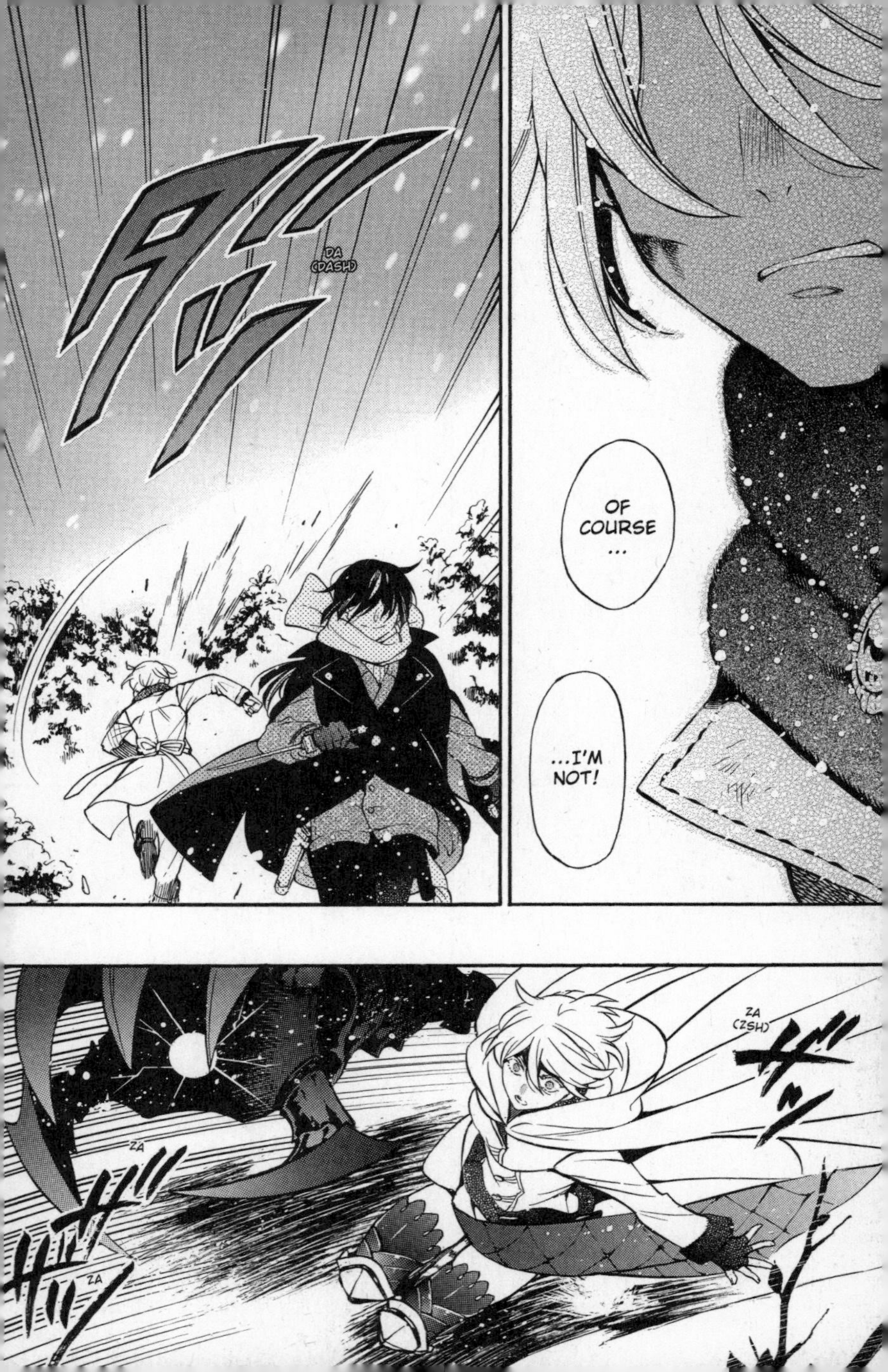
OF COURSE ...
...I'M NOT!
DA (DASH)
ZA (ZSH)
ZA
ZA

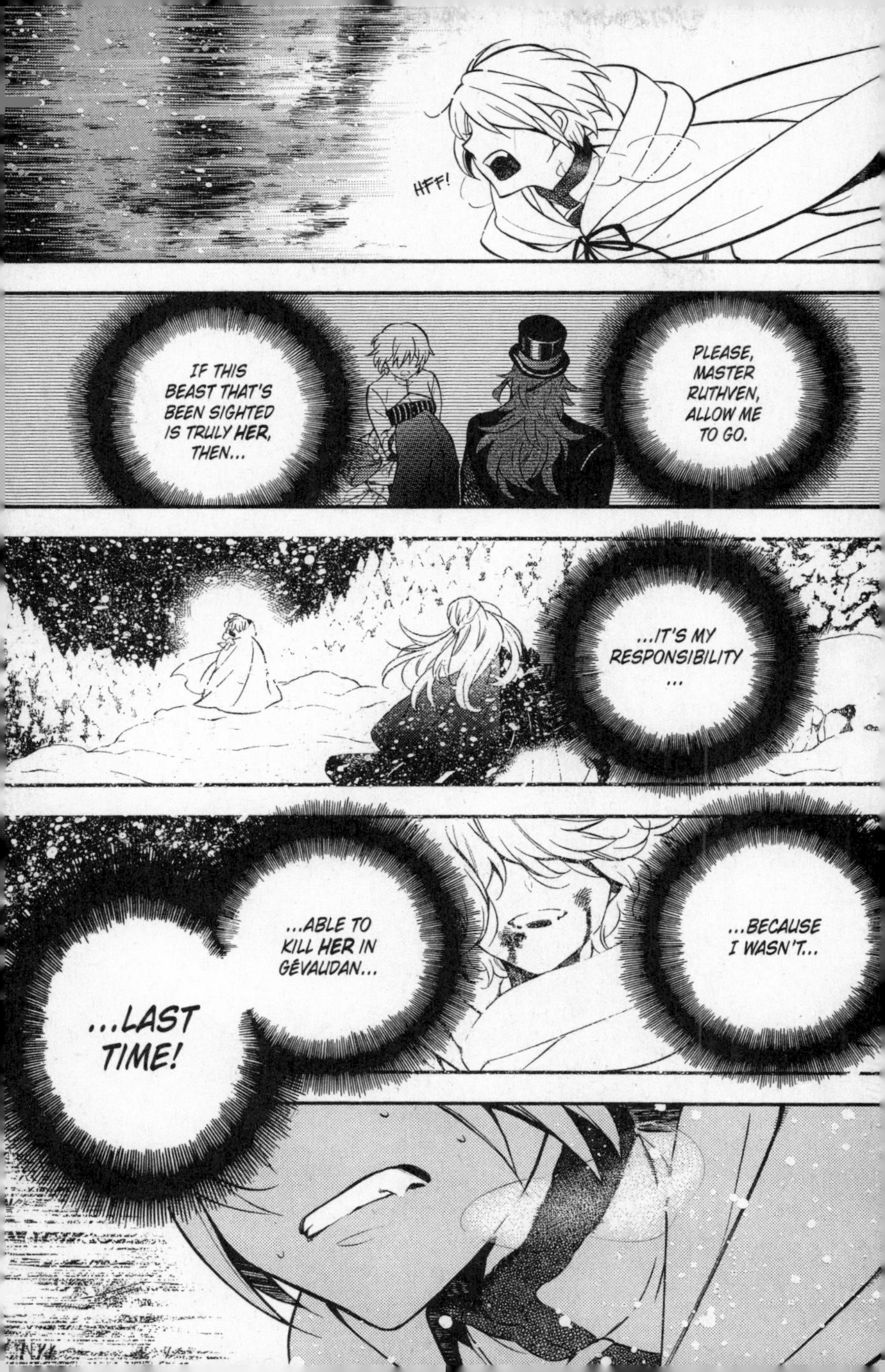
HFF!
PLEASE, MASTER RUTHVEN, ALLOW ME TO GO.
IF THIS BEAST THAT'S BEEN SIGHTED IS TRULY HER, THEN...
...IT'S MY RESPONSIBILITY ...
...BECAUSE I WASN'T...
...ABLE TO KILL HER IN GÉVAUDAN...
...LAST TIME!

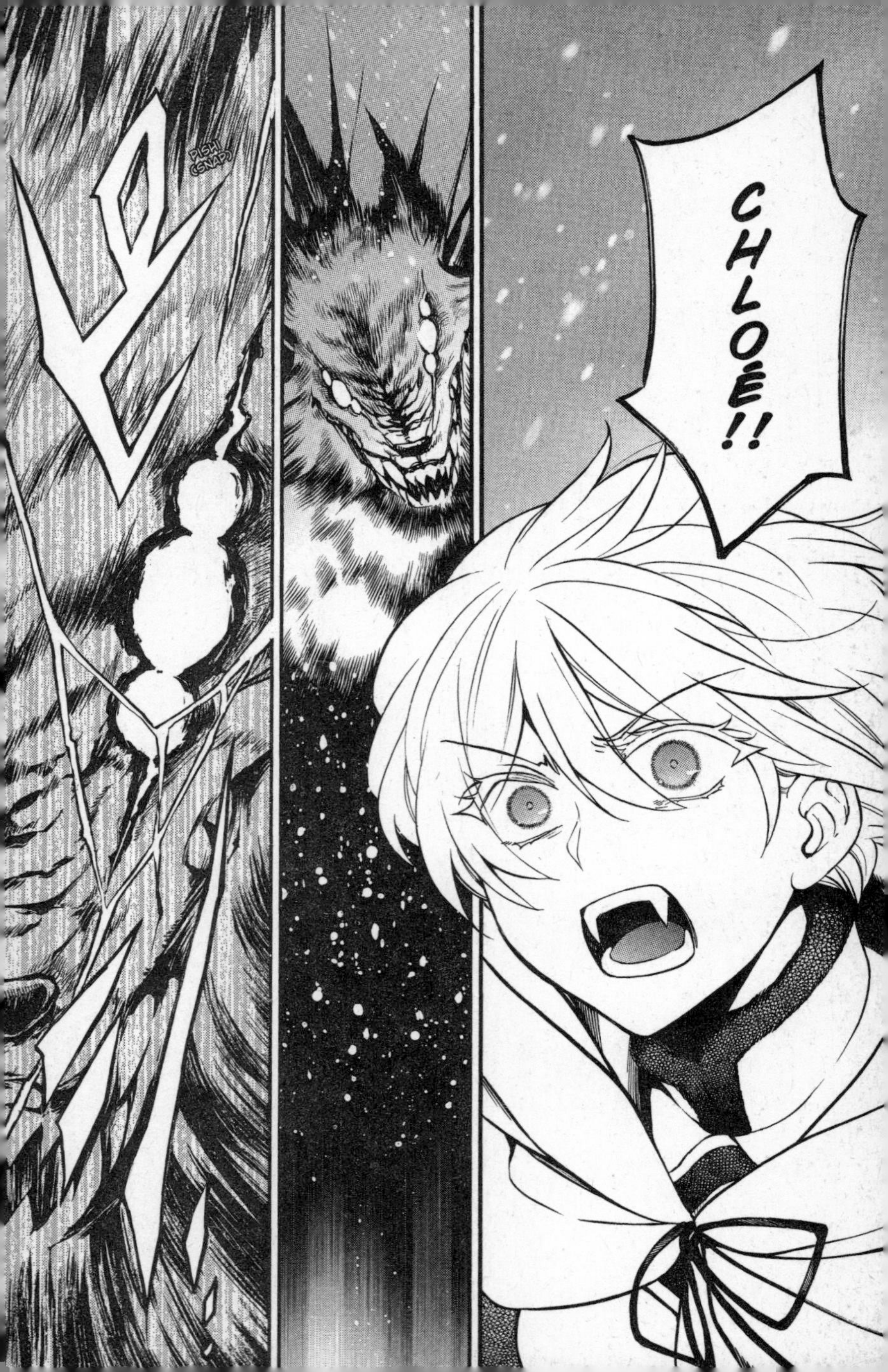
CHLOÉ!!
PISHI (SNAP)

Mémoire 25 Endroit Approprié MELEE

Les Mémoires de Vanitas

THE CASE STUDY OF
VANITAS

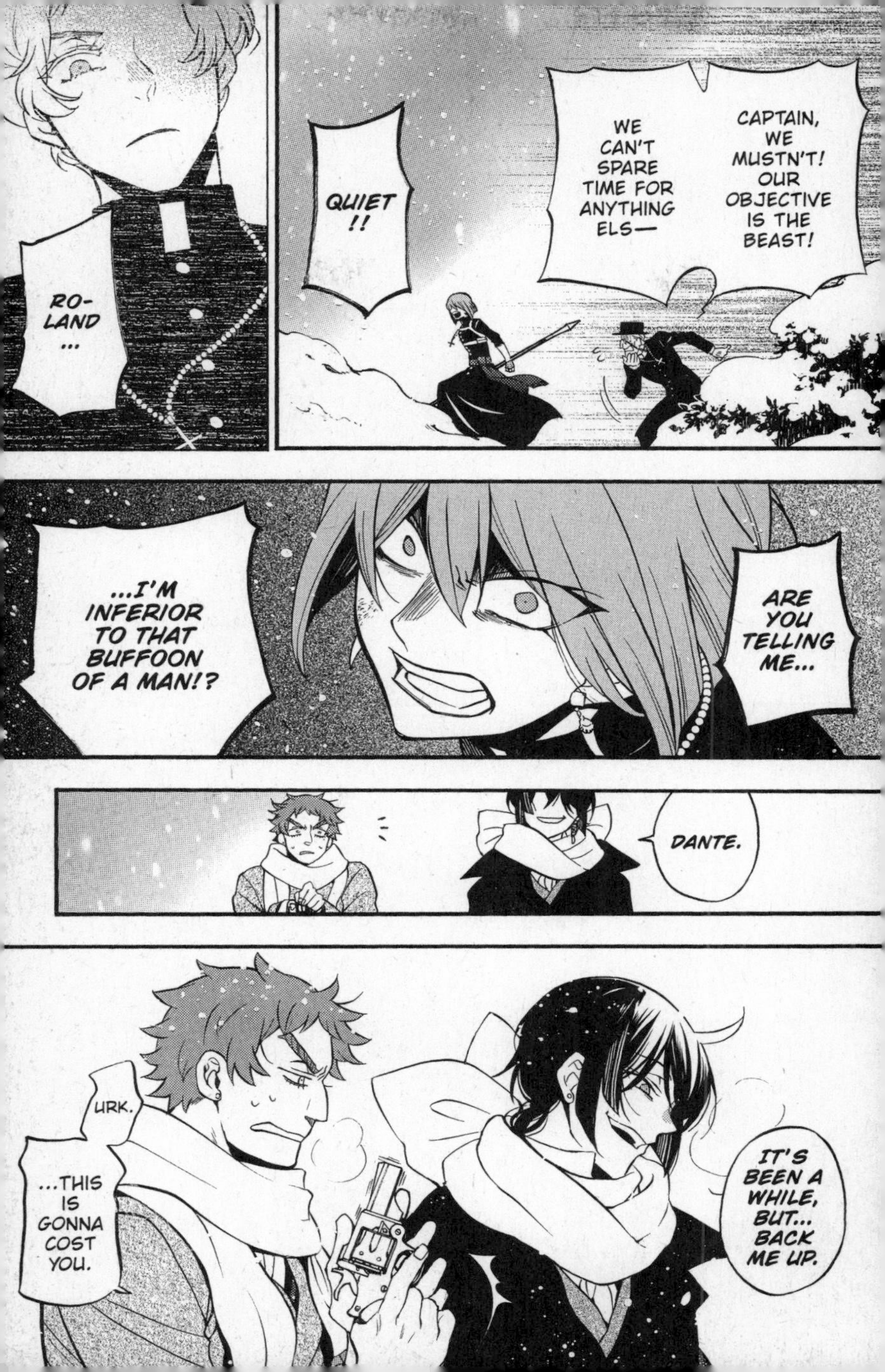
CAPTAIN, WE MUSTN'T! OUR OBJECTIVE IS THE BEAST!
WE CAN'T SPARE TIME FOR ANYTHING ELS—
QUIET !!
RO-LAND ...
ARE YOU TELLING ME...
...I'M INFERIOR TO THAT BUFFOON OF A MAN!?
DANTE.
IT'S BEEN A WHILE, BUT... BACK ME UP.
URK.
...THIS IS GONNA COST YOU.

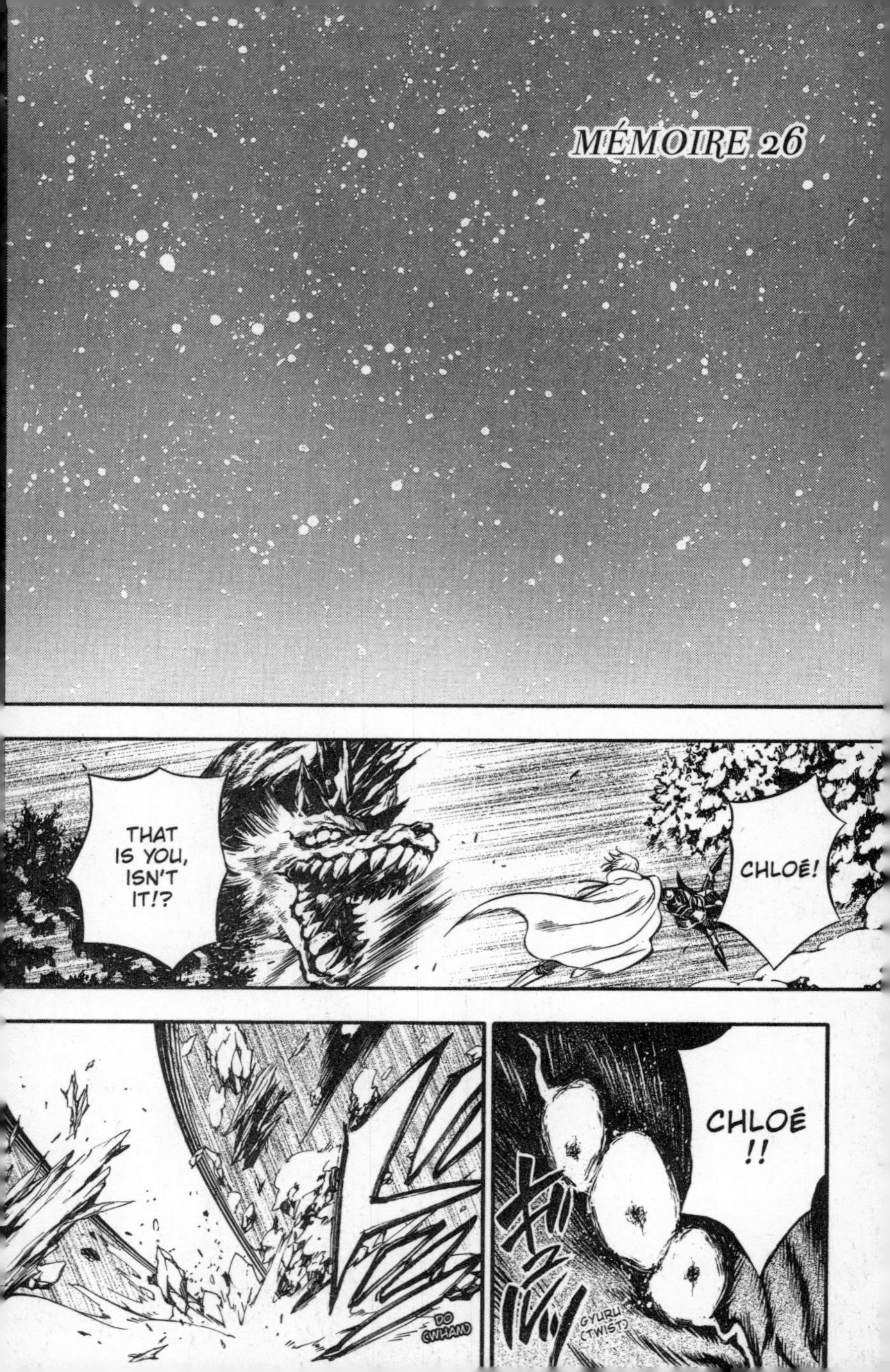
MÉMOIRE 26
CHLOÉ!
THAT IS YOU, ISN'T IT!?
CHLOÉ !!
GYURU (TWIST)
DO (WHAM)

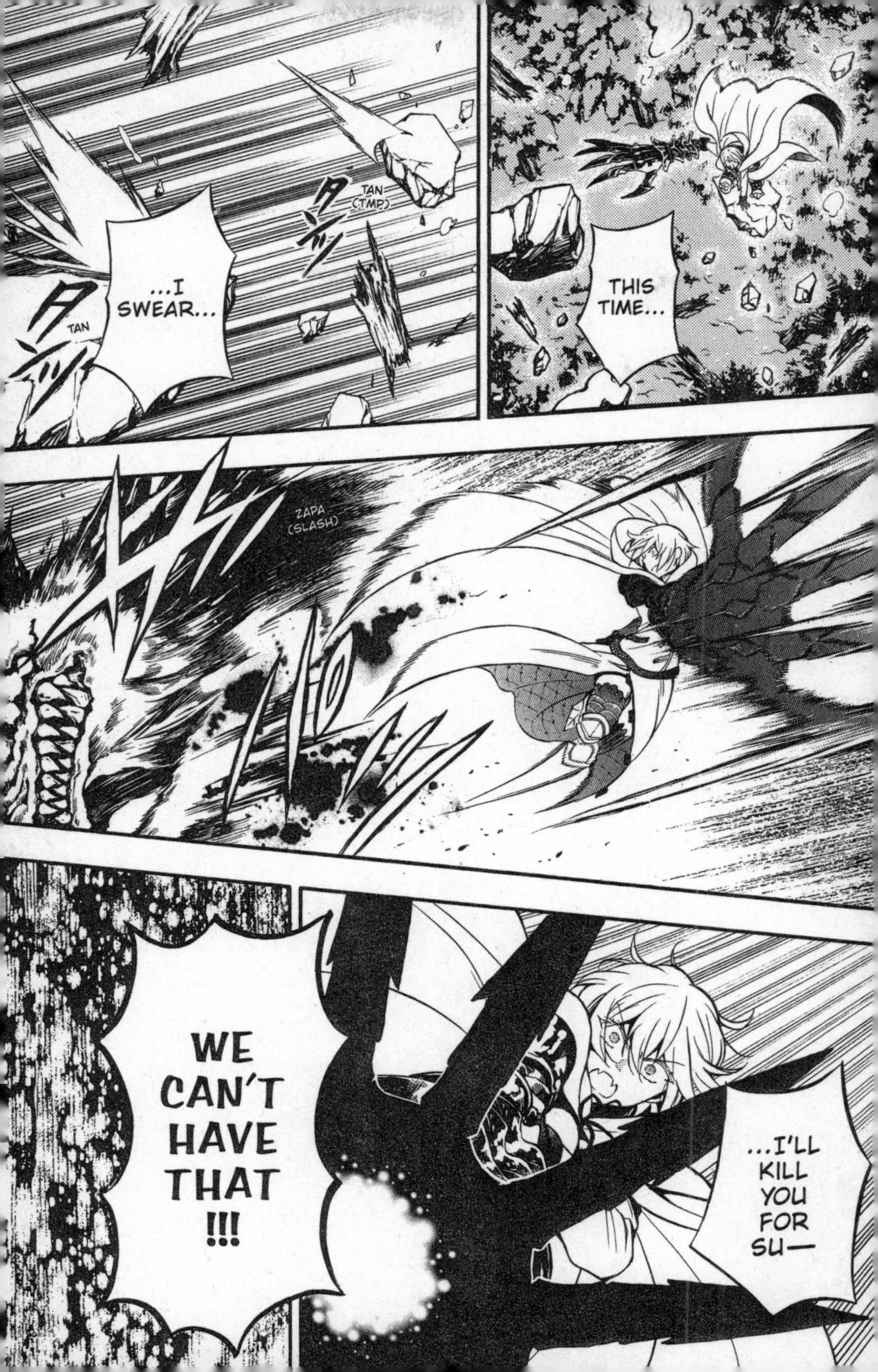
THIS TIME...
TAN (TMP)
...I SWEAR...
TAN
ZAPA (SLASH)
...I'LL KILL YOU FOR SU—
WE CAN'T HAVE THAT!!!

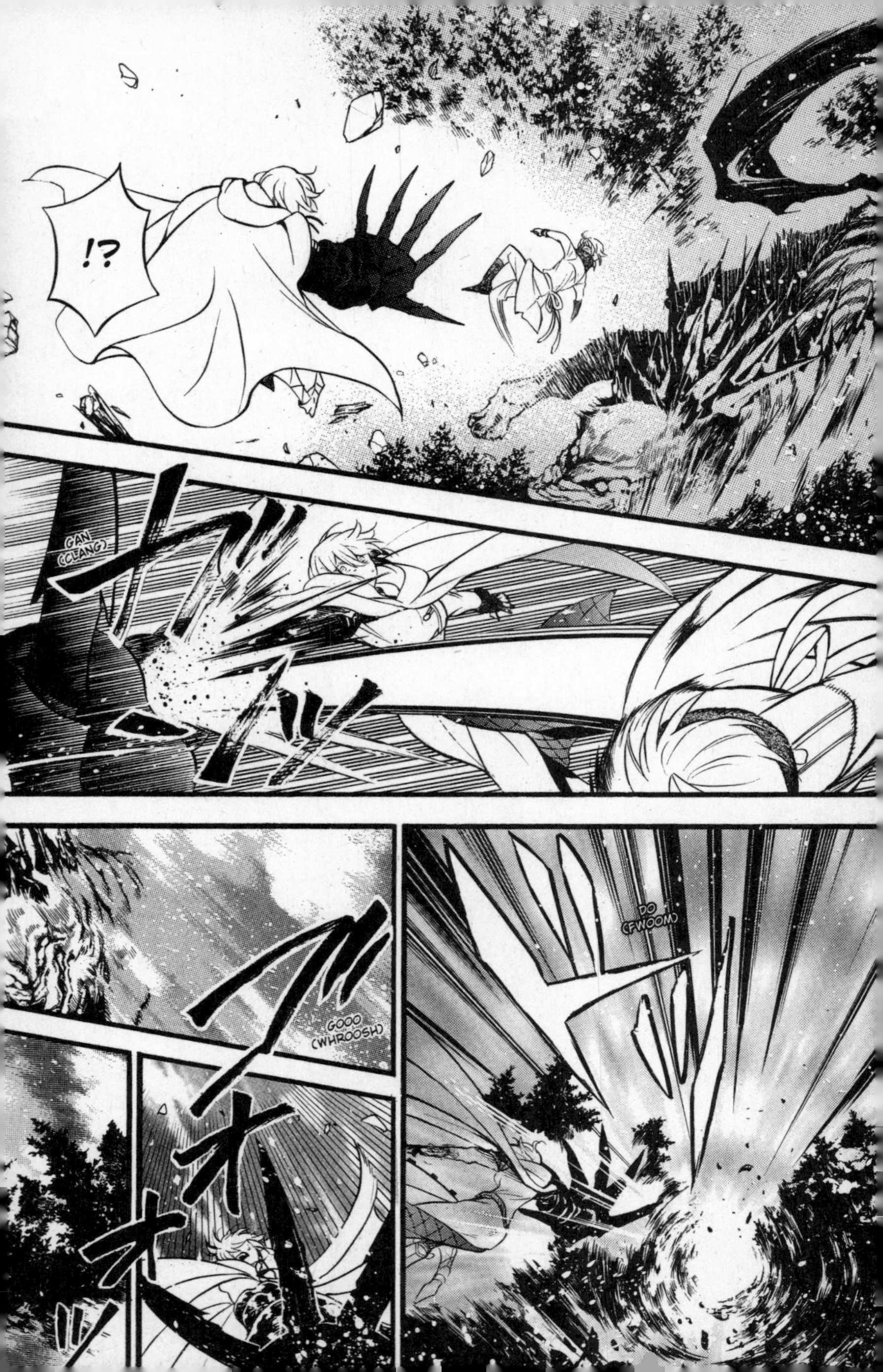
!?
GAN (CLANG)
DO (FWOOM)
GOOO (WHROOSH)

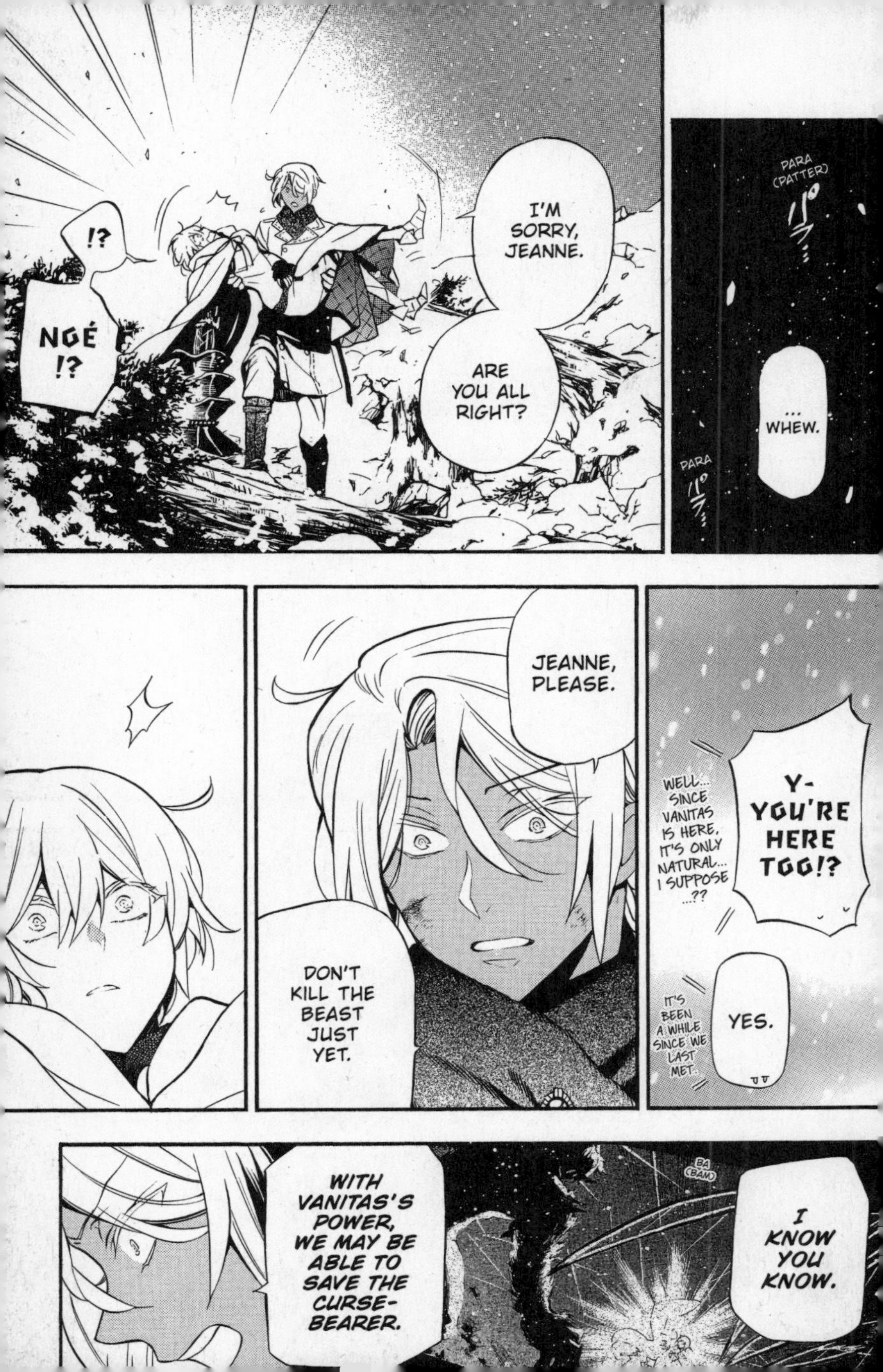
PARA (PATTER)
...WHEW.
PARA
I'M SORRY, JEANNE.
ARE YOU ALL RIGHT?
!?
NGÉ !?
Y-YOU'RE HERE TOO!?
WELL... SINCE VANITAS IS HERE, IT'S ONLY NATURAL... I SUPPOSE ...??
YES.
IT'S BEEN A WHILE SINCE WE LAST MET.
JEANNE, PLEASE.
DON'T KILL THE BEAST JUST YET.
I KNOW YOU KNOW.
BA (BAM)
WITH VANITAS'S POWER, WE MAY BE ABLE TO SAVE THE CURSE-BEARER.

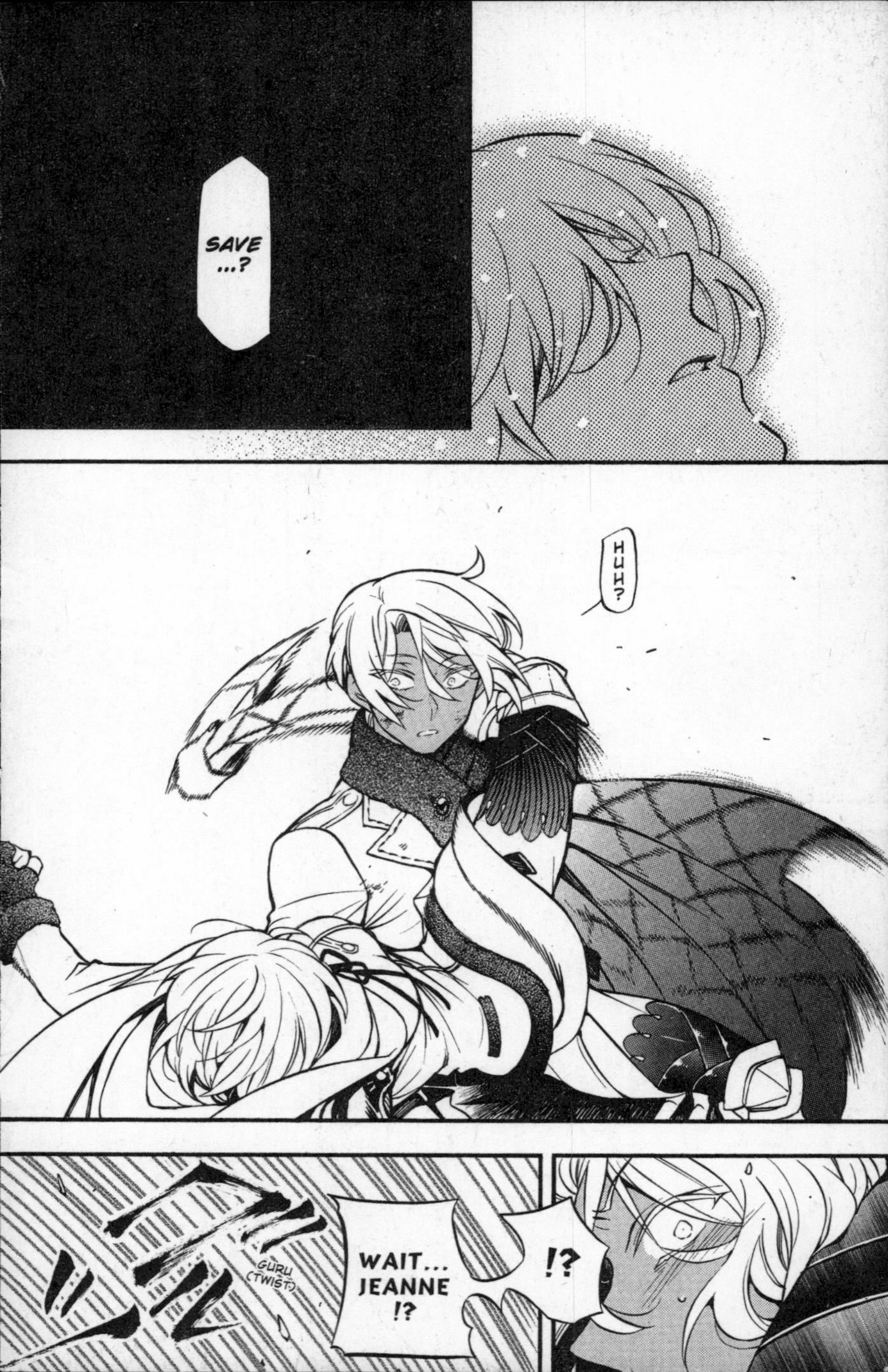
SAVE ...?
HUH?
!?
WAIT... JEANNE !?
GURU (TWIST)

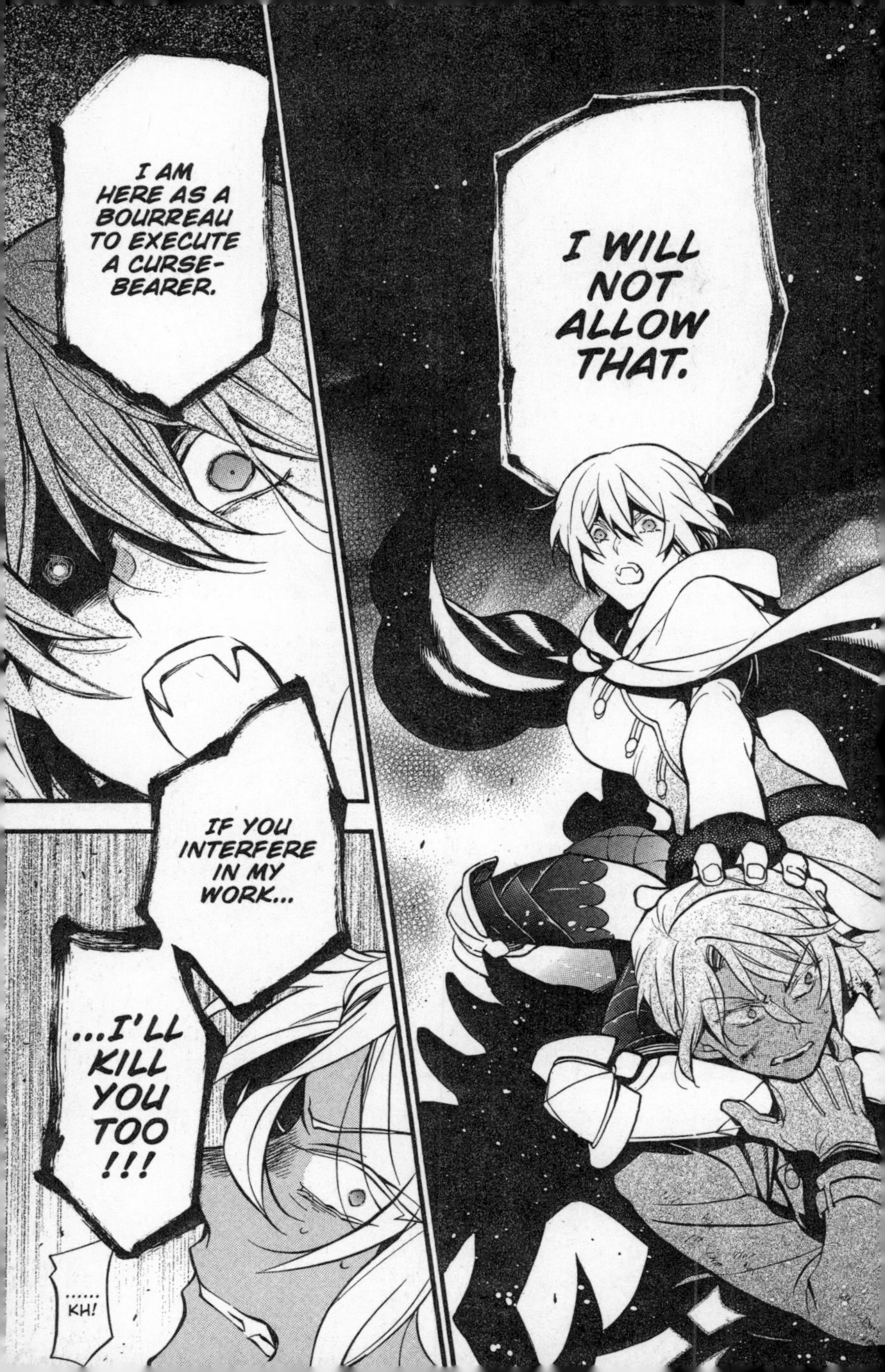
I WILL NOT ALLOW THAT.
I AM HERE AS A BOURREAU TO EXECUTE A CURSE-BEARER.
IF YOU INTERFERE IN MY WORK...
...I'LL KILL YOU TOO!!!
......KH!

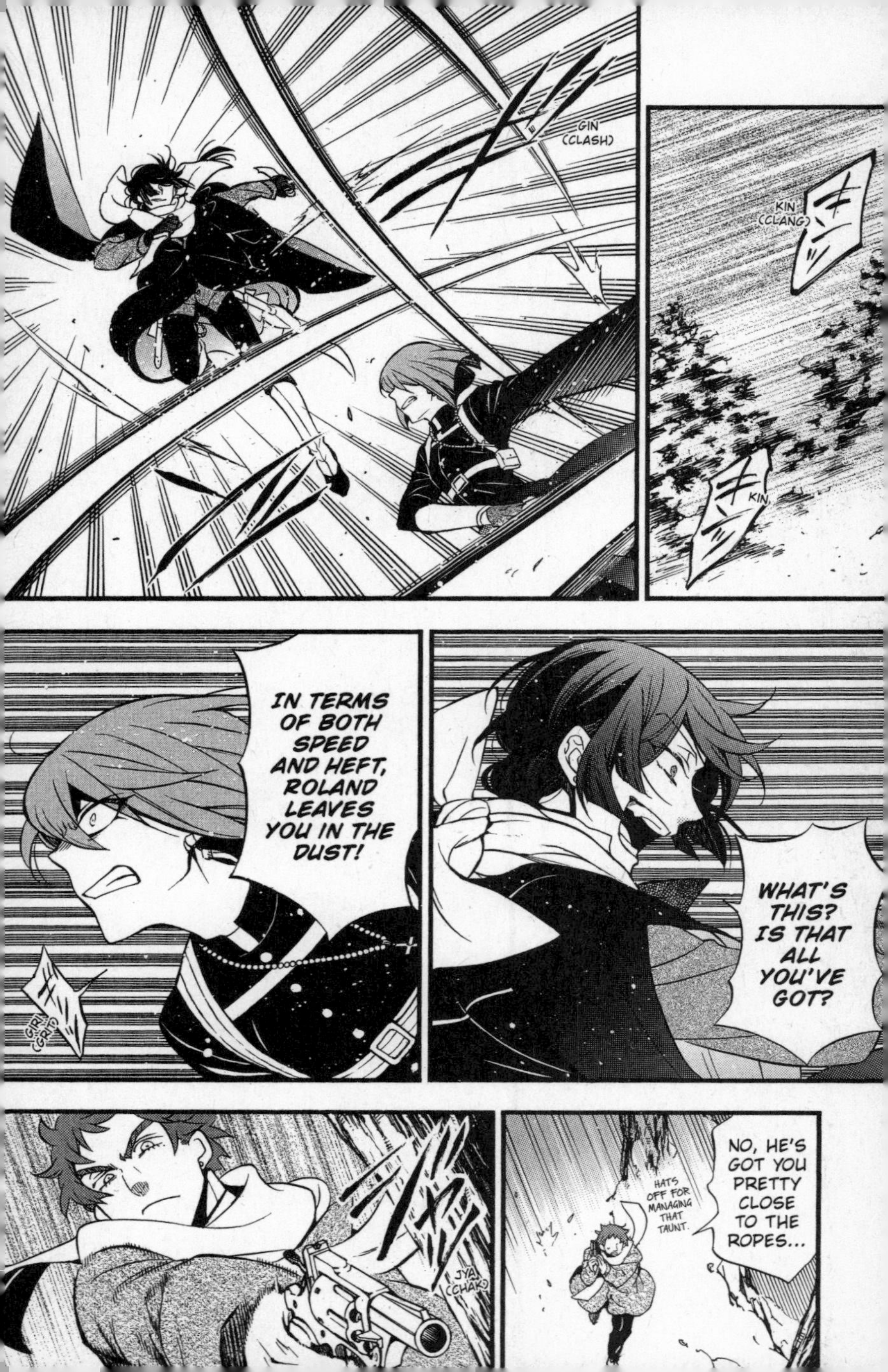
KIN (CLANG)
KIN
GIN (CLASH)
WHAT'S THIS? IS THAT ALL YOU'VE GOT?
IN TERMS OF BOTH SPEED AND HEFT, ROLAND LEAVES YOU IN THE DUST!
GIRI (GRIT)
NO, HE'S GOT YOU PRETTY CLOSE TO THE ROPES...
HATS OFF FOR MANAGING THAT TAUNT.
JYA (CHAK)

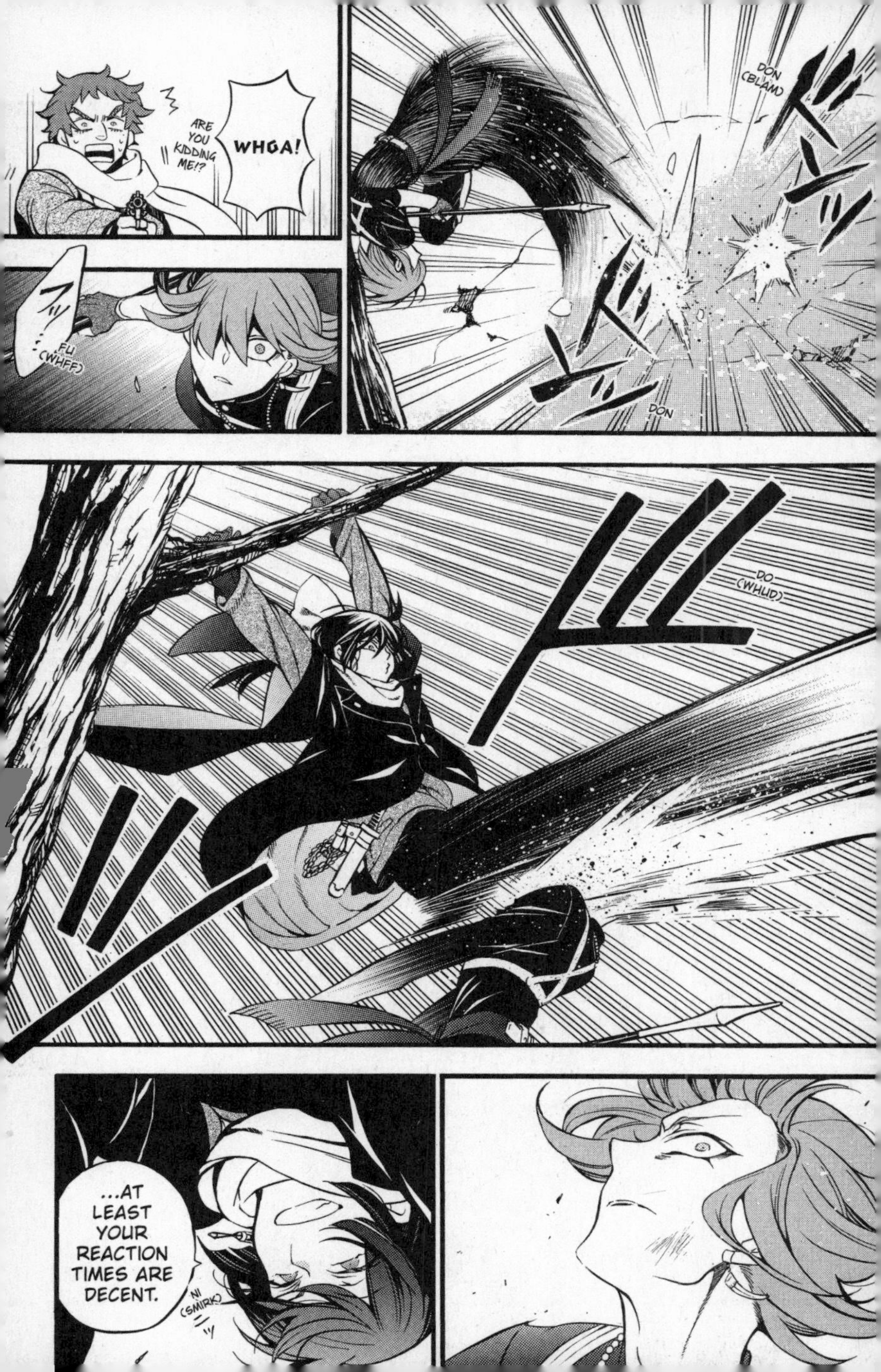
DON (BLAM)
DON
WHGA!
ARE YOU KIDDING ME!?
FU (WHFF)
DO (WHUD)
...AT LEAST YOUR REACTION TIMES ARE DECENT.
NI (SMIRK)

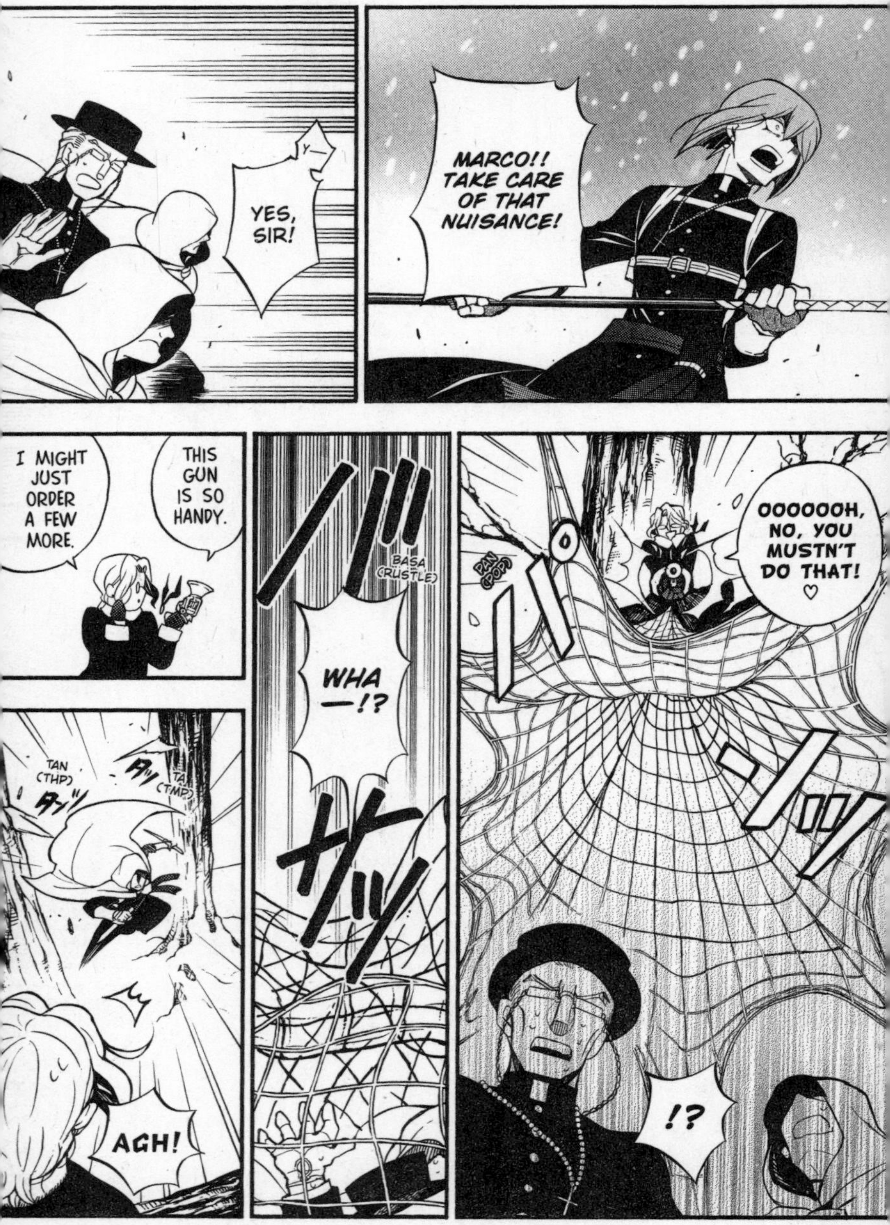

MARCO!! TAKE CARE OF THAT NUISANCE!
Y—
YES, SIR!
PAN (POP)
OOOOOOH, NO, YOU MUSTN'T DO THAT! ♡
!?
BASA (RUSTLE)
WHA—!?
THIS GUN IS SO HANDY.
I MIGHT JUST ORDER A FEW MORE.
TAN (THP)
TA (TMP)
AGH!

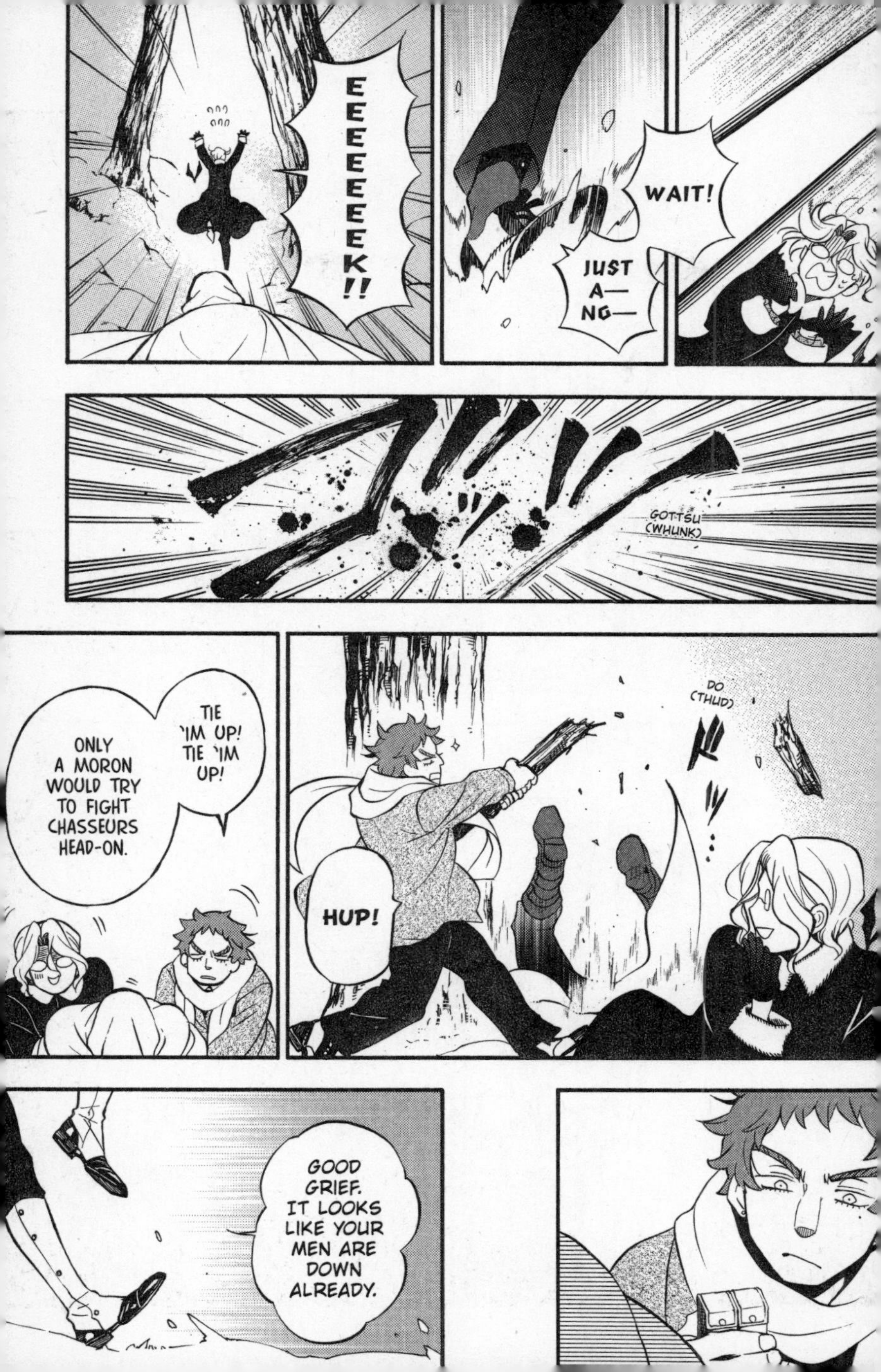
WAIT!
JUST A— NG—
EEEEEEEK!!
GOTTSU (WHUNK)
DO (THUD)
HUP!
TIE 'IM UP! TIE 'IM UP!
ONLY A MORON WOULD TRY TO FIGHT CHASSEURS HEAD-ON.
GOOD GRIEF. IT LOOKS LIKE YOUR MEN ARE DOWN ALREADY.

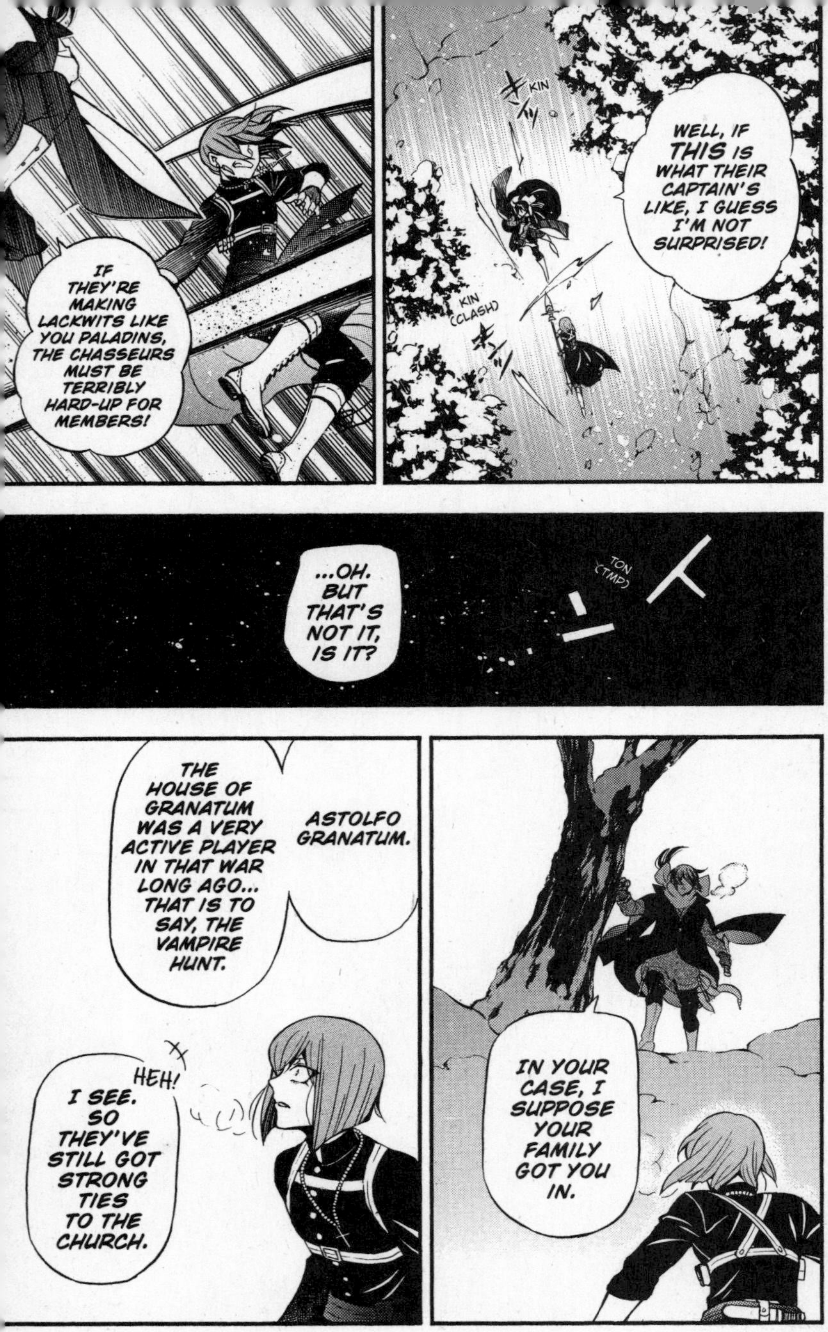
WELL, IF THIS IS WHAT THEIR CAPTAIN'S LIKE, I GUESS I'M NOT SURPRISED!
KIN
KIN (CLASH)
IF THEY'RE MAKING LACKWITS LIKE YOU PALADINS, THE CHASSEURS MUST BE TERRIBLY HARD-UP FOR MEMBERS!
TON (TMP)
...OH. BUT THAT'S NOT IT, IS IT?
IN YOUR CASE, I SUPPOSE YOUR FAMILY GOT YOU IN.
ASTOLFO GRANATUM.
THE HOUSE OF GRANATUM WAS A VERY ACTIVE PLAYER IN THAT WAR LONG AGO... THAT IS TO SAY, THE VAMPIRE HUNT.
HEH!
I SEE. SO THEY'VE STILL GOT STRONG TIES TO THE CHURCH.

LET ME GUESS! YOU BEGGED YOUR FATHER, DIDN'T YOU?

"WAAAAAAH, DADDY! I'VE JUST GOT TO BE A PALADIN, NO MATTER WHAAAAT! DOOO SOME-THIIIING!"

HA-HA-HA! HOW WAS THAT? A PRETTY GOOD IMITATION, NO!?

WELL, YEAH. DUH.

...

HE'S, ER... SAYING THIS WITH FULL KNOWLEDGE OF THAT BOY'S FAMILY CIR-CUMSTANCES, ISN'T HE?

URGH ...

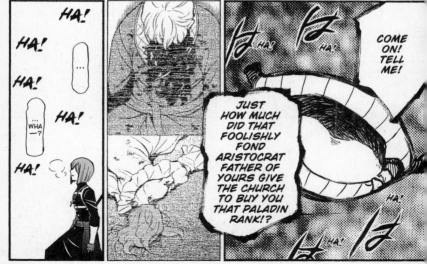

HA!

HA!

HA!

...

HA!

... WHA —?

HA!

HA!

COME ON! TELL ME!

JUST HOW MUCH DID THAT FOOLISHLY FOND ARISTOCRAT FATHER OF YOURS GIVE THE CHURCH TO BUY YOU THAT PALADIN RANK!?

HA!

HA!

HA!

145

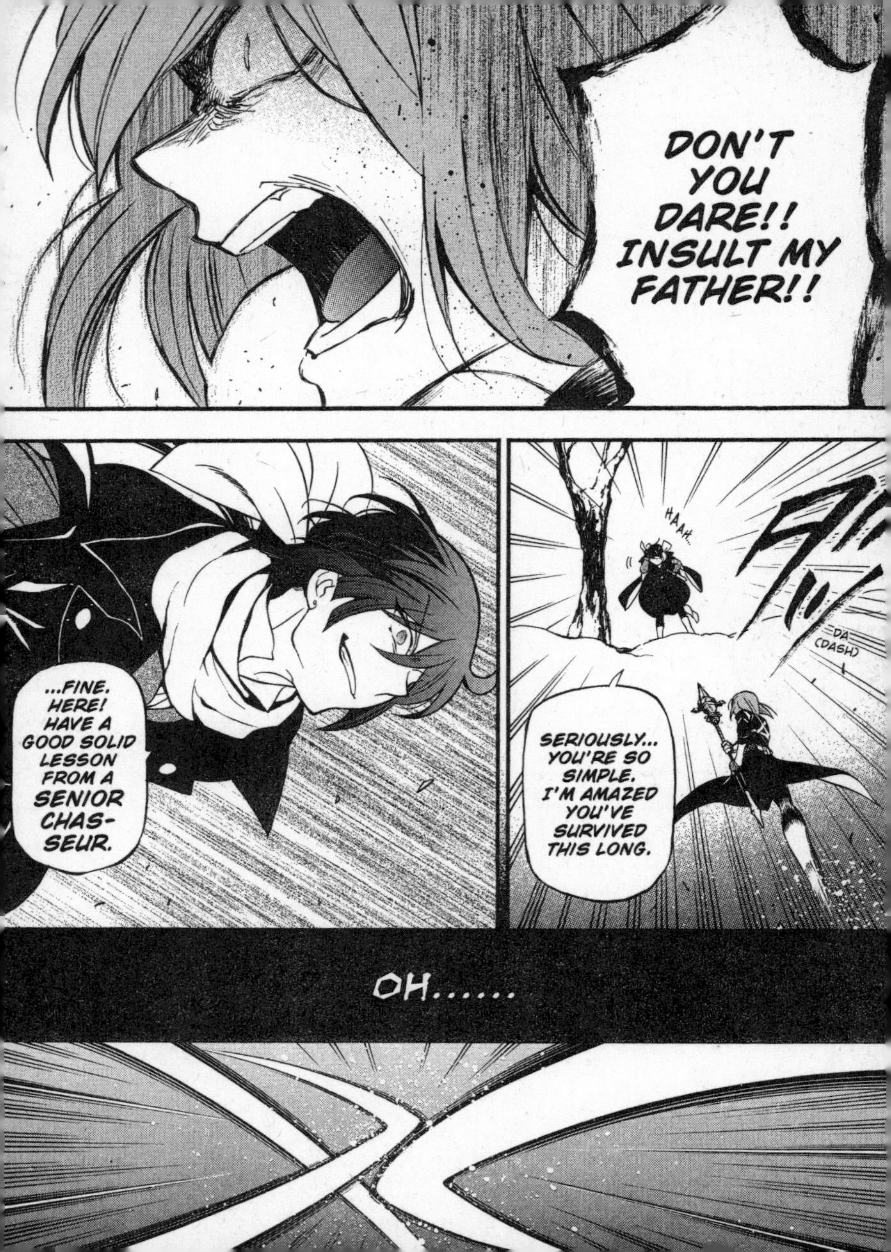
DON'T YOU DARE!! INSULT MY FATHER!!
HAAH..
DA (DASH)
SERIOUSLY... YOU'RE SO SIMPLE. I'M AMAZED YOU'VE SURVIVED THIS LONG.
...FINE. HERE! HAVE A GOOD SOLID LESSON FROM A SENIOR CHASSEUR.
OH......

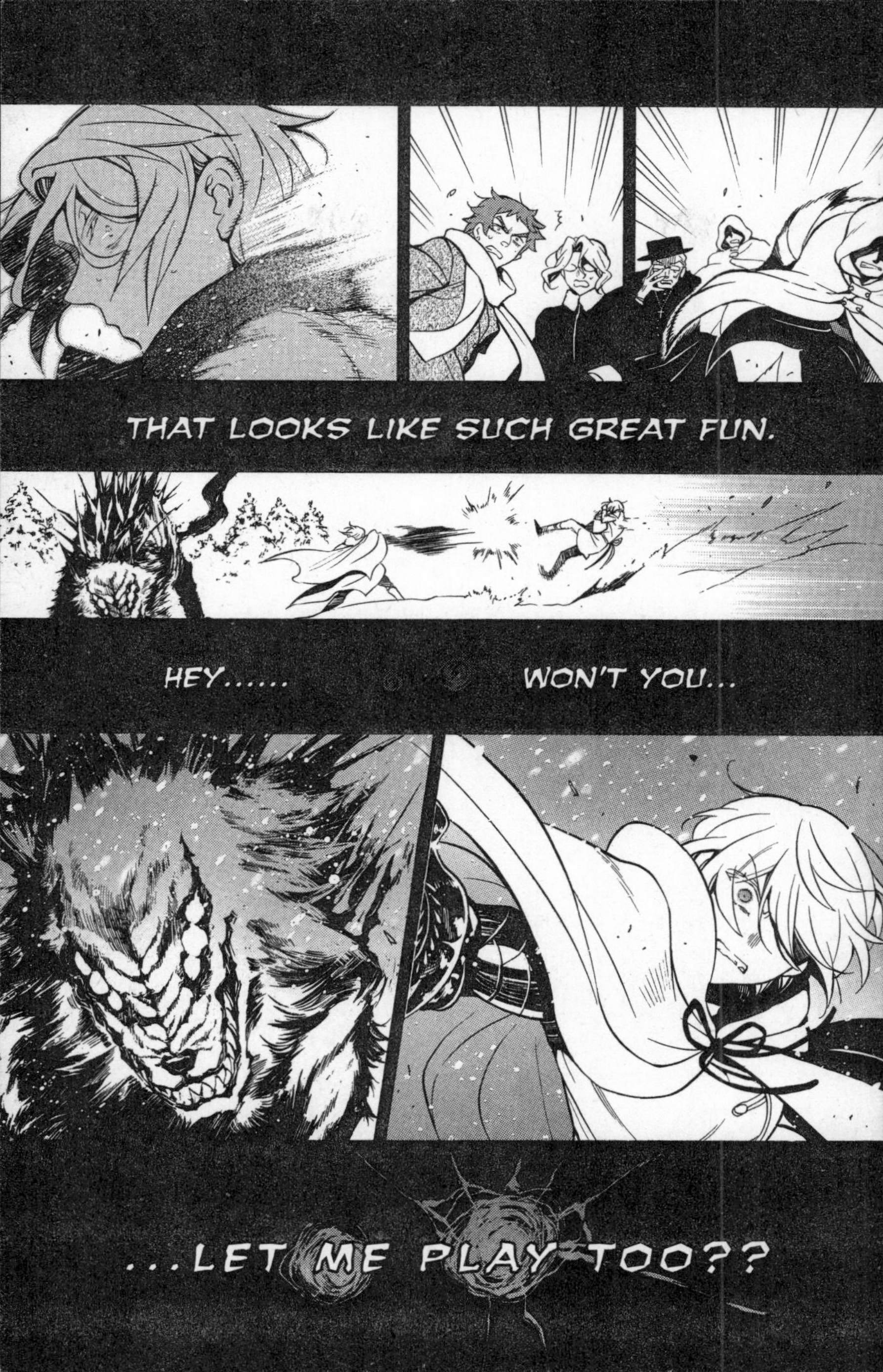
THAT LOOKS LIKE SUCH GREAT FUN.
HEY......
WON'T YOU...
...LET ME PLAY TOO??

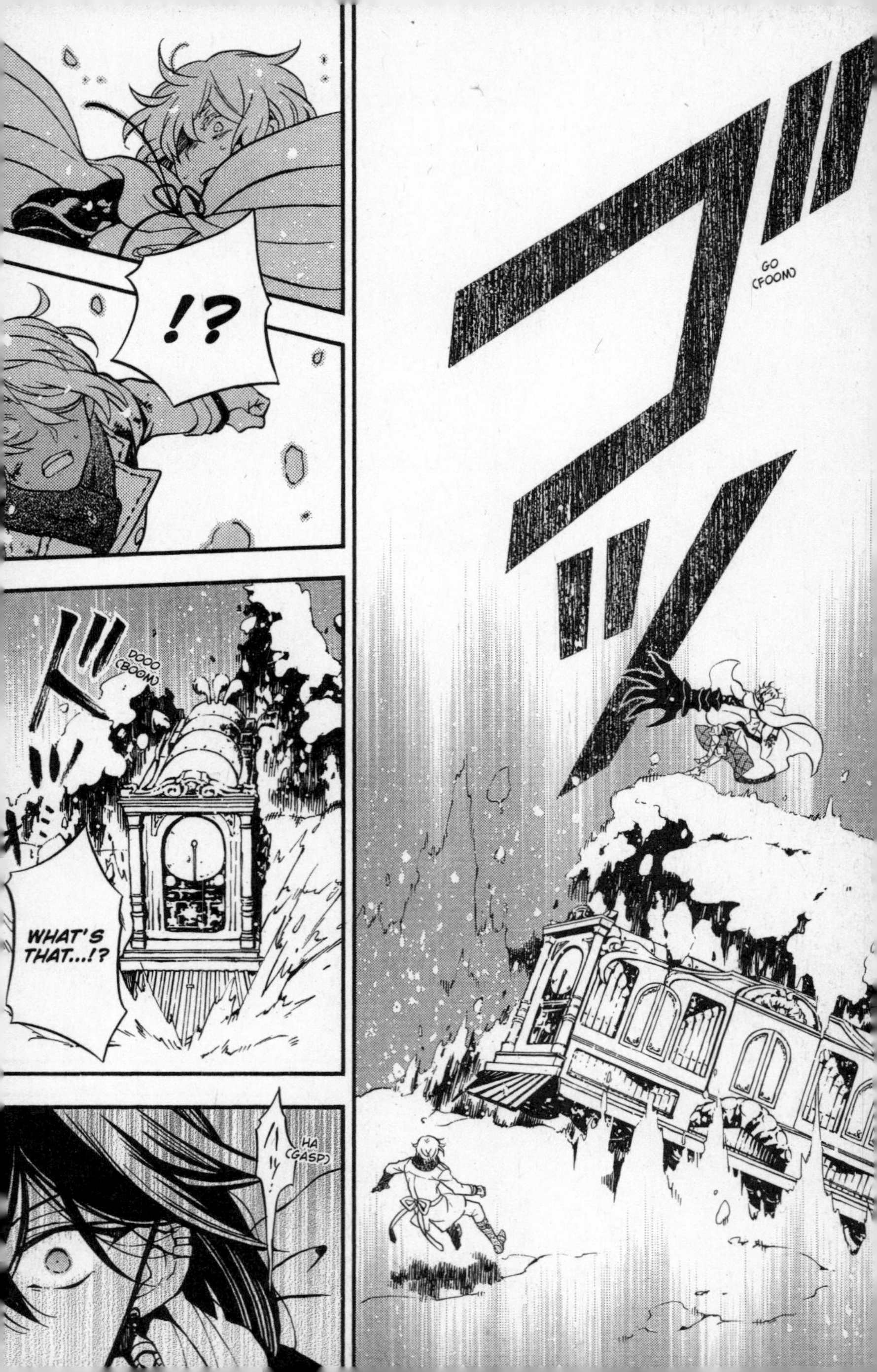
GO
(FOOM)
!?
DOOO
(BOOM)
WHAT'S THAT...!?
HA
(GASP)

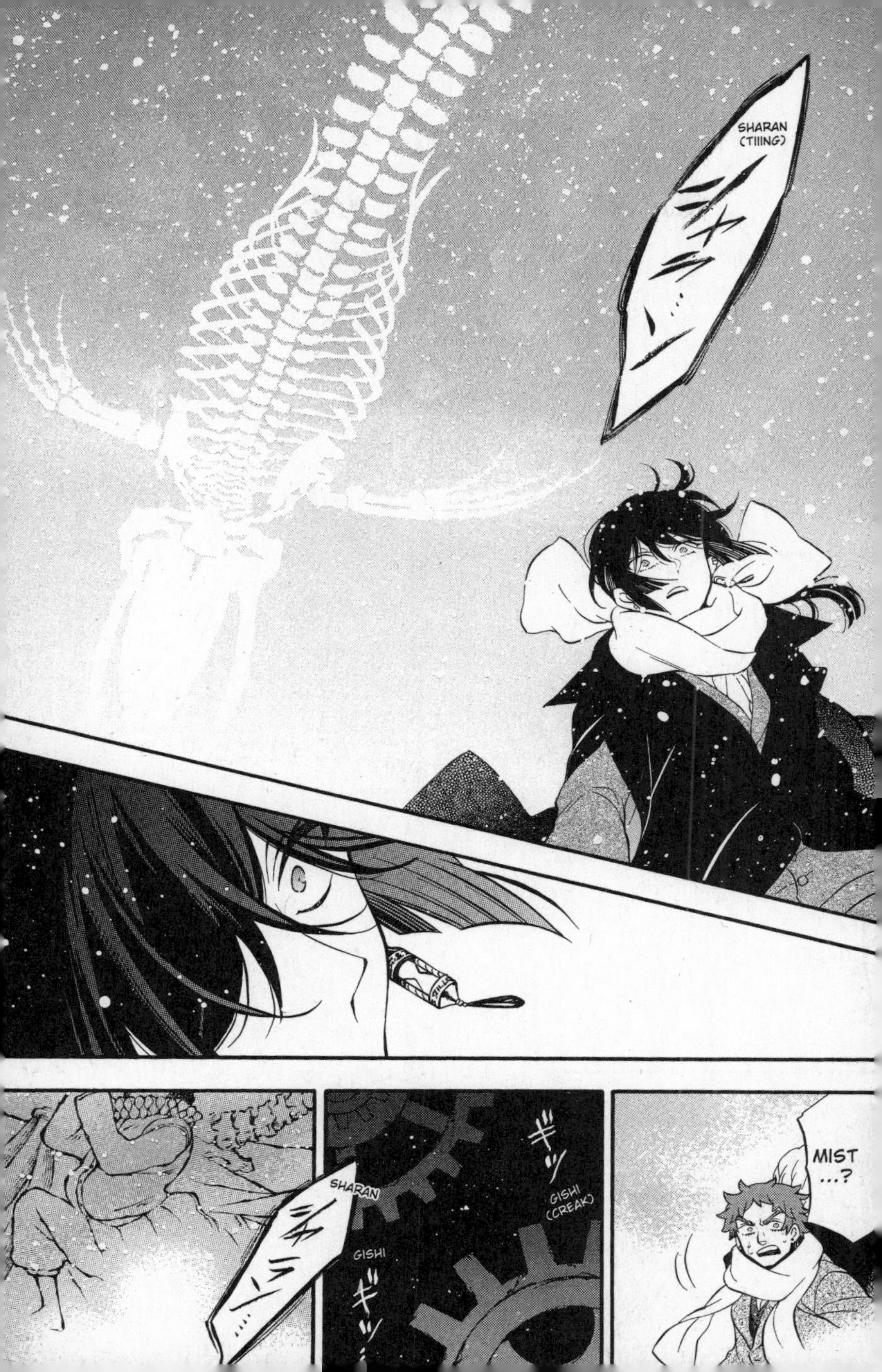
SHARAN (TIIING)
MIST ...?
GISHI (CREAK)
GISHI
SHARAN

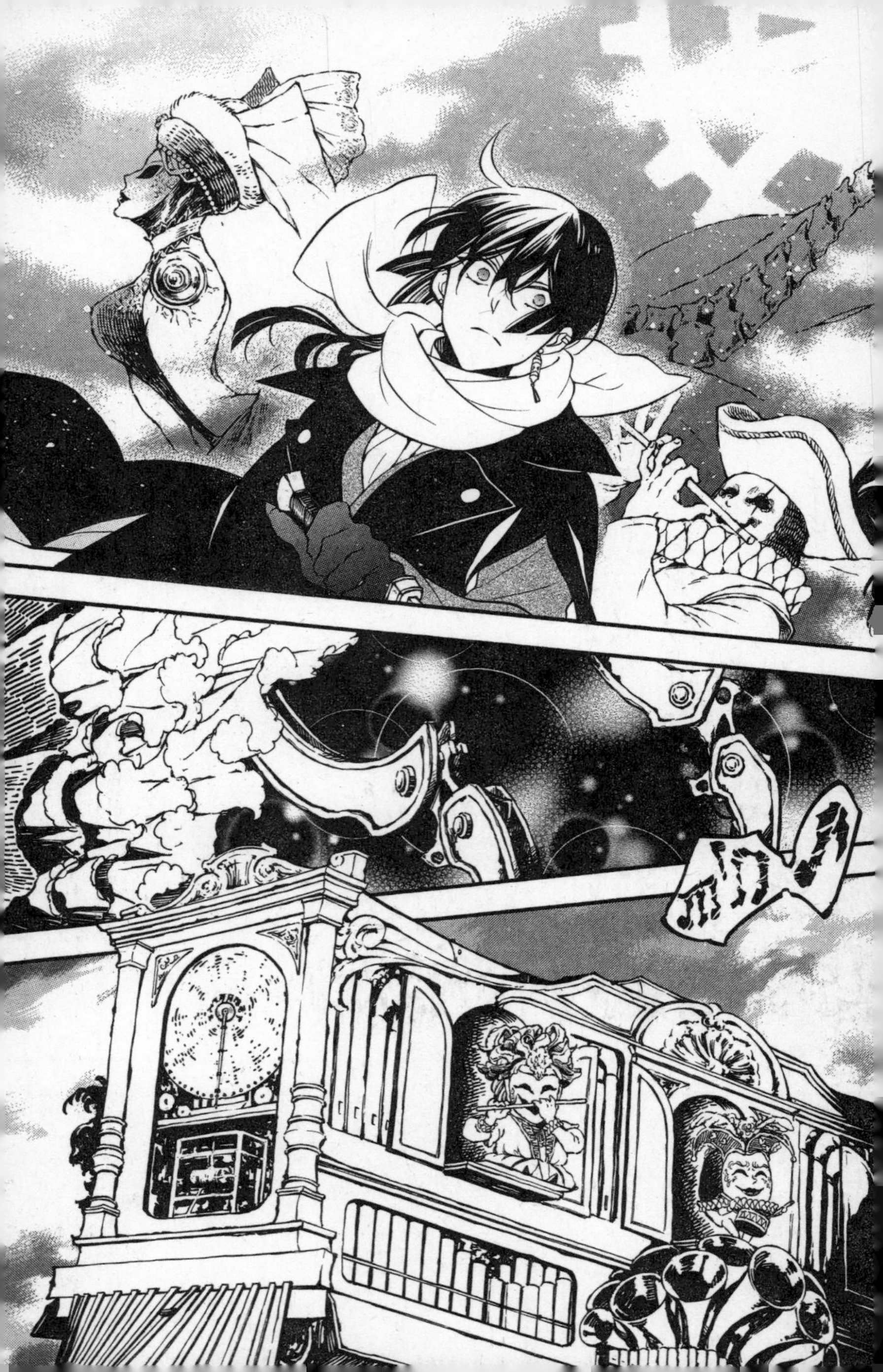

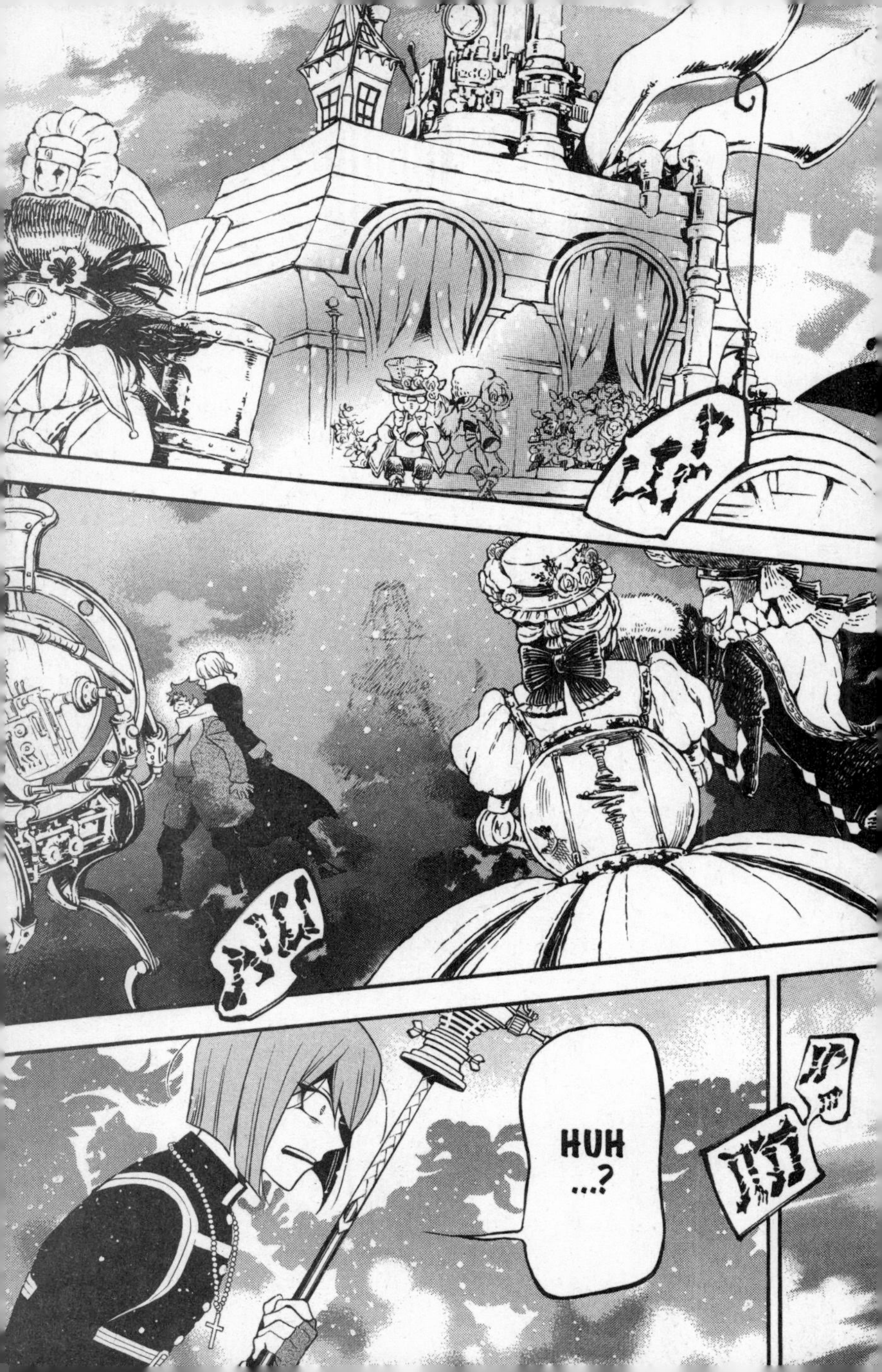
HUH ...?

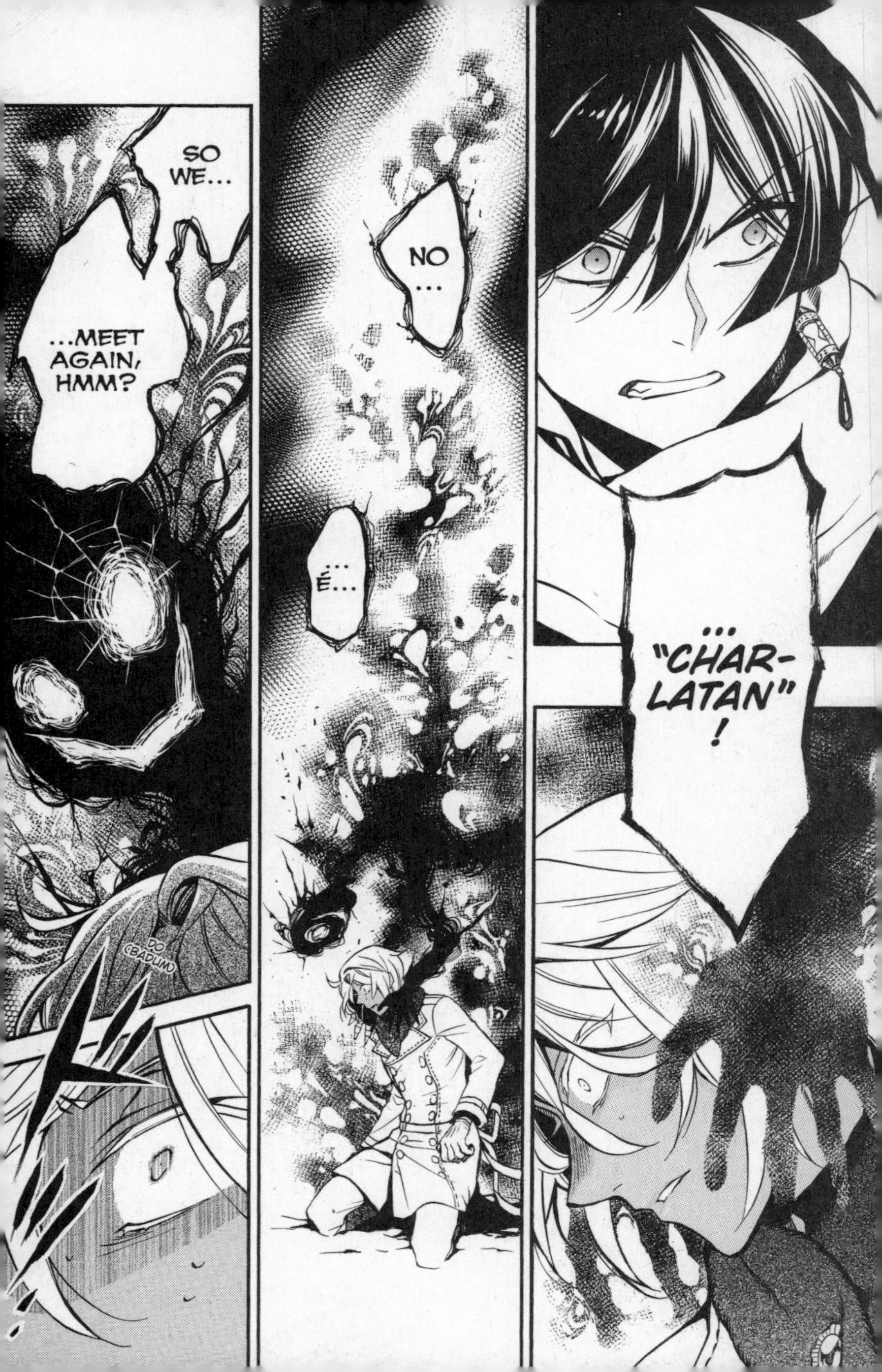
..."CHAR-LATAN"!
NO ...
...É...
SO WE...
...MEET AGAIN, HMM?
DO (BADUM)

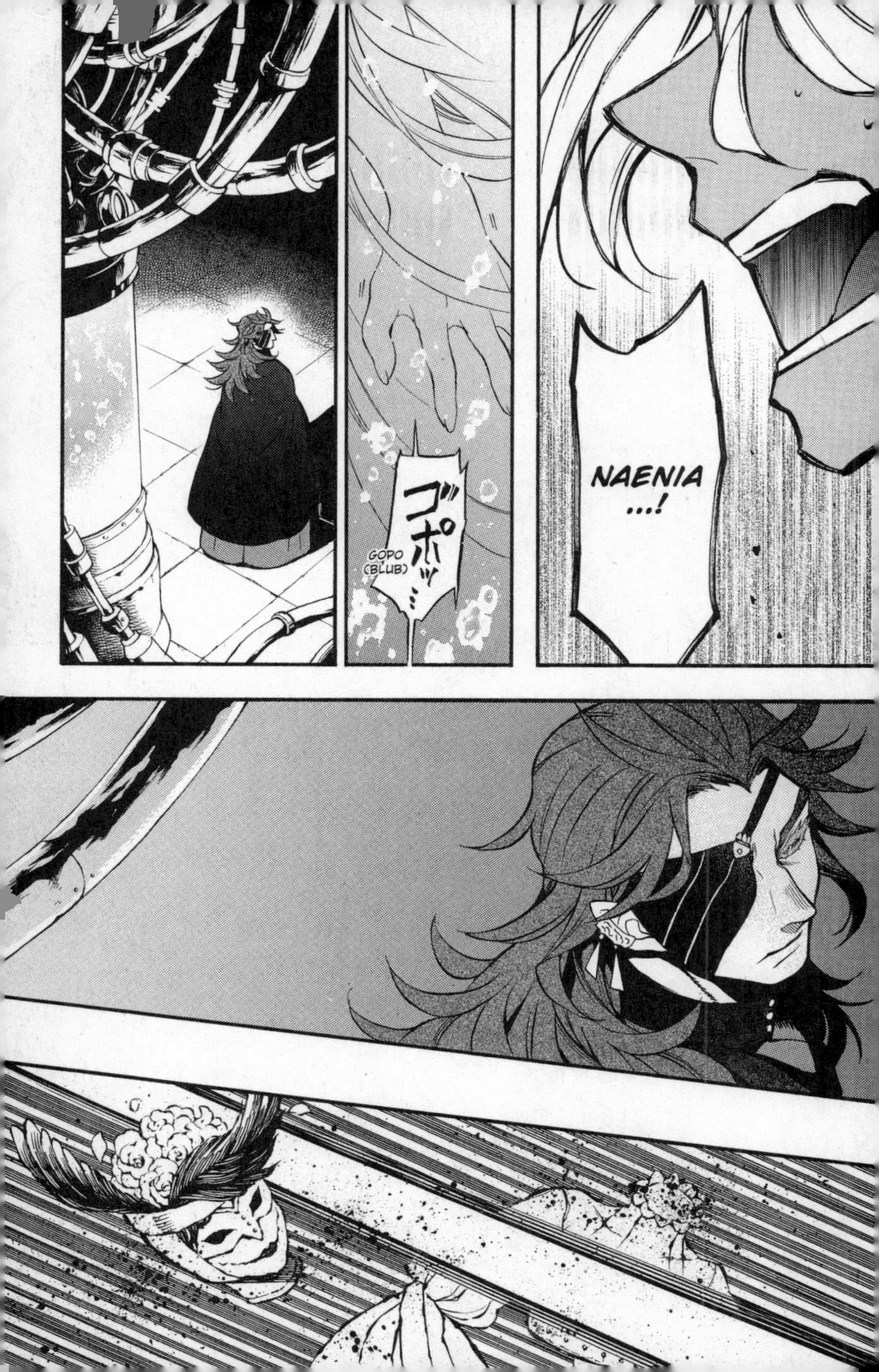
NAENIA
...!
ゴポッ
GOPO
(BLUB)

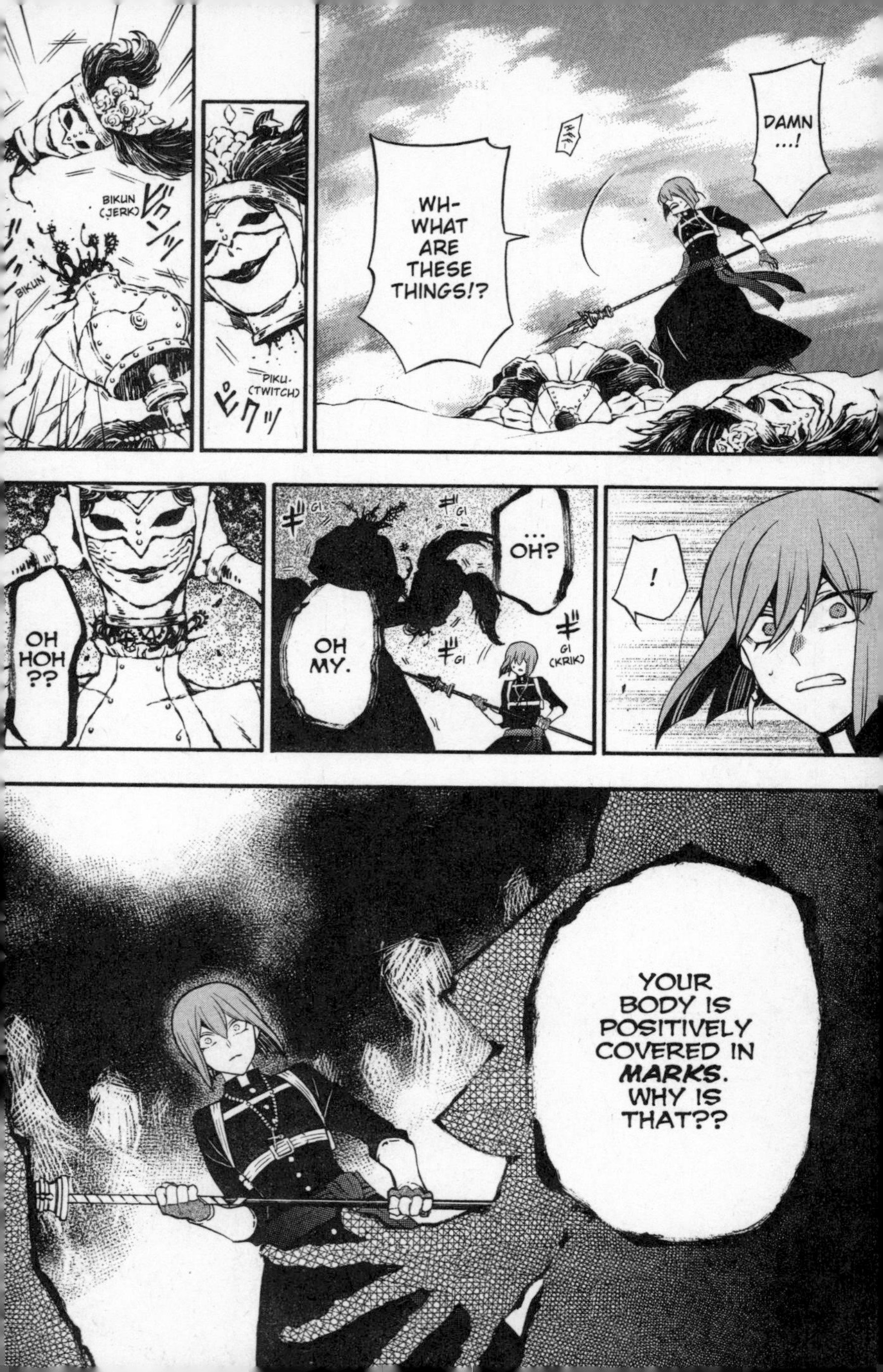
DAMN ...!
WH- WHAT ARE THESE THINGS!?
PIKU (TWITCH)
BIKUN (JERK)
BIKUN
!
... OH?
GI
GI
OH MY.
GI
GI (KRIK)
OH HOH ??
YOUR BODY IS POSITIVELY COVERED IN *MARKS*. WHY IS THAT??

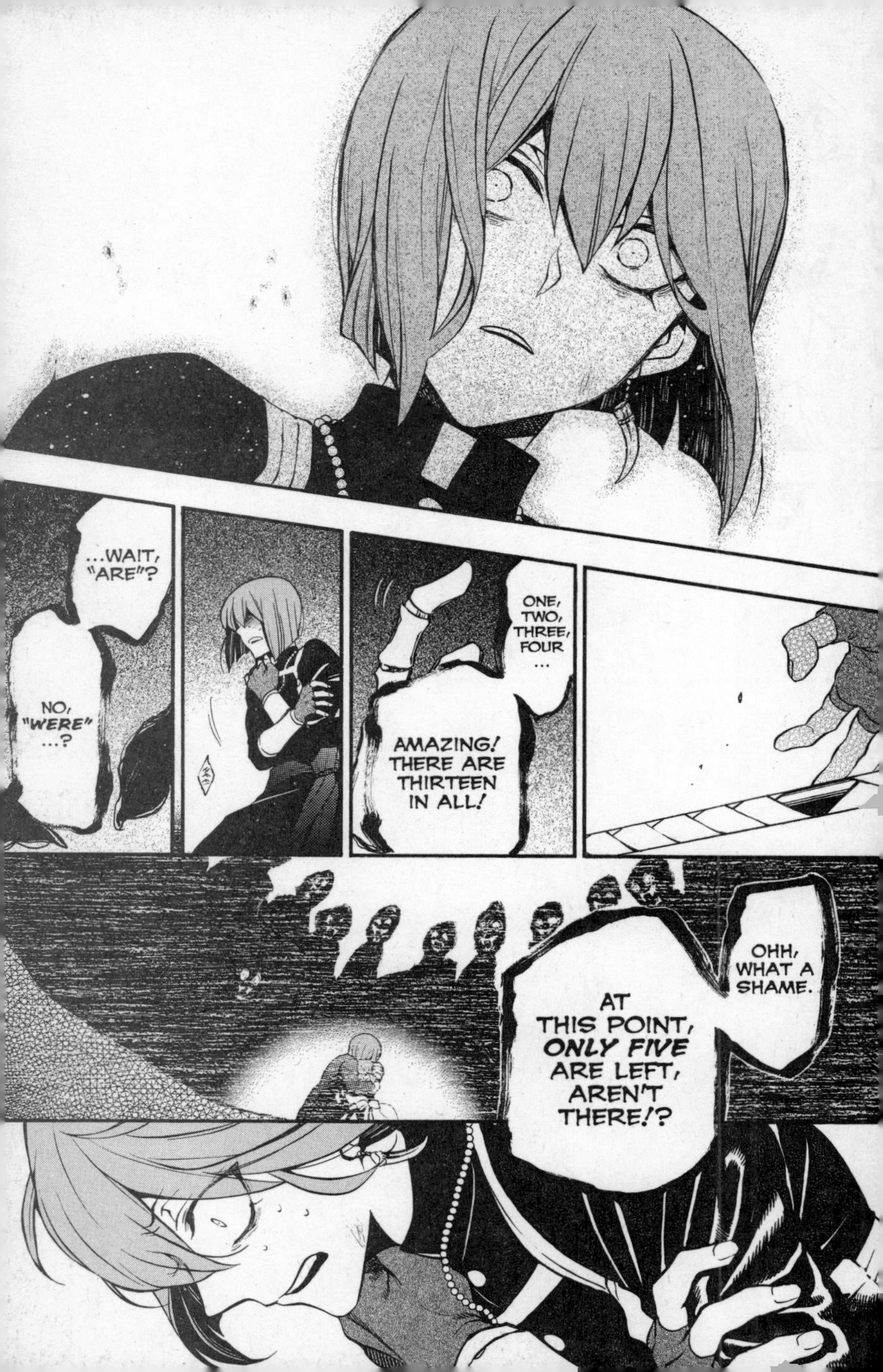
ONE, TWO, THREE, FOUR ...
AMAZING! THERE ARE THIRTEEN IN ALL!
...WAIT, "ARE"?
NO, "WERE" ...?
OHH, WHAT A SHAME.
AT THIS POINT, ONLY FIVE ARE LEFT, AREN'T THERE!?

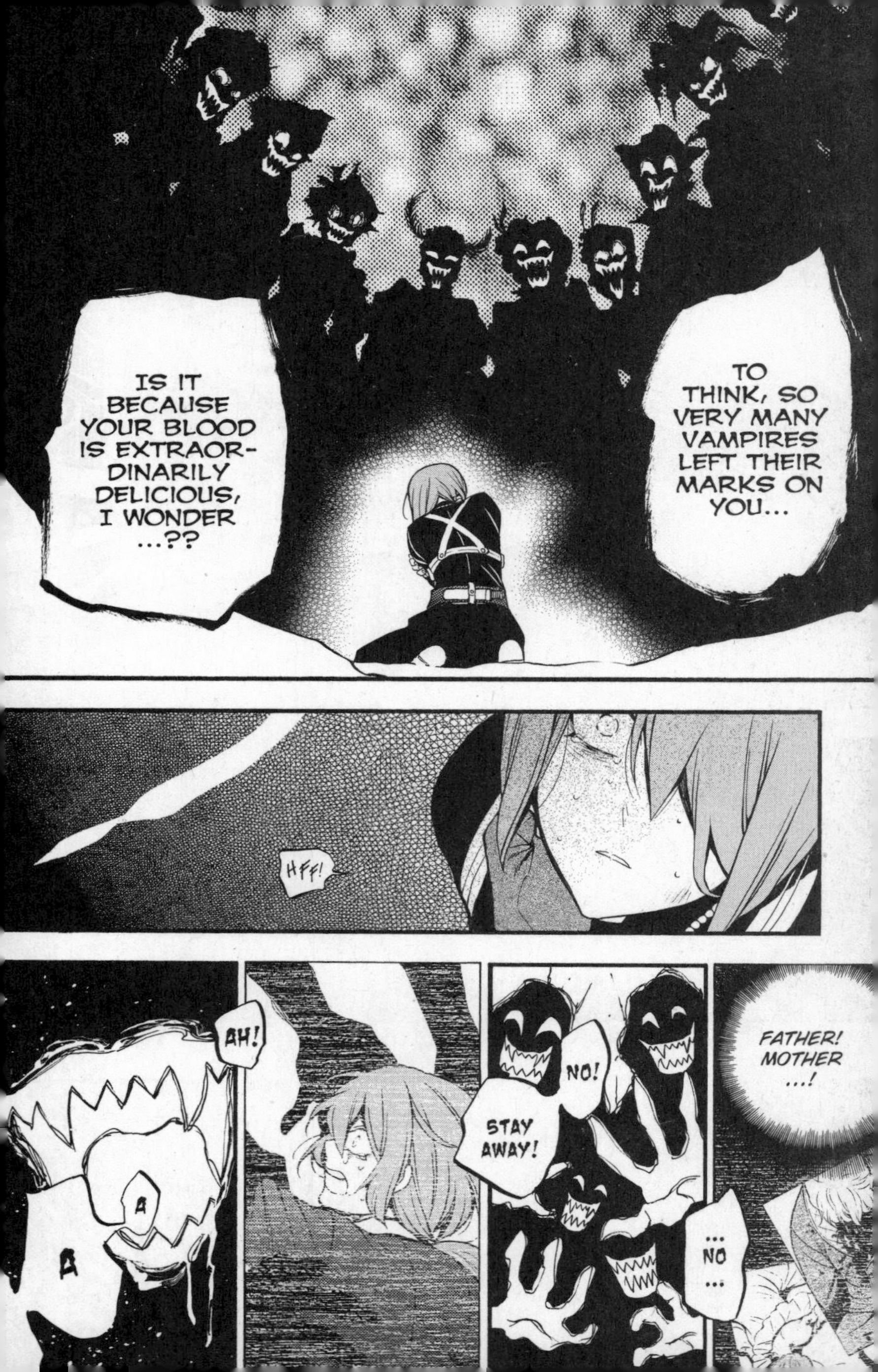
TO THINK, SO VERY MANY VAMPIRES LEFT THEIR MARKS ON YOU...
IS IT BECAUSE YOUR BLOOD IS EXTRAOR-DINARILY DELICIOUS, I WONDER ...??
HFF!
FATHER! MOTHER ...!
NO!
STAY AWAY!
... NO ...
AH!
A
A

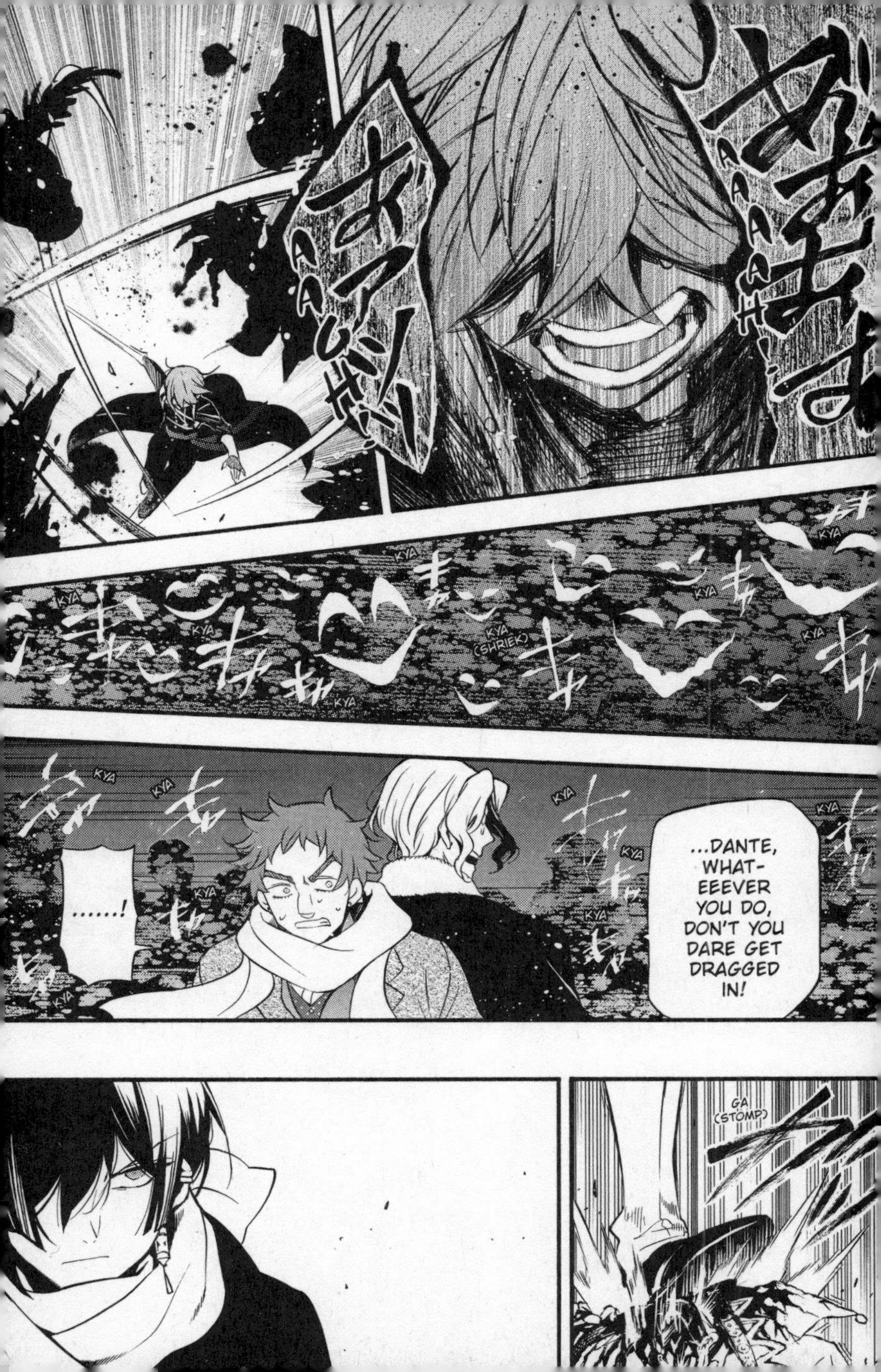
AAAAAH!
AAA
KYA
KYA
KYA
KYA (SHRIEK)
KYA
KYA
KYA
KYA
KYA
KYA
KYA
...DANTE, WHAT-EEEVER YOU DO, DON'T YOU DARE GET DRAGGED IN!
KYA
KYA
KYA
......!
KYA
GA (STOMP)

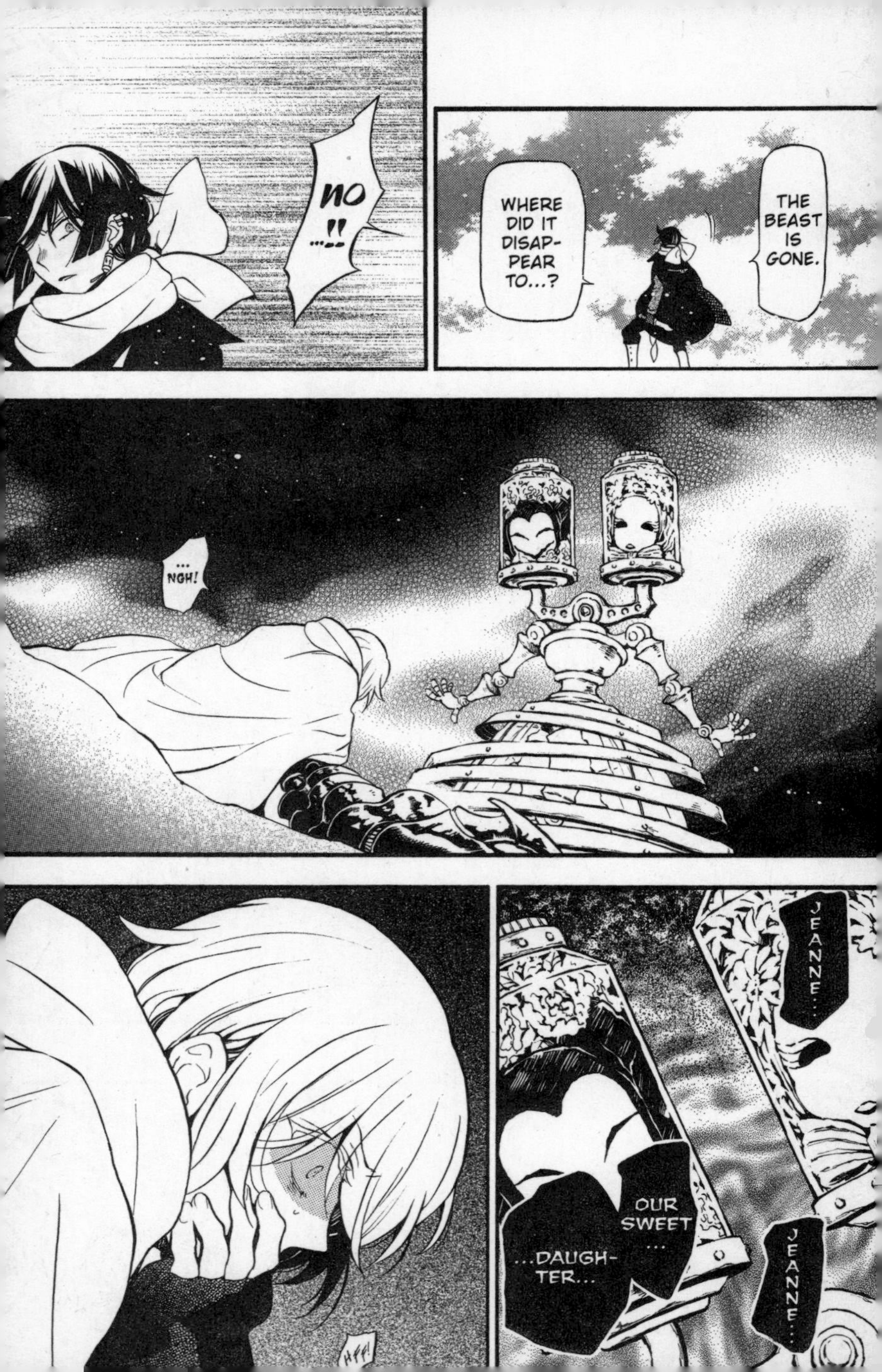
THE BEAST IS GONE.
WHERE DID IT DISAPPEAR TO...?
NO...!!
...NGH!
JEANNE...
OUR SWEET...
JEANNE...
...DAUGHTER...
HFF!

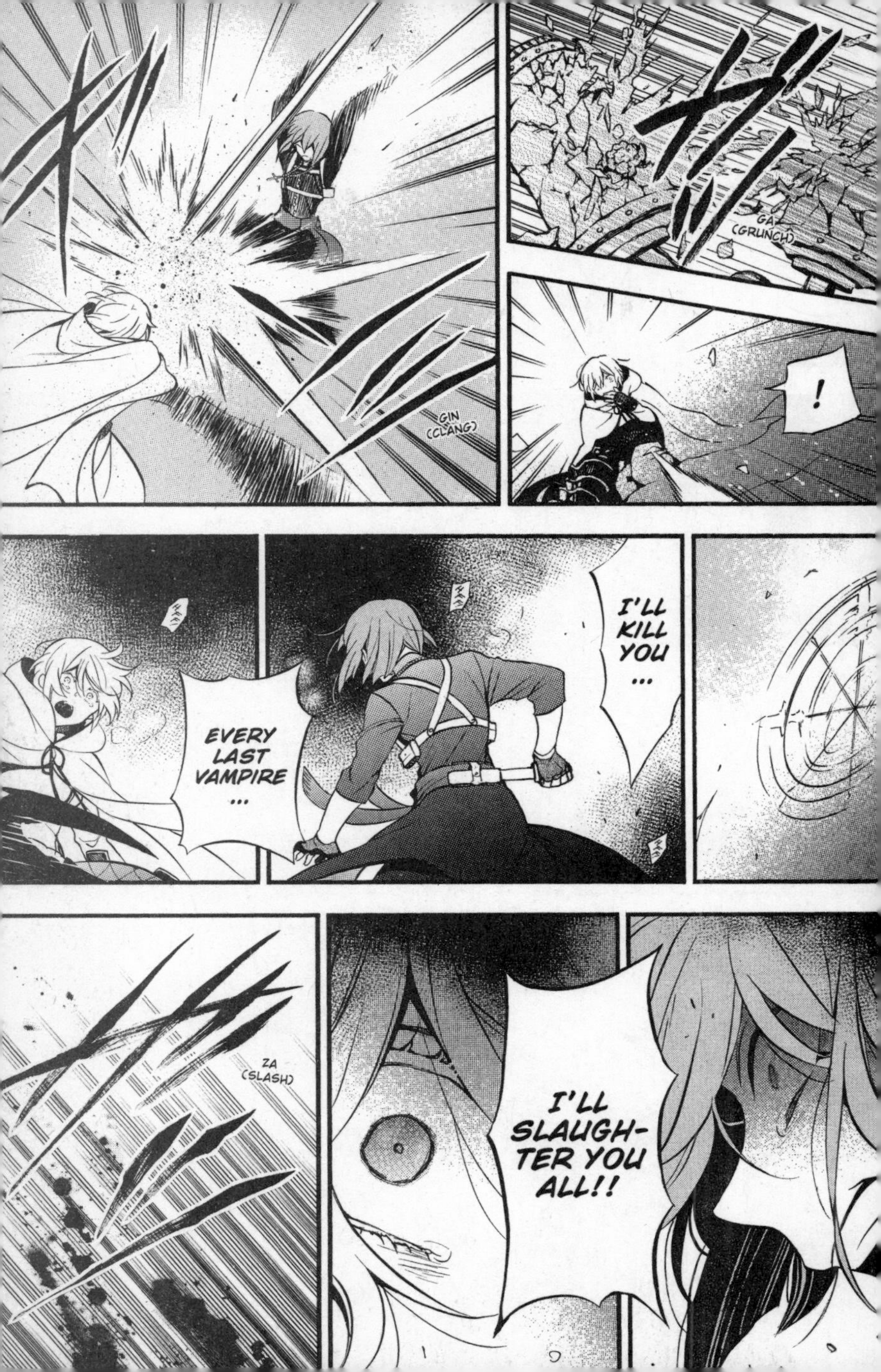
GA (GRUNCH)
!
GIN (CLANG)
I'LL KILL YOU ...
EVERY LAST VAMPIRE ...
I'LL SLAUGH-TER YOU ALL!!
ZA (SLASH)

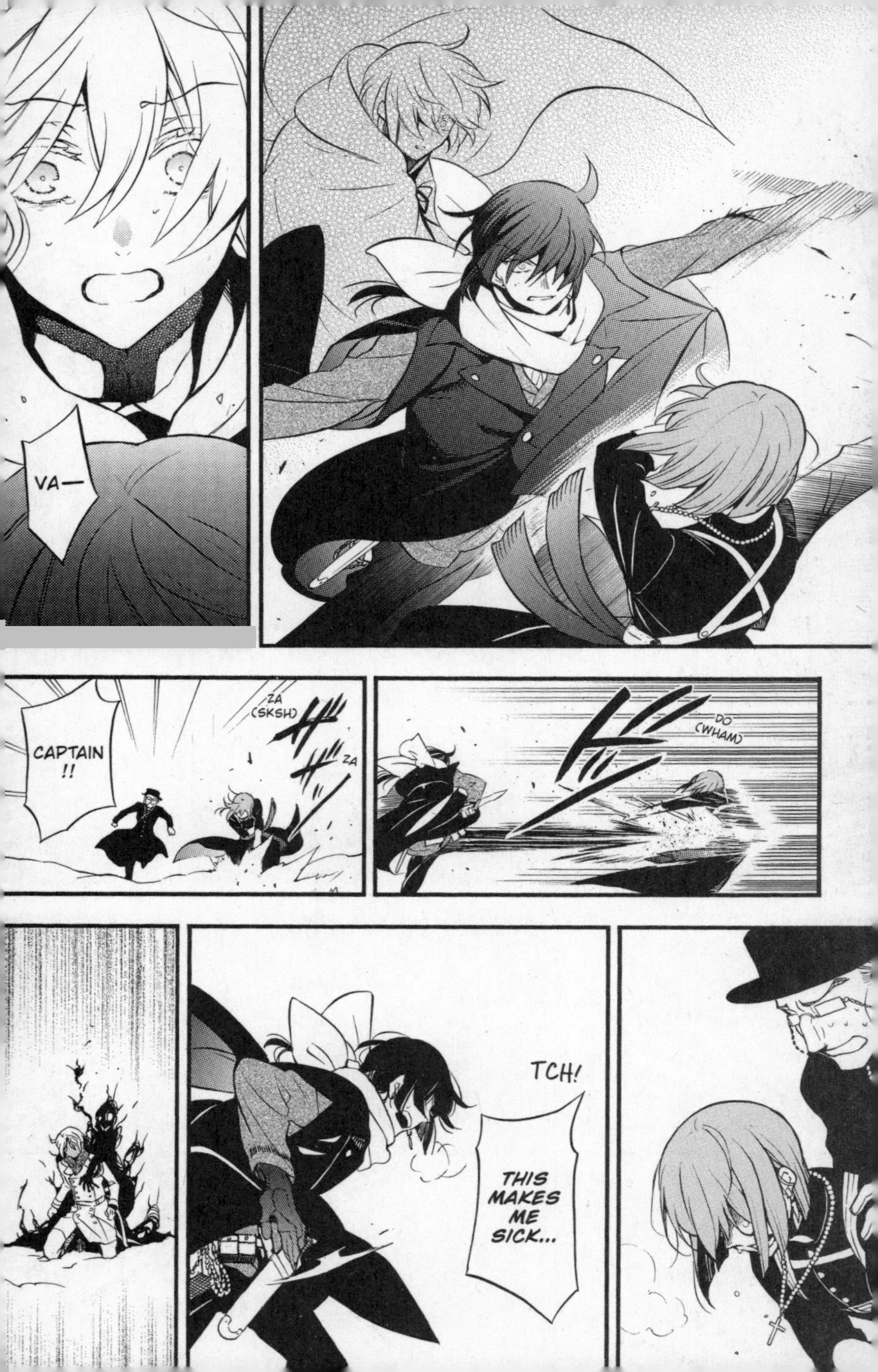

VA—
DO (WHAM)
ZA (SKSH)
ZA
CAPTAIN !!
TCH!
THIS MAKES ME SICK...

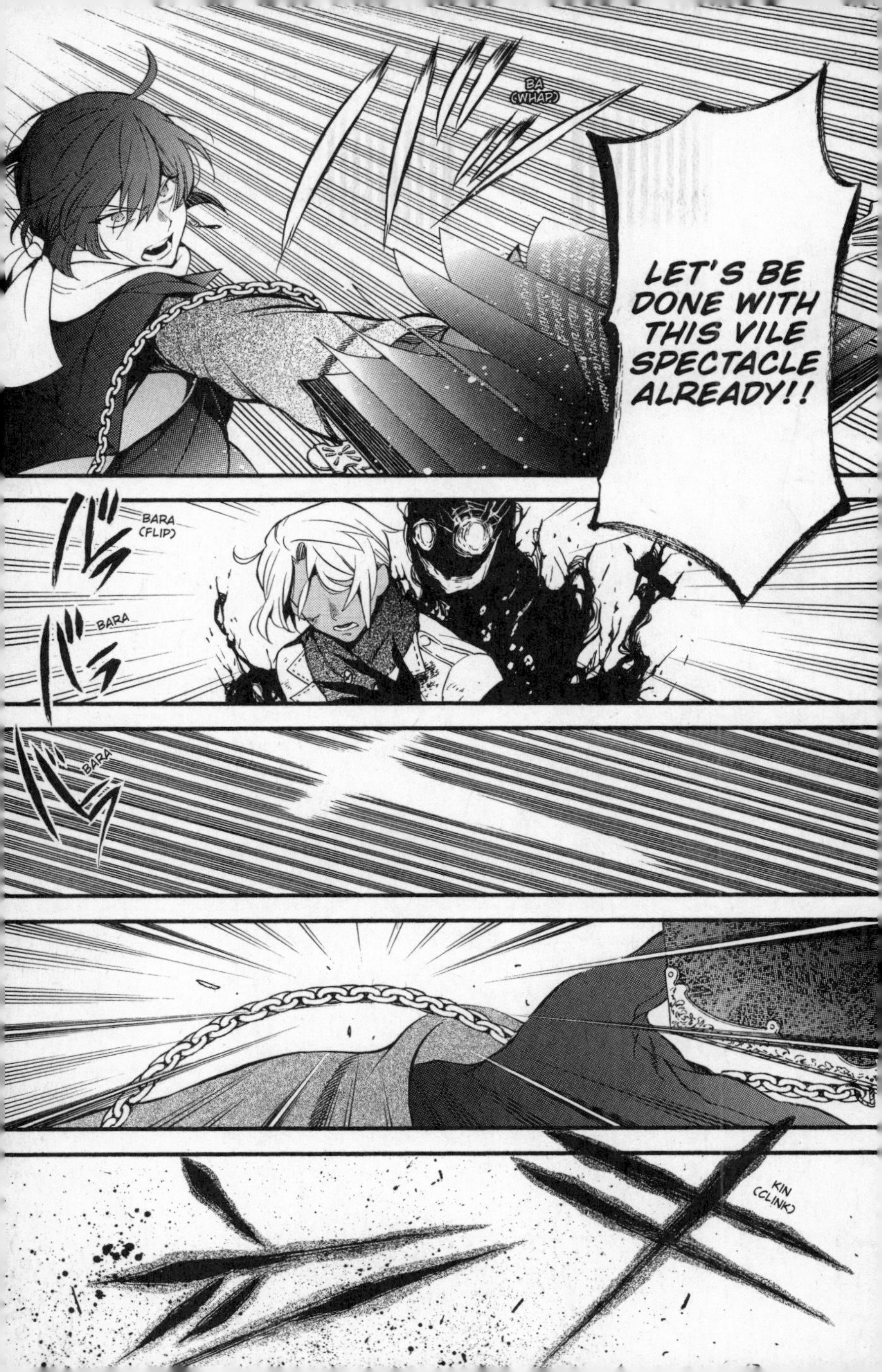
BA (WHAP)
LET'S BE DONE WITH THIS VILE SPECTACLE ALREADY!!
BARA (FLIP)
BARA
BARA
KIN (CLINK)

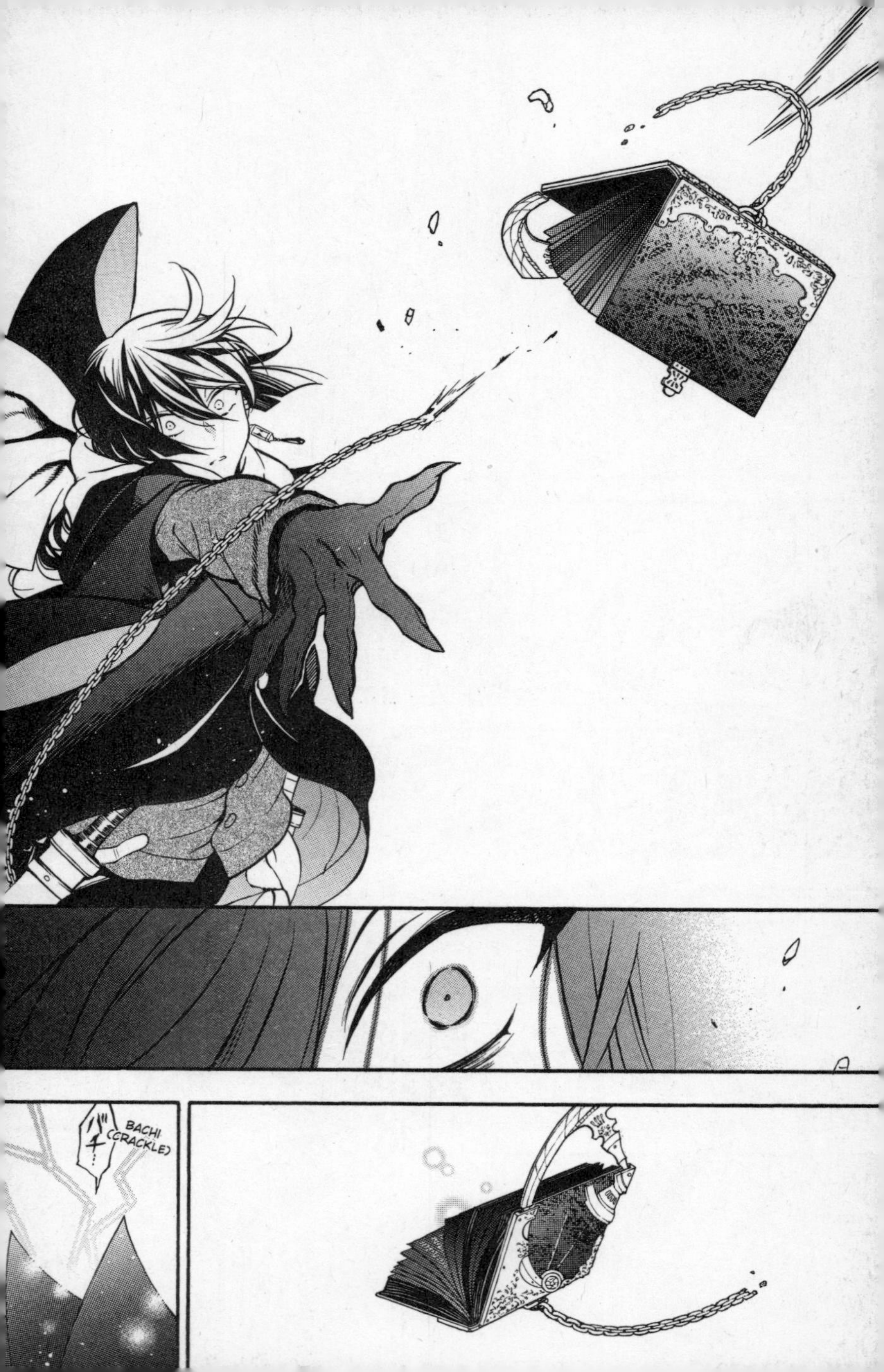
バチ
BACHI (CRACKLE)

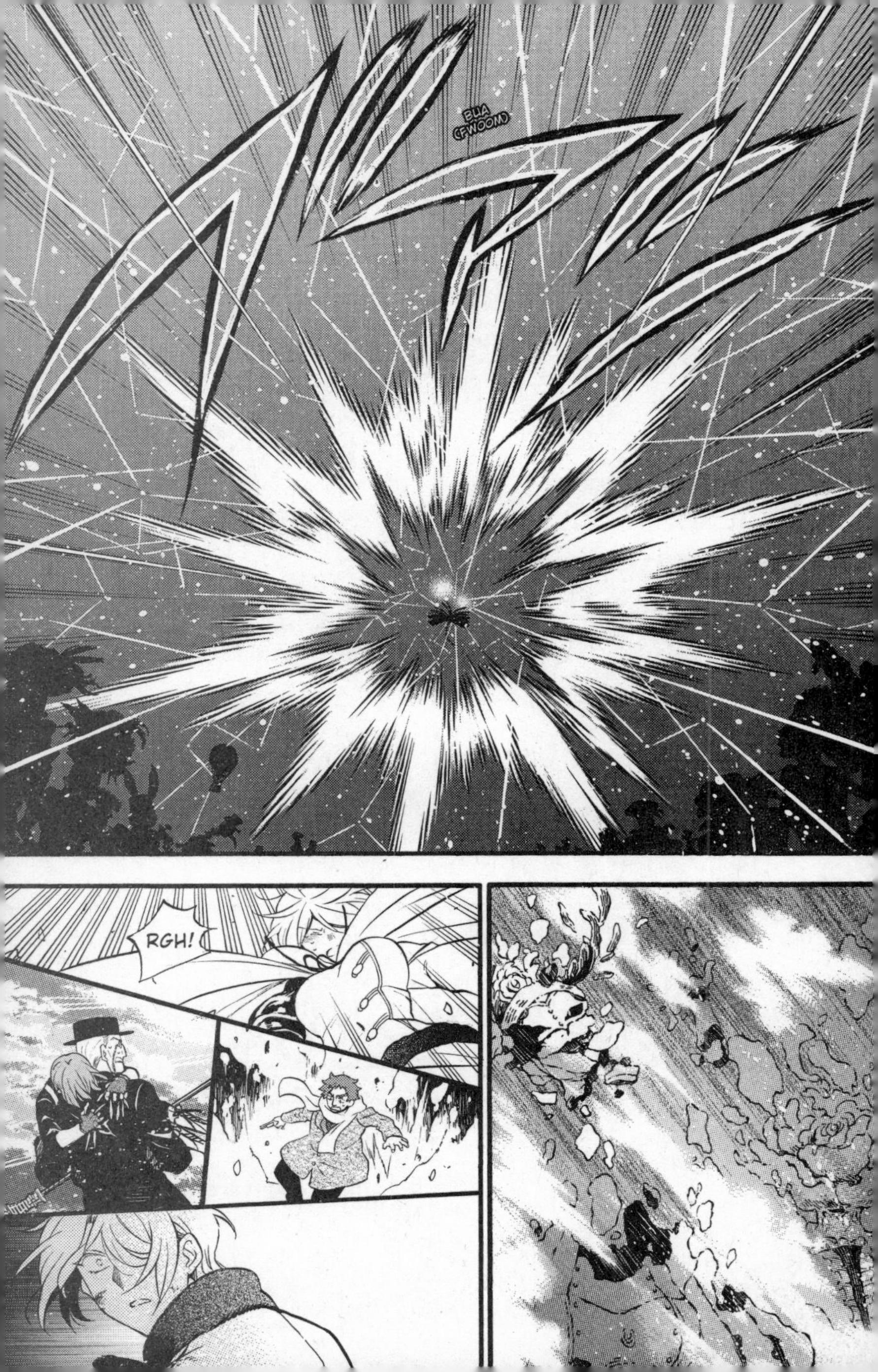
BUA
(FWOOM)
RGH!

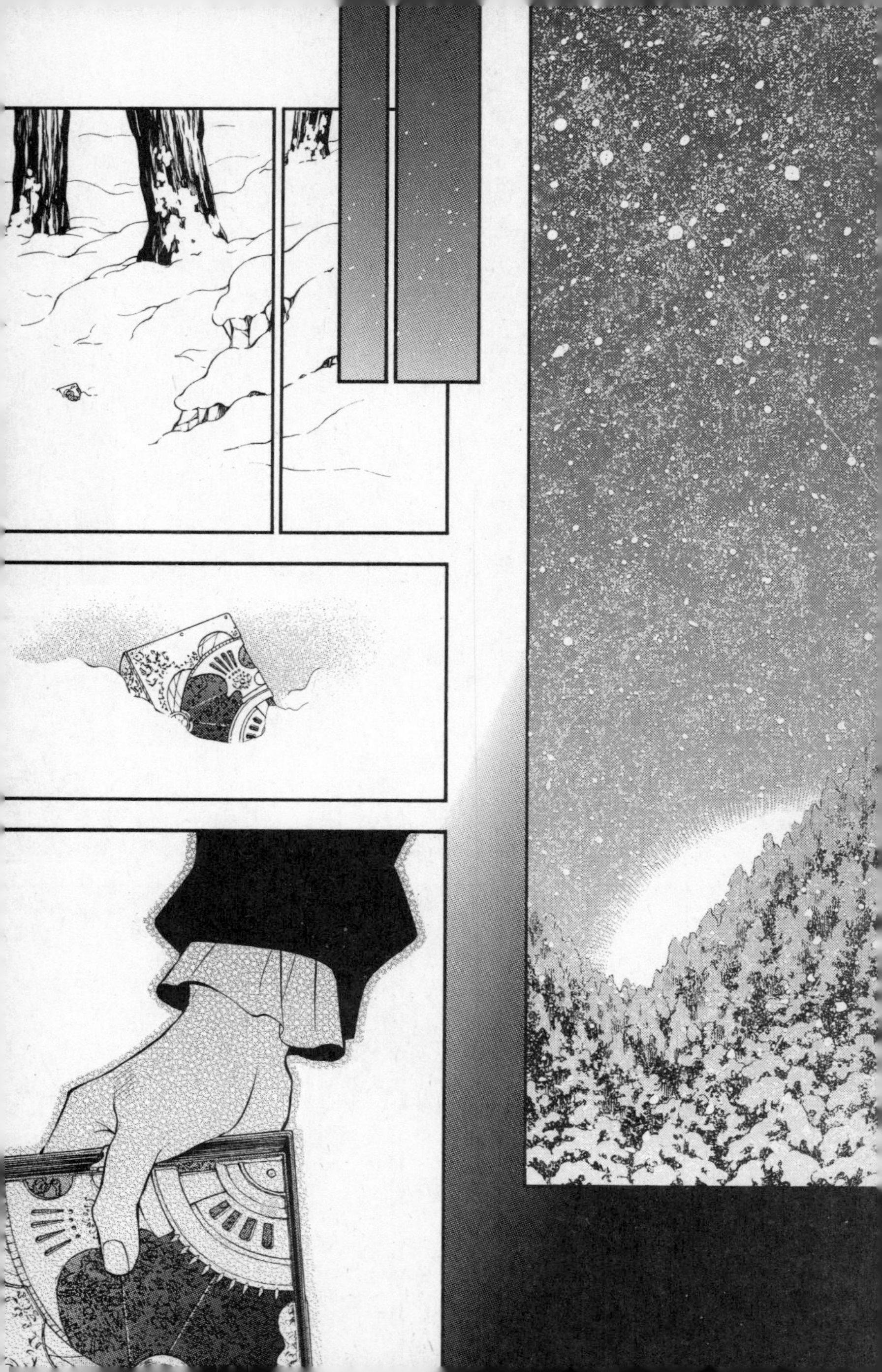

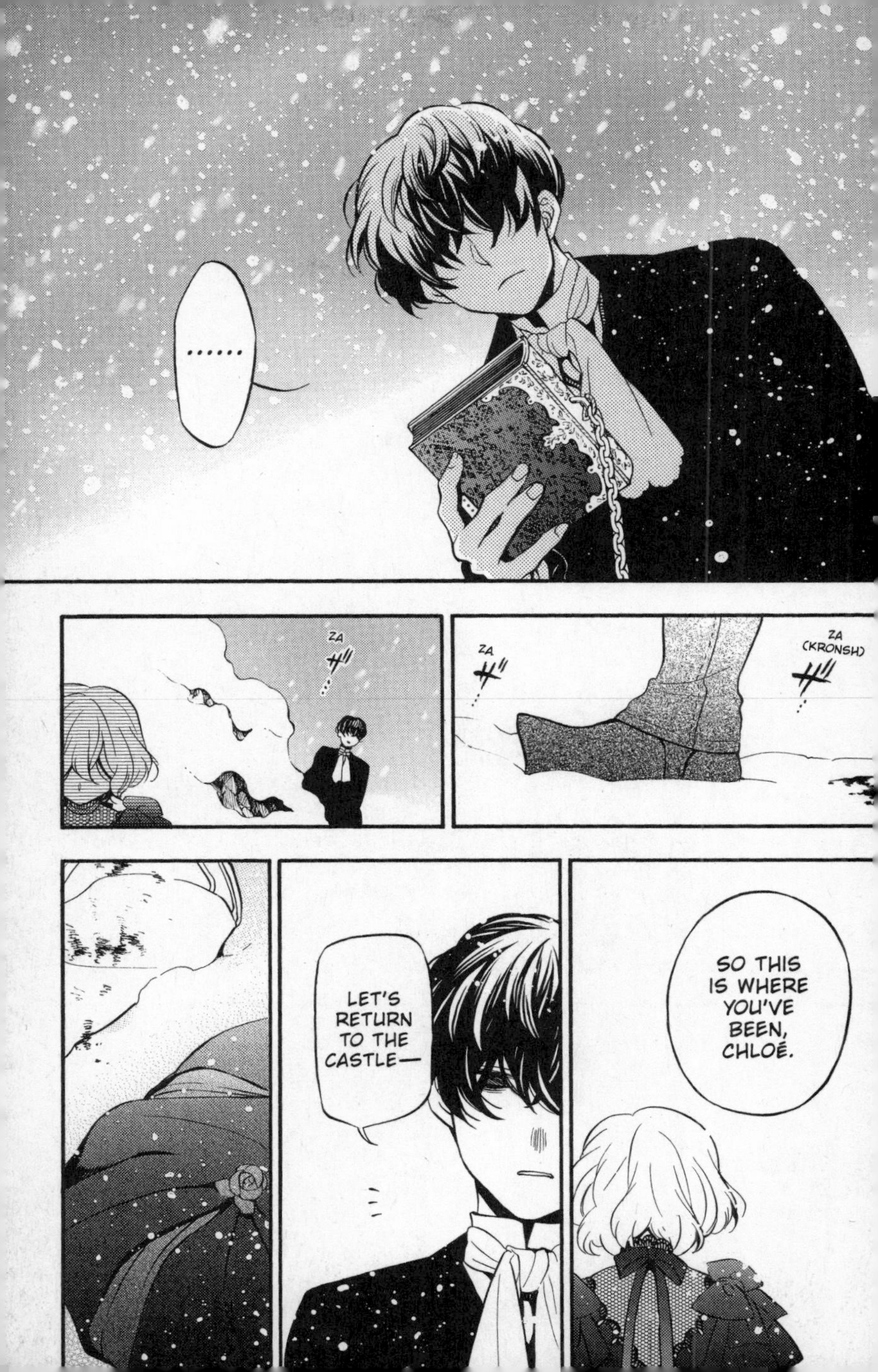
......
ZA (KRONSH)
ZA
ZA
SO THIS IS WHERE YOU'VE BEEN, CHLOÉ.
LET'S RETURN TO THE CASTLE—

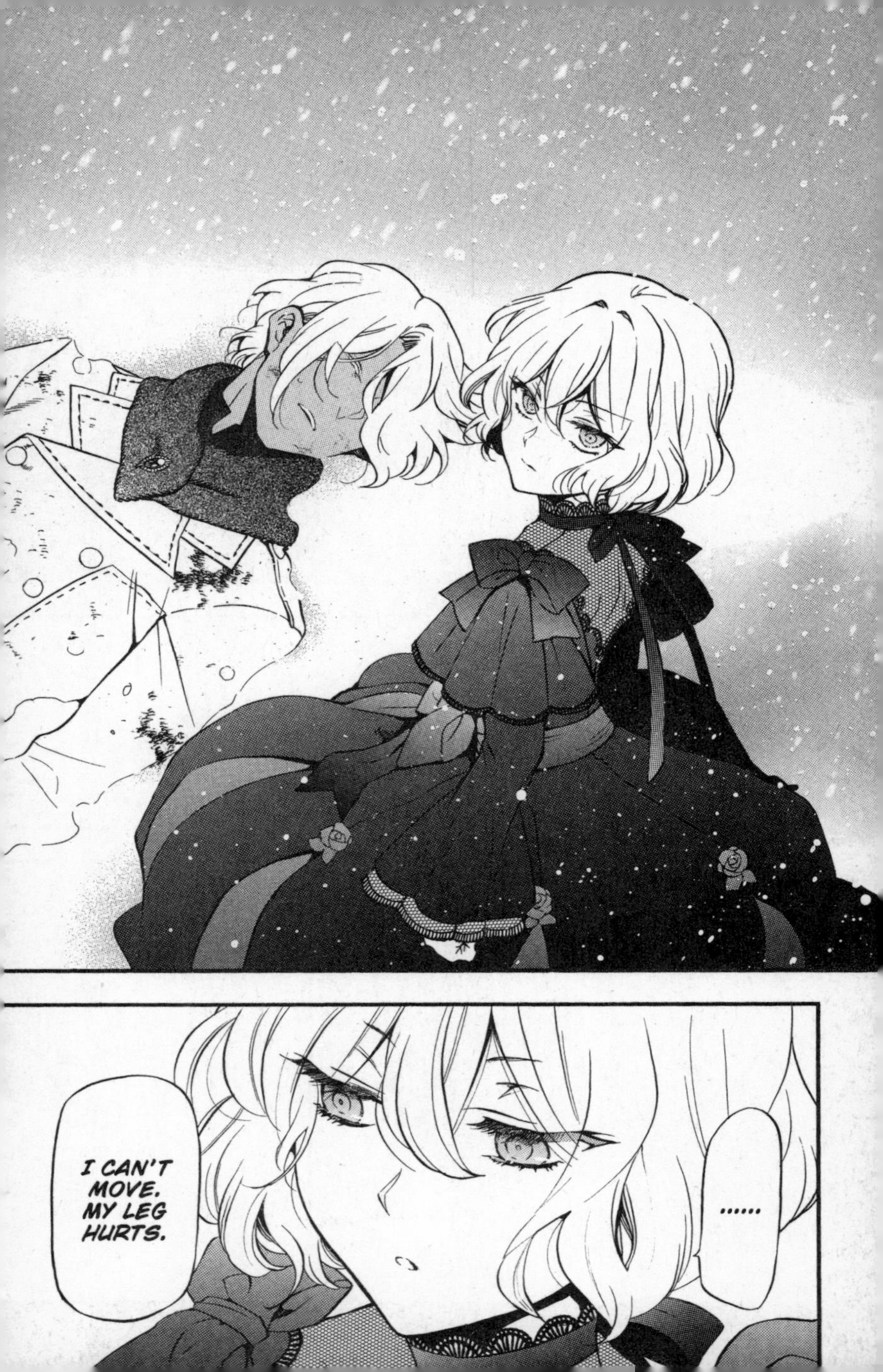
......
I CAN'T MOVE. MY LEG HURTS.

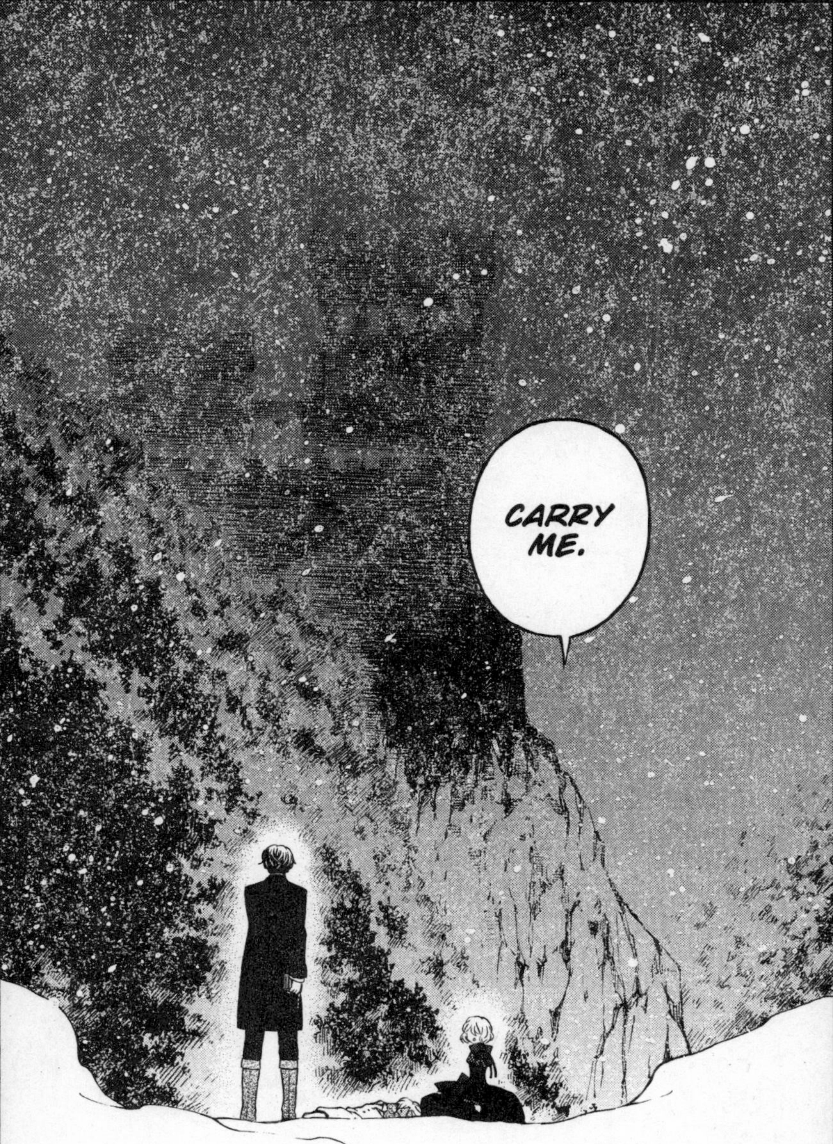
CARRY ME.

Mémoire 26 Dissonance CREAKING LAUGHTER

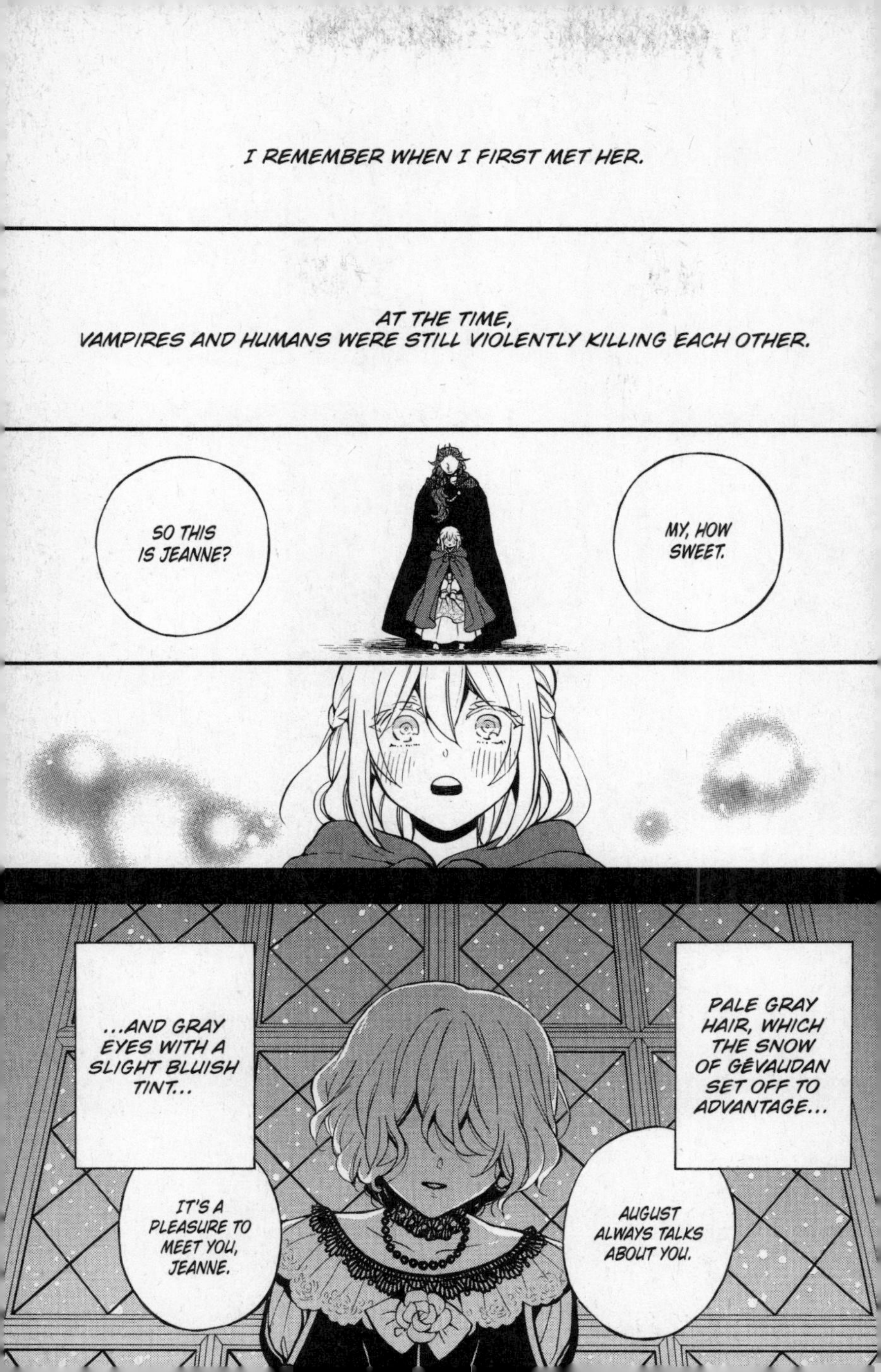
I REMEMBER WHEN I FIRST MET HER.
AT THE TIME, VAMPIRES AND HUMANS WERE STILL VIOLENTLY KILLING EACH OTHER.
MY, HOW SWEET.
SO THIS IS JEANNE?
PALE GRAY HAIR, WHICH THE SNOW OF GÉVAUDAN SET OFF TO ADVANTAGE...
...AND GRAY EYES WITH A SLIGHT BLUISH TINT...
AUGUST ALWAYS TALKS ABOUT YOU.
IT'S A PLEASURE TO MEET YOU, JEANNE.

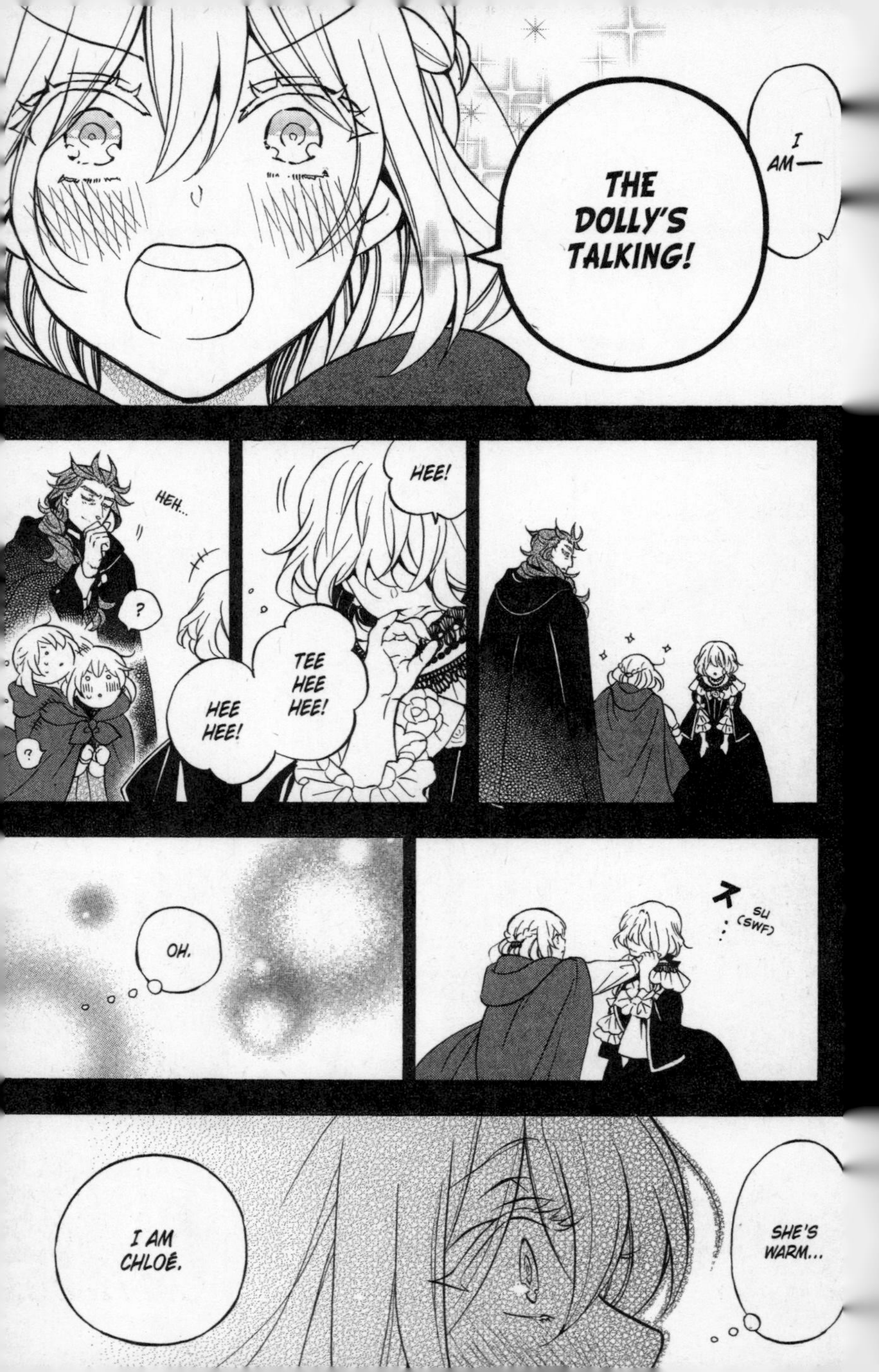
I AM—
THE DOLLY'S TALKING!
HEE!
TEE HEE HEE!
HEE HEE!
HEH...
?
?
ス
SU (SWF)
OH.
SHE'S WARM...
I AM CHLOE.

MÉMOIRE 27

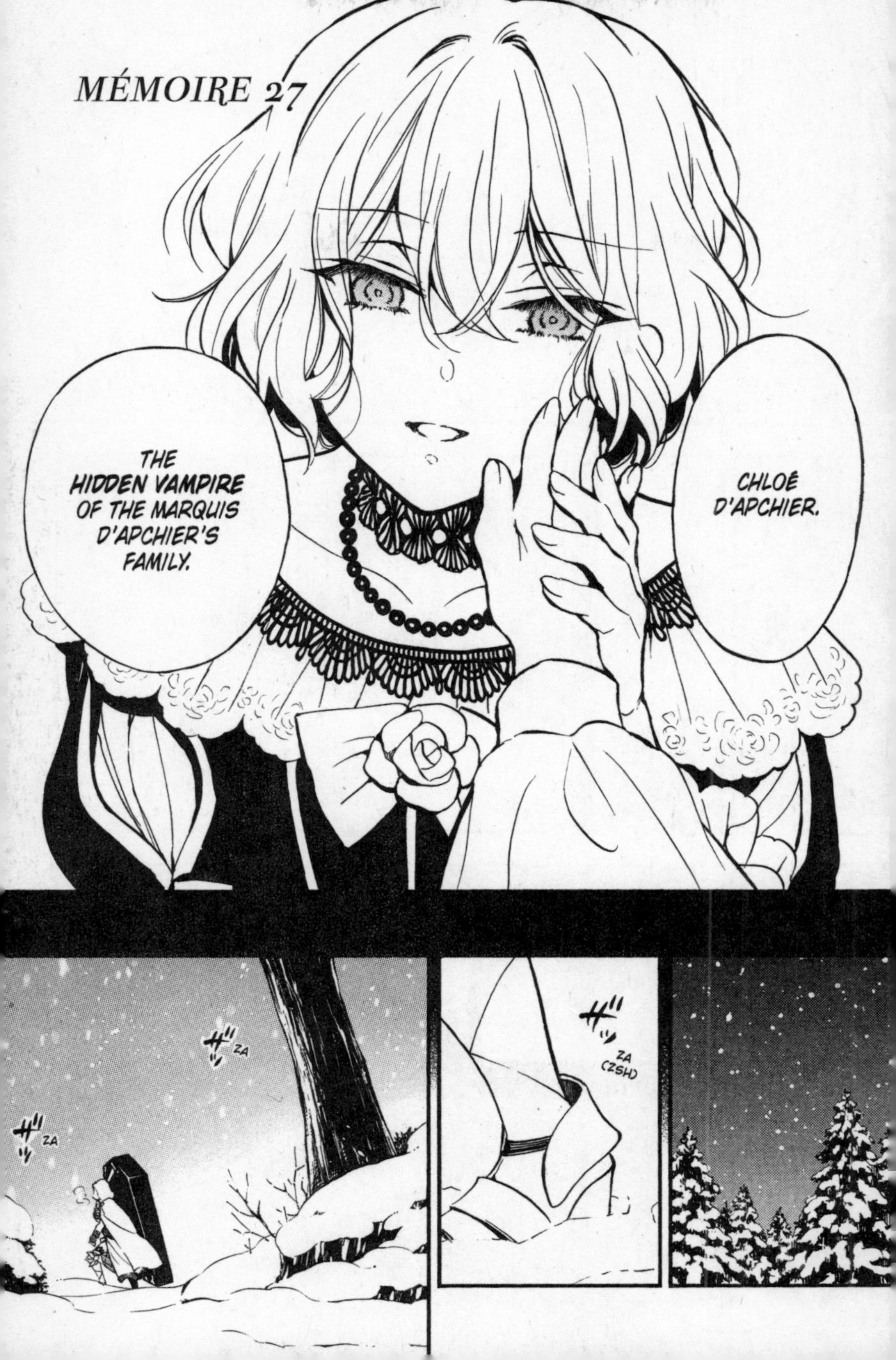
CHLOÉ D'APCHIER.
THE HIDDEN VAMPIRE OF THE MARQUIS D'APCHIER'S FAMILY.
ZA (ZSH)
ZA
ZA

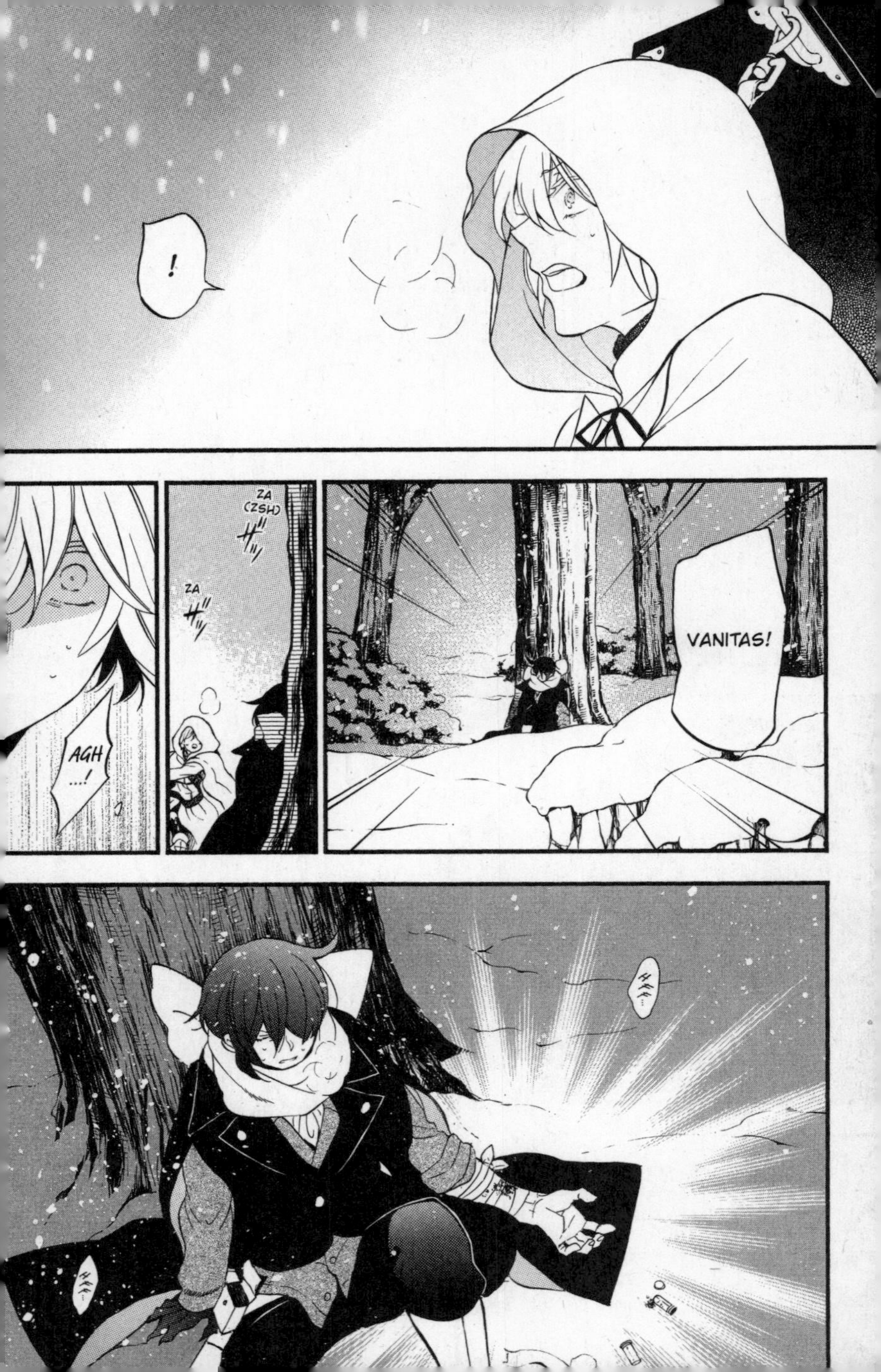
!
VANITAS!
ZA (ZSH)
ZA
AGH ...!

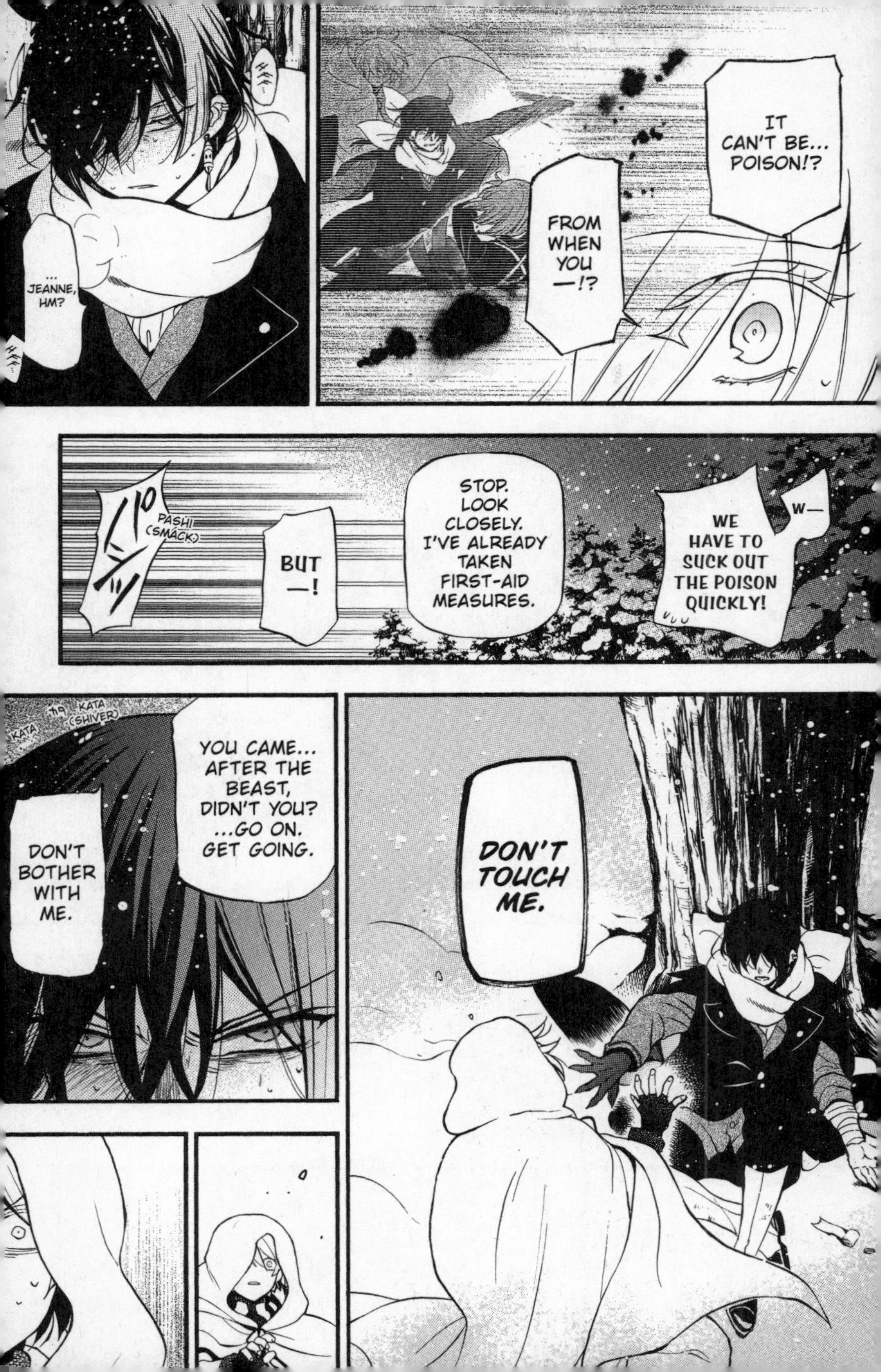
IT CAN'T BE... POISON!?
FROM WHEN YOU —!?
... JEANNE, HM?
W—
WE HAVE TO SUCK OUT THE POISON QUICKLY!
STOP. LOOK CLOSELY. I'VE ALREADY TAKEN FIRST-AID MEASURES.
BUT —!
PASHI (SMACK)
DON'T TOUCH ME.
KATA KATA (SHIVER)
YOU CAME... AFTER THE BEAST, DIDN'T YOU? ...GO ON. GET GOING.
DON'T BOTHER WITH ME.

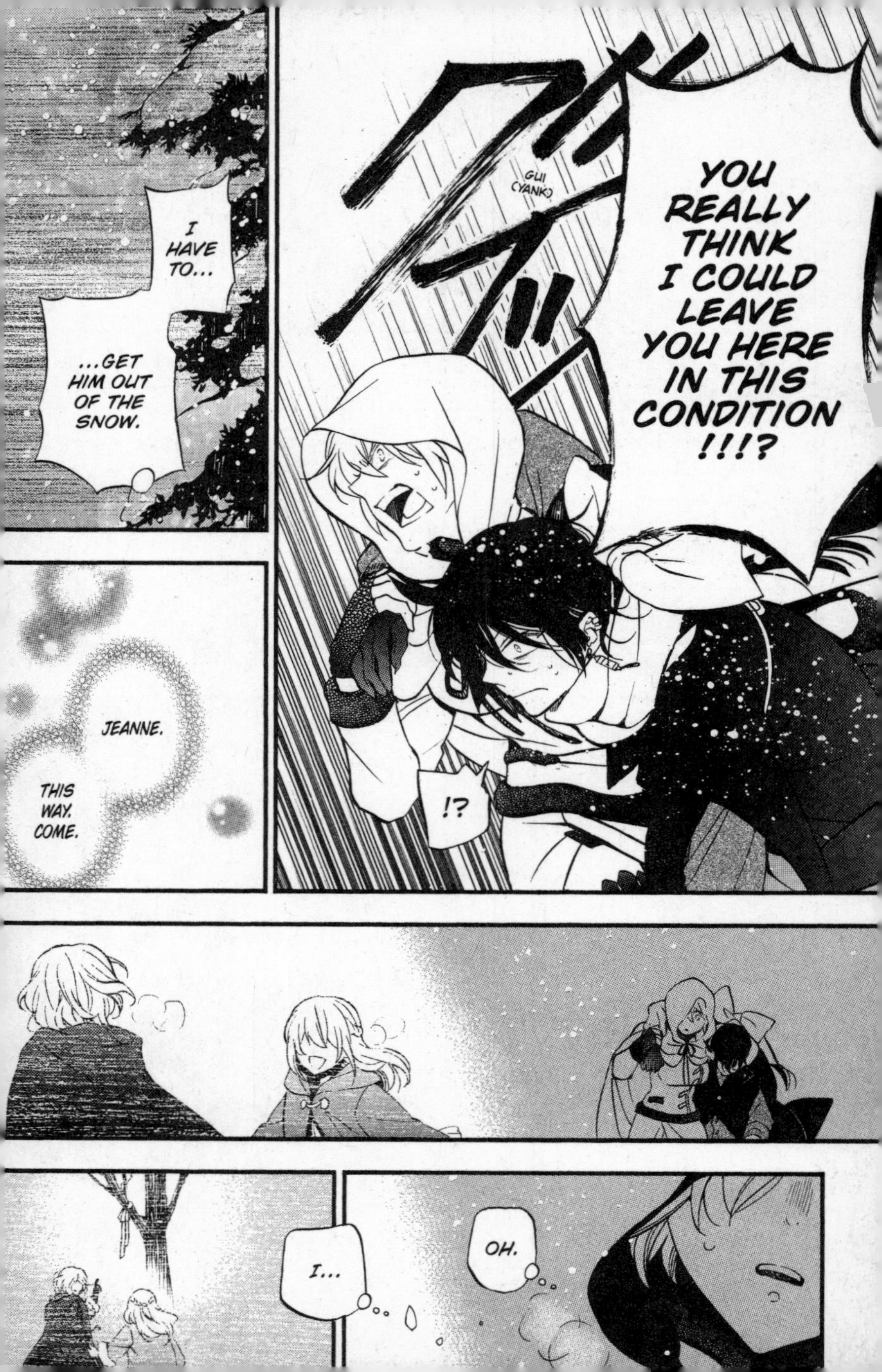
GUI (YANK)
YOU REALLY THINK I COULD LEAVE YOU HERE IN THIS CONDITION !!!?
!?
I HAVE TO...
...GET HIM OUT OF THE SNOW.
JEANNE.
THIS WAY. COME.
OH.
I...

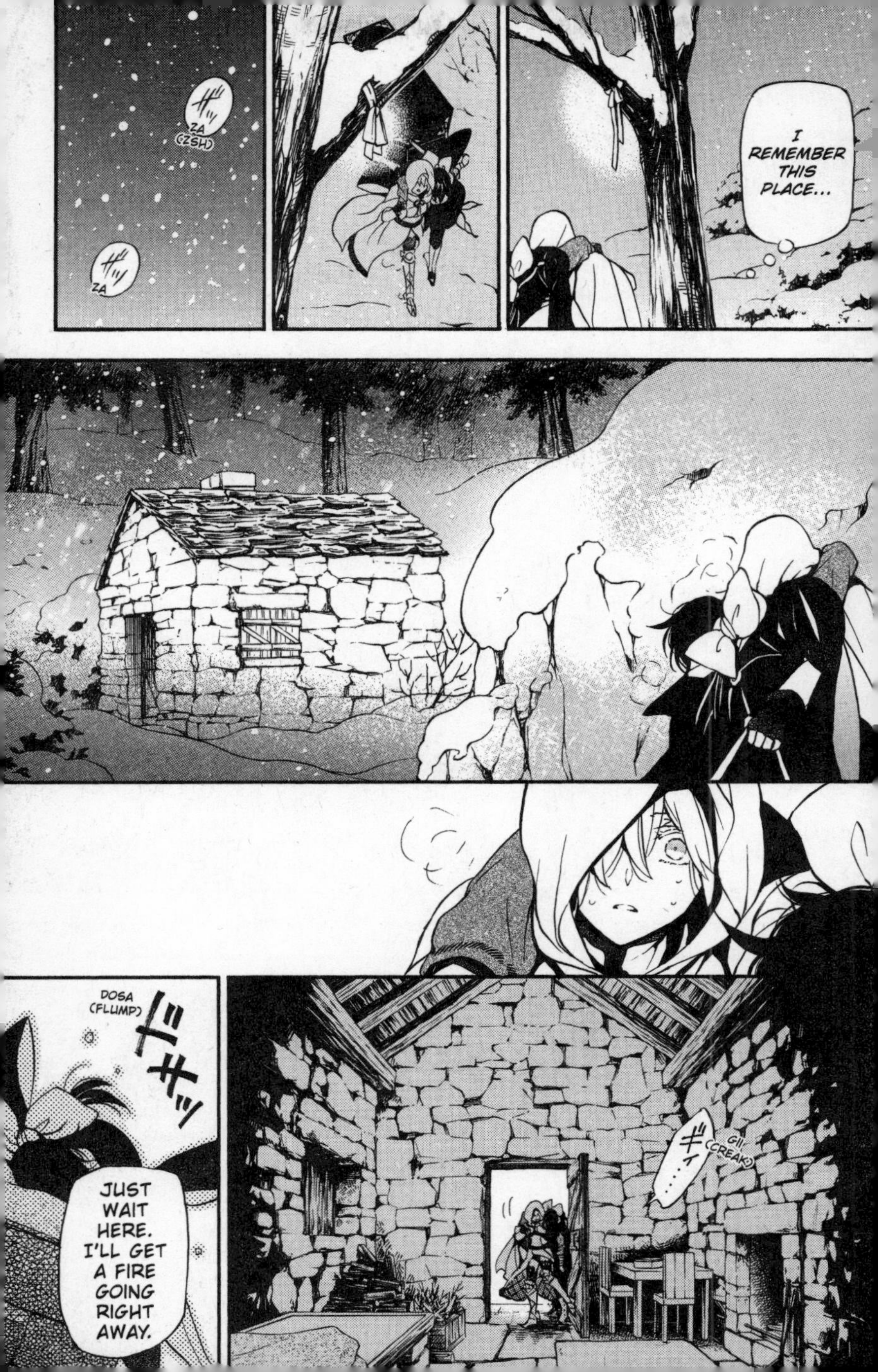
I REMEMBER THIS PLACE...
ZA (ZSH)
ZA
GII (CREAK)
...
DOSA (FLUMP)
JUST WAIT HERE. I'LL GET A FIRE GOING RIGHT AWAY.

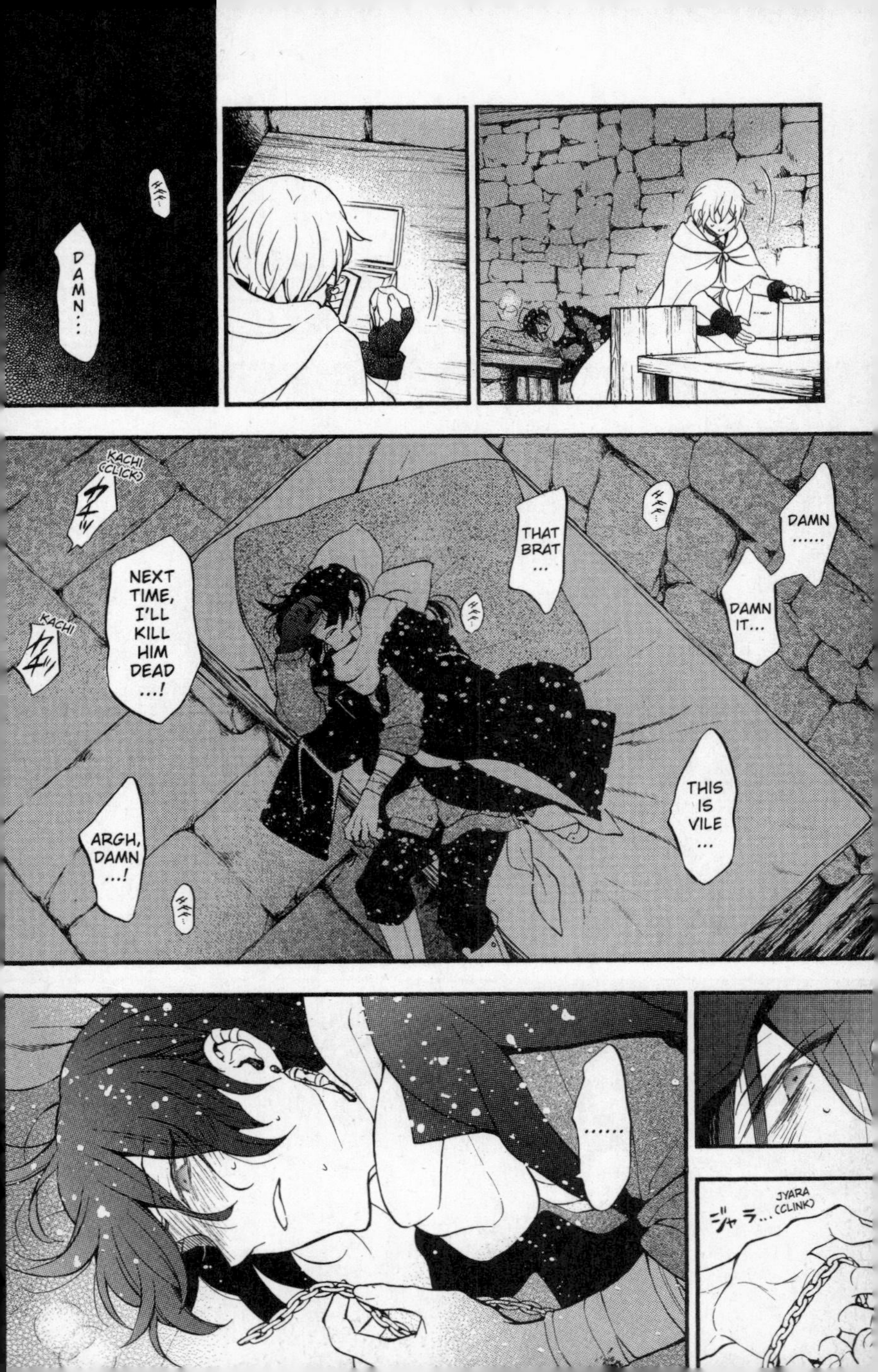
DAMN...
DAMN ......
DAMN IT...
THAT BRAT ...
KACHI (CLICK)
NEXT TIME, I'LL KILL HIM DEAD ...!
KACHI
THIS IS VILE ...
ARGH, DAMN ...!
JYARA (CLINK)
ジャラ…
......

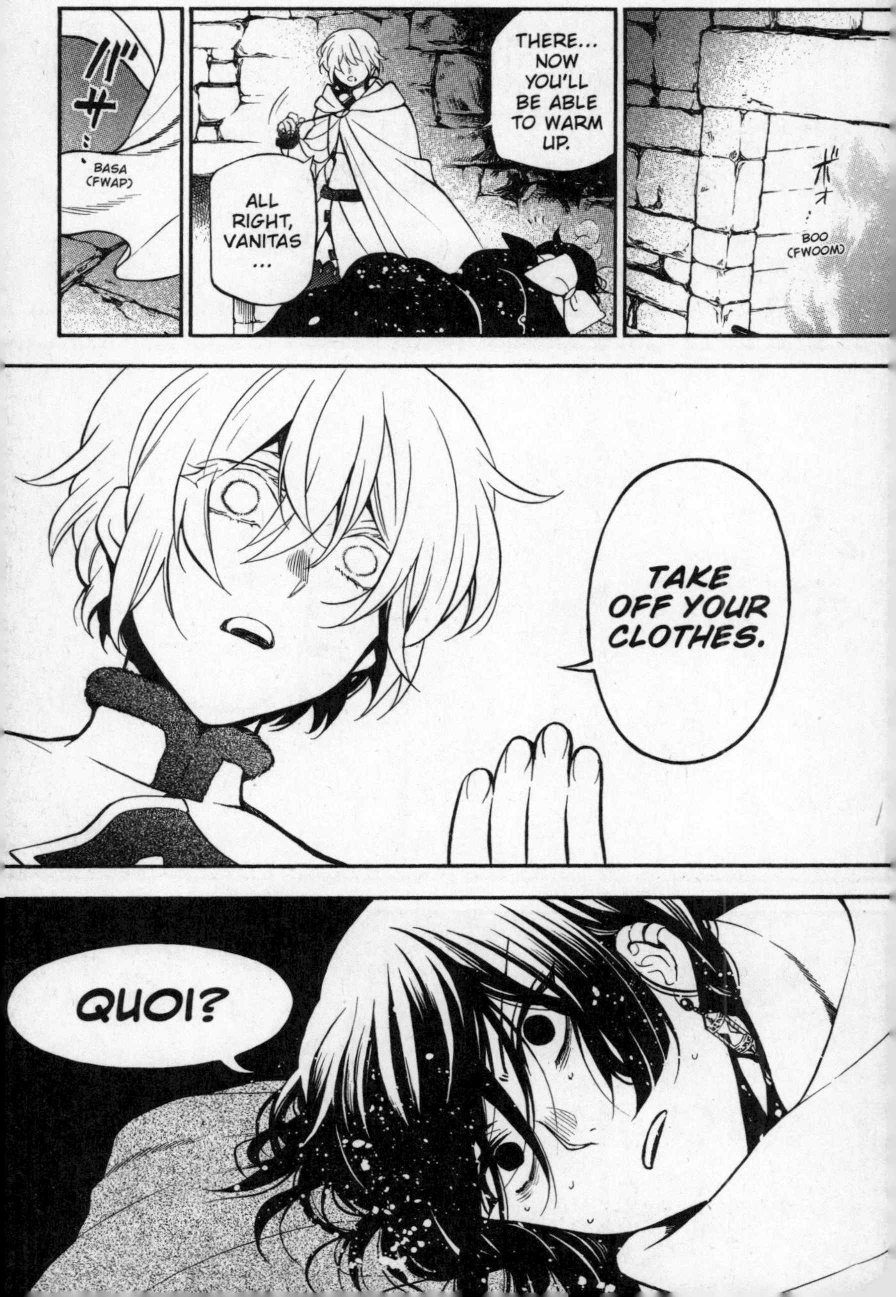
ボオ…
BOO (FWOOM)
THERE... NOW YOU'LL BE ABLE TO WARM UP.
ALL RIGHT, VANITAS...
バサ…
BASA (FWAP)
TAKE OFF YOUR CLOTHES.
QUOI?

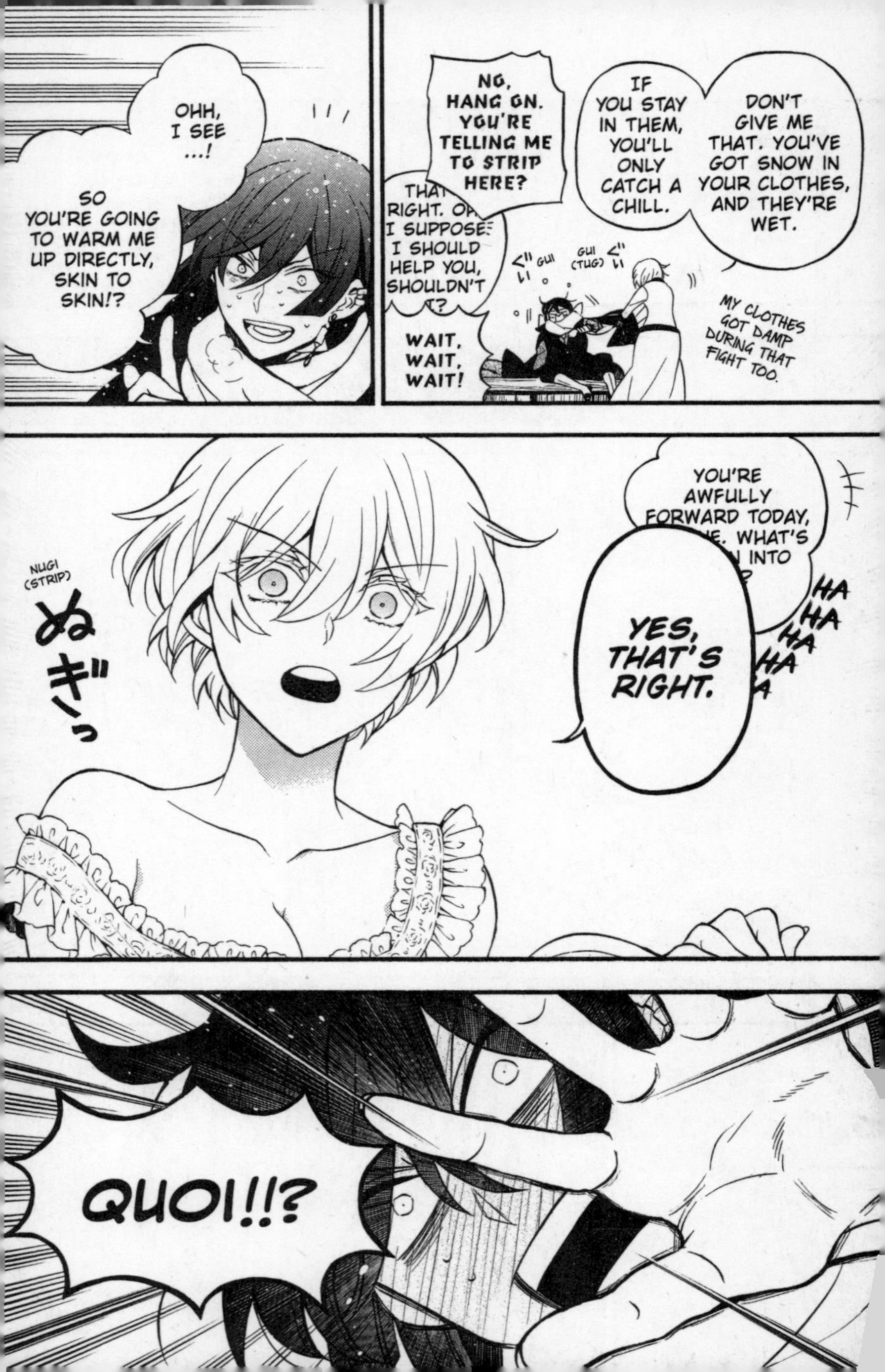
DON'T GIVE ME THAT. YOU'VE GOT SNOW IN YOUR CLOTHES, AND THEY'RE WET.
IF YOU STAY IN THEM, YOU'LL ONLY CATCH A CHILL.
NO, HANG ON. YOU'RE TELLING ME TO STRIP HERE?
MY CLOTHES GOT DAMP DURING THAT FIGHT TOO.
GUI (TUG)
GUI
RIGHT. I SUPPOSE I SHOULD HELP YOU, SHOULDN'T
WAIT, WAIT, WAIT!
OHH, I SEE ...!
SO YOU'RE GOING TO WARM ME UP DIRECTLY, SKIN TO SKIN!?
YOU'RE AWFULLY FORWARD TODAY,
WHAT'S
INTO
YES, THAT'S RIGHT.
HA HA HA HA
NUGI (STRIP)
ぬぎっ
QUOI!!!?

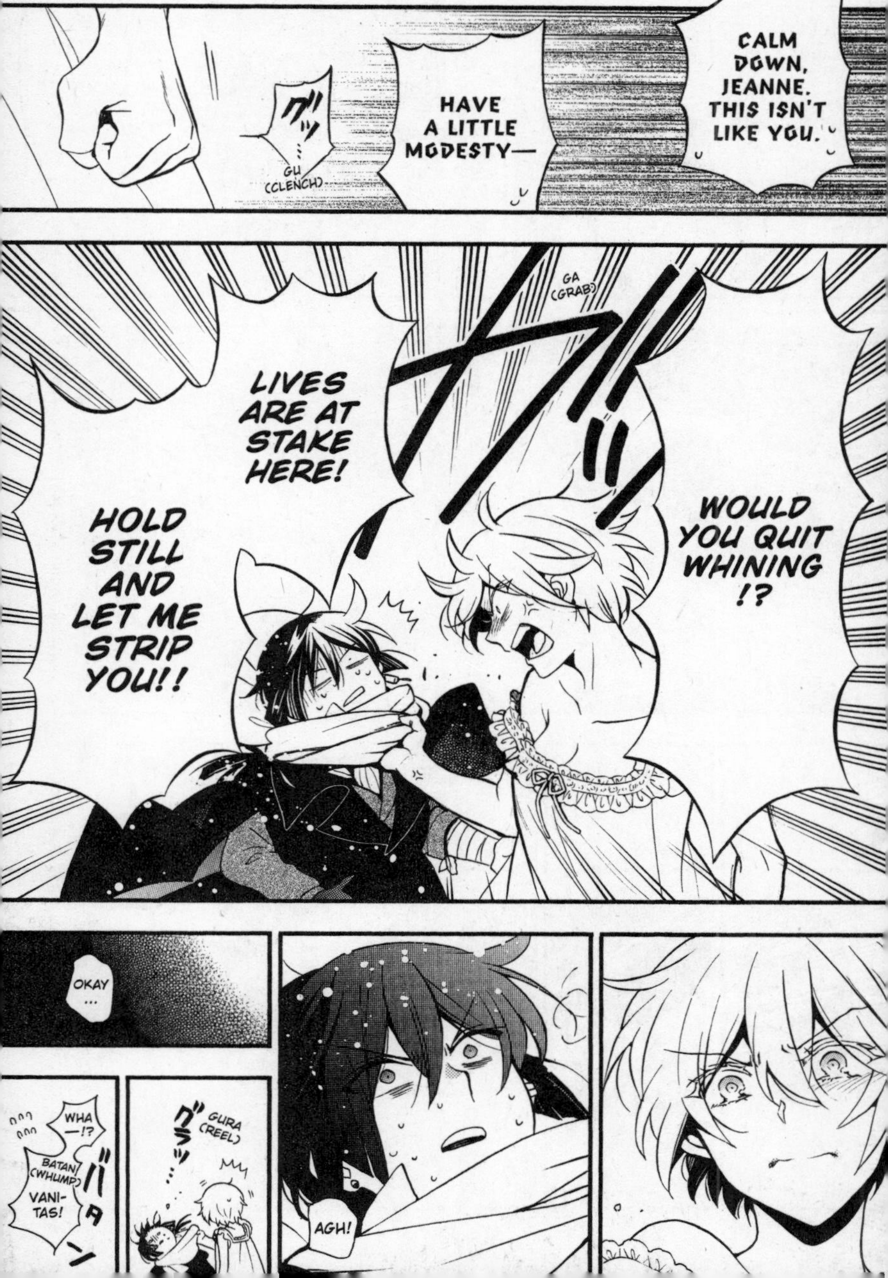
CALM DOWN, JEANNE. THIS ISN'T LIKE YOU.
HAVE A LITTLE MODESTY—
GU (CLENCH)
GA (GRAB)
WOULD YOU QUIT WHINING!?
LIVES ARE AT STAKE HERE!
HOLD STILL AND LET ME STRIP YOU!!
AGH!
OKAY...
GURA (REEL)
WHA—!?
BATAN (WHUMP)
VANI-TAS!

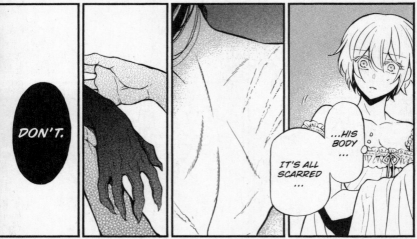

DON'T.

IT'S ALL
SCARRED
...

...HIS
BODY
...

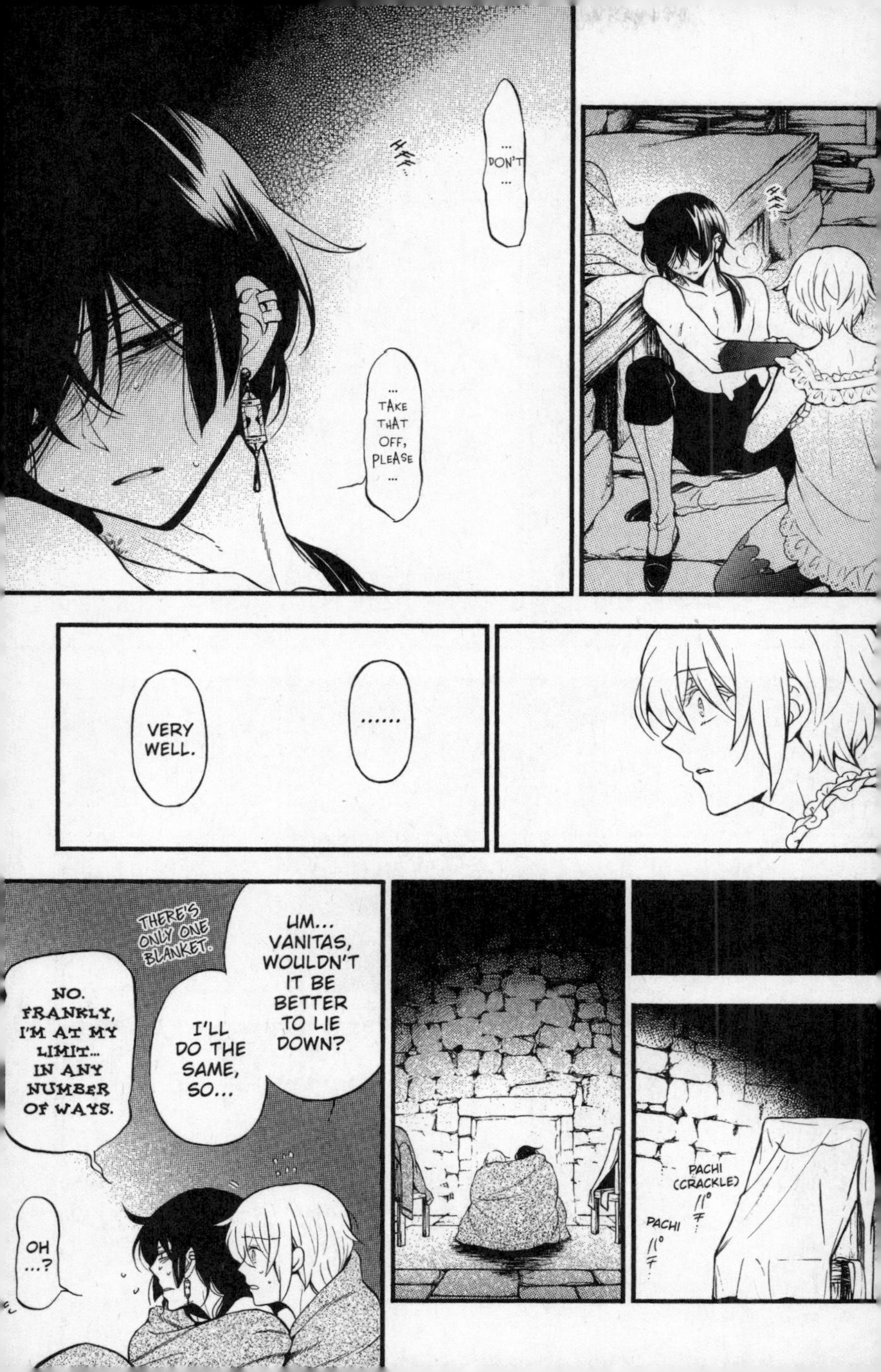
HFF...
...DON'T...
HFF...
...TAKE THAT OFF, PLEASE...
......
VERY WELL.
PACHI (CRACKLE)
PACHI
UM... VANITAS, WOULDN'T IT BE BETTER TO LIE DOWN?
THERE'S ONLY ONE BLANKET.
I'LL DO THE SAME, SO...
NO. FRANKLY, I'M AT MY LIMIT... IN ANY NUMBER OF WAYS.
OH...?

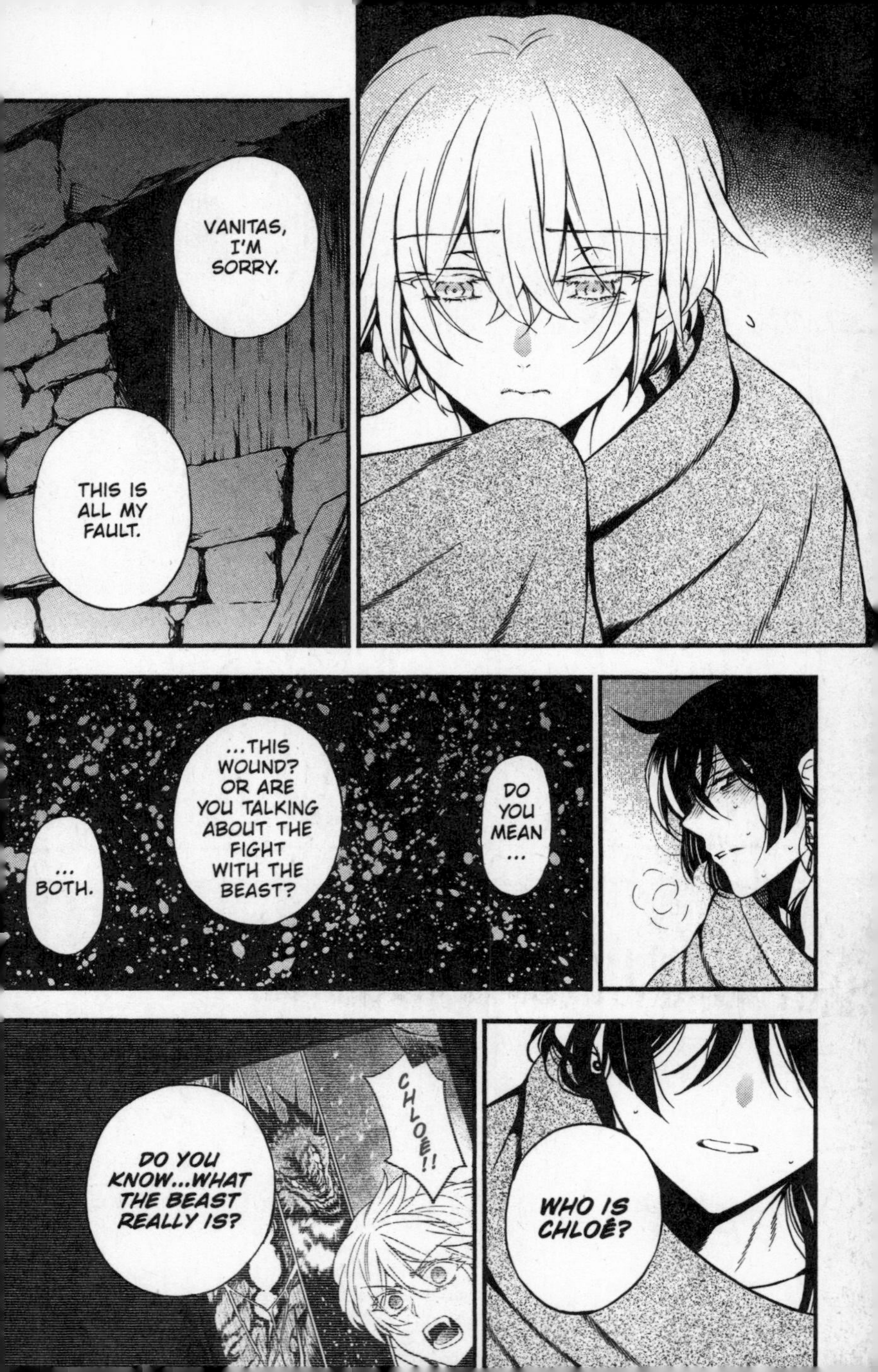
VANITAS, I'M SORRY.
THIS IS ALL MY FAULT.
DO YOU MEAN...
...THIS WOUND? OR ARE YOU TALKING ABOUT THE FIGHT WITH THE BEAST?
...BOTH.
WHO IS CHLOÉ?
CHLOÉ!!
DO YOU KNOW...WHAT THE BEAST REALLY IS?

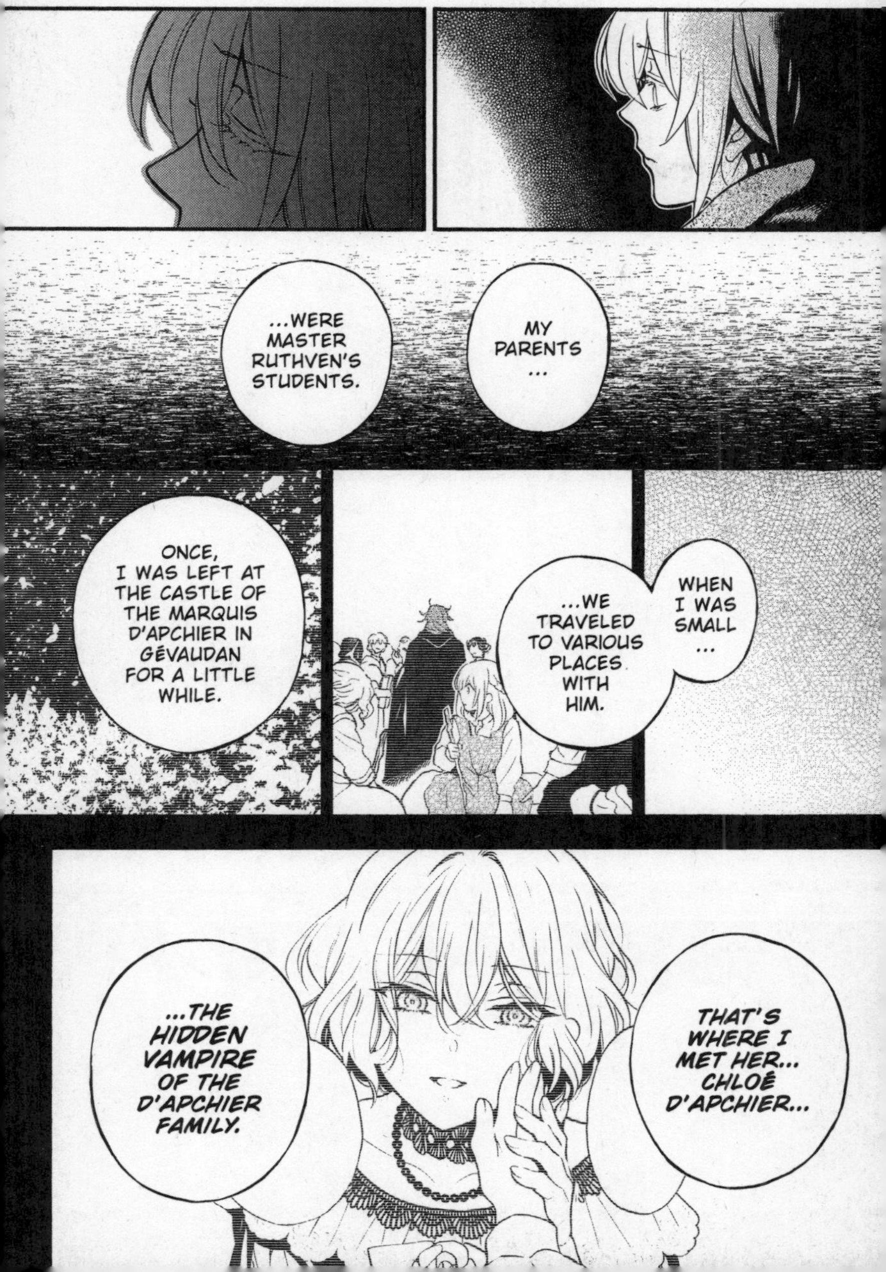
MY PARENTS ...
...WERE MASTER RUTHVEN'S STUDENTS.
WHEN I WAS SMALL ...
...WE TRAVELED TO VARIOUS PLACES WITH HIM.
ONCE, I WAS LEFT AT THE CASTLE OF THE MARQUIS D'APCHIER IN GÉVAUDAN FOR A LITTLE WHILE.
THAT'S WHERE I MET HER... CHLOÉ D'APCHIER...
...THE HIDDEN VAMPIRE OF THE D'APCHIER FAMILY.

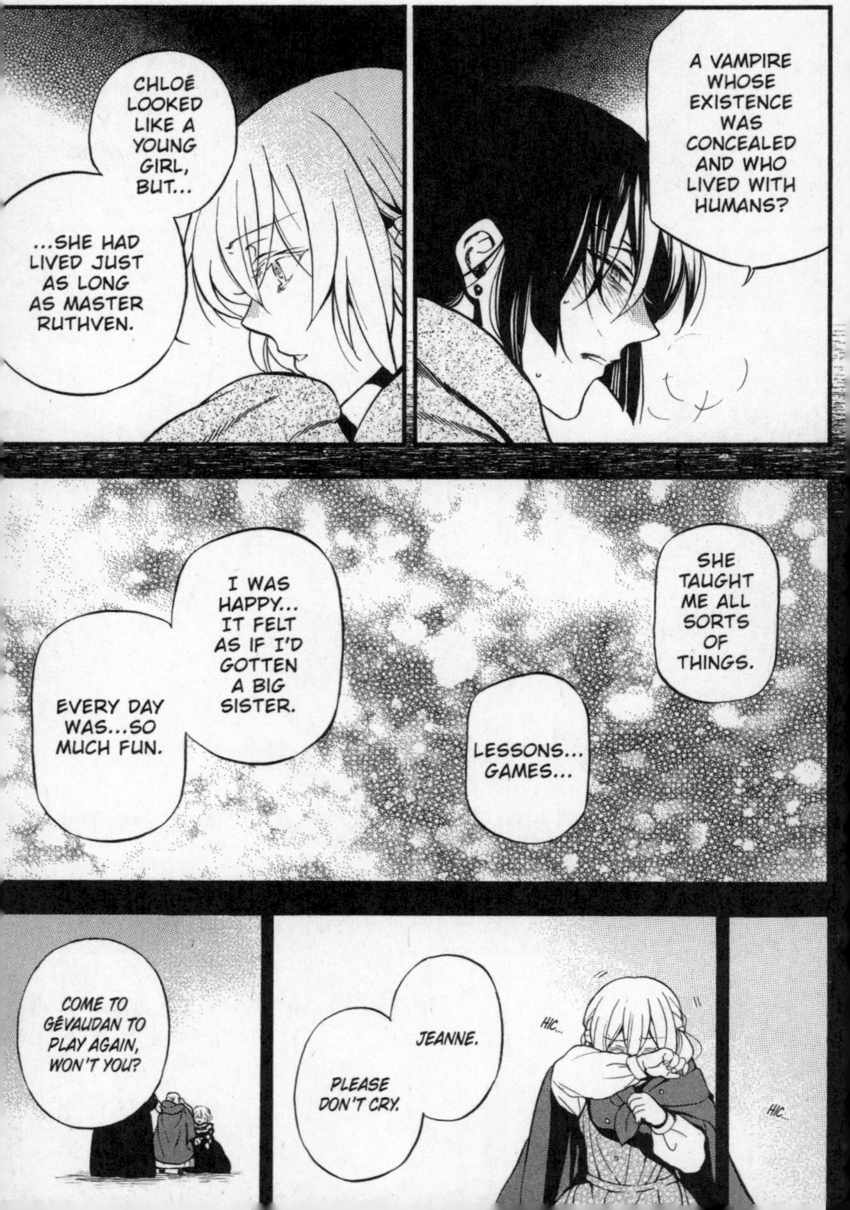
A VAMPIRE WHOSE EXISTENCE WAS CONCEALED AND WHO LIVED WITH HUMANS?
CHLOÉ LOOKED LIKE A YOUNG GIRL, BUT...
...SHE HAD LIVED JUST AS LONG AS MASTER RUTHVEN.
SHE TAUGHT ME ALL SORTS OF THINGS.
LESSONS... GAMES...
I WAS HAPPY... IT FELT AS IF I'D GOTTEN A BIG SISTER.
EVERY DAY WAS...SO MUCH FUN.
HIC...
JEANNE.
HIC...
PLEASE DON'T CRY.
COME TO GÉVAUDAN TO PLAY AGAIN, WON'T YOU?

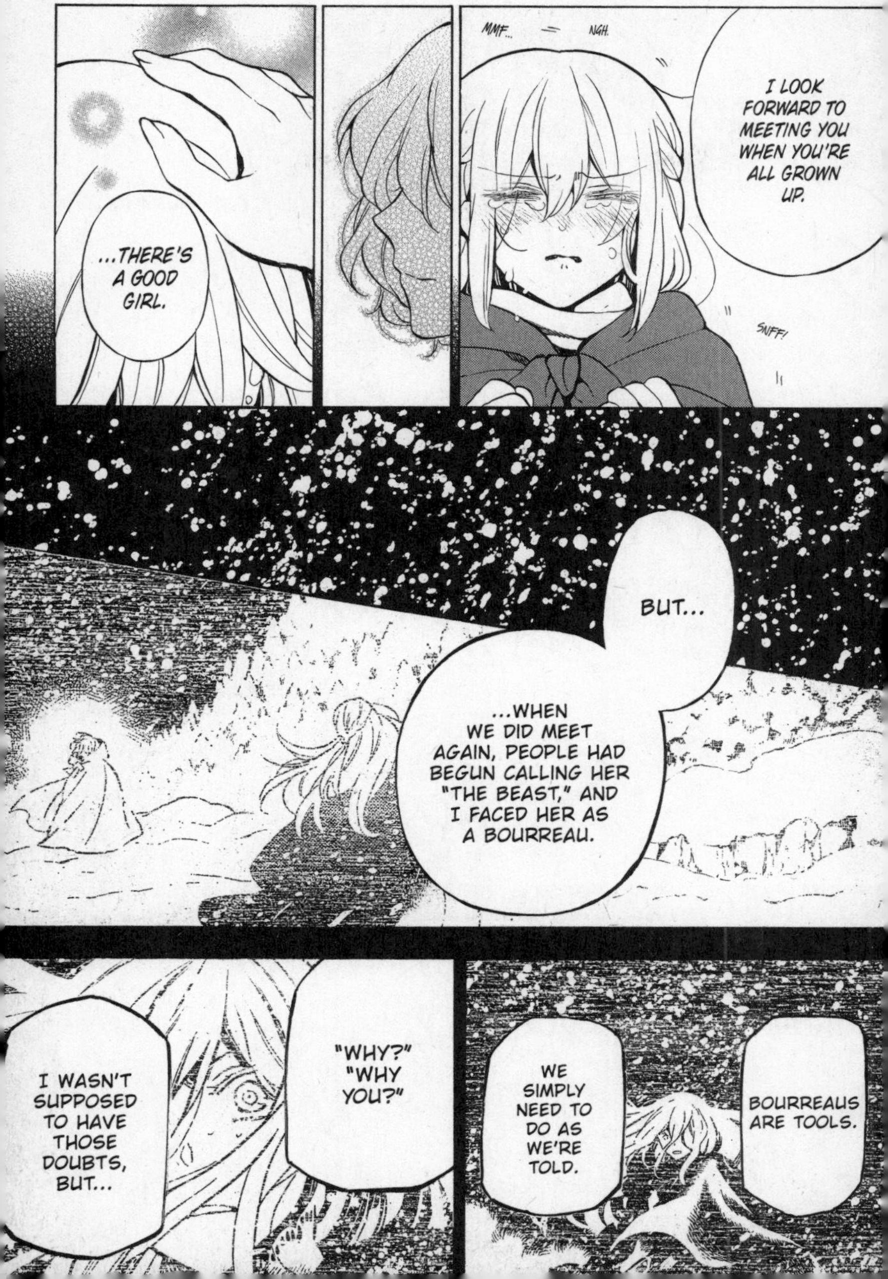
MMF...
NGH.
I LOOK FORWARD TO MEETING YOU WHEN YOU'RE ALL GROWN UP.
SNFF!
...THERE'S A GOOD GIRL.
BUT...
...WHEN WE DID MEET AGAIN, PEOPLE HAD BEGUN CALLING HER "THE BEAST," AND I FACED HER AS A BOURREAU.
BOURREAUS ARE TOOLS.
WE SIMPLY NEED TO DO AS WE'RE TOLD.
"WHY?" "WHY YOU?"
I WASN'T SUPPOSED TO HAVE THOSE DOUBTS, BUT...

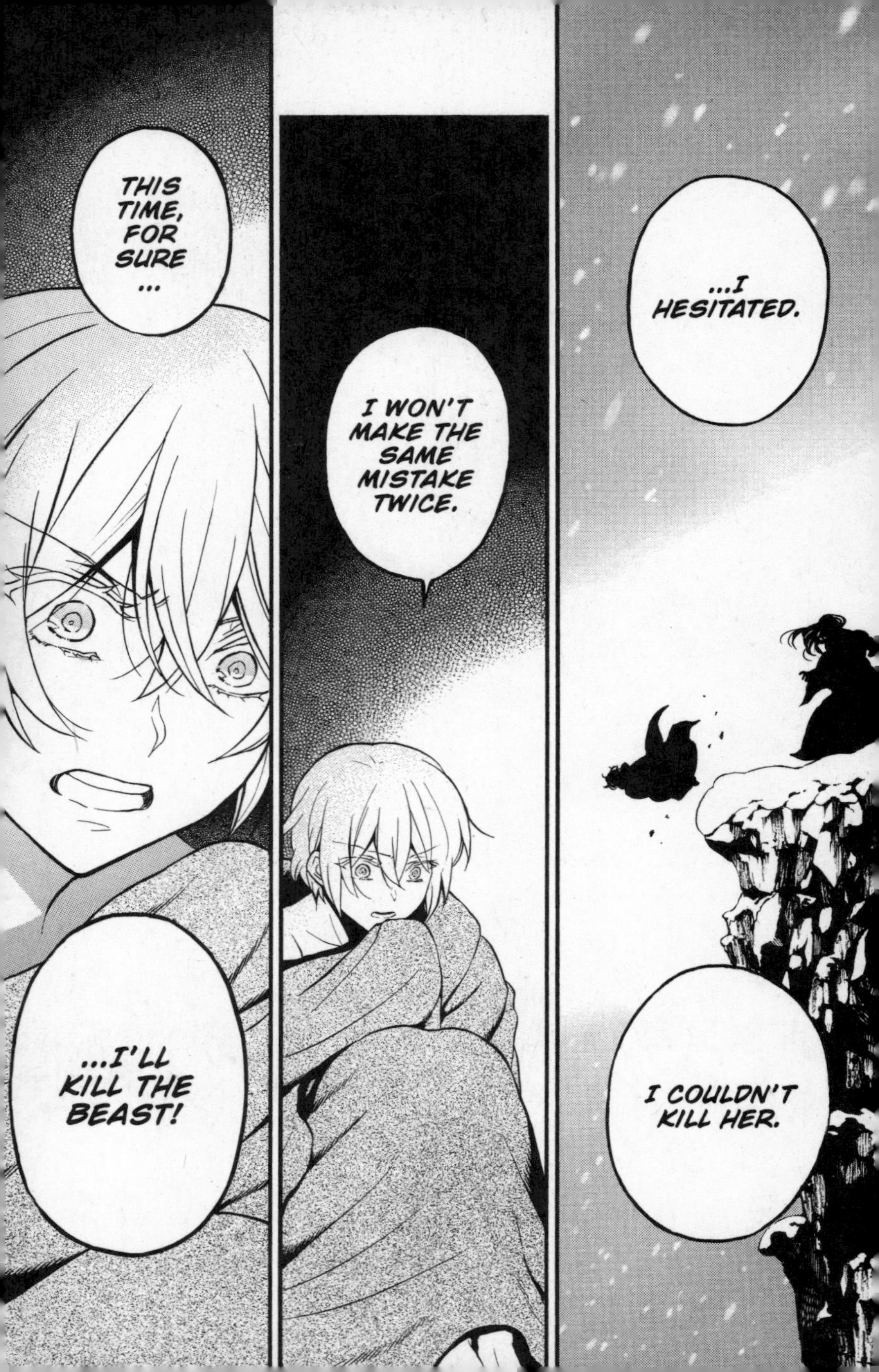
...I HESITATED.
I COULDN'T KILL HER.
I WON'T MAKE THE SAME MISTAKE TWICE.
THIS TIME, FOR SURE ...
...I'LL KILL THE BEAST!

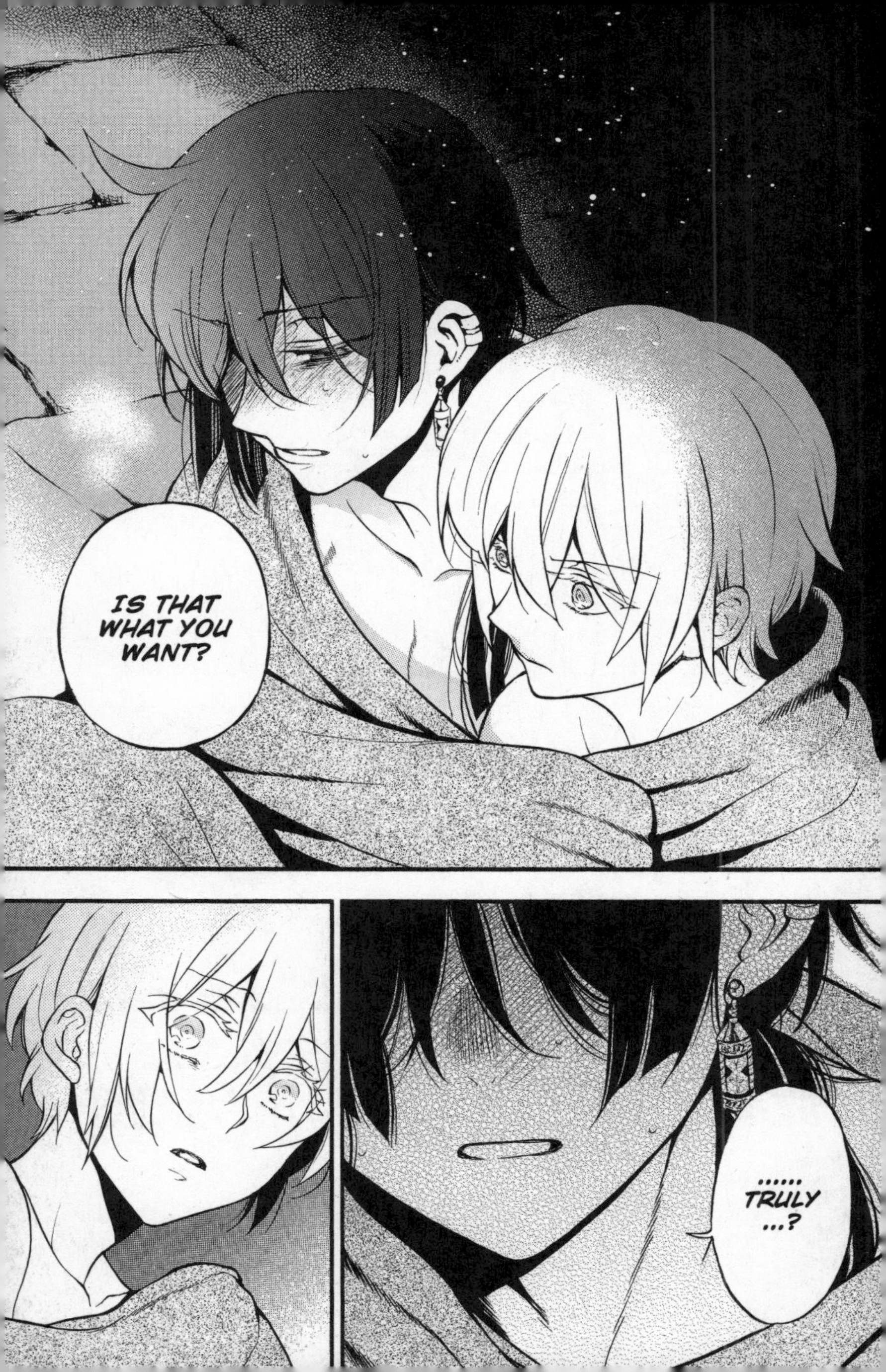
IS THAT WHAT YOU WANT?
......TRULY ...?

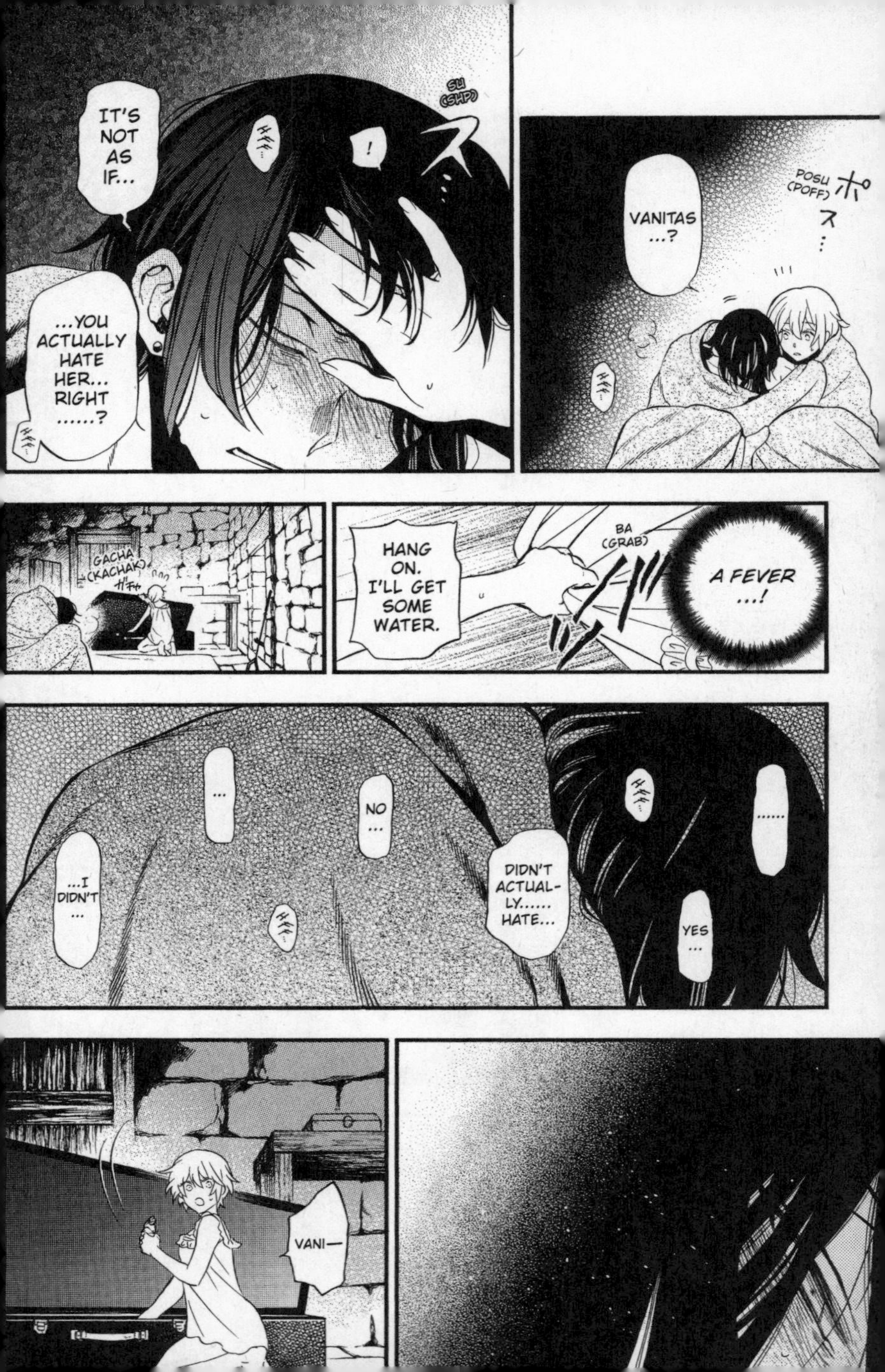
POSU (POFF) ポス…
VANITAS …?
SU (SHP)
!
IT'S NOT AS IF…
…YOU ACTUALLY HATE HER… RIGHT ……?
BA (GRAB)
A FEVER …!
HANG ON. I'LL GET SOME WATER.
GACHA (KACHAK) ガチャ
……
YES …
DIDN'T ACTUAL-LY…… HATE…
NO …
…
…I DIDN'T …
VANI—

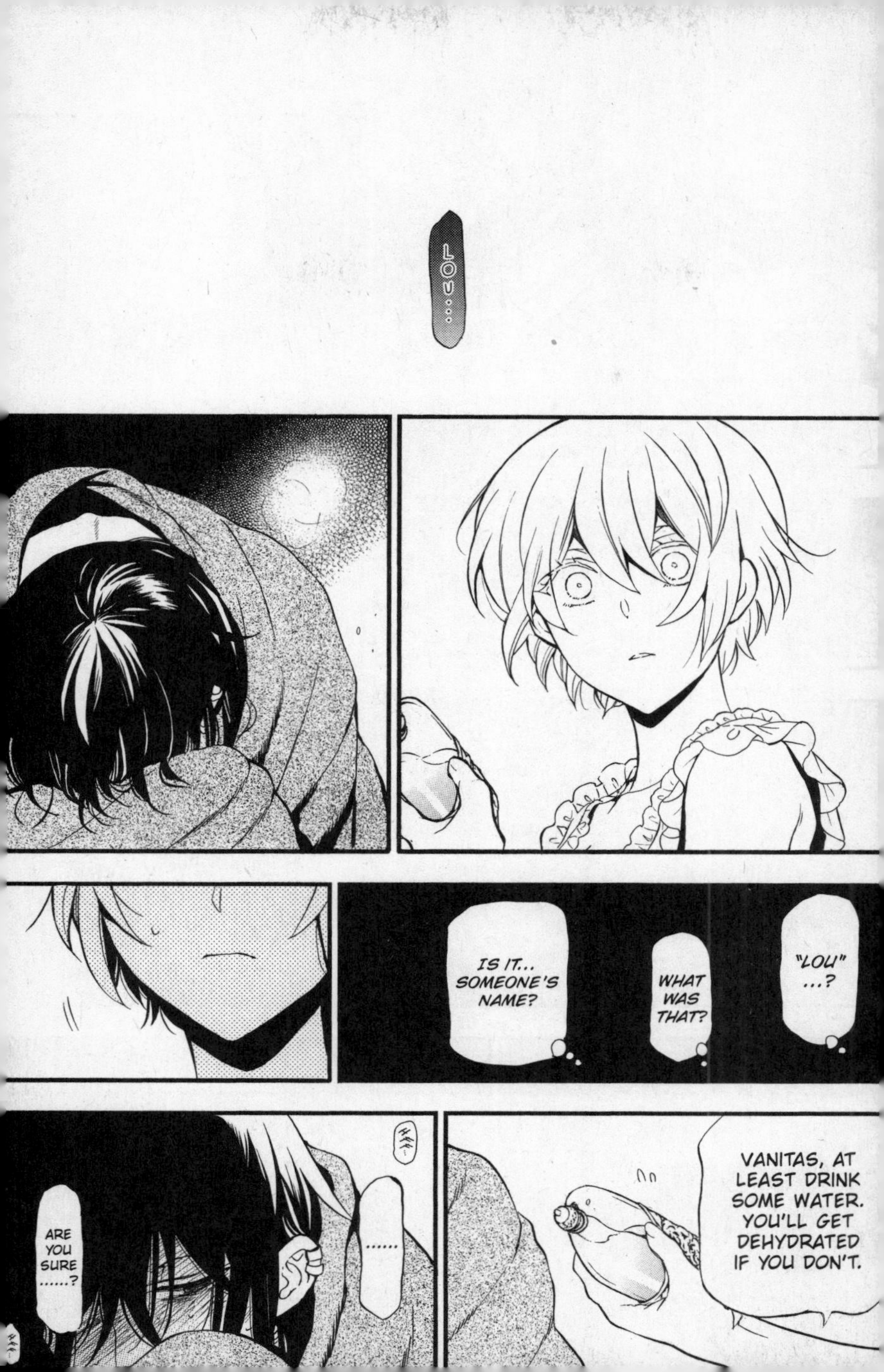
LOU...
"LOU" ...?
WHAT WAS THAT?
IS IT... SOMEONE'S NAME?
VANITAS, AT LEAST DRINK SOME WATER. YOU'LL GET DEHYDRATED IF YOU DON'T.
......
ARE YOU SURE ......?

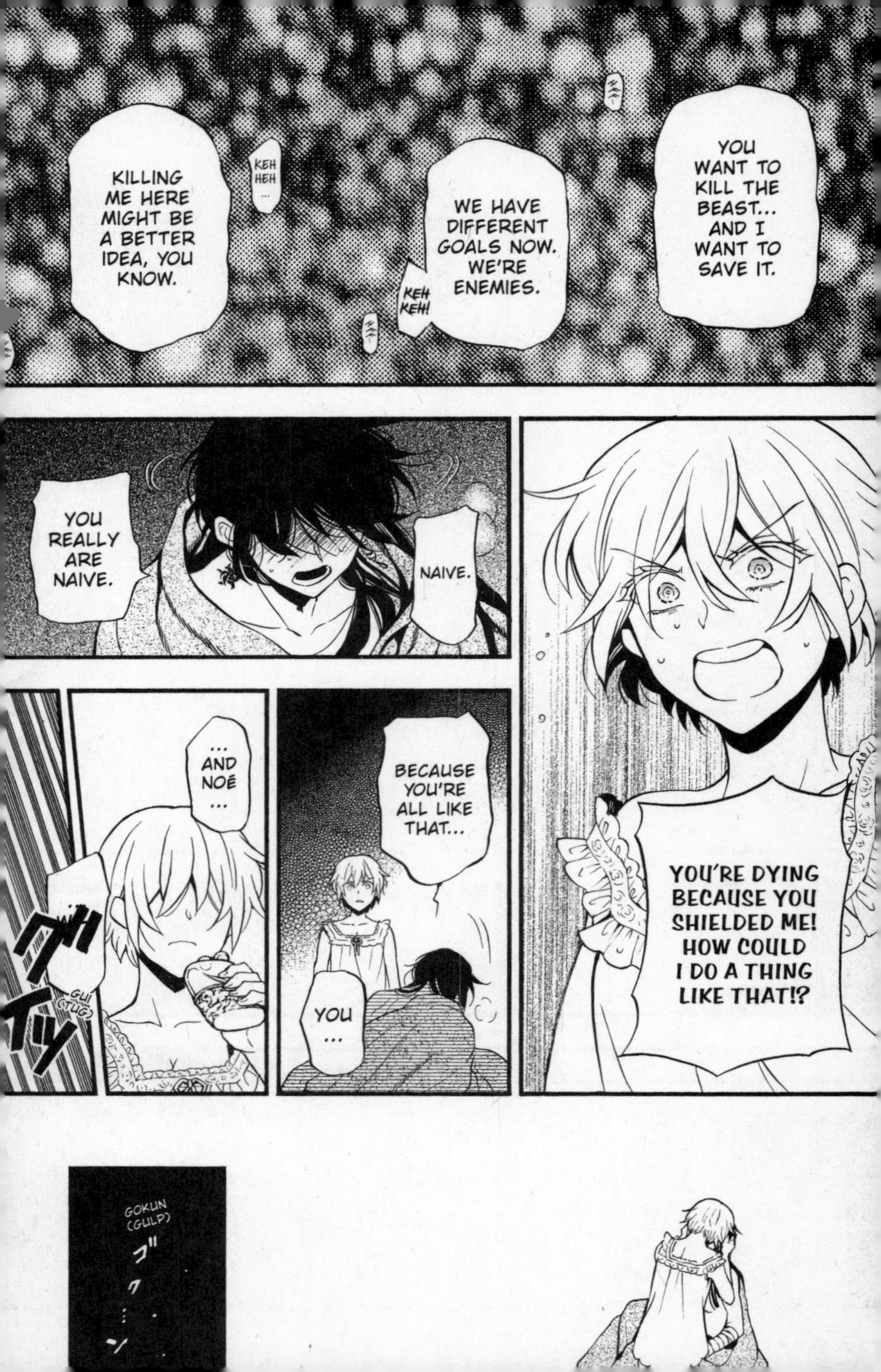
YOU WANT TO KILL THE BEAST... AND I WANT TO SAVE IT.
WE HAVE DIFFERENT GOALS NOW. WE'RE ENEMIES.
KEH KEH!
KEH HEH ...
KILLING ME HERE MIGHT BE A BETTER IDEA, YOU KNOW.
YOU'RE DYING BECAUSE YOU SHIELDED ME! HOW COULD I DO A THING LIKE THAT!?
NAIVE.
YOU REALLY ARE NAIVE.
BECAUSE YOU'RE ALL LIKE THAT...
YOU ...
... AND NOÉ ...
GUI (TUG)
GOKUN (GULP)

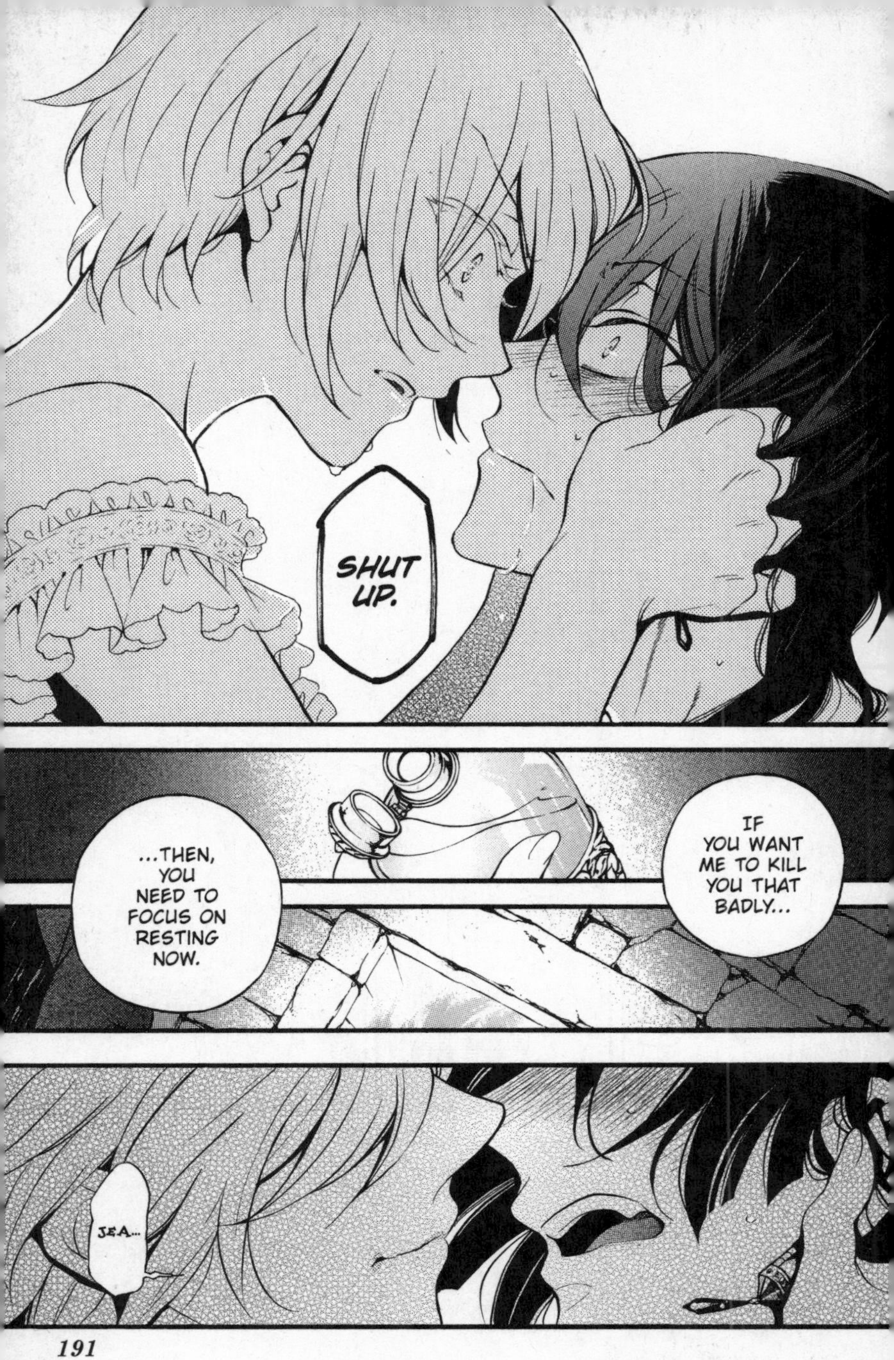
SHUT UP.
IF YOU WANT ME TO KILL YOU THAT BADLY...
...THEN, YOU NEED TO FOCUS ON RESTING NOW.
JEA...

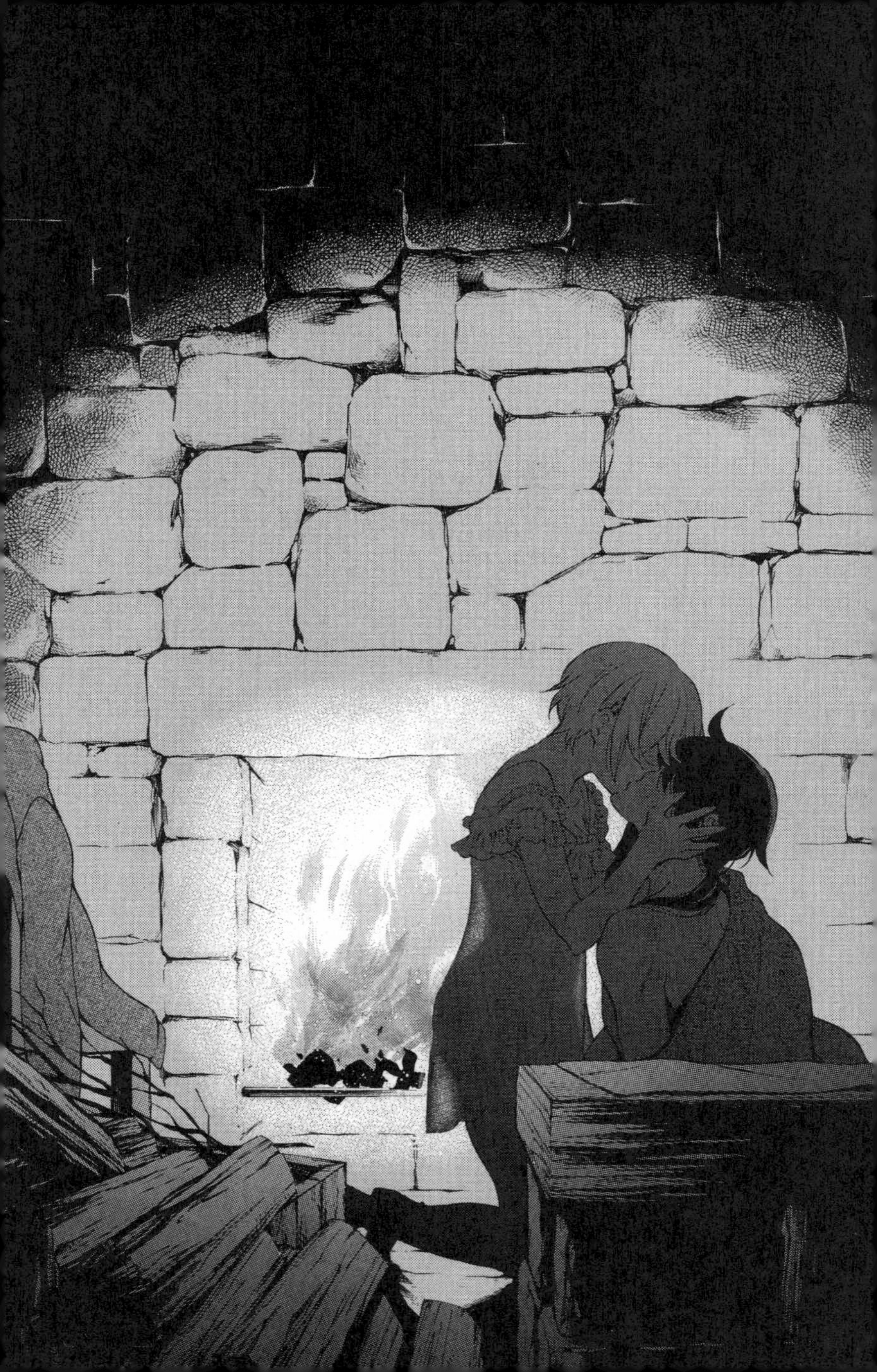

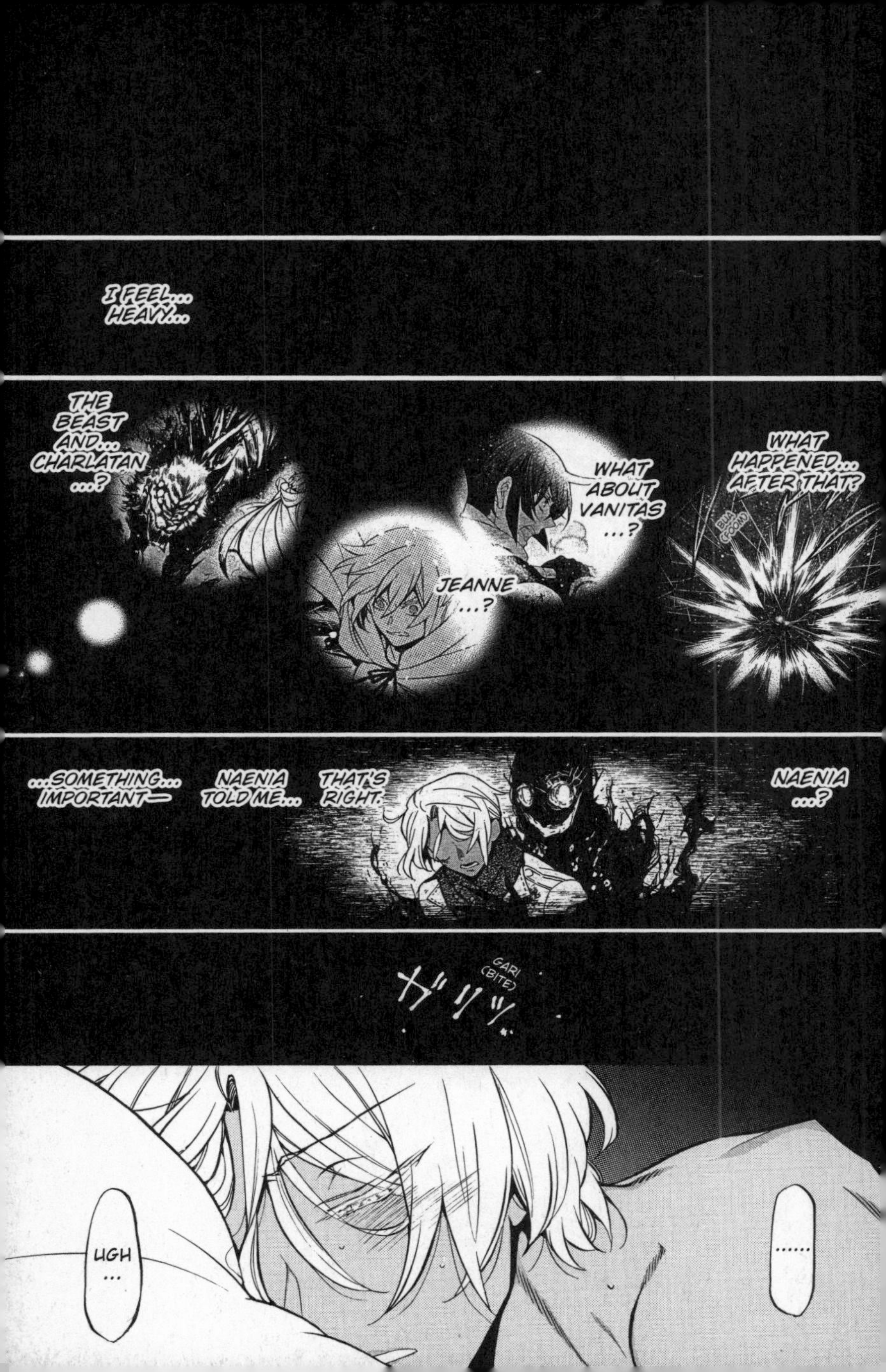
I FEEL... HEAVY...
WHAT HAPPENED... AFTER THAT?
BUA (FOOM)
WHAT ABOUT VANITAS ...?
JEANNE ...?
THE BEAST AND... CHARLATAN ...?
NAENIA ...?
THAT'S RIGHT.
NAENIA TOLD ME...
...SOMETHING... IMPORTANT—
GARI (BITE)
......
UGH ...

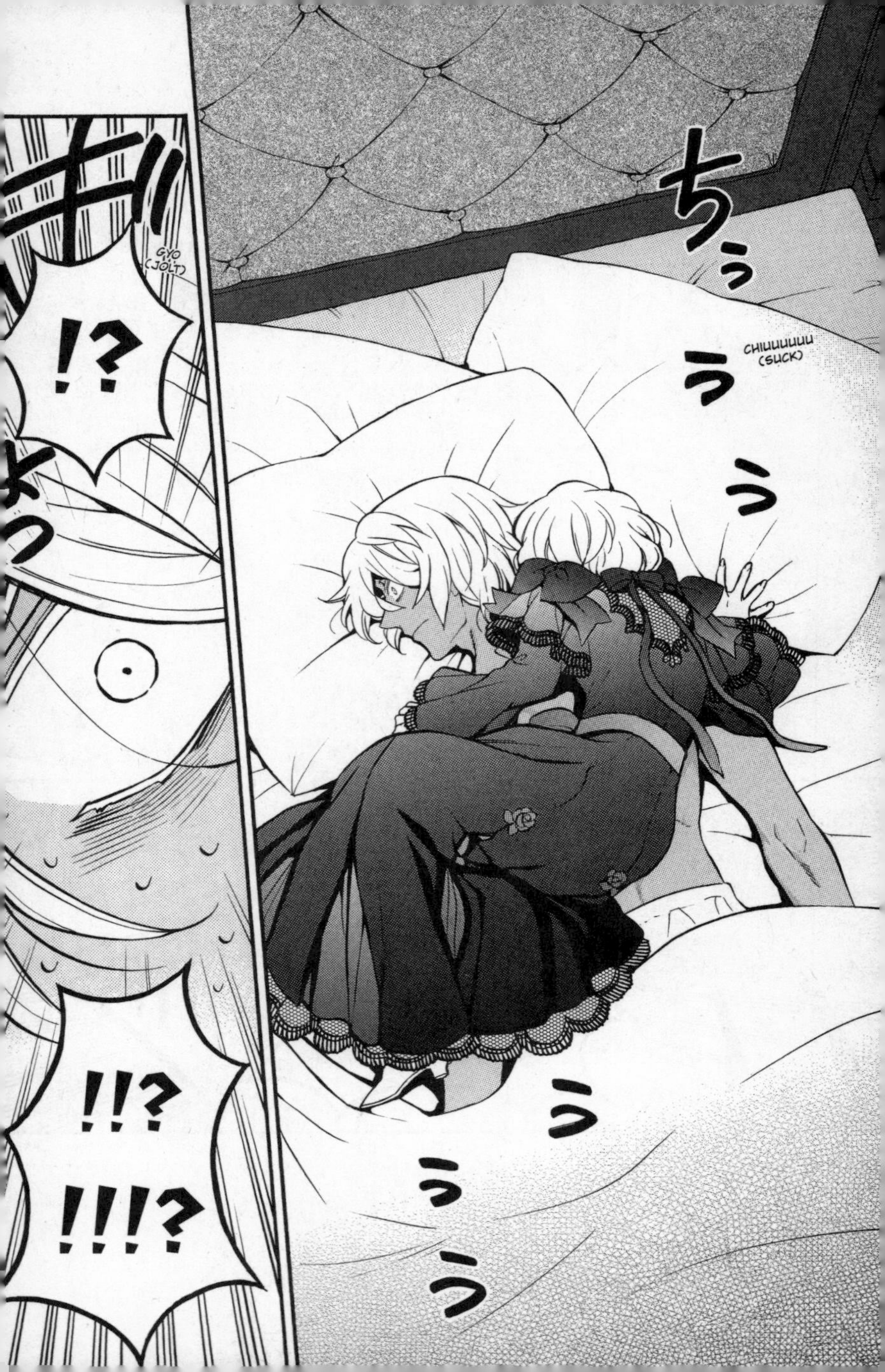
CHIUUUUUUU
(SUCK)
GYO
(JOLT)
!?
!!?
!!!?

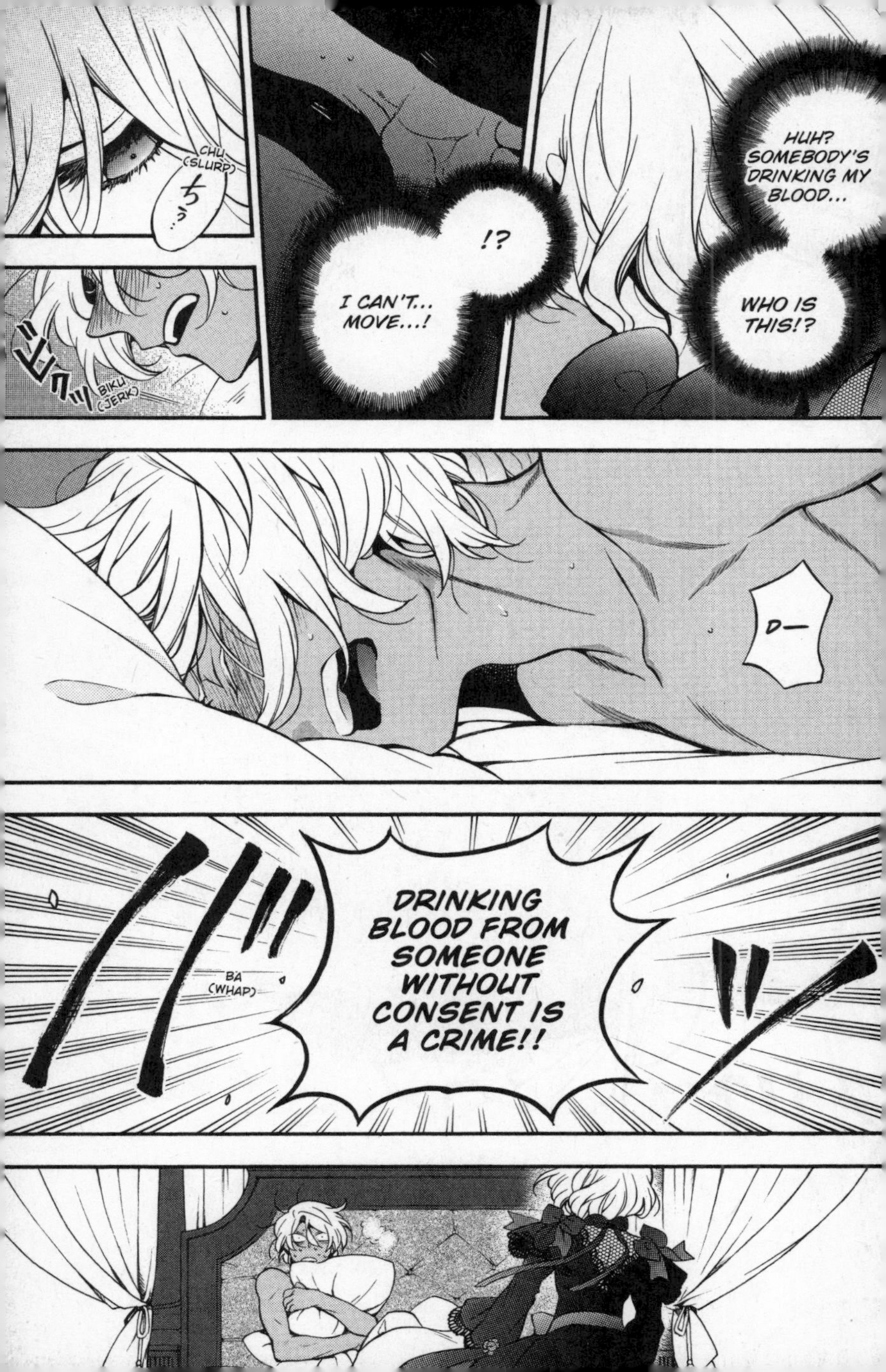
HUH? SOMEBODY'S DRINKING MY BLOOD...
WHO IS THIS!?
!?
I CAN'T... MOVE...!
CHU (SLURP)
BIKU (JERK)
D—
DRINKING BLOOD FROM SOMEONE WITHOUT CONSENT IS A CRIME!!
BA (WHAP)

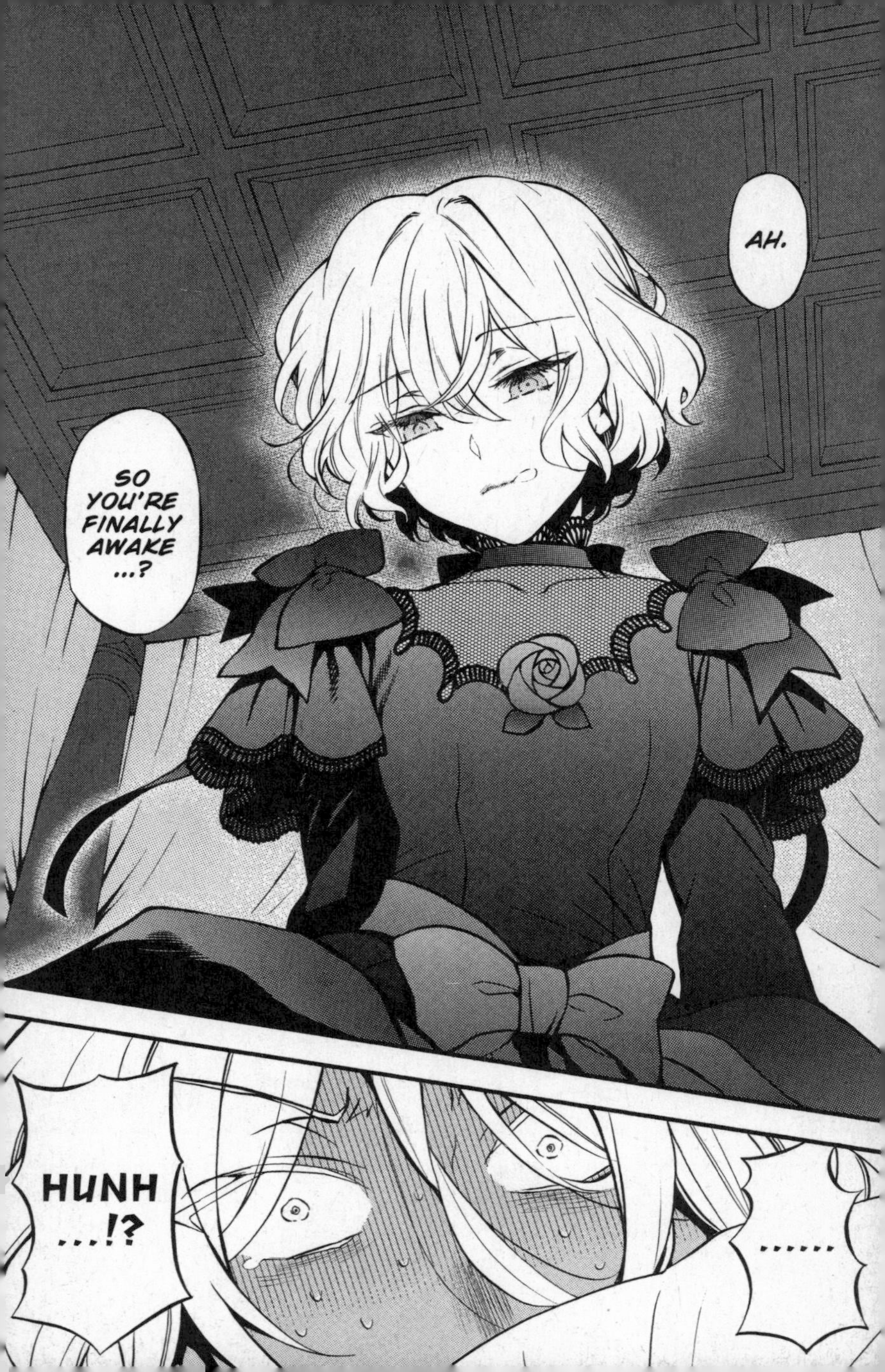
AH.
SO YOU'RE FINALLY AWAKE ...?
......
HUNH ...!?

Mémoire 27 Cage de Neige DREGS

Entracte (INTERLUDE)

Chambre d'enfants A DREAM OF THE SOUND OF RAIN

This side story was technically supposed to be printed in Volume 4.
In chronological terms, it falls during Mémoire 13, when Vanitas and Noé return from the other world

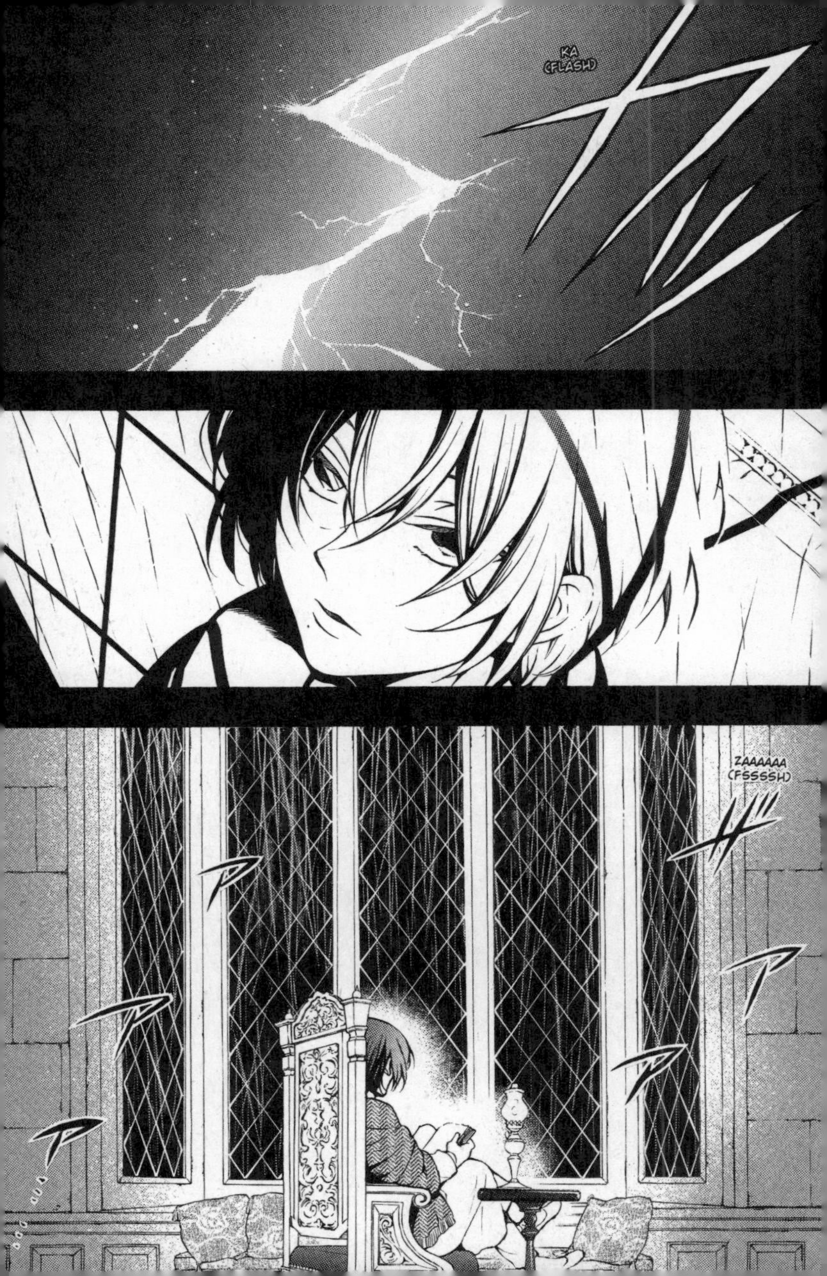
KA
(FLASH)
ZAAAAAA
(FSSSSH)

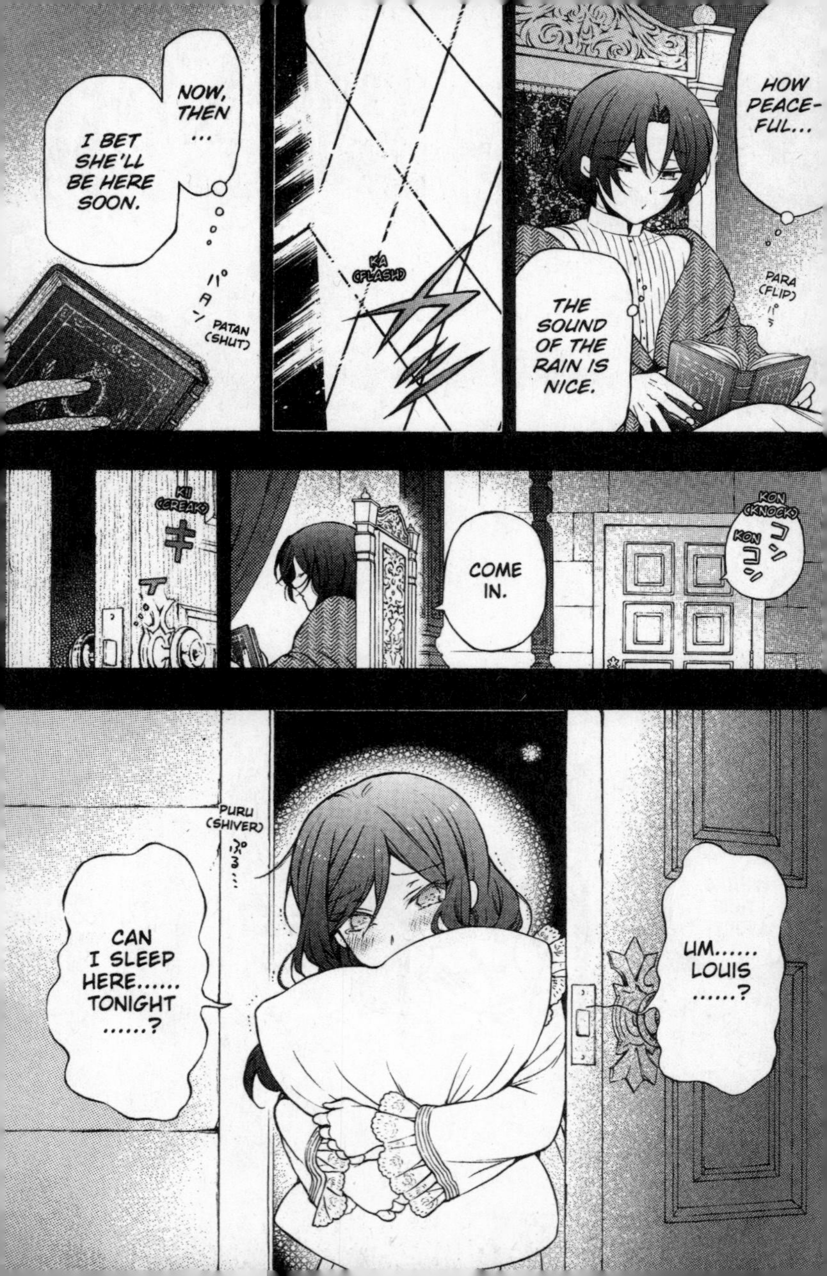
HOW PEACE-FUL...
THE SOUND OF THE RAIN IS NICE.
PARA (FLIP)
パラ
KA (FLASH)
NOW, THEN ...
I BET SHE'LL BE HERE SOON.
パタン
PATAN (SHUT)
KON (KNOCK)
コン
KON
コン
COME IN.
KII (CREAK)
キイ
UM...... LOUIS ......?
PURU (SHIVER)
ぷる…
CAN I SLEEP HERE...... TONIGHT ......?

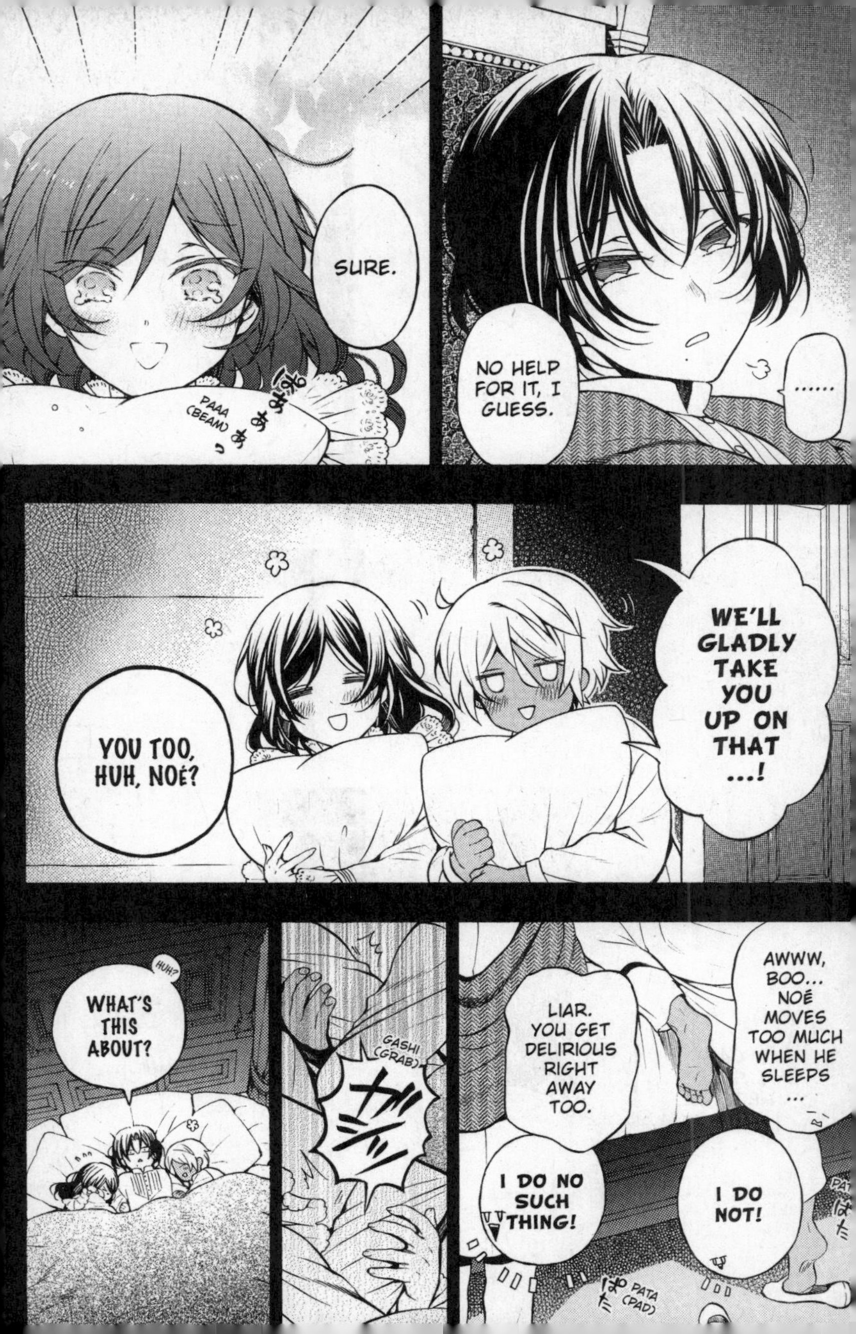
......
NO HELP FOR IT, I GUESS.
SURE.
PAAA (BEAM)
WE'LL GLADLY TAKE YOU UP ON THAT...!
YOU TOO, HUH, NOÉ?
AWWW, BOO... NOÉ MOVES TOO MUCH WHEN HE SLEEPS...
LIAR. YOU GET DELIRIOUS RIGHT AWAY TOO.
I DO NOT!
I DO NO SUCH THING!
PATA (PAD)
GASHI (GRAB)
HUH?
WHAT'S THIS ABOUT?

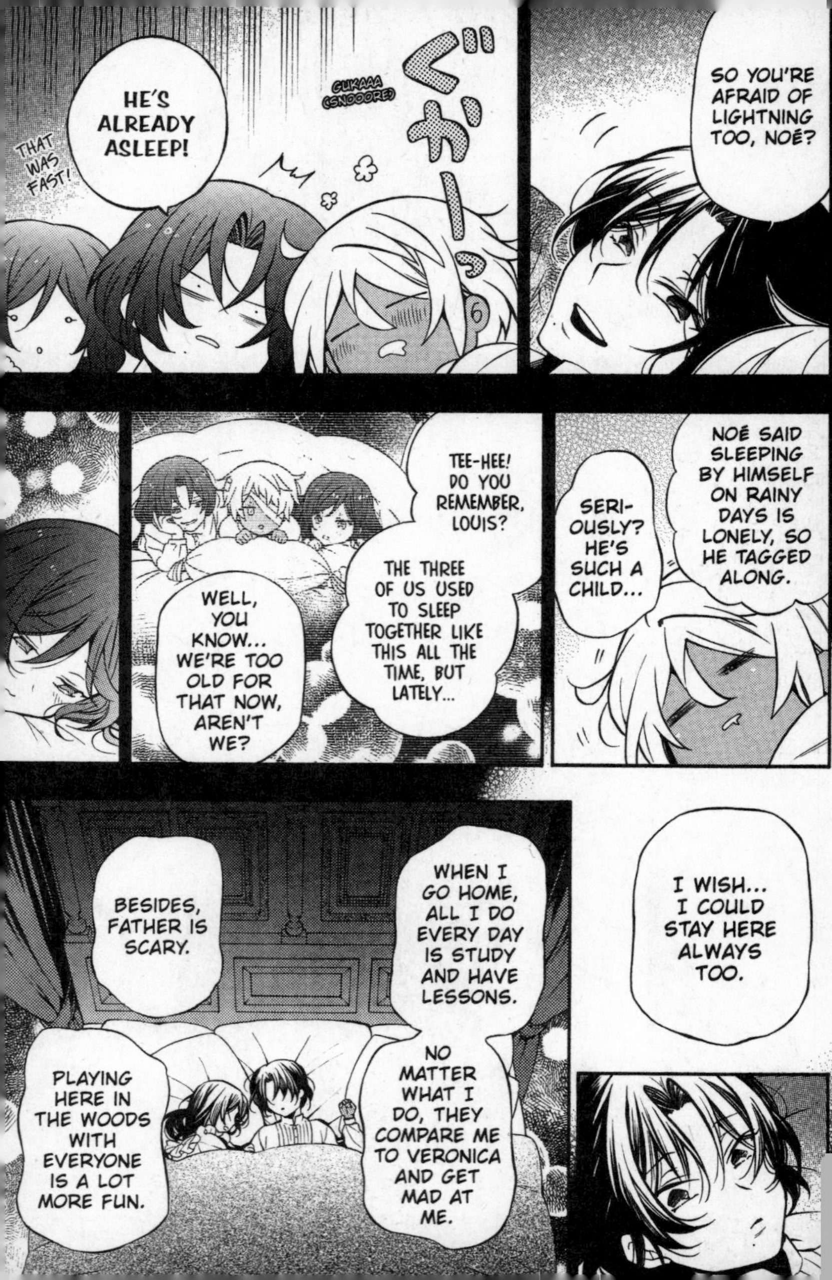
SO YOU'RE AFRAID OF LIGHTNING TOO, NOÉ?
GUKAAA (SNOOORE)
HE'S ALREADY ASLEEP!
THAT WAS FAST!
NOÉ SAID SLEEPING BY HIMSELF ON RAINY DAYS IS LONELY, SO HE TAGGED ALONG.
SERIOUSLY? HE'S SUCH A CHILD...
TEE-HEE! DO YOU REMEMBER, LOUIS?
THE THREE OF US USED TO SLEEP TOGETHER LIKE THIS ALL THE TIME, BUT LATELY...
WELL, YOU KNOW... WE'RE TOO OLD FOR THAT NOW, AREN'T WE?
WHEN I GO HOME, ALL I DO EVERY DAY IS STUDY AND HAVE LESSONS.
BESIDES, FATHER IS SCARY.
NO MATTER WHAT I DO, THEY COMPARE ME TO VERONICA AND GET MAD AT ME.
PLAYING HERE IN THE WOODS WITH EVERYONE IS A LOT MORE FUN.
I WISH... I COULD STAY HERE ALWAYS TOO.

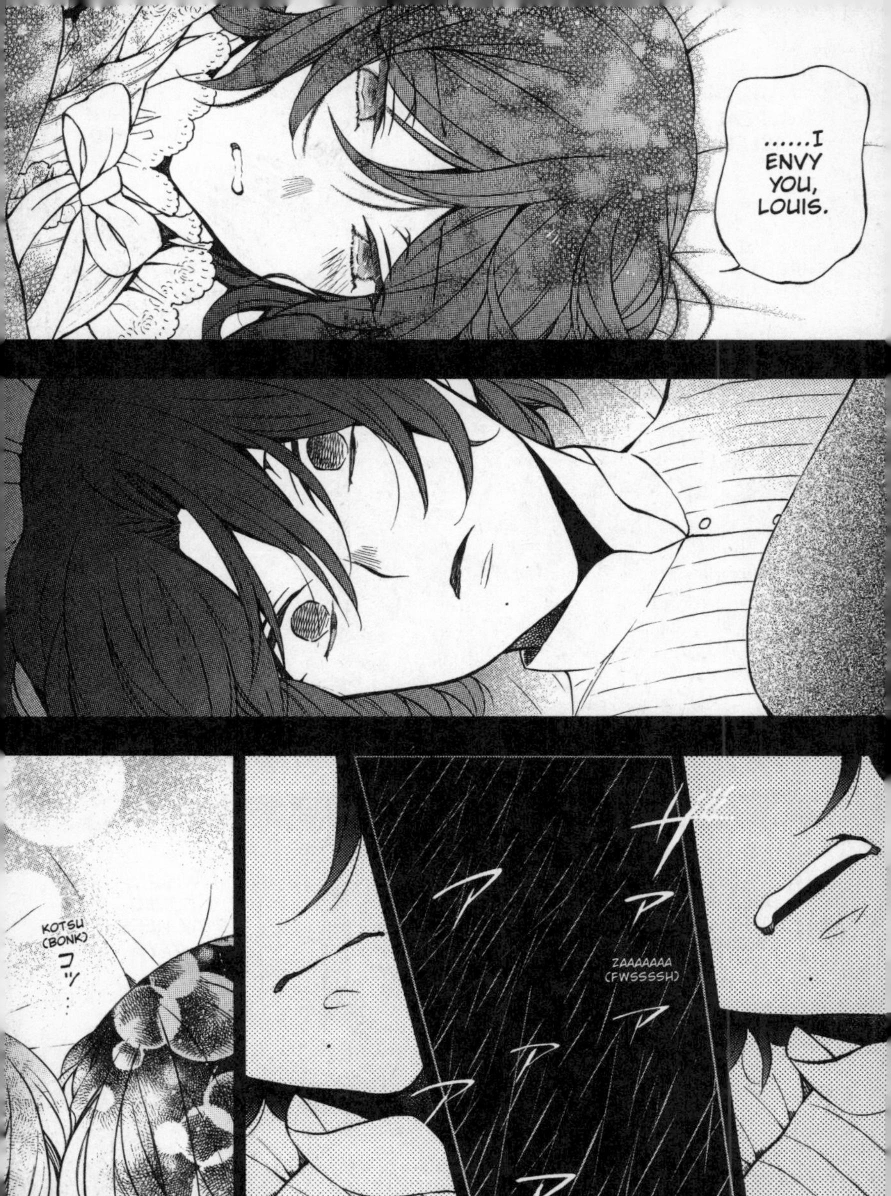
......I ENVY YOU, LOUIS.
ザァァァァァァ
ZAAAAAAA (FWSSSSH)
KOTSU (BONK)
コッ…

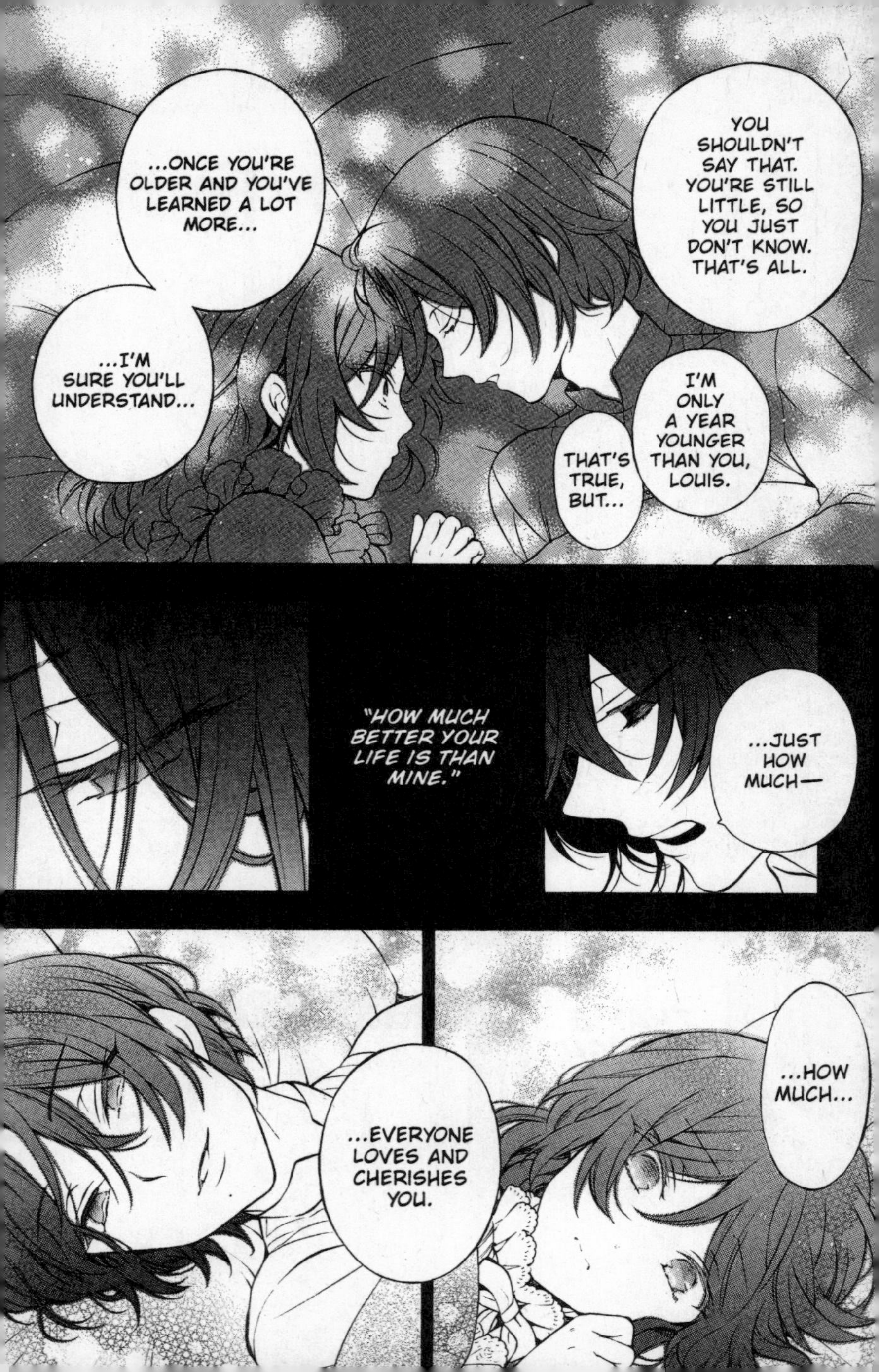
YOU SHOULDN'T SAY THAT. YOU'RE STILL LITTLE, SO YOU JUST DON'T KNOW. THAT'S ALL.
I'M ONLY A YEAR YOUNGER THAN YOU, LOUIS.
THAT'S TRUE, BUT...
...ONCE YOU'RE OLDER AND YOU'VE LEARNED A LOT MORE...
...I'M SURE YOU'LL UNDERSTAND...
...JUST HOW MUCH—
"HOW MUCH BETTER YOUR LIFE IS THAN MINE."
...HOW MUCH...
...EVERYONE LOVES AND CHERISHES YOU.

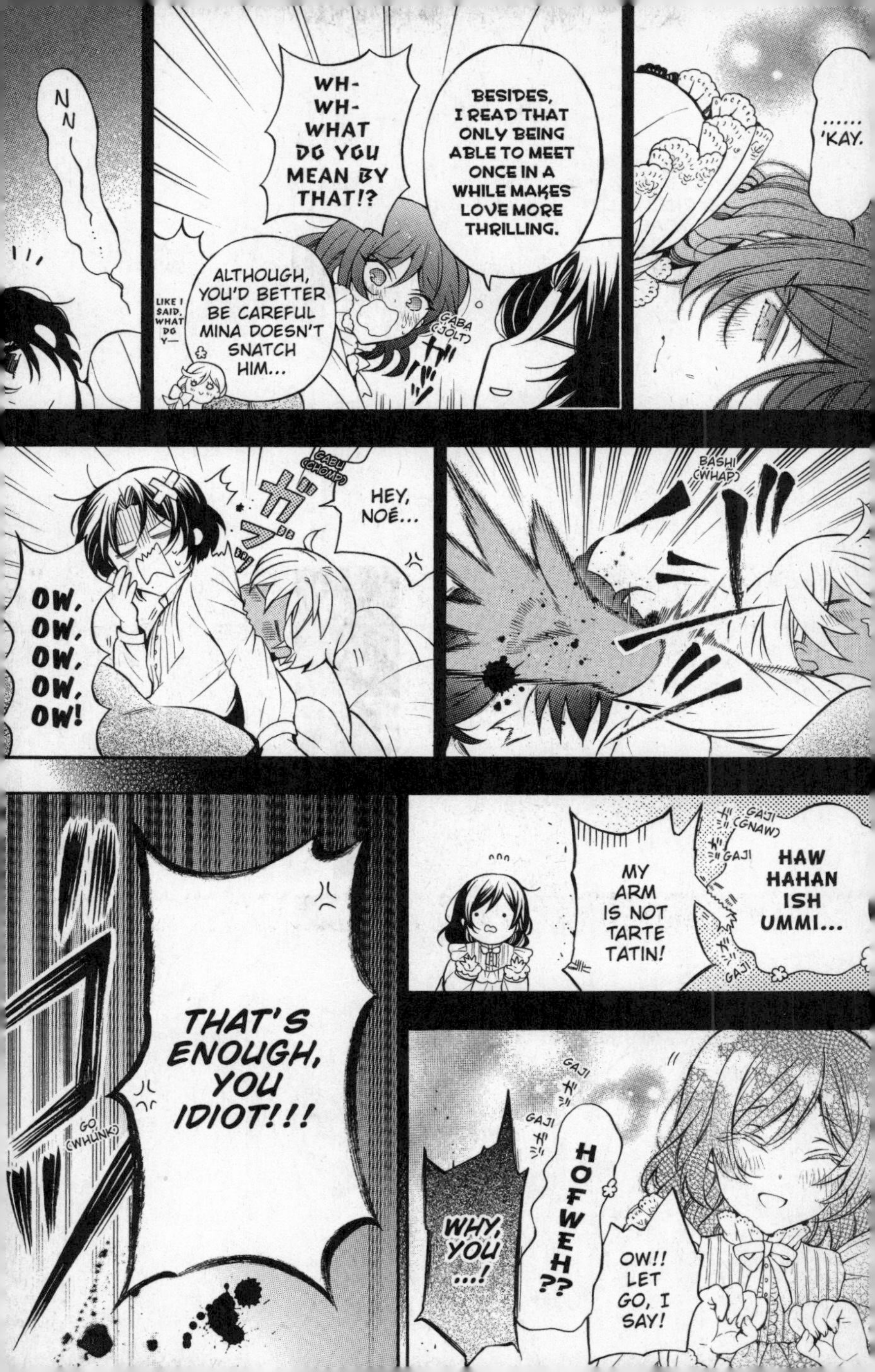
......'KAY.
BESIDES, I READ THAT ONLY BEING ABLE TO MEET ONCE IN A WHILE MAKES LOVE MORE THRILLING.
WH-WH-WHAT DO YOU MEAN BY THAT!?
GABA (JOLT)
ALTHOUGH, YOU'D BETTER BE CAREFUL MINA DOESN'T SNATCH HIM...
LIKE I SAID, WHAT DO Y—
NN
BASHI (WHAP)
HEY, NOÉ...
GABU (CHOMP)
OW, OW, OW, OW, OW!
HAW HAHAN ISH UMMI...
GAJI (GNAW)
GAJI
GAJI
MY ARM IS NOT TARTE TATIN!
OW!! LET GO, I SAY!
HOFWEH??
GAJI
GAJI
WHY, YOU...!
THAT'S ENOUGH, YOU IDIOT!!!
GO (WHUNK)

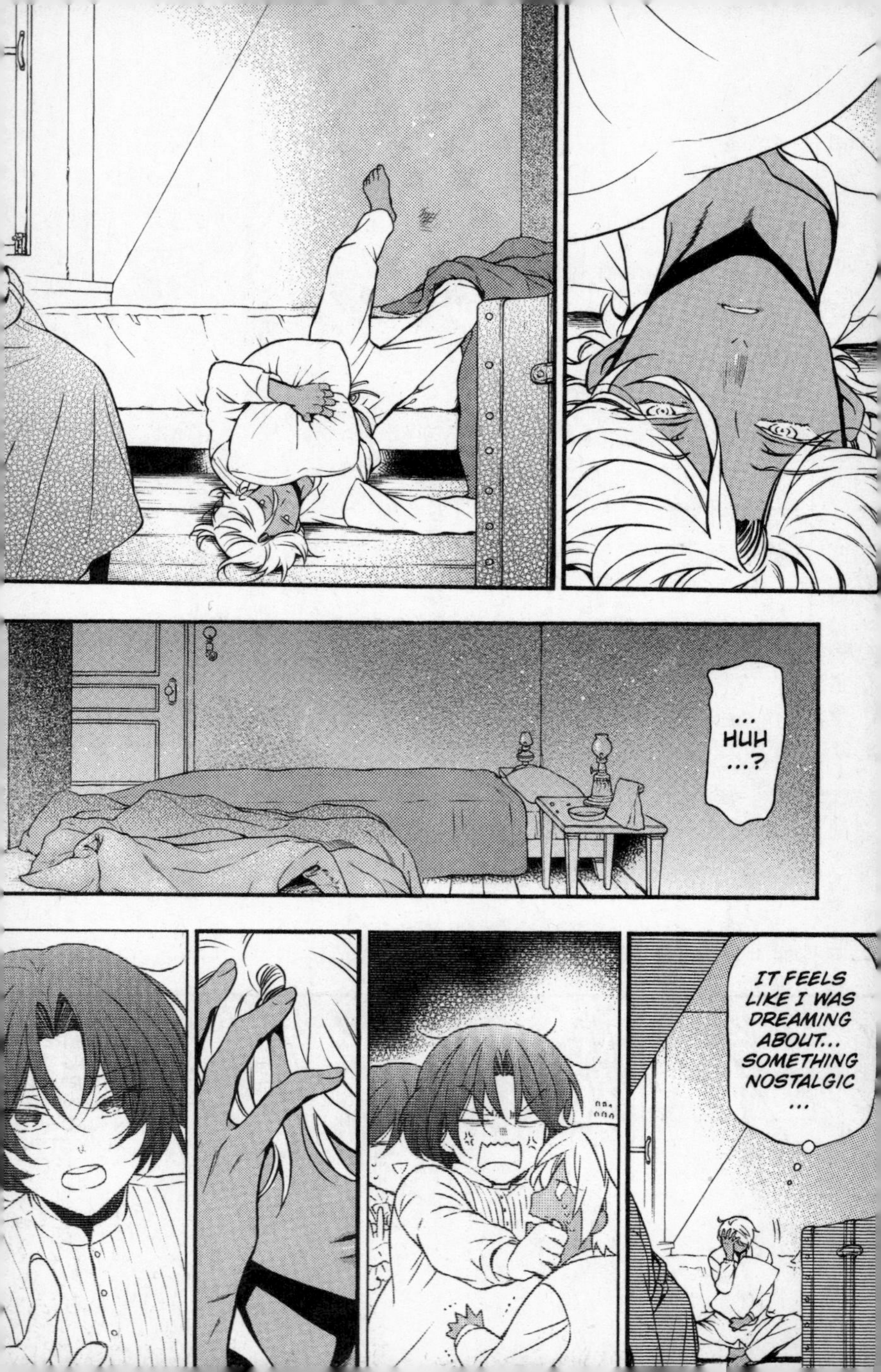
...
HUH
...?
IT FEELS LIKE I WAS DREAMING ABOUT... SOMETHING NOSTALGIC...

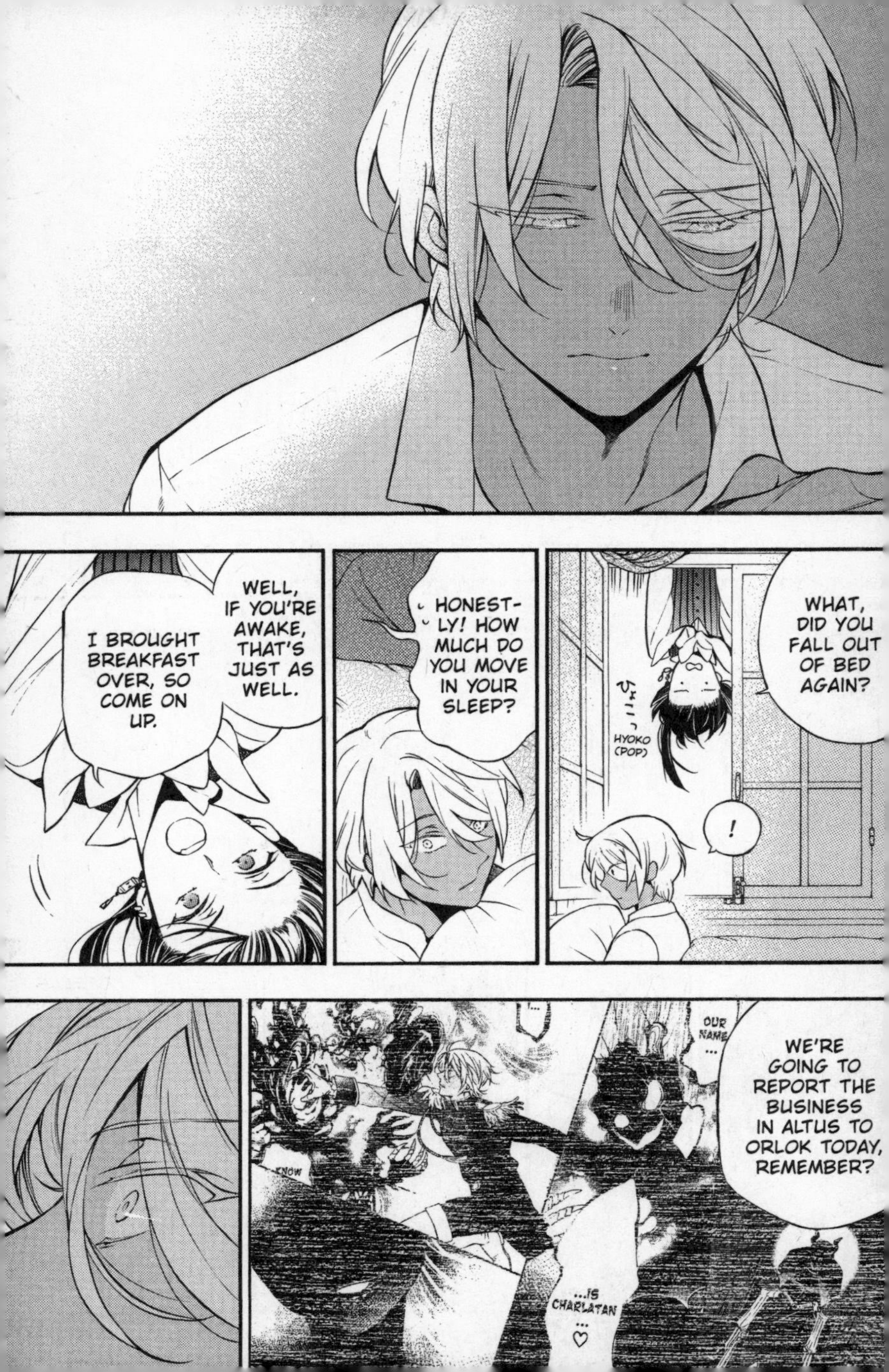
WHAT, DID YOU FALL OUT OF BED AGAIN?
HYOKO (POP)
!
HONEST-LY! HOW MUCH DO YOU MOVE IN YOUR SLEEP?
WELL, IF YOU'RE AWAKE, THAT'S JUST AS WELL.
I BROUGHT BREAKFAST OVER, SO COME ON UP.
WE'RE GOING TO REPORT THE BUSINESS IN ALTUS TO ORLOK TODAY, REMEMBER?
OUR NAME ...
...
KNOW
...IS CHARLATAN ... ♡

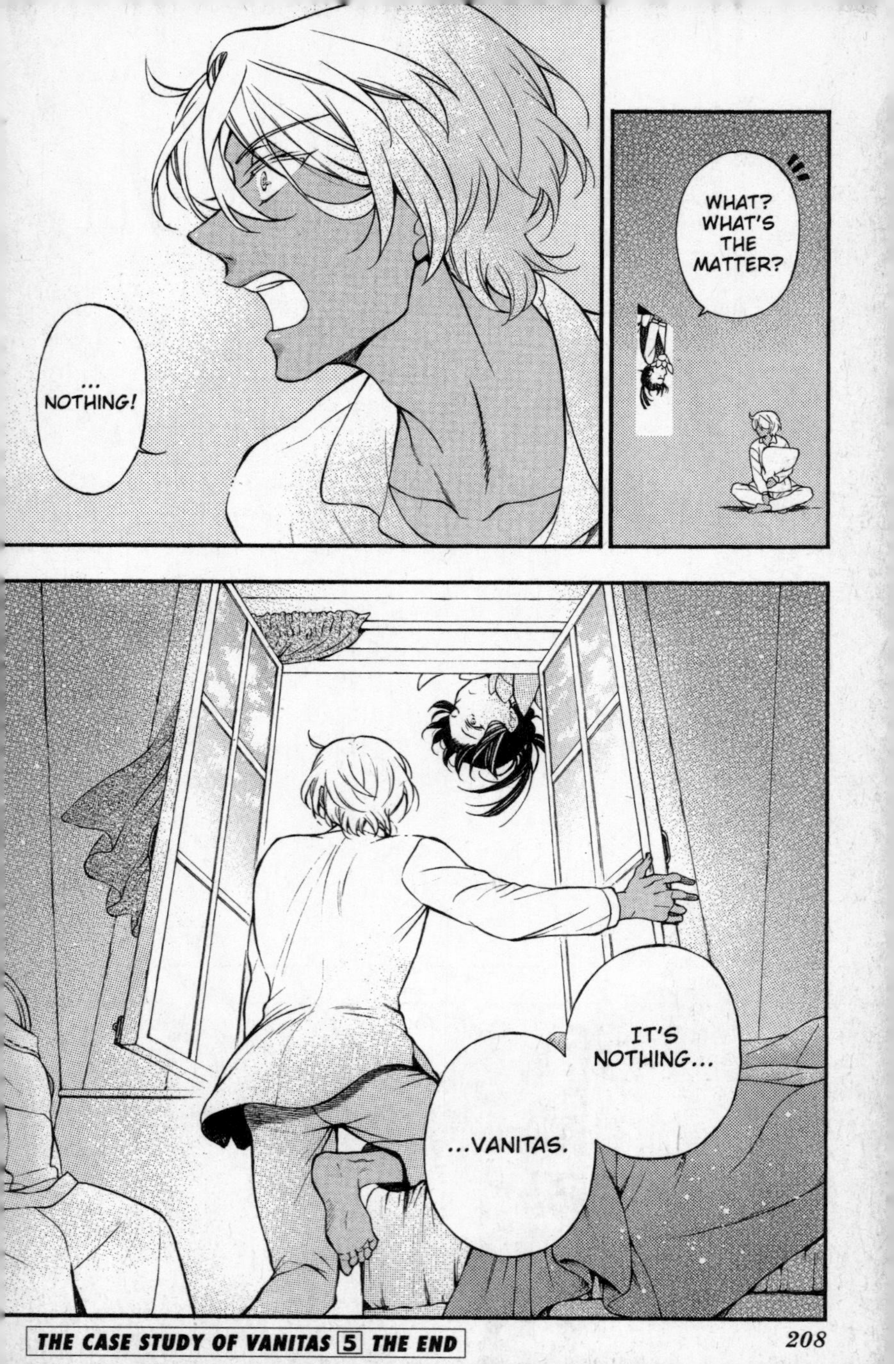
WHAT? WHAT'S THE MATTER?
... NOTHING!
IT'S NOTHING...
...VANITAS.

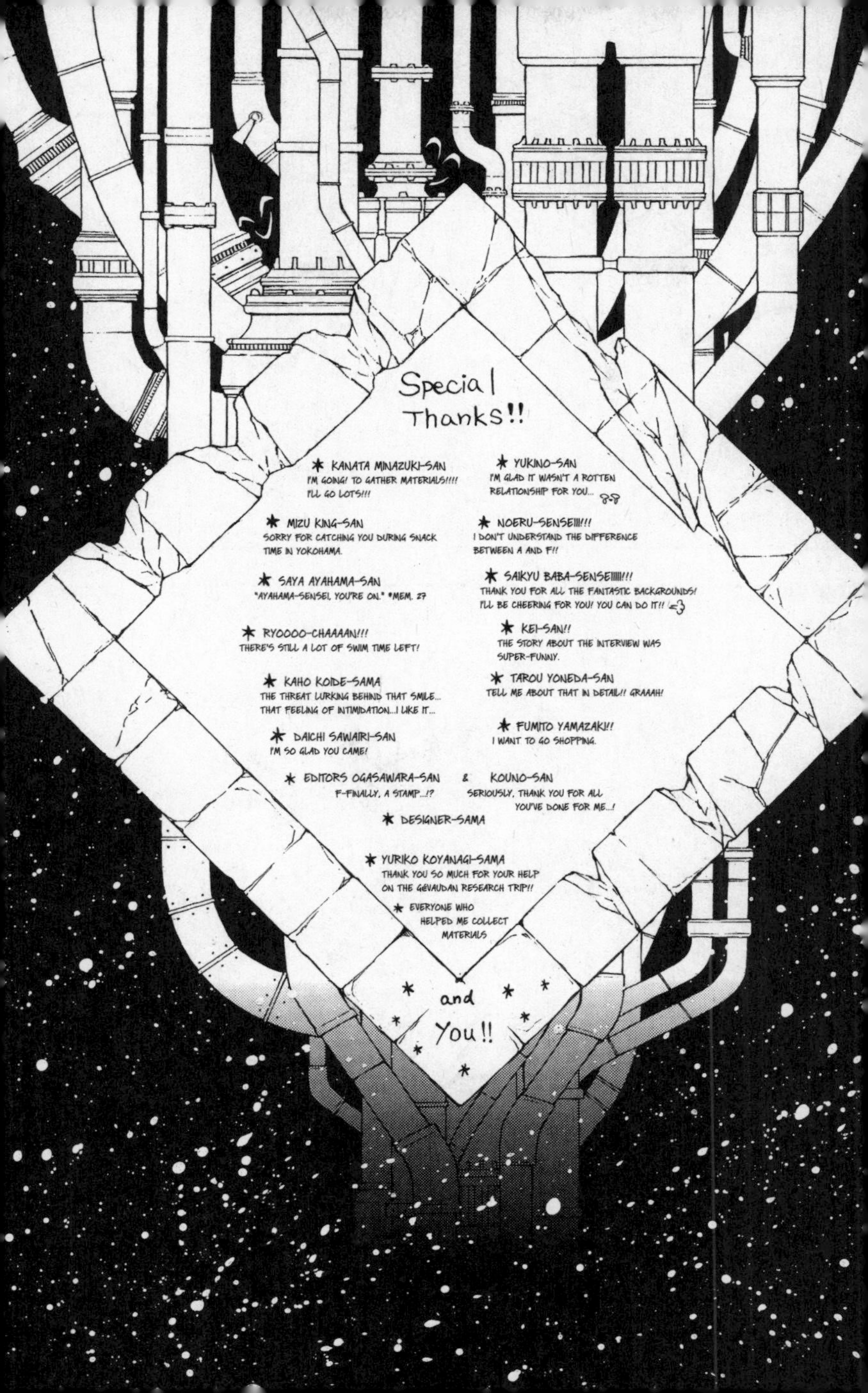
Special Thanks!!
* KANATA MINAZUKI-SAN
I'M GOING! TO GATHER MATERIALS!!!!
I'LL GO LOTS!!!
* MIZU KING-SAN
SORRY FOR CATCHING YOU DURING SNACK TIME IN YOKOHAMA.
* SAYA AYAHAMA-SAN
"AYAHAMA-SENSEI, YOU'RE ON." *MEM. 27
* RYOOOO-CHAAAAN!!!
THERE'S STILL A LOT OF SWIM TIME LEFT!
* KAHO KOIDE-SAMA
THE THREAT LURKING BEHIND THAT SMILE...
THAT FEELING OF INTIMIDATION...I LIKE IT...
* DAICHI SAWAIRI-SAN
I'M SO GLAD YOU CAME!
* YUKINO-SAN
I'M GLAD IT WASN'T A ROTTEN RELATIONSHIP FOR YOU...
* NOERU-SENSEIIII!!!
I DON'T UNDERSTAND THE DIFFERENCE BETWEEN A AND F!!
* SAIKYU BABA-SENSEIIIIII!!!
THANK YOU FOR ALL THE FANTASTIC BACKGROUNDS!
I'LL BE CHEERING FOR YOU! YOU CAN DO IT!!
* KEI-SAN!!
THE STORY ABOUT THE INTERVIEW WAS SUPER-FUNNY.
* TAROU YONEDA-SAN
TELL ME ABOUT THAT IN DETAIL!! GRAAAH!
* FUMITO YAMAZAKI!!
I WANT TO GO SHOPPING.
* EDITORS OGASAWARA-SAN & KOUNO-SAN
F-FINALLY, A STAMP...!?
SERIOUSLY, THANK YOU FOR ALL YOU'VE DONE FOR ME...!
* DESIGNER-SAMA
* YURIKO KOYANAGI-SAMA
THANK YOU SO MUCH FOR YOUR HELP ON THE GEVAUDAN RESEARCH TRIP!!
* EVERYONE WHO HELPED ME COLLECT MATERIALS
and You!!

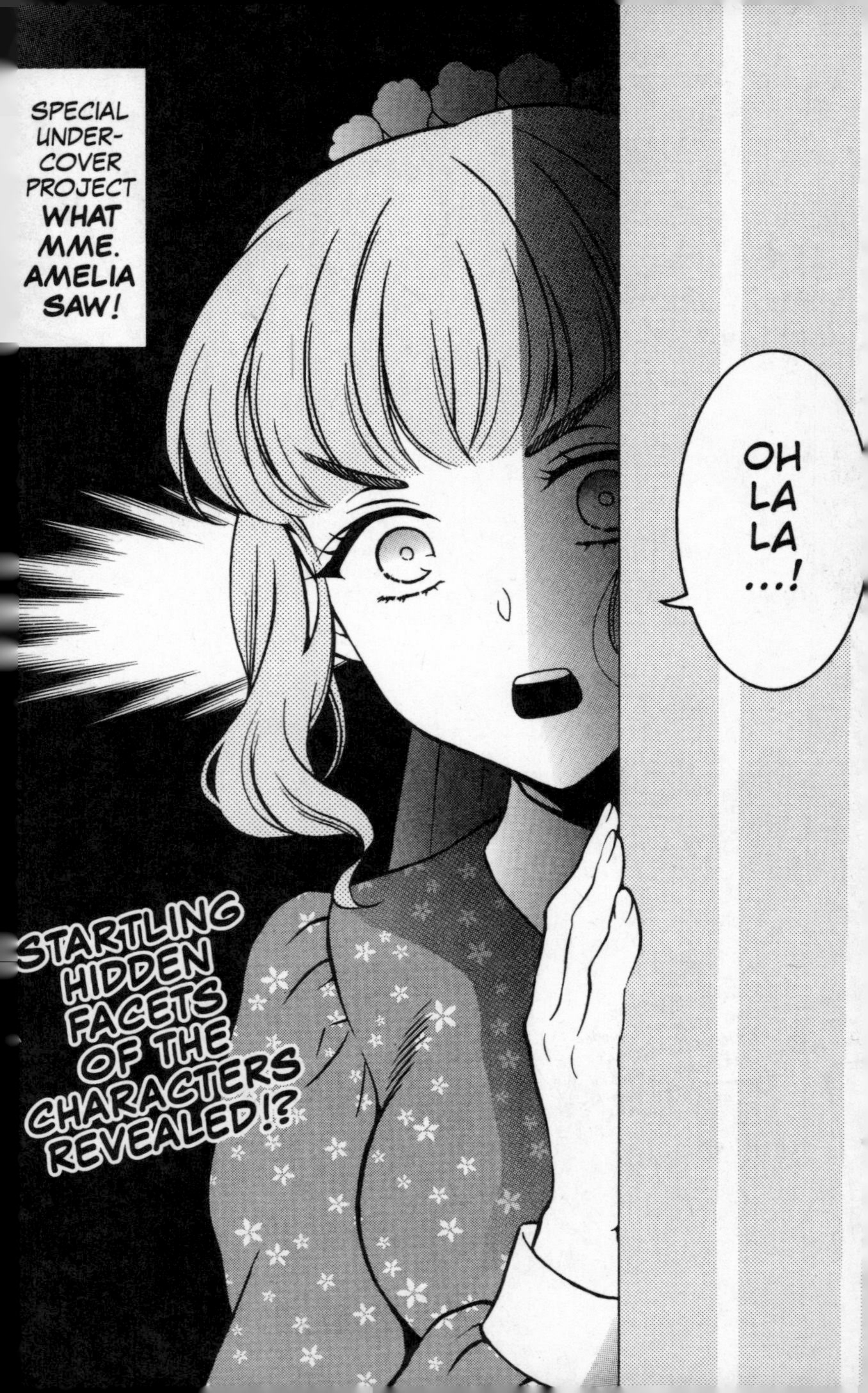
OH LA LA...!
SPECIAL UNDER-COVER PROJECT WHAT MME. AMELIA SAW!
STARTLING HIDDEN FACETS OF THE CHARACTERS REVEALED!?

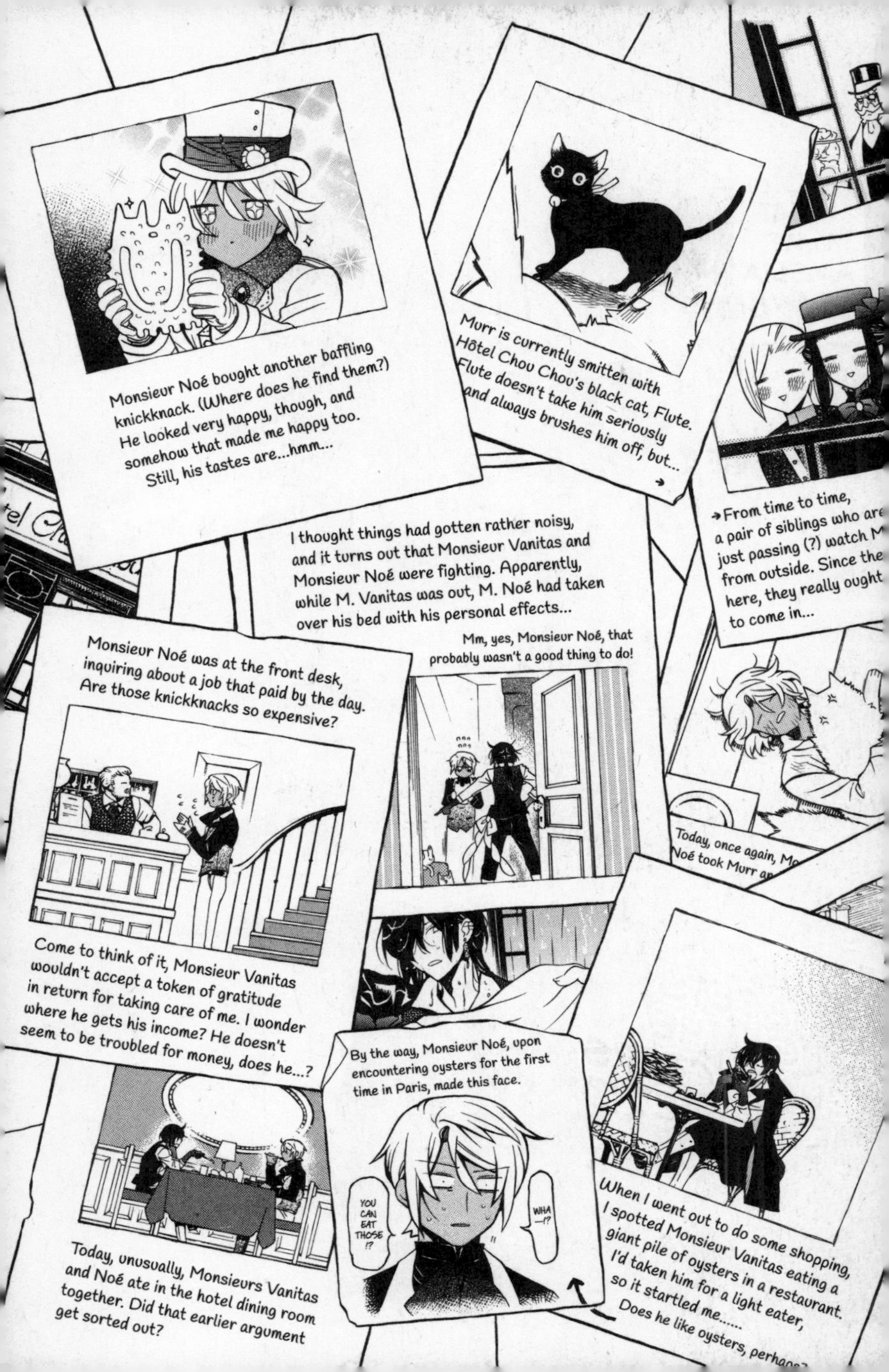
→From time to time,
a pair of siblings who are
just passing (?) watch M
from outside. Since the
here, they really ought
to come in...
Murr is currently smitten with Hôtel Chou Chou's black cat, Flute. Flute doesn't take him seriously and always brushes him off, but... →
Monsieur Noé bought another baffling knickknack. (Where does he find them?) He looked very happy, though, and somehow that made me happy too. Still, his tastes are...hmm...
Today, once again, Mo
Noé took Murr an
I thought things had gotten rather noisy, and it turns out that Monsieur Vanitas and Monsieur Noé were fighting. Apparently, while M. Vanitas was out, M. Noé had taken over his bed with his personal effects...
Mm, yes, Monsieur Noé, that probably wasn't a good thing to do!
Monsieur Noé was at the front desk, inquiring about a job that paid by the day. Are those knickknacks so expensive?
Come to think of it, Monsieur Vanitas wouldn't accept a token of gratitude in return for taking care of me. I wonder where he gets his income? He doesn't seem to be troubled for money, does he...?
When I went out to do some shopping, I spotted Monsieur Vanitas eating a giant pile of oysters in a restaurant. I'd taken him for a light eater, so it startled me...... Does he like oysters, perhaps?
By the way, Monsieur Noé, upon encountering oysters for the first time in Paris, made this face.
WHA—!?
YOU CAN EAT THOSE !?
Today, unusually, Monsieurs Vanitas and Noé ate in the hotel dining room together. Did that earlier argument get sorted out?

IT WAS FUN AND... EDUCATIONAL...

...BUT BOY, WAS IT EVER COLD!

Jun Mochizuki

AUTHOR'S NOTE

For the arc that starts in Volume 5, I visited a village called Saugues in France for research. However, there was heavy snow on the very day I planned to visit. The transportation network was paralyzed, and I wasn't sure whether to go on or turn back...or whether— assuming I managed to reach the village safely—I'd be able to leave again. Let's just say...it was an eventful trip and lots of fun!

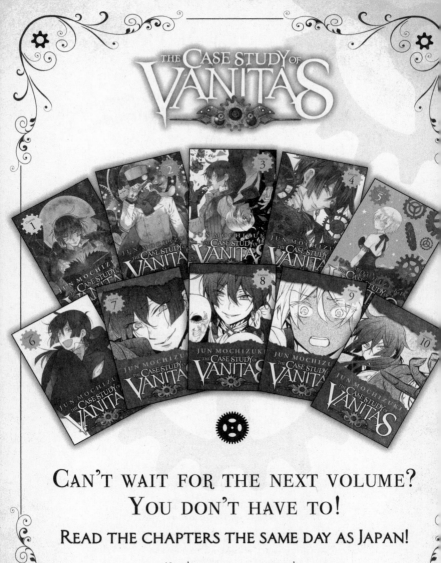

CAN'T WAIT FOR THE NEXT VOLUME?
YOU DON'T HAVE TO!

READ THE CHAPTERS THE SAME DAY AS JAPAN!

New chapters come out every month,
available worldwide wherever e-books are sold!

THE CASE STUDY OF VANITAS
VOLUME 5

JUN MOCHIZUKI

TRANSLATION: TAYLOR ENGEL
LETTERING: BIANCA PISTILLO

Vanitas no Carte Volume 5 ©2018 Jun Mochizuki/SQUARE ENIX CO., LTD.
First published in Japan in 2018 by SQUARE ENIX CO., LTD. English translation rights arranged with SQUARE ENIX CO., LTD. and Yen Press, LLC through Tuttle-Mori Agency, Inc., Tokyo.

English translation ©2019 by SQUARE ENIX CO., LTD.

Yen Press
1290 Avenue of the Americas
New York, NY 10104

Visit us at yenpress.com
facebook.com/yenpress
twitter.com/yenpress
yenpress.tumblr.com
instagram.com/yenpress

First Yen Press Edition: January 2019
The chapters in this volume were originally published as ebooks by Yen Press.

Yen Press is an imprint of Yen Press, LLC.
The Yen Press name and logo are trademarks of Yen Press, LLC.

The publisher is not responsible for websites (or their content) that are not owned by the publisher.

Library of Congress Control Number: 2016946115

ISBNs: 978-1-9753-8368-8 (paperback)
978-1-9753-8369-5 (ebook)

10 9 8 7 6 5 4 3 2 1

WOR

Printed in the United States of America